Visions of Tiwanaku

UCLA COTSEN INSTITUTE OF ARCHAEOLOGY PRESS
Monograph Series
Contributions in Field Research and Current Issues in Archaeological Method and Theory

Monograph 77

Advances in Titicaca Basin Archaeology-2

Alexei Vranich and Abigail R. Levine (eds.)

Monograph 76

The Dead Tell Tales

María Cecilia Lozada and Barra O'Donnabhain (eds.)

Monograph 75

The Stones of Tiahuanaco

Jean-Pierre Protzen and Stella Nair

Monograph 71

Crucible of Pueblos: The Early Pueblo Period in the Northern Southwest

Richard H. Wilshusen, Gregson Schachner, and James R. Allison (eds.)

Monograph 70

Chotuna and Chornancap: Excavating an Ancient Peruvian Legend

Christopher B. Donnan

Monograph 68

The Chanka: Archaeological Research in Andahuaylas (Apurimac), Peru

Brian S. Bauer, Lucas C. Kellett, and Miriam Aráoz Silva

VISIONS OF TIWANAKU

Edited by
Alexei Vranich and
Charles Stanish

Monograph 78
Cotsen Institute of Archaeology Press
2013

THE COTSEN INSTITUTE OF ARCHAEOLOGY PRESS is the publishing unit of the Cotsen Institute of Archaeology at UCLA. The Cotsen Institute is a premier research organization dedicated to the creation, dissemination, and conservation of archaeological knowledge and heritage. It is home to both the Interdepartmental Archaeology Graduate Program and the UCLA/Getty Master's Program in the Conservation of Archaeological and Ethnographic Materials. The Cotsen Institute provides a forum for innovative faculty research, graduate education, and public programs at UCLA in an effort to positively impact the academic, local and global communities. Established in 1973, the Cotsen Institute is at the forefront of archaeological research, education, conservation and publication and is an active contributor to interdisciplinary research at UCLA.

The Cotsen Institute Press specializes in producing high-quality academic volumes in several different series, including Monographs, World Heritage and Monuments, Cotsen Advanced Seminars, and Ideas, Debates, and Perspectives. The Press is committed to making the fruits of archaeological research accessible to professionals, scholars, students, and the general public. We are able to do this through the generosity of Lloyd E. Cotsen, longtime Institute volunteer and benefactor, who has provided an endowment that allows us to subsidize our publishing program and produce superb volumes at an affordable price. Publishing in nine different series, our award-winning archaeological publications receive critical acclaim in both the academic and popular communities.

The Cotsen Institute of Archaeology at UCLA
Charles Stanish, Director
Gregory Areshian, Assistant Director
Willeke Wendrich, Editorial Director
Randi Danforth, Publications Manager

EDITORIAL BOARD OF THE COTSEN INSTITUTE OF ARCHAEOLOGY:
Willeke Wendrich	Area Editor for Egypt, North, and East Africa
Richard G. Lesure	Area Editor for South and Central America, and Mesoamerica
Jeanne E. Arnold	Area Editor for North America
Aaron Burke	Area Editor for Southwestern Asia
Lothar Von Falkenhausen	Area Editor for East and South Asia and Archaeological Theory
Sarah Morris	Area Editor for the Classical World
John Papadopoulos	Area Editor for the Mediterranean Region
Ex-Officio Members:	Charles Stanish, Gregory E. Areshian, and Randi Danforth
External Members:	Kusimba Chapurukha, Joyce Marcus, Colin Renfrew, and John Yellen

Copyediting by Peg J. Goldstein
Text and cover design by Leyba Associates

Library of Congress Cataloging-in-Publication Data

Visions of Tiwanaku / edited by Alexei Vranich and Charles Stanish.
    pages cm
Includes bibliographical references and index.
ISBN 978-0-917956-09-6 (alk. paper)
1. Tiwanaku Site (Bolivia)--Congresses. 2. Tiwanaku culture. 3. Indians of South America--Tiwanaku River Valley (Bolivia)--Antiquities--Congresses. 4. Excavations (Archaeology)--Tiwanaku River Valley (Bolivia)--Congresses. 5. Tiwanaku River Valley (Bolivia)--Antiquities--Congresses. I. Vranich, Alexei, 1968- author, editor of compilation. II. Stanish, Charles, 1956- author, editor of compilation.

F3319.1.T55V58 2013
984'.01--dc23

2013031790

Copyright © 2013. Regents of the University of California
All rights reserved. Printed in the United States of America

Contents

Authors vi
List of Figures vii
List of Tables x
Preface xi
    Alexei Vranich

Chapter 1: Visions of Tiwanaku 1
    Alexei Vranich

Chapter 2: Stylistic Variation and Seriation 11
    Michael Moseley

Chapter 3: Tiwanaku: A Cult of the Masses 27
    Patrick Ryan Williams

Chapter 4: Tiwanaku and Wari State Expansion:
    Demographic and Outpost Colonization Compared 41
    Paul Goldstein

Chapter 5: The Cultural Implications of Tiwanaku and Huari Textiles 65
    William J Conklin

Chapter 6: Tiwanaku Influence on the Central Valley of Cochabamba 87
    Karen Anderson

Chapter 7: Tiwanaku Ritual and Political Transformations
    in the Core and Peripheries 113
    Matthew T. Seddon

Chapter 8: Tiwanaku Origins and the Early Development:
    The Political and Moral Economy of a Hospitality State 135
    Matthew Bandy

Chapter 9: What Was Tiwanaku? 151
    Charles Stanish

Chapter 10: Nature of an Andean City: Tiwanaku and the Production of Spectacle 167
    William H. Isbell

Chapter 11: Social Diversity, Ritual Encounter, and the
    Contingent Production of Tiwanaku 197
    John W. Janusek

Chapter 12: Tiwanaku's Coming of Age: Refining Time and Style in the Altiplano 211
    Patricia J. Knobloch

Chapter 13: Concluding Thoughts 235
    Alexei Vranich

Index 239

AUTHORS

Karen Anderson
University of California, Santa Barbara

Matthew Bandy
SWCA Environmental Consultants, Albuquerque

William J Conklin
The Textile Museum, Washington, D.C.

Paul Goldstein
University of California, San Diego

William Isbell
State University of New York, Binghamton

John W. Janusek
Vanderbilt University, Nashville

Patricia J. Knobloch
Institute of Andean Studies, La Mesa

Michael Moseley
University of Florida, Gainesville

Charles Stanish
University of California, Los Angeles
Santa Fe Institute, Santa Fe, New Mexico

Matthew T. Seddon
Church Divinity School of the Pacific, Berkeley

Alexei Vranich
Cotsen Institute of Archaeology, Los Angeles

Patrick Ryan Williams
The Field Museum, Chicago

Figures

Figure 2.1. The two axes of stylistic variation portrayed as perpendicular to one another, with different variants of the same style represented by different boxed symbols 19

Figure 2.2. Interaxial stylistic variation portrayed in a social temporal matrix, with different variants of the same style represented by different boxed symbols 22

Figure 3.1. Moquegua Valley map 28

Figure 3.2. Plan of the Wari colony at Cerro Baúl 28

Figure 3.3. Plans of the Tiwanaku colonies at (a) Chen Chen and (b) Omo 29

Figure 3.4. Comparative plans of Tiwanaku monumental architecture 30

Figure 3.5. Monumental architecture on the summit of Cerro Baúl 31

Figure 3.6. Comparative plans of three classes or scales of residential architecture at Cerro Baúl and Cerro Mejía 33

Figure 3.7. Examples of Tiwanaku residential architecture at Tumilaca la Chimba and Omo 34

Figure 4.1. The south-central Andes, showing vectors of Tiwanaku colonization, Wari's southernmost outpost, and the Moquegua study area 42

Figure 4.2. Principal Tiwanaku and Wari sites in the Osmore drainage, showing the middle Moquegua Valley 46

Figure 4.3. The indigenous setting. Map of Pre-Tiwanaku Huaracane settlements of the middle Moquegua Valley ... 47

Figure 4.4. Moquegua Archaeological Survey, radiocarbon dates (1σ calibrated range). 48

Figure 4.5. The Tiwanaku colonies. Map of Tiwanaku settlements of the middle Moquegua Valley 51

Figure 4.6. Tiwanaku caravan route geoglyphs, including llamas and *keros*: (a) Chen Chen M1; (b) Omo M10 52

Figure 4.7. Tiwanaku site group at Río Muerto, showing separation of contemporary Omo (M70)- and Chen Chen (M43)–style sectors 53

Figure 4.8. Tiwanaku red-slipped serving ware: front-face god *keros* from Isla del Sol (AMNH Bandelier Collection), Copacabana (Copacabana Museo del Sitio), and Omo M12 53

Figure 4.9 (a) Tiwanaku black polished vessels in the form of reclining llamas, Ciriapata cemetery, Island of the Sun (AMNH Bandelier Collection) and Omo M12, Moquegua; (b)Tiwanaku black polished serving ware:Titin Uuayani and Ciriapata cemeteries, Island of the Sun (AMNH Bandelier Collection); and Omo style, Omo M12, Moquegua 54

Figure 4.10. Wari chicheria patio group, Trapiche M7, structure 3 56

Figure 4.11. Wari serving ceramics, Trapiche M7, Huaracane neckless olla utilitarian vessel 57

Figure 4.12. Relative surface frequencies of Wari and Huaracane ceramics, Middle Horizon sectors, Trapiche M7 57

Figure 5.1. Portions of two painted textiles, each of which contains an example of a Chavín figure: left, an apparently low-status Chavín figure; right, a high-status figure 66

Figure 5.2. A breechcloth is shown on this Pucará sculptural figure 67

Figure 5.3. A sculptural stela found at Khonkho 67

Figure 5.4. The two-dimensional figures incised onto the Kantatayita stone architrave wear body banding similar to figures in Chavín and Pucará art but have very different headdresses and ritual paraphernalia 68

Figure 5.5. A fragment of a Tiwanaku textile from a burial on Quebrada Vitoria, Chile 69

Figure 5.6. A group of Huari statues photographed after their discovery and assembly but before they were transferred to the local museum 70

Figure 5.7. Reconstruction drawing of the Akapana pyramid as it would have been viewed from the northeast 71

Figure 5.8. The Bennett Stela, the largest and perhaps best preserved of the many Tiwanaku stelae, was recovered by American archaeologist Wendell Bennett 72

Figure 5.9. A reconstruction drawing of a ceremonial Huari textile believed to have been found near Ica, Peru, but now in the Textile Museum's collection. 73

Figure 5.10. Left, a digital reconstruction of a Tiwanaku tunic from a burial excavated by Padre Gustavo LePaige in San Pedro de Atacama, Chile; right, a Huari tunic 74

Figure 5.11. Typical figures used repeatedly in the compositions of the two tunics in Figure 5.10;
left, Tiwanaku; right, Huari 74

Figure 5.12. The weft interlocking creates sharp demarcations between colors in this detail
of a Huari tunic. Cotton warp (vertical), camelid weft (horizontal) 75

Figure 5.13. A Tiwanaku tunic textile fragment from a Tiwanaku site west of Moquegua
displays camelid weft interlocking but also uses camelid fiber warp 75

Figure 5.14. A Tiwanaku loom reconstruction, illustrating how a Tiwanaku tunic from the Coyo Oriente burial
grounds in San Pedro de Atacama, Chile, would have appeared in a Tiwanaku loom 76

Figure 5.15. A Huari loom, showing how one part of the tunic would have looked in its loom 76

Figure 5.16. The attendant figure in the center is from the carved Sun Gate; the figure
on the left is a detail from the Tiwanaku tunic shown in Figure 10; the figure on the right
is from the early Huari sleeved tunic shown in Figure 10 77

Figure 5.17. A diagram showing an image of a Tiwanaku tunic on a human figure and an image
of the Gate of the Sun 78

Figure 5.18. The mythological figures on Tiwanaku and Huari tunics seem to represent an image
of horizontally flying mythological figures that recede in size and into the apparent distance 79

Figure 5.19. A diagram showing an array of the figures characteristic of the arrangement
of Tiwanaku and Huari tunics as perceived from the wearer's point of view 79

Figure 5.20. The back side of the Gate of the Sun portal 80

Figure 5.21. A checkerboard Huari tunic 80

Figure 5.22. This *khipu*, which is quite unlike Inca *khipu* and is attributed to Huari, makes
extensive use of multicolor wrapping 81

Figure 5.23. Sun Gate undulating band 81

Figure 5.24. A comparison of three undulating bands, each with an animated head
at the turning points. Bottom, the Tiwanaku Sun Gate band; center, a reconstruction drawing
of the central band from the early Textile Museum Huari ceremonial textile; top, a characteristic
Huari tunic design band 82

Figure 5.25. Left, a Tiwanaku square hat; right, a Huari square hat 83

Figure 5.26. Left, detail image of a Tiwanaku hat consisting of knotted construction; right,
detail image of a Huari hat with pile construction 83

Figure 5.27. A group of cut stones in the site of Wari whose geometry and workmanship
seem remarkably like those found in Tiwanaku 84

Figure 5.28. A reconstruction drawing of a typical Inca checkerboard tunic as it would
have appeared during its creation on the loom 85

Figure 6.1. Map of the south-central Andes showing Tiwanaku and relative distances to peripheries
Cochabamba and Moquegua. 88

Figure 6.2. Map of Cochabamba's valleys and sites mentioned in the text. 89

Figure 6.3. Cochabamba Central Valley chronology and ceramic styles. 92

Figure 6.4: Comparison of Illataco- and Piñami-phase decorated style frequencies as a percentage
of decorated sherds from Piñami 93

Figure 6.5. Increasing frequency of decorated ceramics from the Late Formative through the Middle Horizon 93

Figure 6.6: Examples of common CVCT-style drinking vessels from Piñami, including variations
on *kero* forms and *challadores* (funnel-shaped cups) 94

Figure 6.7. Comparison of Illataco- and Piñami-phase decorated style frequencies as a percentage of the
total assemblage at Piñami 95

Figure 6.8. Late Piñami rectilinear domestic architecture from Piñami...97

Figure 6.9. Camelid jaw scraper tools from Middle Horizon contexts at Piñami 98

Figure 6.10. A Tiwanaku-style snuff spoon from a Late Piñami context 99

Figure 6.11. Stone *trompos* from Middle Horizon contexts at Piñami 99

Figure 6.12. Diagram of various early Middle Horizon tomb types at Piñami: (a) rectangular
stone-lined and stone-covered tomb; (b) rectangular cut pit tomb with a stone rim;
(c) round cut pit tomb with a stone rim and cover; (d) circular cut-walled tomb 102

Figure 6.13. Comparison of changes in pitcher and cup forms from the Middle Horizon (right) and the
    Late Intermediate period (left). All vessels are from Piñami 105
Figure 7.1. Inca *ch'alla* offerings...118
Figure 7.2. An Inca king consults with *huacas* 118
Figure 7.3. Small canals located in the Tiwanaku IV–period occupation of Chucaripupata 122
Figure 7.4. A complex of circular pits located in the Tiwanaku IV–period occupation of Chucaripupata 122
Figure 7.5. Serving vessel sherds from the Tiwanaku IV–period occupation of Chucaripupata.....................123
Figure 7.6. Circular pits in the Tiwanaku IV–period occupation of Chucaripupata, post-excavation 123
Figure 7.7. *Keros* from tombs, late Tiwanaku IV–period occupation of Chucaripupata................................124
Figure 7.8. View of portion of massive outer retaining wall, Tiwanaku V–period occupation
    of Chucaripupata..125
Figure 7.9. Overview of possible Kalasasaya structure at Chucaripupata 126
Figure 7.10. View of interior storage structures, a possible Kalasasaya structure, Chucaripupata 126
Figure 7.11. Plan of a possible Kalasasaya structure at Chucaripupata 127
Figure 8.1. The Ponce Monolith 137
Figure 8.2. Left hand of the Ponce Monolith...138
Figure 8.3. Right hand of the Ponce Monolith 138
Figure 8.4. Modes of commensality inferred from serving vessels: (a) Middle Formative;
    (b) Late Formative and Middle Horizon..139
Figure 8.5. Kalasasaya-style serving bowl, characteristic of the Late Formative 1 139
Figure 8.6. The Ponce Monolith left hand; directional indicators marked by arrows......................................145
Figure 8.7. Details of the Gateway of the Sun; directional indicators marked by arrows:
    (a) central figure; (b) attendant figure, lower row 145
Figure 8.8. The flow of *sami* in the gateway frieze 146
Figure 9.1. The area of greater Tiwanaku, an approximate 25-km radius from the city center......................155
Figure 10.1. Tiwanaku vessel forms 174
Figure 10.2. Contour map overlying an aerial picture of the monumental area of Tiwanaku........................180
Figure 10.3. Photograph from Max Uhle (1893) showing the flat area to the south of the Akapana............181
Figure 10.4. Plan view of the palace at Puruchuco 182
Figure 10.5. Comparison of monumental buildings in the Andes that have been interpreted as palaces 183
Figure 10.6. Omo M10 complex in Moquegua 185
Figure 12.1. Map of Tiwanaku...212
Figure 12.2. A museum-curated example of a Qeya-style vessel with incised decoration of a Rayed Head deity.......212
Figure 12.3. A museum-curated example of a Qeya-style *escudilla* with avian mythical figures
    on the interior rim..212
Figure 12.4. A museum-curated example of a Qeya-style *escudilla* with avian mythical figures
    on the interior rim..213
Figure 12.5. Map of the Putuni Palace Courtyard area excavated by Nicole Couture and
    Kathryn Sampeck, between the Kherikala enclosure to the west and the Putuni Palace
    to the east, indicating Late Formative 2– and Tiwanaku IV–period occupations 213
Figure 12.6. Map of the Akapana East 1 area excavated by John Janusek..214
Figure 12.7. A museum-curated example of a Qeya-style *incensario* with stylized mythical
    icons painted on the exterior and a modeled feline head at the scalloped rim..215
Figure 12.8. A museum-curated example of a Qeya-style *incensario* with stylized mythical
    icons painted on the exterior and a modeled feline head at the scalloped rim..215
Figure 12.9. A museum-curated example of a Qeya-style *vasija* 215
Figure 12.10. A museum-curated example of a Tiwanaku-style red-slipped *tinaja* 216
Figure 12.11. Map of the Akapana A and B sectors in the northwestern terrace area,
    excavated by Linda Manzanilla and María Renée Baudoin 217
Figure 12.12. The Akapana A and B sectors' northwestern terrace area with: (a) a view of the top
    surface of wall 1, the first terrace, and wall 2, looking southeast; (b) north–south section of wall 1,
    looking northeast..218

Figure 12.13. A museum-curated example of a portrait cup..219
Figure 12.14. A museum-curated example of a Tiwanaku-style *kero* with a rounded double torus............................220
Figure 12.15. Map of Akapana East 1 Mound area excavated by John Janusek 223
Figure 12.16. Map of Putuni Palace Courtyard area excavated by Couture and Sampeck,
 between the Kherikala enclosure to the west and the Putuni Palace to the east, indicating
 Tiwanaku V–period occupations 225
Figure 12.17. A museum-curated example of a Tiwanaku-style *kero* with a Rayed Head deity icon 228

TABLES

Table 4.1. A Continuum of Archaic State Traits...43
Table 4.2. Radiocarbon Dates from the Moquegua Middle Valley..49
Table 4.3. Moquegua Mid-Valley Survey Results by Cultural Affiliation...50
Table 6.1. Cochabamba Western, Eastern, and Far Valleys, Compared with Moquegua and Tiwanaku Valleys 91
Table 6.2. ^{14}C Dates for Central Valley Sites for the Beginning of the Middle Horizon..91
Table 6.3. Tomb Construction Techniques for Seated-Flexed and on-the-Side-Flexed Burials by
 Middle Horizon Phase at Piñami...101
Table 6.4. Vessel Forms by Style in Early and Late Burials at Piñami..103
Table 12.1 Comparison of Correlated ^{14}C Samples for Omo and Chen Chen Styles..229

PREFACE

ALEXEI VRANICH

Mesopotamia, the Indus Valley, the Nile River Valley, China, the Titicaca Basin, the North Coast of Peru, Central America, lowland Amazonia. These are the places where civilizations developed independently, largely untouched by any outside influence. They are, in effect, locations where archaeology can address two major questions about the human condition: (1) Why, after thousands of years, did people change from nomadic to sedentary agricultural lifestyles; and (2) why, after thousands of years, did these small, sedentary groups become builders and move into cities? One might conclude that there would be substantial synergy among scholars working in these places, since they seek answers to similar questions and face comparable challenges. Furthermore, their publications are driven by the same terms—for example, *complexity, state, urbanism, hierarchy,* and *specialization,* to name a few. Exchanges between these scholars are frequent and often formalized into organized symposia and edited volumes. However, in the end, the results tend to disappoint, if not confound, when we realize that we're employing a similar vocabulary to describe radically different data sets. As archaeologists, we first have to decide whether it is possible to compare on a global scale abstract concepts generated exclusively from material remains, and if the answer is yes, then we have to determine how we can efficaciously incorporate and reconcile the results of this cross-cultural research short of becoming experts in each respective area. This volume offers at best a partial yet focused stab at this challenge by taking the aforementioned fifth geographic area, the Titicaca Basin, and gathering contributions from a dozen of the leading scholars in the field with active research.

In the spring of 2006, the Cotsen Institute of Archaeology hosted a conference with invited speakers, with a view to having each presenter allow time for questions and discussion, which would continue into break periods and mealtimes. The result of those presentations and the dynamic discussion during and after the conference are published in this volume. Our rules were simple and straightforward: Present your data set and, from the perspective of your research, answer the question: What was Tiwanaku? The paucity of data is such that there is a danger that Tiwanaku becomes an abstraction—similar to the role that Atlantis played in Plato's *Republic*—a platform for scholars to showcase their writing and rhetorical skills. We did not want the conference and resulting volume to become an exercise in rhetoric, with the outcome based on the debating abilities of each presenter. Every opinion needed to be informed, and consequently the editors have tried to draw upon a representative sample of scholars working on various aspects and in different regions of the Tiwanaku phenomenon. The contributors could criticize previous and present models, but in the end, all had to propose and justify their own models.

In the first chapter, Vranich provides a general overview of the changing views, or visions, of the meaning and place of Tiwanaku over the last half millennium. Thereafter, Michael Moseley describes how the political climate of the middle of the twentieth century marginalized Tiwanaku from mainstream developments across the Andes. Tiwanaku's decades-long theoretical and intellectual isolation has put present-day scholars at a disadvantage. On the other hand, these lacunae make Tiwanaku and the Titicaca Basin some of the more exciting places to work because of the potential to redefine entire periods of prehistory. Moseley possesses the authority to relate persuasively such a controversial story about recent and present-day personalities and institutions, not only because of his broad experience in the Andes but also because his own project, Programa Contisuyo in the Moquegua Valley, was a result of tension that forced scholars to conduct research outside of the political borders of Bolivia.

As a result, areas outside Tiwanaku are better understood than the actual site itself. That situation is changing quickly with new research, but it would be fair to say that most of our recent ideas have been developed outside the immediate heartland. The order of the following chapters takes the reader from the farthest-known reaches of the Tiwanaku phenomenon to the Titicaca Basin and then to the ruins themselves. The continuation the Programa Contisuyu in the Tiwanaku "paradise" of Moquegua—a description that refers to its pleasant climate and excellent preservation of archaeological materials—has created a level of resolution of data sufficiently fine that it has been possible to make deeper inquiries into the identity of the people who ascribed to a Tiwanaku way of life. Paul Goldstein and Ryan Patrick Williams are two scholars who have continued and expanded on the research goals of the Programa Contisuyo Moquegua. Goldstein primarily concentrates on the Tiwanaku occupation, while Williams has been developing research on the impressive Huari outpost on the summit of Cerro Baúl. Both scholars consider defining the relation between the colonist and indigenous populations of the valley to reveal the basic organizational structure of these two complex polities.

The elaborate weavings described and analyzed by William Conklin originated in the dry coastal valleys and oases, areas that are distant from the highland capital. An architect by training, Conklin has published extensively on Andean architecture but has also found time to become an expert in textiles. One reason for these seemingly divergent interests is that Conklin sees little difference in the manner in which cloth and architecture are designed and conceptualized. Early in the development of Andean studies, the iconographic similarities between Tiwanaku and Huari led some investigators to conflate both cultures into a single entity. The two sites were identified and differentiated long ago; since then, their relationship has been one of the burning questions in Andean prehistory. Conklin considers both the mechanics of weaving and the arrangement of symbolism to distinguish between Tiwanaku and Huari, and he hypothesizes on their social and political structures.

Although the fertile Bolivian valley of Cochabamba offers neither the research synergy of the drier valleys of coastal Peru nor optimum conditions for preservation, Karen Anderson's stratigraphic excavation of one of the few intact mound sites in the valley complements previous large-scale surveys of the Cochabamba. Anderson notes a process similar to the one that Matt Seddon describes on the Island of the Sun, where imitation of key Tiwanaku elements—such as the *kero*—by the indigenous population preceded any evidence that could attest to the highland site's direct control.

Circling geographically closer to the southern Titicaca Basin, Matt Seddon presents the results of his excavation on the sacred Island of the Sun, thereby documenting the first confirmed incursions of the Tiwanaku polity outside the heartland. Fortunately for Tiwanaku specialists, the comparatively modest Tiwanaku platform escaped the notice of Inca architects who monumentalized the nearby area of exposed bedrock, as well as the notice of later colonial looters who targeted the same area when searching for fabled treasures. Seddon's broad and deep excavation on this Tiwanaku monument presents a relatively intact testament to the role of rite and ideology in the expansion of a complex polity, from the initial contact to what Seddon interprets as a forceful intervention of architecture of social and political control.

Charles Stanish traces his academic genealogy to the Programa Contisuyu. The influence of this project is evident in his emphasis on directing large-scale surveys, followed by selective excavation of sites guided by specific research goals. In a series of publications, Stanish has presented a case for a selective Tiwanaku occupation around the lakeshore and along routes leading to important lowland and tropic resources outside the basin. Though his research is cited by scholars aiming to temper previous claims of a monolithic and militarized Tiwanaku Empire, Stanish remains steadfast in his conviction that within much smaller, redefined boundaries, Tiwanaku acted with intentionality and, if requisite, with force. Stanish regularly visits many of the Cotsen Institute's active research projects around the world. These experiences are evident in his contribution, in which he draws upon analogy to other premodern civilizations that, like Tiwanaku, possessed a social and political infrastructure that one would associate with a developed state despite small primary centers and limited territorial extent.

John Wayne Janusek is often cast as the advocate of a decentralized Tiwanaku, in contrast to Stanish's centralized model. However, the reality is far more complex. Though both scholars disagree on key points related to the foundations of power in Tiwanaku society, they overlap in many other areas, including a similar concern about the wide gaps in our knowledge, where an entrenched opinion is indefensible. Janusek's ideas are based on more than a decade of work at the core of the site of Tiwanaku, where he personally directed and oversaw the excavation of residential, monumental, and agricultural remains.

The search for the origins of social complexity took Janusek away from the heavily modified Tiwanaku site to the neighboring valley of Jesús de Machaca. The well-preserved and shallow Formative-period site of Khonko Wankane provided an opportunity to expose broad architectural patterns and would form the basic blueprint for the design of the mature Tiwanaku site. Just as influential to the model Janusek proposes in this volume was the ethnographic setting for the ruins, where he was able to observe how the archaeological site became the venue for yearly reunions of the communities of the valley.

Matthew Bandy directed excavation and analysis on a project new to the southern basin. The Taraco Archaeological Project, based on the peninsula of the same name, founded by Christine Hastorf at the University of California, Berkeley, produced a generation of scholars attuned to the value of the most modest of remains, such as seeds and fish scales. Cold objective quantification would be the best way to describe Bandy's previous research on prehistoric demographics. On the basis of an extensive survey of the Taraco Peninsula, followed by a valley-wide resurvey of the valley bottom of the southern basin, Bandy has systematically evaluated models for the development and growth of the site of Tiwanaku. In this contribution, Bandy presents a more speculative, and more theoretical, approach to the foundations of political power at a mature Tiwanaku from the perspective of the use of space and the iconography of the monoliths.

The research of William Isbell and his colleagues in southern Peru was cut short by the violent Peruvian civil war of the 1980s, but not before Huari became the archaeological exemplar of expansion and hierarchy. Isbell's familiarity with the archaeological correlates of intentional, centralized planning is the basis for his critique of previous models of the organization of the site and polity of Tiwanaku. Patricia Knobloch systematically reviews ceramic pottery styles within their excavation context and relative or absolute dates with a view to refining the basic Tiwanaku chronology. Knobloch concludes that the period of Tiwanaku expansion was far shorter than previously thought, lasting approximately 200 years, from A.D. 800 to 1000.

In conclusion, I would like to thank the contributors for their patience and their willingness to review and modify their contributions over the long period between the conference and the publication of this volume. I would like to personally thank Lloyd Cotsen for his continuing support in the institute and its mission to investigate, preserve, and disseminate our global archaeological heritage.

*For Freddy Arce (1948-2011),
friend and dedicated Tiwanaku scholar*

1
VISIONS OF TIWANAKU

ALEXEI VRANICH

On January 21, 2006, in a valley 13,000 feet above sea level, a former coca leaf farmer from the subtropics of the eastern slopes of the Bolivian Andes walked barefoot past shattered blocks of stone to the summit of an eroding mound. Donning a colorful poncho, he gave thanks to the gods for a good year and walked to the edge of the temple, where his private moment of communion and gratitude was interrupted by the roar of an estimated 30,000 people. Evo Morales had become the first indigene elected to the highest office in Bolivia, and on that day he was celebrating his symbolic inauguration costumed as a pre-Columbian priest. His message proclaiming the end of 500 years of resistance, the start of 500 years of power, and the "beginning of a new year for the original inhabitants of our land" resonated well with the mostly indigenous crowd. The moment of his symbolic inauguration was marked by the presentation of the traditional staff of office, which was ceremoniously handed to him by the leaders of the Aymara Indians, the indigenous people living in the highlands of Bolivia.

A new and powerful political force, the Aymara had tumbled the previous two governments and now had brought Evo, as he is known to one and all in Bolivia, to power. Thus, by celebrating his inauguration at Tiwanaku in a traditional costume, Evo was publicly acknowledging his gratitude to the indigenous Aymara, who viewed him as one of their own. The presidential personnel made sure that the press reported that the staff, historically made of wood and bands of silver, contained signature material from each of the provinces of modern Bolivia. Literally, Evo became the leader of all the indigenous communities in the highlands; symbolically, he held all of Bolivia—from the indigenous highlanders to the white colonists of the Amazon—in the palm of his hand.

Even for his detractors, this ceremony was an awe-inspiring event that appeared for one moment to unite a country perpetually on the verge of dissolution. As unique as this may have felt to the enraptured audience, similar scenes had been played out several times in the past. Two hundred years earlier, a general leading an army seeking independence from Spain had passed through the ruins and ordered that a notable but much abused piece of sculpture be returned to its upright position. Calling forth the local inhabitants to witness the event, he declared the end of foreign tyranny and the start of a new, and free, republic. Nearly 200 years before that, Spanish priests discovered that the strange and demonic-looking statues were still being worshiped by the natives. Uprooting and dumping these stone monoliths into a prepared pit, the priests called for the natives of the area to witness the end of pagan darkness and the start of the enlightened Christian era. And two centuries before that, even before anyone in Europe was aware of the existence of an entire continent to the west, a man held to be the direct descendant of the sun arrived at the head of the largest army ever assembled in the land. Seeing the ruins, he ordered that the most beautiful temple be cleared and its fallen stones reset. Calling forth the local natives, he proclaimed the return of their legitimate ruler and the start of a new period of fertility and abundance.

In the following sections I delve in greater detail into the methods and motivations behind various interpretations of and interventions on the ruins. Though the format is chronological, there is clearly no implication of evolution. This selective review of half a millennium of interpretations, written on paper, painted on canvas, or physically etched into the stones on the site, serves to contextualize this publication and its contributions as part of a longer tradition of presenting a vision and the implication of the ruins of Tiwanaku. Even if we declare neutrality, our visions exist with a highly charged political and social context, in which archaeology and the archaeologist are elements in a high-stakes game involving global forces. We do have the advantage of nearly unlimited access to centuries of descriptions and extensive funding for specialized analysis that can source and date materials in a manner unimaginable just decades ago. Nevertheless, these are all just tools, and history has shown us that with enough time, our interpretations, or at least most of our interpretations, will fade as new data come to the forefront and new theoretical models make the previous frameworks seem anachronistic.

Setting

The site of Tiwanaku is located in the republic of Bolivia, in an area known as the altiplano, meaning "high plain" or "high plateau." Set between the two primary mountain ranges of the Andean continent, the altiplano is known for its high altitude (average 11,000 feet above sea level) and piercingly cold climate. At the lowest point of the altiplano lies Lake Titicaca, the world's highest navigable lake. The presence of this massive body of water moderates some of the more extreme aspects of the climate of the altiplano and has provided its residents with a continuous supply of lake and shoreline resources for more than 10,000 years.

At the near end of a funnel-shaped valley, 10 km from the shoreline, is the site of Tiwanaku. Most of the monuments one can see at the site date to a period from A.D. 500 to 1000. Prior to that epoch, Tiwanaku was one of several villages in the Titicaca Basin with a small temple and a cluster of associated houses. After A.D. 500, Tiwanaku evolved into the largest site in the basin both in terms of population and monumentality. The stylized icons of the Tiwanaku culture, such as the Staff God and the Decapitator, were extensively reproduced on stone, clay, wood, textile, and metal. At Tiwanaku's apogee, these artifacts were coveted by inhabitants of the shoreline of Lake Titicaca and several distant valleys along the slopes of the basin. The site itself was a collection of stepped platforms and sunken courtyards in various stages of construction and decay. Adobe houses concentrated near the monuments but spread out across the valley bottom as far as the eye could see. Monumental construction and the use of Tiwanaku imagery on artifacts come to an end around A.D. 950. The basin remains heavily populated and productive, but nothing comparable to Tiwanaku is built during the pre-Columbian period. Over the next half millennium, the story of Tiwanaku—the rise and collapse of a powerful society—was told in the form of a narrative in which the narrator stood at the end of history. Visitors would puzzle over the huge stones and wonder why the ruins appeared to be sui generis: there was nothing as monumental either before or after Tiwanaku.

The Inca

At its height, the Inca Empire stretched the length of the Andes, from modern-day Santiago de Chile to Quito, Ecuador. This remarkable achievement was reached through a combination of force, alliances, bribery, and a flexible and forceful use of religion. The Inca religion readily accepted other deities into its pantheon, as well as—to the confusion of the Spanish, who attempted to create a universal history of the Andes of their own—a wide range of creation myths revered by the various groups the Inca conquered. However, the Inca were uncompromising in the belief that their own creation myth was supreme and that their status as firstborn to the world gave them the right to conquer and subjugate. This claim was sorely tested when Inca armies entered the Titicaca Basin and stood before the eroding stones and towering monoliths of a civilization far older than theirs.

With a tweak of mythic history and a great deal of creative construction, the Inca transformed this potential liability into a powerful symbolic resource. Cycles of destruction and creation are common themes in Andean cosmology, and the Inca ingeniously interpreted the ruins of Tiwanaku as the remains of a previous world destroyed by the creator god Viracocha. Disillusioned with the behavior of its inhabitants, Viracocha turned its residents to stone and then made the sun, moon, and stars and subsequently created the first ancestors of all human nations, with the Inca being the first among first. This having been accomplished, he left Tiwanaku and journeyed across the landscape, naming places and calling out the first couples from their *pacarina*, or "dawning places," to populate their respective homelands. In the meantime, the first Inca couple traveled underground to the valley of Cuzco with instructions to conquer and bring all the trappings of civilization to the people of the Andes. Inca rule was now based on their firstborn status at Tiwanaku, and, as if to clear up any potential doubt, the sun himself gave the first Inca, Manco Capac, a specific mandate of rule over other Andean groups. Having been descended from the sun, their supreme deity, the Inca could thus claim special privilege and declare his legitimacy as a pan-Andean ruler.

To make this history tangible, the Inca invested a huge amount of energy in constructions across the entire Titicaca Basin, modifying and enhancing important ritual places. Tiwanaku became the terminal point on an important ritual pilgrimage route that began in the Inca capital of Cuzco. The best-preserved structure at Tiwanaku, the Pumapunku, was renovated and refurbished, and a royal and religious settlement, complete with a palace, bath (essential for Inca rituals), kitchen, and associated plaza, was built against this temple. The Incas even intervened in a more aggressive fashion on the platform, emptying out fill between the retaining walls to form three chambers overlooking the plaza. Arriving in Tiwanaku, visitors and pilgrims would be hosted in the refurbished and Incanized temple, where the mythic history would be told through ritual performance.

The Inca, then, essentially carried out the first excavation and interpretation-driven restoration project and, to continue this modern touristic metaphor, built a complete planned settlement to receive, house, and entertain visitors.

European Invasion and Colonization

For the Inca, Tiwanaku was the end of one world and the start of the next. However, within a few decades, the Spaniards would arrive with the clear intent of razing the Andean world and starting a new Spanish Catholic world. By the time Cieza de León, a young Spanish soldier contracted to write the first official history of the Andes, arrived in Tiwanaku a few short years after Spain's incursion into the Inca Empire, the site had been in ruins for nearly half a millennium. Deriving no answers from the site itself as to the purpose of the huge eroding pillars and the strangely cut stone blocks or the identity of the builders, he interviewed the local Aymara Indians and asked them if the Inca built these ruins. Laughing, they said no and instead related the story of a race of giants who moved the huge stones in a single night. Their reason and motivation behind such a story are of course speculation, but based on my own personal experience and a well-documented history of interactions between the Aymara and more powerful foreigners, I am firm in the belief that nothing is said in a casual manner. In that light, this story would serve the Aymara well by divorcing them from the tangible evidence of a pagan past. They could then claim, as indigenous writers would in the coming decades, that they had always been Catholic, though with a slight variation on the particulars. More immediate was the partition of the former empire and its wealth. Land that belonged to the Inca was being confiscated for the Spanish Crown or divided up by the conquistadors. Land that belonged to those conquered by the Inca (and subsequently "liberated" by the Spanish) could ostensibly revert to its original owners. The largest, most visible claim by the Inca to the fertile Titicaca Basin was debunked; consequently, the question of tangible proof of ownership retreated into a nonhuman past. The next of kin would be the Aymara.

The Spaniards found this explanation compatible with their own agenda. Like the Inca, their mandate to rule was divine, and their justification for the destruction of the Inca Empire was based on the idea that they had liberated the continent from tyrants who were in fact recent interlopers. The ruins of Tiwanaku were not Inca and thus served to ridicule their mythic history by showing that other societies, perhaps even more amazing cultures that had been destroyed by the tyrant Inca, had existed in the past. The Spanish priest Sarmiento de Gamboa, commissioned to write an official history of the Incas and to find a justification for the conquest, would present this and other information to the remaining Inca nobility and force them sign a document admitting their crimes. Indigenous writer Guaman Poma would retort with a 1,000-page illustrated letter to the king of Spain, presenting a Christianized version of Inca creation and laying claim to the ruins on the basis that the Inca emperor had built Tiwanaku after hearing of the buildings of Babylon and the Temple of Solomon.

Age of the Traveler-Scholar

After the first century of the conquest, the site and what it represented began to fade from the public imagination. The economic and political center of the Andes had shifted to the coast and the new city of Lima; the high Andes and its ruins of stone became a dangerous backwater subject to periodic indigenous rebellions. Even though abandoned for half a millennium and disassociated (at least officially) by the local indigenous population, the silent monoliths and carvings would occasionally offend Catholic sensibilities and become targets of ritual mutilation and burial. The ruins were rediscovered by a series of traveler-scholars in the late eighteenth and the nineteenth century after the colonies achieved their independence from Spain. Though the site had changed from a sacred location to a convenient quarry for the haciendas, churches, and civic architecture of the new colonial order, enough remained to draw wonder and awe. The Tiwanaku had a curious way of building walls and revetments by placing large pillars in between sections of ashlars. When all the small well-dressed stone had been quarried, the remaining pillars brought to the Western mind familiar places like Stonehenge and Baalbek. A few of the much abused monoliths remained, including the celebrated Gateway of the Sun, reset as a noble gesture to the indigenous people but, unfortunately for archaeologists, without note of its original location. Most curious were two monoliths set directly at the entrance to the church in the town plaza. According to early travelers, these monoliths were brought from the ruins by the local priest and commissioned to be carved into statues of the saints Peter and Paul. One could interpret this story, if true, as either the resourceful Aymara's way of both preserving a portion of their past and avoiding the expense of making from scratch one more set of saints for their colonial masters, or as proof of the degree of accommodation that had been reached by the Catholic authorities and their indigenous charges.

It is of interest to note that Tiwanaku also became known to the outside world through popular travel books that often highlighted, if not exaggerated, the mysterious and exotic aspect of the wilds of the Americas. Descriptions of human sacrifices and drawings of strangely dressed and impoverished natives fed readers' appetites for the dangerous and exotic. Notwithstanding, many of the drawings, maps, and later photographs of these early traveling scholars are invaluable resources for the present-day researcher, since they show many structures that have been substantially modified or lost. Their other activities—collecting artifacts for European museums, elaborating theories on the origins of the Tiwanaku people based on hyper-diffusion concepts of the time, and spinning romanticized ideas about the rise and fall of civilizations—would eventually lead to a backlash in the mid–twentieth century that continues to affect the field today.

Building Tiwanaku

In the turbulent years after emancipation from Spain, Bolivia lost a series of wars and ceded substantial parts of territory to its stronger neighbors. The last major war—the tragic War of the Chaco (1932–1935)—destroyed the country both economically and psychologically. The exhausted soldiers of the defeated army retained their army-issued firearms and straggled back to their villages, harboring a deep mistrust for the state that had thrown them into a useless conflict. Even before that disaster, the loss of access to the sea in the War of the Pacific (1879–1884) had been etched deeply into the national psyche. To this day, a facsimile of a historic map of Bolivia before the War of the Pacific is displayed in government offices and private homes. The banner of the lost coastal province of Litoral is carried along with the colors of the present-day provinces in the quasi-military parades endemic to every plaza space in the country.

It was in this environment of defeat, xenophobia, and mistrust that Carlos Ponce Sanginés, an archaeologist and politician, formed an audaciously nationalistic agenda aimed at reconstructing Tiwanaku as the pre-Columbian symbol of Bolivian national identity. Whereas the broken beauty of the isolated and eroding gigantic stones on the windswept plains might represent the height of romance and mystery to the foreign traveler and scholar, to Ponce Sanginés the stones must have been symbolic of the impotence of his poor and landlocked country. As excavations began in the late 1950s, rifle fire from the rusty guns of the Chaco War—already antiquated in the 1930s—rang out sporadically from the village in the direction of the ruins; Ponce Sanginés, with a machine gun emplaced on the summit of the largest eroding building, responded in kind.

From his perspective, Ponce Sanginés was firm in the belief that foreigners had held sway in Tiwanaku for centuries and that the time for a Bolivian perspective was overdue. Fine Tiwanaku pieces, perhaps even finer than those on display in Bolivia, were exported under suspicious circumstances and placed on display in European museums. He dedicated a large space in his publications to attacking and discrediting previous ideas—especially exaggerated accounts and outlandish ideas—while promoting Tiwanaku as just as large and powerful as any ancient equivalent in the Old World. He would draw upon the Incas as the theoretical analogue for his vision of an aggressive and expansive empire. The heavily cemented and overly reconstructed pyramids of Teotihuacán in Mexico would serve as the inspiration for his methods. The problem was that Tiwanaku had neither the magnificent setting of a Machu Picchu nor the monumentality and size of Teotihuacán. Even more ironic was the fact that the more he excavated, the less monumental the site appeared to be. The celebrated standing pillars that seemed to sprout from the ground were, in reality, part of a retaining wall covered for most part behind thickly mortared revetments.

Ponce initially respected the archaeological evidence and rebuilt the primary building of the core, the Kalasasaya, as a low stepped platform. Though authentic, the effect was unsatisfying. Rather than instilling a sense of awe, the stepped sides of the platform became an obstacle course challenging visitors to scramble up the sides. Ponce halted and then dismantled his initial reconstruction. In the future, remains that were not sufficiently monumental were labeled "colonial" or, worse, "Inca" and were taken apart and reused in the reconstructions. What survived were those remains that were considered to be from the "classic" or "imperial" period. The Kalasasaya was transformed from a low, stepped plaza with multiple points of entry into a fortified platform bounded by a single wall of monumental pillars. As the national and international outcry over the reconstructions increased, Ponce withheld the field notes and promised that soon all the data would be published in a manner that would redeem his reconstructions.

Instead of containing objective data, Ponce's publications were for the most part a forceful discourse on the despotic and coercive power of Tiwanaku. The boundaries of this empire, defined by the distribution of a generously defined Tiwanaku style of artifacts, corresponded rather well with the present borders of Bolivia, but with the addition of access to the sea. Tiwanaku was now an empire like that of the Aztecs and the Egyptians and accordingly needed a pyramid in the center of the site. The heavily eroded and damaged Akapana was the best candidate, but for the previous half millennium it had been described as a fortress or a hill surrounded by rings of stone. Recent archaeological investigations support the theory that the Akapana was the most monumental version of a long tradition of raised stepped plazas. With a terminological sleight of hand, the suffix *pyramid* was added and repeated in all publications (books, newspapers, pamphlets) until it became inconceivable to say "Akapana" without adding "pyramid." In artistic reconstructions, the summit was reduced to increase its pyramidal form. Bolivia now had a claim to its original prewar boundaries; the evidence for this claim was a monumental pre-Columbian capital, complete with a pyramid.

Rise of the Aymara

The twilight of Ponce's tenure at Tiwanaku corresponded with the return of democratically elected governments to Bolivia (1982), and a process of political and economic decentralization began to redirect resources to local governments. Politically and economically astute, the local Aymara Indians clearly perceived the mutual value of the ruins as a powerful symbol and as a source of sustainable income from tourism and research. A near half century of archaeological work created an experienced labor force that organized itself into a formal labor syndicate. Foreign and national projects pumped money into the local economy in the form of wages for work that involved much less labor than cultivating potatoes or grazing animals over hundreds of kilometers of grassland. The number of visitors to Tiwanaku increased from several hundred a year around the middle of the twentieth century to an estimated 45,000 in 2008. (European and North American travelers visit during the summer months of June, July, and August, whereas national and South American visitors arrive during the rest of the year.) Gradually, the ruins at Tiwanaku became an iconic stop along the campaign trail for any aspiring or elected official. The usual format for such a visit was for the candidate, most likely a mestizo dressed in a Western suit, to preside over a small Aymara ceremony (a *pago,* or gift to Mother Earth for good luck) and then deliver a speech about the importance of heritage, the proud history of the Bolivian people, and the need to continue investigations in the form of large-scale excavations that would employ a number of people. Both sides would see the exchange as political theater, but this inexpensive and purely symbolic offering would resonate with both the countryside and the increasingly active urban Aymara.

In recent decades, the management of the site and its budget was controlled from La Paz by two government agencies: the Department of Culture—in charge of cultural events that range from a soccer program for youths to the investigation and preservation of historic sites—and the Institute of Archaeology, a smaller and usually subordinate branch dedicated exclusively to the protection and investigation of an estimated 30,000 archaeological sites from the high Andes to the Amazon Basin. It was easy to figure out the primary interest of this institute: located on Tihuanacu Street, this early twentieth-century building was covered with brightly colored Tiwanaku imagery both inside and out. Starting in the early 1990s, local Aymara communities and the municipality of Tiwanaku began a series of maneuvers to gain greater control over the management of and the profits derived from the increasingly popular ruins. After several years of escalating acrimonious negotiations, the defining moment came in 2000 when a coalition of indigenous leaders took over the ruins and adjacent facilities and expelled all state employees. Archaeological projects, both national and foreign, would continue to follow the norms established by the Department of Culture and the Institute of Archaeology, though occasionally a ministry in La Paz would block a foreign research permit as a means to bait the Aymara back to the negotiating table. Hiring was decided at the local level by a complex process that divided up the scarce jobs with incredible accuracy across the 23 different communities in the valley. The most profitable day of ticket sales, a festival held on the day of the winter solstice, was completely under local control: traditional leaders of the communities, attired in red ponchos and wielding staffs of authority, would collect tickets at the entrance. The funds from this event and from ticket sales during the year became an important part of the working budget for the communities of the valley and a constant source of friction as different communities and local organizations vied for a larger share.

The roles and responsibilities of the local government, indigenous organizations, the national government, and international agencies would be the subject of future negotiations and even conflict. Notwithstanding, there have been moments of authentic collaboration and goodwill between local and state authorities. The most high-profile collaboration was the repatriation of the largest piece of Tiwanaku sculpture from its much abused location in a traffic circle in front of the football stadium in La Paz. The monolith had been uncovered in the 1930s and was moved several decades later by Arthur Posnansky—first to the main avenue of the city, then to a mock Tiwanaku sunken temple in what was then a quiet area slightly outside the main congested area of the capital. In subsequent years, the capital expanded exponentially, and the tranquil faux temple become isolated in a congested traffic circle, suffering from the effects of urban pollution and neglect. The return of the monolith was a stirring event: a movable party carried it along the 72 km from La Paz to the ruins. Indigenous-based ceremonies shared the stage along with the usual ribbon cutting and presentation of plaques and speeches that are the mainstay of politicians. The moment the monolith was reset at Tiwanaku was an emotional one; the Aymara said that their giant had returned home; the mestizos felt they had done their part to right centuries of wrong.

The goodwill between the agencies in La Paz and the local community lasted for several years. At the time of the writing of this contribution, a critical evaluation from UNESCO on the quality of excavation and restoration became the catalyst to expel all the archaeologists of the institute from the ruins. The new mayor of Tiwanaku, a young Aymara woman with deep family roots in the town but educated and socialized in the nearby capital, appointed a close group of young archaeologists—both Aymara and mestizo—from the university in La Paz to assess the situation. The news of a protracted argument and litigation among the archaeologists and government agencies and ministries went viral across the Internet. The accusation that a pyramid was being reconstructed reprehensibly struck a chord with the Web-browsing public; images of the reconstruction of the pyramid became "pictures of the week." Modern technology assured that nearly identical versions of the original story were reported across various news agencies.

Experience Globalized

The ruins must have been a remarkable sight when they were a singular and difficult destination to reach rather than one of the dozens of sites that your average tour package will see in a given week. The massive stones of Tiwanaku appear even larger to the traveler who has spent days moving across the seemingly inhospitable altiplano, seeing little else than brown grass, brown adobe houses, and a few roughly shaped stones that pass for an archaeological site. Within the cultural context of the Titicaca Basin, the achievement of Tiwanaku is nothing less than incredible. However much affection I feel for Tiwanaku, I recognize that the ruins themselves can be a rather underwhelming experience. Misleading reconstructions dismay the increasingly savvy tourist, and a failure to control growth has marred the site and vistas with modern buildings of exposed brick and rebar. Spread out over several square kilometers, the site has no recognizable natural boundaries apart from a barbed-wire fence that runs around the main concentration of platforms. Most tour groups are not even taken to the slightly isolated ruins of Pumapunku, the temple the Inca refurbished to commemorate the birth of humanity that is now widely considered by experts to be the most remarkable pre-Columbian construction in the Andes. After two hours in the withering sunlight and thin air, few have the energy to complain when the tour bus drives by these remarkable ruins directly to the highway and back to the capital. Unfortunately, part of this indifference is the product of modern travel. Most tourists arrive from the direction of Peru and by then not only have seen Machu Picchu but are most likely suffering from what guides call "temple fatigue": the inability to appreciate ruins or to differentiate one set from the next. The general feeling one gets from tour books is that Peru is the place to go to see ruins; Bolivia is the place to go for natural wonders and to avoid the crush of tourists in Peru.

The same global forces that thrust Tiwanaku into an unfair popularity contest with Machu Picchu, Tikal, and Angkor Wat have also provided access to a well-developed and lucrative market. Every June 21, thousands of people brave subzero temperatures to stand in the early morning hours inside the low platform of the Kalasasaya. As the horizon over the low mountains to the east begins to lighten, the crowd becomes quiet; all eyes focus on the silhouetted figure of an important indigenous leader standing on the lintel of a monumental gateway and waving the multicolored indigenous flag of the Aymara. At 7:21 a.m. the sun breaks over the horizon several meters to the north of the gateway. Film crews aligned with the center of the gateway quickly snap up their tripods and move to the right, lowering their cameras close to the ground in order to frame the sun with the jambs of the gateway. The rest of the crowd, packed shoulder to shoulder along the near-kilometer length of the platform, may not even notice that the anticipated alignment never takes place. Even fewer know that the celebration began in 1986, when a dozen Bolivian archaeologists and their friends were inspired to revive a solstice festival rumored to have existed in the past.

The first festival was conducted with no reference to ethnographies and no consultations with ritual Aymara specialists in the valley. In fact, the organizers' primary sources of information were descriptions written by the Spanish of Inca ceremonies that occurred 500 years after the collapse of Tiwanaku. The attendees of this first re-creation, numbering no more than 15, were all urban residents with either a strong interest or formal training in anthropology; they brought with them a basic "ritual kit" that can be purchased in the indigenous market for special events such as the construction of a new house. The second re-creation, done the following year, required a bit more preparation; a serious attempt to contextualize the festival within the local culture was made. An Aymara ritual specialist made the basic preparations, and other indigenous authorities were invited. With lit torches, the mixed group of urban mestizos and rural Aymara processed into the Kalasasaya platform while two photographers recorded the event. In the emotional moments of the light of sunrise, two goals were established by the core group: one was to have the large monolith in La Paz returned to Tiwanaku, and the second was to "revive" the solstice ceremony. Twenty years later, a boisterous and rather intoxicated crowd of 15,000 greeted the solstice sunrise in the Kalasasaya while the original group either stayed home or stood by the side with rather mixed feelings about what they had created.

The irony of the present-day June 21 solstice ceremony is that the sun does actually pass through the gate, both on sunrise and sunset, during the equinoxes. There are also several other archaeologically confirmed solar, lunar, and stellar alignments that are more revealing about Tiwanaku society. The choice of the solstice sunrise as the important ceremony is based on some basic rules of event planning: the other alignments are either too small, are too subtle, or take too long to be appreciated by a large group of people. In the case of the March 22 equinox, the solar alignment is perfect and dramatic, but it takes place at the lowest moment of tourist visitation—that is, during the highest period of rain. Sunrise over a desolate landscape 13,000 feet above sea level after a terribly cold and dark night is an impressive sight that can be appreciated by thousands of people at the height of the tourist season. The dramatic setting and the pageantry of the event are part of the draw, but what is being marketed is the idea that the past can be experienced without enduring the complications of culture or society, or by going through stacks of books that are, according to public perception, difficult to understand, often contradictory, and lacking a satisfactory answer to the questions of how and why. Outside of a concert or a political rally, most visitors will have never felt such solidarity with such a large group of strangers. This model has been developed and tested at other archaeological sites around the world, such as Cuzco in Peru, Chichén Itzá in Mexico, and Stonehenge in England. Tiwanaku has bought into the successful solstice franchise with a ready-made market and financially has benefited.

Restarting the Aymara World

The fact that Evo's inauguration was so similar to the solstice festival comes as no surprise: decades of planning and organizing have provided the local expertise and a blueprint for managing the large and often unruly crowds that gather on the fragile archaeological site. The claim, privately whispered, that Evo Morales would be no one were it not for the ruins of Tiwanaku ignores a series of globalizing forces and a tenacious, well-run campaign that lasted for several turbulent and occasionally violent years. But politics is in large part both timing and performance, and in this situation Morales was a consummate performer, making his entrance at the most opportune moment. Setting the stage was a time-consuming process going back to the mid–twentieth century, when the Agrarian Reform Law (1953) swept away vestiges of the Spanish colonial land tenure system and allowed the Aymara to vote, own property, and migrate to the city. This act also had the effect of dissolving centuries-old bonds between family, community, and land. Several decades later the Aymara had become a powerful political force of related families and kin groups living in the city or in the countryside. The festival took on a special significance in 1992, when it became both a protest against and an alternative celebration to the quincentenary of the voyage of Columbus. The solstice would mark the start of the Aymara New Year, and the date of 5499 was calculated by adding the number of years since 1492, plus five cycles of 1,000 years. The explanation for this date is hazy at best, but the implication is clear: the Aymara world had existed before this date and continued to exist afterward.

By 2005, the year of the election, tens of thousands had attended the event, and braving the coldest night of the year was considered to be a rite of passage and a reaffirmation of indigenous identity. The entire country had become accustomed to the image of thousands of people standing around the ruins waving indigenous Aymara flags with mouths full of coca leaves. However, after an evening in the bitter cold and in very basic accommodations, most urban people were done reconnecting to their traditional rural roots and were ready to return to the comforts of the city. The rural Aymara, on the other hand, remained in the countryside and continued to work in basic if not arduous conditions. Nevertheless, the festival ingrained the idea of deep-seated identity through a common experience.

Tiwanaku provided the perfect setting for a major dramatic event, although it lacked the players. Previous politicos had donned ponchos and appeared among the ruins, conducting Aymara rituals with severe solemnity. Nevertheless, after the event, the candidate would take off the poncho, shake the confetti out of his hair, and, dressed in his Western-style suit and tie, return to the backseat of his chauffeured vehicle and be driven back to the capital. For several reasons Evo could play the role on a national scale, not the least of which was that he was Aymara and as a result had inherited a motivated audience already familiar with the euphoric feelings of unity and solidarity that a proper performance could induce. After his successful campaign and inauguration, he also became heir to the ruins themselves, which, unlike the hundreds of other locales that served as settings for political rallies, would become a mnemonic reminder for the story of Evo and the place of the Aymara in the Bolivian republic.

Since the inauguration in 2006, the solstice festival has acquired an even greater symbolic significance: a united Aymara have elected one of their own to the nation's highest office. Morales, dressed in a modest-looking alpaca sweater, still attends the festivals, but he sits in a spot that affords him a good view of the sunrise and renders him nearly invisible to the crowd. Politics require taking the center stage; but politicians also must possess a degree of humility and evince recognition; that is to say, there is no need to be blatant when the obvious will do. Evo and the Aymara no longer need to dominate center stage to stake their claim for representation and power; the mere existence of the ruins serves as a daily reminder of this claim—until, of course, the next successful reinterpretation.

2
STYLISTIC VARIATION AND SERIATION

Michael Moseley

This essay examines relationships between style and seriation. It was provoked by the question at the core of this symposium: "What was Tiwanaku?" This query has been asked repeatedly over the last 200 years, and one can imagine that it has been asked over the course of a millennium since the demise of the great urban center of Tiwanaku. A long history of research yields a consensus that the archaeological complex was a unique nexus of power—ideological, economic, political, and social—and enduring symbolism. Yet what the sprawling ruins signified for their creators vanished with their passing long ago. Subsequent generations have therefore continually interpreted the monument anew as an emblem of what they wish Tiwanaku was.

For the Inca it was a very special place where the creator, Viracocha, sculpted the first humans from Lake Titicaca clay. Yet the Inca encountered the metropolis in ruins, according to Cieza de León (1976 [1553–1554]), one of the site's early colonial visitors. As a kind of monumental Rorschach test, Tiwanaku has represented diverse things to different people and to various social and political movements. These changeable readings of the ruins are well reviewed by Stanish (2002), and further dimensions will be added as future generations redefine the past anew (Albarracin-Jordan 1999, 2014).

The one common denominator to visions of Tiwanaku is that it was a *center* of some ilk. Such acknowledgment reflects the physical facts that the scale of corporate construction and the elaboration of monumental arts at the complex are both unprecedented and unsurpassed in the Andes south of Cuzco. Consequently, it has long been recognized as a special place in the Andean landscape and imagination. For the Inca it was a nexus of divine creation and political authority; its status as a fountainhead of the Inca ruling elite and their right to rule was invoked by later communities as well, from national states to small farming communities.

For archaeology its "centrality" has long been associated with presumptions about core, expansion, and periphery and linked inseparably with art, style, and change. Tiwanaku was integral to basic ideas that arose a century ago in Americanist archaeology. These persistent concepts go unstated, but they profoundly influence modern understanding of the past. Elucidating the critical suppositions that have crept into the foundations of contemporary interpretation can contribute to a more refined appreciation of what ancient centers like Tiwanaku may have been.

I therefore review the very curious intellectual history of what Tiwanaku has been to the discipline because its trials and tribulations tell an insightful story about theoretical approaches to the past that the present is still tied to. The "origin center → horizon of civilization" concept that Tiwanaku fostered is reviewed next in the context of how and why phases of seriated sequences change. Finally, I elucidate the two different axes of stylistic variation.

Well recognized is the fact that styles change over time and the diachronic axis of variation is essential to the construction of seriated chronologies. Ignored is the fact that, as in linguistics, dialects of style constitute a significant synchronic axis of variation. Schools of fashion differentiate people who share the same culture. Yet this blatant reality remains unacknowledged by the discipline because seriation cannot distinguish which axis is the source of variation. It can only assume that all significant differences are products of change over time due to cultural change. Consequently, the methodology can and has delivered misleading sequences that obfuscate the dynamics of concurrent social differentiation.

From Core to Periphery

Of all the great ancient centers of the Andes, Tiwanaku was the first to receive broad international recognition. Many early visitors published commentary on and illustrations of the ruins (Stanish 2002). However, it was the German investigator Alphons Stübel who initiated a vital turn toward systematic description by methodically measuring, drawing, and recording the many archaeological remains in 1876–1877. Upon returning to Berlin, Stübel brought in a young museum assistant, Max Uhle, to help digest and report on the large compendium of data that was published as *Die Ruinenstätten von Tiwanaku* in 1892. As the title implies, the monument was considered a ruined city, and its lavishly illustrated arts differed from those of the Inca represented by collections in European museums that Uhle and other scholars had studied. Furthermore, the style could be recognized as pre-Inca on the basis of early Spanish chroniclers' observation about the relative antiquity of the site (Stübel and Uhle 1892). The well-received volume appeared when the discipline of archaeology was in its infancy, and it promoted immediate international recognition of the imposing ruins as a premier New World monument. Consequently, Tiwanaku has long been a privileged center of attention, scholarly debate, and intense speculation.

Upon first traveling to South America, Uhle planned to excavate at Tiwanaku. Visiting the ruins in 1894, he found the military using stelae for target practice. Horrified, he publicly denounced the destruction and created a scandal in the press. The government then prohibited all excavation. Completely stalled on receiving a permit, the frustrated investigator moved to Lima the next year (Rowe 1954). Uhle supported his endeavors by generating collections for foreign museums. Grave accompaniments provided high returns, and a grand ceremonial center, Pachacamac, a short trip south of Lima, was long known for producing numerous tombs, so he excavated there for 10 months in 1896. Deep deposits yielded a fourfold stratified sequence of mortuary remains that Uhle was able to sort out on the basis of his prior museum studies and Bolivian visit. Inca-related remains occurred at the top. They were followed by graves with local styles of pottery found above and below a layer of burials with goods that he recognized as Tiwanaku. The research results were written up in 1897 and published in 1903 (Kaulicke 1998). The monograph was a milestone because time-depth, stratigraphy, and seriation were previously unacknowledged in the New World. With sponsorship from the University of California, Berkeley, Uhle broadened his investigations of coastal cemeteries, and by 1901 his studies had ranged from the southern Ica drainage through the northern Moche Valley (e.g., Uhle 1913). Most remains were not stratified, but local sequences could be roughly seriated by comparison with the Pachacamac stratigraphic sequence. This led to the conclusion that Inca and Tiwanaku materials were very widespread in comparison with intervening local styles that varied from region to region.

How could these coastal discoveries be explained? As in any pioneering investigation, variation and heterogeneity came across as "noise," whereas similarity and consistency commanded his attention. Focusing upon the latter, Uhle turned to Spanish accounts about Tahuantinsuyu to fathom Tiwanaku (Kaulicke 1998; Menzel 1977; Rowe 1954). He extracted four interpretative tenets from the chronicles. First, prior to the ascendancy of Cuzco, conditions of barbarism and savagery reigned in the Andes. Second, civilization was singularly invented at Cuzco by a creative monarch, Pachacuti. Third, it was then disseminated across the Cordillera as a horizon of enlightenment by Inca legions within a historically very rapid period of time. Fourth, the short-lived imperium collapsed abruptly in the wake of Francisco Pizarro's military campaign.

Finding these tenets attractive, by way of analogy Uhle (1903, 1913) proposed that ancient Tiwanaku was the origin center and capital of an advanced pre-Hispanic polity that had incorporated much of the central Andes for a relatively brief period. Furthermore, the far-flung arts issuing from the capital constituted a distinct horizon style, similar to that of the Inca, and thus the Tiwanaku style became a chronological marker for ordering the local and regional archaeological sequences. With this bold stroke of interpretation he transformed Tiwanaku from its 1892 *Ruinenstätten* status as a major archaeological city into a nexus that was the fountainhead of a far-flung horizon of ancient civilization. Thus the age-old question "What was Tiwanaku?" could be asked of both the core and its periphery, as the present volume does.

Uhle's vision of Tiwanaku is credited for introducing the "horizon" concept to American archaeology (Willey and Phillips 1958). Historically, his origin center → horizon of civilization vision was also exceptionally important as the pioneering use of an indigenous analogue, the Inca, to interpret pre-Columbian archaeological remains. Uhle could well have drawn upon classical antiquity, other Old World, or evolutionary schemes to explain Tiwanaku. Instead, he developed an original Andean model that was highly appropriate for the region. Unfortunately, this innovative lead in pursuing indigenous interpretative models was not pursued by subsequent foreign investigators.

Uhle's formulations might have attracted scant attention due to his dearth of substantive publications other than the 1903 Pachacamac report. Fortunately, Phoebe Apperson Hearst was the patron of his explorations from 1899 to 1905, and the majority of his important coastal collections from the Ica through the Moche valleys ended up at the University of California in Berkeley, where A. L. Kroeber had founded the Department of Anthropology (Menzel 1977). Kroeber had been skeptical of time-depth in the Americas until 1915, when he collected and seriated surface sherds from around Zuñi Pueblo in the Southwest. This sparked his interest in working in either Mexico or Peru. The latter won out because of the availability of the Uhle collections and because Kroeber could have the field virtually to himself, which he did for several decades. This led to the establishment of the "Berkeley School" of Peruvian archaeology, which long dominated the course of scholarship pursued by U.S. and foreign investigators.

Uhle's legacy came about because Kroeber had a young student, William Duncan Strong, who needed support and was put to work on the Peruvian collections in 1922. Other students joined Kroeber in the undertaking, and by 1927 all of the materials had been published. The study procedures entailed spatially laying out all the pieces in a particular collection. Those with the most obvious similarities were then grouped together to create stylistically discrete entities. Finally, seriation was employed to order the entities chronologically (Rowe 1962c). The end results largely confirmed and formalized Uhle's more intuitive seriations. Publication was critical in making the materials clearly intelligible and useful to other scholars (Rowe 1954). In so doing, it reaffirmed the contention that Tiwanaku was an ancient cultural and stylistic wellspring of expansive geographic scope, broadly analogous to imperial Cuzco.

It is curious that Kroeber followed Uhle's lead down several questionable paths. Provided the opportunity to excavate in Peru in 1925 and 1926, he focused almost exclusively on the recovery of tombs, as had his predecessor. Yet in the Nazca Valley he did open a cut in a refuse deposit using the "European model" of excavating in 50-cm arbitrary levels. Unfortunately, change in domestic ceramics was not readily evident in sequential levels. Nonetheless, Kroeber's protégé, William Duncan Strong, later pursued such excavations when he and students Gordon Willey and John Corbett investigated sites on the central coast in 1941–1942. Digging into sloping natural strata at Pachacamac and elsewhere often resulted in the recovery of mixed assemblages. Nonetheless, these assemblages included a far greater range of ceramic forms—particularly domestic utilitarian wares—than were represented in mortuary assemblages. Yet there were few such excavations.

Confronted with creating a ceramic chronology from surface sherds for the 1946 Virú Valley Project, James Ford (1949:31) observed, "Indeed, with few exceptions of fairly recent date, it can be said that virtually all published knowledge of the archaeology of the Peruvian-Bolivian areas has dealt with tomb furnishings. This emphasis has an effect on current interpretations of Peruvian prehistory" because, as he noted, the mortuary focus excluded 95-plus percent of the broader ceramic record and the domestic settlements of common folk associated with it. Kroeber (1944) may have become aware of the broader archaeological potentials by the time of his last trip to Peru, in 1942, when he toured and recorded insightful observations on a large number of sites and monuments. Nonetheless, the Berkeley School never deviated from Uhle's focus on mortuary remains.

When Uhle worked at Pachacamac and New World archaeology was devoid of time-depth, it is understandable that he envisaged Inca and Tiwanaku arts as standardized and relatively homogeneous. These qualities made them regional temporal markers. Indeed, the essence of "horizon styles" has always rested on the unity, not variability, of their arts. Kroeber and his students accepted these tenets as the Uhle collections were studied and published. Given chronological concerns, notions of stylistic homogeneity spilled over to Ica and Moche fine arts. With the publication of the Uhle collections, the discipline was well disposed to conceptualize these and other bodies of mortuary ceramic arts as "whole cultural styles," as Kroeber would call them in 1957. Stylistic homogeneity is an essential premise of seriation, and this is the means by which chronologies have been constructed for a century. What Kroeber practiced in Peru was curiously divorced from what he preached theoretically in *Style and Civilization*. This 1957 volume defined "whole cultural style" and attacked it as a misleading notion that failed to capture variable aesthetic expressions reflecting cultural diversity and heterogeneity. Curiously, the book was not listed as a relevant archaeological publication in Kroeber's *American Antiquity* obituary (Rowe 1962a). The discipline remained content with the vision of style that Kroeber and his students set forth in publishing the Uhle collections. These publications reaffirmed the sanctity of horizon styles and cemented the horizon concept into the foundations of Andean archaeology as foreign investigators have practiced it.

Beginning with Julio C. Tello, Peruvian scholars have been far less sanguine about the utility of the horizon concept than their overseas counterparts (e.g., Lumbreras 1974). If for no other reason, this reticence reflects the fact that the rugged topography of the Cordillera fosters and shelters ethnic, social, and artistic diversity that conquests, including those of the Inca and Spanish, failed to homogenize into tidy epochs of cultural unity. It is my understanding that Julio Tello viewed the evolution of indigenous societies as a highly intertwined process with roots and branches that diverged out but often merged back together (Burger 2014; Tello 1960). This vision seems remarkably akin to Kroeber's (1948) "tree of culture" with diverging and converging evolutionary paths. Yet Tello's views were anathema to his North American colleagues. These colleagues literally "straightened things out" (Willey 1945). Temporal continuities were linearized into "traditions" and Chavín de Huántar was co-opted as the hearth of a new "early horizon." The latter prompted the first methodological scrutiny of the horizon concept, particularly by Gordon Willey (1948; Willey et al. 1956). Inspection focused largely upon the horizon style notion and its characterization. Although there has never been a horizon without an origin center, centers went unexamined and the Inca archetype went unquestioned.

Horizon styles figured in a marvelous 1946 experiment in Andean archaeology: the Virú Valley Project. This was the first broad-perspective, multidisciplinary undertaking of its kind to focus on long-term human adaptations in a single study. Excavations were undertaken at a number of different sites by a number of archaeologists, and they brought to light a wealth of artifacts and data that had received little prior attention. It also marked the first systematic survey of a broad range of prehistoric sites. The survey required dating sites from surface sherds, which James Ford (Ford and Willey 1949) undertook using innovative methods of quantitative frequency seriation that brought common utilitarian ceramics into focus. These controls, in turn, allowed the temporal and spatial distributions of sites to be analyzed as changing settlement patterns, and this opened an entirely new vista for archaeological inquiry.

The pathbreaking Virú Valley Project might have spurred Andean archaeology to move beyond its traditional fixation with seriating mortuary remains. However, none of the participating archaeologists returned to actively engage in field studies. Rather, many elected to work elsewhere or to pursue museum studies. This created a profound void in Peruvian studies. It was shortly filled in 1948 when John Rowe joined the Berkeley faculty and found that he had the field to himself, as Kroeber had before him. Hired to teach both linguistics and archaeology, Rowe was a brilliant scholar with an impeccable command of Latin and Greek and deep intellectual roots in classical archaeology (Menzel 2006; Schreiber 2006). Classical education led him to view ancient objects—individual ceramics and other specimens—in the manner of an art historian, emphasizing style rather than the typology that characterized the Virú research. Consequently, the course of Peruvian archaeology turned back to Uhle's original focus on tombs and seriation.

Tiwanaku had reigned supreme in Andean archaeology for nearly half a century before the sierra center of Huari was acknowledged to be the source of broadly similar arts and influences in Peru that Uhle and his disciples had erroneously attributed to Bolivia. The recognition of Huari reconfigured the spatial scope of the Tiwanaku horizon but did not eliminate it. Significantly, it raised the very fascinating evolutionary spectrum of two first-generation archaic states emerging concurrently in the Andes. Unfortunately, critical research issues surrounding the emergence of paired states were quickly obfuscated. In 1960 John Rowe advocated a new, unified chronological system for the central Andes. Previously, foreign investigators had employed rather idiosyncratic schemes, often invoking evolutionary stages that blended style and time (Rowe 1945). Therefore, standardizing procedures to clearly distinguish between cultural and temporal change was certainly needed.

To this end, Rowe (1960) proposed two interrelated things. The first was that the discipline should organize dating and interpretation on the basis of a sequence of temporal units, each strictly defined and subdivided on the basis of calendrical dates. The commendable intent was to divorce the components of chronology from the vicissitudes of cultural change, thereby avoiding problems inherent in developmental stages (Rowe 1962c). The calendrical brackets of archaeological time might have been labeled in an entirely neutral framework by tagging them numerically or alphabetically. Instead they were labeled "horizons" and "periods." Unfortunately, this nomenclature did little to divorce the discipline from thinking along the lines of differences in cultural content, much as Uhle and Kroeber had done. Thus today, when archaeologists talk about the Late Horizon, they tend to envisage the Inca rather than a narrow 42-year span of absolute time.

This narrow time span is a product of Rowe's second proposition. It contended that the temporal units of his pan-Peruvian system were to be defined and dated on the basis of a "master sequence" that Rowe and his Berkeley associates were formulating for the coastal Ica Valley (e.g., Menzel et al. 1964). To paraphrase Menzel (2006), the foundations of this formulation held that archaeological style analysis dealt with "communities" of art created in workshops adhering to standard models of widely acceptable visual communication in a culture. Arts could therefore be analyzed by procedures analogous to those of linguistics to elucidate the structure and vocabulary of aesthetic expression and to chart, in detail, their changes over time. Indeed, these procedures produced a very fine-grained sequence for Ica that was essential to the pan-Peruvian calendrical system it supported. The system's Late Horizon began in 1476, when the Inca conquered the valley, and ended with its Spanish incorporation in 1534. This 42-year precision dating came not from seriation but from Rowe's interpretation of ethnohistoric documents. What, then, is the dating precision of earlier periods and horizons of the calendrical superstructure? They were derived from ^{14}C assays. Because the assays and the master sequence did not always agree, there was very little incentive for the Berkeley School to invest in statistically significant suites of radiometric constraints. Indeed, because few absolute dates were run, a pick-and-choose philosophy prevailed, and the only acceptable ^{14}C dates where those that agreed with the master sequence.

That Uhle's Ica grave lots underwrote the longest detailed sequence in the Andes is a scholarly monument to Rowe. Rowe was not an excavator except on rare occasion. He disdained cultural evolution and was highly suspicious of the chronological efficacy of stratigraphy because excavation by arbitrary levels had characterized most U.S.-led investigations in the 1940s and often resulted in mixed assemblages (Rowe 1961). His penchant lay with the nuances of seriation—specifically qualitative versus quantitative seriation—and he believed that ancient styles could be dissected into very short divisions spanning a generation or two (Schreiber 2006). Consequently, the Ica master sequence was based upon seriated mortuary ceramics in collections made by Uhle and collections of looted pieces assembled by others.

Although the chronological framework proposed by Rowe is now prevalent, it did not arise out of scholarly deliberation and consensus. It was delivered by fiat. And it was imposed because Rowe was the dominant foreign archaeologist working in Peru at the time. Furthermore, Berkeley was the principal center for U.S. graduate studies in Andean archaeology, and it produced cadres of disciples. Expectably, Peruvian archaeologists working in the tradition of Tello did not embrace the scheme. However, foreign investigators were strongly compelled to do it the Berkeley way if they contemplated working in Peru.

Rowe's chronological system effectively purged Tiwanaku from the purview of the Middle Horizon by recognizing Huari as the origin center of stylistic influence reaching Ica and the other coastal valleys where Uhle had collected. This left Tiwanaku looming large but literally beyond the horizon. Indeed, "out of sight, out of mind" was the case, because the Bolivian center is not acknowledged on any of Rowe's chronological charts.

Methodologically, it can be asked if the Berkeley "horizon" scheme could possibly accommodate two concurrent centers of regional influence. Obviously not if one, Huari, was 250 km away and the other, Tiwanaku, was 750 km away from the Ica master sequence. In theory, banishing the altiplano center to the periphery was not important because Huari manifestations in Ica marked a temporal horizon that could be projected to the highlands of Bolivia. In reality, this presumption never worked due to cross-dating problems. Radiocarbon assays for the Ica sequence are not always internally consistent. Furthermore, sequences in other Andean areas are not always well calibrated. Thus cross-correlations made on the basis of absolute dates can be tenuous, particularly as distance increases. Cross-correlations made on the basis of trade items or items exhibiting stylistic influence become more tenuous with increasing distance from the master sequence. In part, this is because the small Ica Valley did not regularly export art to adjacent drainages or exert regional influence. Consequently, temporal horizons are defined by foreign influence arriving in Ica, not by Ica influence flowing to other centers. Again, distance is a critical variable. Cuzco and Huari are relatively close to the coastal drainage, and their stylistic influence is quite evident. This cannot be said of Chavín de Huántar some 600 km away. Its stylistic influence in Ica requires a greater stretch of the imagination. Obviously, things would be organized very differently if the master sequence lay in a Pacific drainage north of Lima or south of Arequipa. Consequently, the temporal framework of Peruvian archaeology, as practiced by foreigners, is tied by historical accident to where Uhle chose to excavate and to which of his Berkeley collections were amenable to detailed seriation. Serendipity, not rational research design, continues to structure interpretation of the past.

No objections were raised to marginalizing Tiwanaku, for various reasons. Rowe had great disdain for Carlos Ponce, a nationalist political figure who controlled Bolivian archaeology and excluded foreign investigation in the country. Thus there was no scholarly constituency to analyze the implications of Rowe's chronological system or to argue against the purge. The net result was that Tiwanaku and its entire Titicaca hinterland were marginalized from the prehistoric "Peruvian" scheme of things. This did not diminish the importance of Tiwanaku in the eyes of Argentinian, Bolivian, or Chilean archaeologists. Indeed, creative insights and provocative proposals about the altiplano center thrived when it was free of Berkeley School constraints. Thus, when barriers to outside research in the Titicaca region ameliorated and the pace of investigation accelerated, there was no allure for alignment with the distant Ica master sequence. Consequently, a very different chronological and organizational framework emerged. It is young, vibrant, and finding its way, as the contributors to this volume illustrate.

Centrality and Variation

Having weathered the slings and arrows of archaeological interpretation, Tiwanaku is not yet liberated from suppositions that accompany the origin center →horizon of civilization concept. Presumptions about art, style, and variation are embedded in the concept, and they extend to other ancient centers as well. Uhle's Inca archetype envisaged Cuzco as the singular fountainhead of imperial-style art and architecture, which was then spread throughout the political realm. Implementing this interpretive model entailed two presumptions. First, Cuzco was stylistically homogeneous and encapsulated the pristine expression of the Inca imperial "whole culture style." And second, as this imperial horizon style radiated across the conquest landscape, more variable expressions transpired in hinterlands, where the arts were not always faithfully duplicated. Faltering hinterland purity of origin-center fashion has long been a problem in accurately identifying horizon-style expressions in peripheral areas.

The problem plagued Chavín when U.S. investigators pronounced it a horizon-style origin center. Recognizing that fashion, like beauty, lies in the eye of the beholder, Willey (1951) cogently proposed that the Chavín horizon style should be strictly defined by the art and iconography carved in stone at the origin center of Chavín de Huántar. Reflecting the supposition that the most pristine expression of the horizon style occurred at the origin center, Willey's proposal remains a highly viable procedure for operationalizing the origin center → horizon of civilization concept. Yet it won few adherents in a profession lacking self-discipline. Investigators instead pursued more idiosyncratic characterizations, to the point that the term *Chavinoid* arose as a catchall for a morass of supposedly early materials. This definitional problem persists, and it afflicts all archaeological centers and their associated styles, including Tiwanaku.

Ensuing scrutiny of the monumental arts and architecture at the Chavín origin center revealed stylistic variation. This did not conform to the Cuzco archetype of presumed homogeneity. How, then, were graphic differences at the early center to be explained? After visiting the ruins and examining their construction, stone carvings, and other arts, John Rowe (1962b) produced a widely acclaimed seriation of the Chavín style that divided the monumental complex into an old temple and a new temple annex and the arts into four chronological phases characterized by different stylistic expressions. The ramifications for the early horizon were far reaching. Equally important, Rowe's Chavín work set important precedents. The first was that whole culture styles were encapsulated at their origin centers. The second was that if stylistic change at the origin centers could be identified and calibrated, then parallel change was expectable in the hinterland areas of influence.

Phasing

This interpretive framework structured my vision of the Huacas del Sol and de la Luna during investigations in the early 1970s. At the time, this Moche complex was considered the center and capital of the first archaic state to arise in the Cordillera. Its art, considered a unified style, had been previously seriated into a fivefold sequence by Rafael Larco (1938–1939, 1948), and this was a very highly respected sequence. Although the manner of vessel painting often differed between phases, Larco's (1948) sequence relied principally upon form differences in the spouts of mold-made stirrup-spout vessels evident in his private collections from the Moche and Chicama valleys. Rowe immediately checked the proposed sequence against the Uhle Moche collection of 31 grave lots with 600-plus objects and pronounced it a viable one (Donnan 1965). Indeed, in many ways the Larco seriation was an ideal one, with simple phase distinctions of broad geographic scope.

Common to all such schemes, Larco's presumed rapid transitions from one phase to the next. Indeed, without short, crisp transformations, seriated units would overlap and lack chronological utility. At Sol and Luna, I assumed that stylistic differences at the center were products of change over time that then radiated out to the broader Moche realm. Yet I was very perplexed by questions about *how* and *why* the seriated phases changed. Archaeological literature provided little guidance because this was not something Andeanists worried about. The technological basis for implementing Moche stylistic change was not a problem. Yet how this was done mystified me. I wondered if a great gong struck atop Huaca del Sol resonated as a grand proclamation rang out to "drop your pots and change your spouts?" Whatever form it took, some sort of proclamation seemed essential. Without an authoritative declaration, how could crisp phase transition transpire rapidly and uniformly in any style sequence? If mandates for punctuated change were absent, then style transformations would lapse into the sphere of artistic drift and temporal ambiguity. If authorities at Sol and Luna ordered style change, then did the capital's artisans quickly fashion new spouts? Did they produce new molds and create appropriate new painting rules? Once formulated at the origin center, was the new-phase production package then shipped to all Moche provinces, thereby facilitating concurrent transformation throughout the realm? This scenario seemed politically and technologically plausible. Yet ensuring hinterland phase-change compliance would have been a conundrum for centralized states and even more problematic for confederated polities. I wondered if "style police" were sent forth to inspect and standardize rural workshop production by Chavín, Moche, Huari, Tiwanaku, and other centers. Did style enforcers also bust old folks who clung to bygone motifs, thereby ensuring concurrent phase changes in seriations? If my former musings now seem amusing, they simply reflect the fact that the profession has been seriating styles for a century without explaining how rapid phase changes in Andean art transpired.

If *how* the style changed is perplexing, *why* is even more so. The Spanish and Inca conquests provide one model of why artistic transformations transpired. Uhle and his followers applied it to what they considered coastal Tiwanaku. The subjugation model defines the Late and Middle horizons in the Ica sequence. In the absence of conquest, the Early Horizon is defined by more shadowy "foreign influence" from a distant center some 600 km away. Yet all seriations have numerous phase transformations that are not readily laid at the feet of foreign interlopers.

What, then, were the cultural conditions that occasioned the sharp transitions in local style that make successive phases of chronological utility? Working at Sol and Luna, I was much vexed by this question. If foreign influence was not particularly evident in the Larco sequence and if artistic drift over time did not result in punctuated change, then what triggered style transformations? Certainly it was not nature! Kroeber defined culture as a "super-organic" phenomenon, and archaeologists continue to conceptualize Andean societies as floating above and beyond their disaster-prone habitats. Therefore, all triggers for artistic change had to be cultural. For Moche, transformations in religious ideology were possible activators, and the thematic content of iconography did differ between phases. Yet "the gods made them do it" seemed a tenuous explanation for why artistic fashion changed. My guess was that there was a correlation with political transformations, such as the ascendancy of new governing dynasties. This could not be demonstrated for Moche, but at origin centers such as Chavín, Huari, and Tiwanaku, the dynamics of governance seemed the best explanatory stimulus for the dynamics of style. Nonetheless, ranging from the Ica and Nazca valleys to many other study areas, there are seriated chronologies for societies that lack evidence of primary centers, focal governance, and centralized production of arts. Why should crisp phase transitions be expected in these contexts, or indeed elsewhere? Artistic expression certainly changes over time, and seriation can gauge this. Yet its abject century-long failure to identify the how and why of aesthetic transformations in the Andes is cause for reflection. The discipline seems to have embraced a methodology that "works" with no attention to why and how it might work, or might be a house of cards.

The Axes of Style Variation

Andean settlement patterns are characterized by relatively frequent shifts in residential foci. Deep stratified deposits that superimpose millennia of continuous occupation are rare, as are site formations akin to Near Eastern tells with very long records of settlement. Consequently, Andean archaeological chronologies are heavily dependent upon seriated sequences of ancient remains. Seriation is remarkably versatile. It will distinguish between three randomly drawn handfuls of red, white, and blue marbles extracted from a pot full of 3,999 marbles, with each color equally represented. Three "grab samples" have a very low probability of being the same or reflecting equal numerical representations of the marble population they were drawn from. In archaeology, the luck of the draw presumes diachronic distinctions. Seriation is a self-contained methodology and a flexible one that can order unprovenienced artifacts, grave lots, excavated assemblages, or surface collections. In the Andes, techniques of seriation have been generally similar for the last century, particularly in the Berkeley School. A whole "community" or cultural style is presumed when dealing with fine arts and grave goods such as those of Ica, Moche, Nazca, Huari, and Tiwanaku. Other than distinctions attributable to function or to social status, all seriations assume that notable differences in aesthetic expressions are chronologically significant. All presume that variation in style is the exclusive product of change over time. All presuppose rapid phase transformations in order to have chronological utility.

Seriation has formed the backbone of Andean inquiry since the days of Uhle. Therefore, to assert that the methodology can and has produced flawed results might seem heretical if it were not for a very simple truth. This reality is that the method can deliver valid chronological results only when style is shared homogeneously among all contemporary members of a society. Artistic unity and presumptions of homogeneous style are critical to the starting premise of seriation, which holds that variation in style is the exclusive product of change over time. Synchronic artistic heterogeneity within a style is anathema to this critical premise. Yet diversity in fashion can transpire if members of a culture or a society use distinctions in aesthetic expression to identify social distinctions among themselves. This is not uncommon. Today there are clothing distinctions between and within Aymara- and Quechua-speaking populations as well as between rural and urban populations. Different fashion dialects tend to have different spatial distributions. However, they can co-occur in profusion at cosmopolitan centers in the highlands and altiplano. At Cuzco, Inti Raymi reenactment is marked by a colorful influx of many different indigenous groups distinguished by different attire.

Methodologically, synchronic aesthetic heterogeneity is very important. It constitutes a second, nontemporal axis of graphic variation: stylistic differences paralleling cultural ones among contemporary people who share similar art. This is diagrammed in Figure 2.1 as two perpendicular axes. In the figure, variants of a single style are represented by different patterns that could align along either axis. In linguistics, patterned variations in shared speech constitute dialects. They are critical elements of linguistic analysis, and analogous variation is expectable in other aspects of cultural behavior. The history of European painting is replete with synchronic "schools" of art. Their supposed absence in the New World cannot be assumed on a priori grounds. The human genome has not identified indigenous people as possessing a gene that predisposed adherence to whole cultural styles. As with linguistic dialects, learning accounts for most of the variation in aesthetic expression that marks social distinctions in the Andes. Yet aesthetic taste could be physically imposed by one generation on the next in the case of cranial deformation. Different deformation patterns characterized different cemeteries surrounding the Tiwanaku Omo M10 complex in Moquegua (Blom et al. 1998; Goldstein 2004; Moseley et al. 1991). That these were kin-based cemeteries of socially distinct M10 residential groups is a reasonable supposition.

Historically, the concept of whole cultural styles was implanted at a time when archaeologists viewed cultures as relatively homogeneous wholes. Excavating at Moche decades ago, I presumed a high degree of cultural unity throughout the geographic realm of Moche arts. Seriation was a logical fit with this perspective. However, the old perspective has constructively shifted toward a more nuanced view that involves ancestor veneration, descent groups, and kinship organization as the cornerstones of indigenous cultures. There are differing views about such organization (e.g., Albarracin-Jordan 1996; Isbell 1997; Moseley 2001). Nonetheless, there is now more attention to differences in the archaeological record than there was twenty years ago. Consequently, synchronic variation in style is currently more expectable, and it can be understood as an indigenous reality used to identify and distinguish diverse groups of people within a broader populace sharing commonalities. Schools of visual communication and dialects of verbal communication enunciate social distinctiveness and social differentiation.

Distinct dialects or schools of fashion are a fact of Andean life, but they have gone unacknowledged in seriation. The reason is that in and of itself, seriation is incapable of distinguishing between the social and

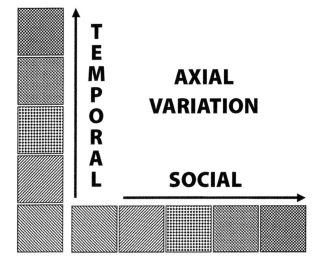

FIGURE 2.1. The two axes of stylistic variation portrayed as perpendicular to each other, with different variants of the same style represented by different boxed symbols.

temporal axes of style variation. It scrutinizes differences in style, but it has no internal means of segregating ethnic or social distinctions from temporal or chronological ones. Powerless to differentiate heterogeneous from homogeneous contexts, it proceeds from the premise that variance in style is the exclusive product of change over time. Methodologically, this is its Achilles heel. In a context of heterogeneity, the methodology orders two very different phenomena along the single axis of temporal change. Consequently, the chronological efficacy of seriated sequences varies relative to the amount of "noise" from concurrent social variation in style that is phased into them.

How much noise might the social axis of aesthetic distinction inject into Andean chronologies? If the Inca Empire was divided into about 80 provinces, each with multiple linguistically, socially, ethnically, and genealogically distinct populations, then heterogeneity was pronounced (Morris 1995). If political formations were characterized by recursive, nested hierarchies of kin-based descent groups, then hierarchy was pronounced. If indigenous distinctions in style of cranial formation, costume, paraphernalia, accoutrements, utensils, housing, and other aspects of material culture defined distinctions in cultural, political, social, and genealogical identity, then variation in fashion was rife among contemporary people in the ancient Andes. Consequently, seriation has been applied to a heterogeneous (not homogeneous) cultural landscape. Because seriation is a self-contained but not self-correcting methodology, the chronological ramifications may prove far-reaching.

The Social Axis

Identifying the social axis of style variation requires dating constraints that are independent of seriation. They can include stratified assemblages, but most commonly they come from radiocarbon (^{14}C) assays. Synchronic social noise in seriated sequences likely varies. When it is present, identification generally requires a minimum of 10 assays for each phase or unit of a seriation. This requirement is rarely met. The reasons are, in part, historical. Incongruities between seriated sequences and associated ^{14}C assays have been recognized for a long time, even though the samples of dates have been relatively small. An early precedent was set for dealing with inconsistencies. The Berkeley School held seriations to be valid and inconsistent carbon dates to be in error (Rowe 1967). Unfortunately, this position transformed seriation into an end in and of itself rather than an independently verifiable means to an end. It reaffirmed the chronological efficacy of seriation and the unstated presumptions of stylistic homogeneity that continue to structure archaeological interpretation. Furthermore, it disparaged the fundamental need for large-scale independent dating of seriated sequences. Consequently, ^{14}C controls have emerged only in areas where there is a great deal of ongoing excavation and fieldwork, and I will touch briefly on several examples.

Independent dating has not been kind to the most venerable of Andean seriations: Larco's (1948) five-phase Moche sequence. Within the last decade, the sequence has largely collapsed, with current investigators using a loose terminology of early (I and II spouts), middle (III and IV spouts), and late (V spouts) Moche. The current terminology is still beset by overlapping ^{14}C dates and, in some cases, elite grave lots containing early and middle stylistic accompaniments. The five different spout forms certainly identify different schools of fashion, but their social correlates remain elusive. Some have varying degrees of geographical focus and may call out social distinctions among groups of people with ties to different areas. Yet who these self-segregating groups were, other than ruling elites, is not understood. Therefore, Moche sociopolitical organization is ill defined. The consequences of a seriated chronology gone awry can have discipline-wide ramifications. In the early 1990s, consensus held that Moche was the first archaic state to arise in the Andes. Now Moche seems to have been a federated elite ideology without marked political centrality.

A much quicker metamorphosis in the axes of stylistic variation transpired in the arid sierra of the Moquegua Valley of southern Peru. Research that began in the early 1980s identified three stylistically distinct expressions of Tiwanaku, each with spatially distinct residence patterns. Methodologically, the first impulse was the traditional one—to seriate the occupations: an altiplano folk colonization, an imperial intrusion from Tiwanaku, and then a collapse-driven reversion to fragmented local expressions of the former order (Goldstein 1989). A significant cadre of ^{14}C assays has negated this interpretation. Populations pursuing different schools of fashion, different forms of cranial deformation, and different patterns of settlement and residential organization overlap in time (Goldstein this volume; Owen and Goldstein 2001). They also co-occur to varying degrees with the Huari imperial colonization of Cerro Baúl in the Moquegua headwaters (Williams this volume). In overview, the importance of this transformation from the temporal to the social axis of variation is that it brings archaeological interpretation into the theater of Andean actualities and what Murra (1972) identified as multiethnic ecological zones.

I conclude these considerations with a case that is still evolving. Rowe's (1962b) seriation of the art and architecture of Chavín de Huántar confronts challenges from ongoing field studies at the center by Stanford University investigators. Their work demonstrates that the old and new temples were not built sequentially. Rather, both exhibit numerous construction stages with interspersed episodes of use and building activities that were often concurrent in both areas of the monument before it assumed final form (Kembel 2001). Thus the seriated architectural sequence of an old edifice followed by a new one is not substantiated. Because the two were ornamented with stone artwork assigned to sequential phases, the temporal validity of the seriation is now open to scrutiny. Assessment of the situation awaits an emerging corpus of ^{14}C dates.

Chavín de Huántar may or may not prove to be a harbinger of things to come. Nonetheless, it raises issues worthy of consideration. The origin center → horizon of civilization concept presumes stylistic homogeneity at Andean nexuses of power. Yet if power was heterogeneous or segmented, and centers were cosmopolitan, then expectations of standardized fashion may be unrealistic.

Sociopolitical differentiation is physically stamped on ancient capitals, such as Cuzco, where high-walled residential compounds forcefully seclude and exclude different cadres of ruling elites. At Chan Chan each major compound was distinguished from all others by the specific motifs and compositions of its wall friezes (Pillsbury 1993, 1996, 2009). Although built sequentially, multiple compounds were in use at the same time. Therefore distinctions in compound ornamentation called out social distinctions at the apex of rule. Differences in the ornamentation of palatial quarters suggest that elite residents also differentiated themselves with elements of costume and material goods. If distinctions in fashion defined who was who, then they would be very important at the top of the sociopolitical hierarchy. If particular areas of foreign conquests or rural estates supported particular compounds at Cuzco (Zuidema 1986) or Chan Chan, then might not the specific stylistic stamps of the "proprietors" be expected on their hinterland holdings? If origin centers were heterarchical, why should archaeologists expect cosmopolitan cores to export homogeneous horizon styles? Horizon styles have been presumed to be homogeneous styles. Yet they are most likely abstractions similar to whole culture styles.

Interaxial Variation

I have portrayed the temporal and social axes of aesthetic variation as perpendicular to one another (Figure 2.1). In doing this and in critiquing seriation, I do not wish to imply that art fails to change over time. It certainly does. Temporal dynamics may have been the dominant trajectory in many cases. But in others, social dynamics were in play. This is expectable in complex cultures embracing assorted populations. Contemporary populations employ stylistic distinctions for many conscious and unconscious reasons. Identifying and analyzing these peculiarities in expression is no less important in studying art than in studying language.

Stylistic distinctions were played out on an interaxial grid framed by temporal and social trajectories of variation. This is illustrated schematically in Figure 2.2, with different variants of a single style represented by different patterns. The figure attempts to show that each variant has its own cultural and chronological history. Some stylistic dialects may have been old, conservative, and enduring. Others may have been innovative and expansive but short-lived. Intermediate mixes can be expected. The challenge is to identify where each dialect falls on the interaxial grid and then explain its cultural and chronological history. Seriation has pioneered inquiry into the identification of stylistic distinctions. The next step is to independently contextualize their temporal and social parameters. This is entirely tractable with good data sets. For example, it is now possible to distinguish substyles within the arts that Larco (1948) called Moche phase V. Furthermore, within the San Jose de Moro substyle, it is feasible to recognize and define the works of individual artisans (McClelland et al. 2007).

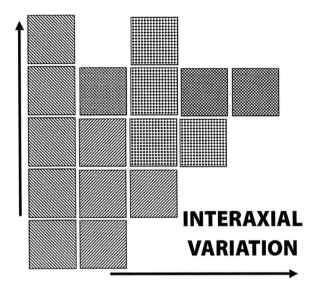

FIGURE 2.2. Interaxial stylistic variation portrayed in a social temporal matrix, with different variants of the same style represented by different boxed symbols.

CONCLUSIONS

Tiwanaku is a remarkable monument, commanding admiration as an ancient central place for centuries. For archaeologists, it became the primordial keystone for the origin center → horizon of civilization concept formulated by Max Uhle. This formulation was very original for its time because it was constructively based on a New World analogue, the Inca, rather than on an Old World template. Historically, Uhle's interpretive model of Tiwanaku was vital to foreign scholars of the twentieth century, who were concerned with the daunting task of sorting out ancient cultural successions in the Andes. Although variation in fashion was common in Uhle's Inca analogue, artistic differences represented background noise to be ignored in the quest for horizon styles that could temporally align prehistory in different regions of the Cordillera.

Originating with Tiwanaku, the horizon style concept reinforced an enduring reliance upon seriation as a method for identifying change and ordering chronologies. Seriation has been applied to many types of remains. However, its dominant and most detailed focus in Peruvian studies has been on mortuary accompaniments, above all those excavated by Uhle and deposited at the University of California. In the quest for relative dating, the Berkeley School emphasized ceramic grave goods as being particularly sensitive to temporal transformation. Consequently, ensuing interpretations of culture history have been time sensitive but relatively myopic due to exclusion of the far broader potential of the archaeological record for addressing issues ranging from everyday life through economic adaptations.

Beginning with Uhle's pioneering orderings of mortuary remains, seriation was refined over time. Kroeber and his students used typology to cluster ceramic grave accompaniments before ordering them chronologically. Rowe turned back to individual grave lots as the primary units for analyzing associations. Rejecting typology, he emphasized qualitative analysis of stylistic expression as the basis for developing very nuanced seriation. His methodology was explicated in a masterful series of very insightful articles of contemporary relevance. Drawing upon Uhle's collections from the Ica Valley, Rowe's approach was manifested in a very long, very detailed seriation of local ceramics. Indeed, some phases reputedly spanned no more than a generation or two, and this remains by far the most comprehensive seriation in the Cordillera.

Rowe considered his rigorous analysis of style to be similar to the analysis of language. Confident in this vision, he proposed two things. The first was that the Ica relative chronology served as the master sequence for a system of calendar-defined horizons and intermediate periods applicable to all of the central Andes. This scheme has structured archaeological interpretation by foreigners for decades. Rowe's second proposal held that if relative dating by Berkeley's method of seriation disagreed with absolute dating by ^{14}C, then the latter was in error. This pronouncement transformed seriation into an end in itself, immune to assessment by other means! Consequently, there are few ^{14}C constraints on the master sequence. With scant independent verification, the discipline's adherence to the sequence's overarching scheme of calendrical horizons and periods is largely "faith based."

There is a long-standing faith in seriation because it delivers relative chronologies through attention to variation in material remains. This is consistent with the fact that arts and artifacts are not static but change, as the discipline of art history attests. As practiced in the Andes, seriation rests upon two keystone premises. The first is that styles are broadly homogeneous synchronically. This, in turn, sustains the second premise, which holds that stylistic variation is the exclusive product of change diachronically. Without these keystones, the methodology loses viability. Maintaining the first premise may explain why practitioners of seriation tend to treat ancient arts as uniform whole cultural styles. Preserving the second premise may explain why the discipline has not recognized that stylistic variation occurs along two axes. One is temporal and diachronic, as the methodology requires. The other axis, however, is social and synchronic. Seriation distinguishes variation, yet in and of itself, it cannot distinguish if the difference falls on the synchronic or diachronic axis or both.

The social axis of variation is important in both visual and oral communication. Dialects of speech and dialects of style are nodal road maps that set the stage for appropriate interaction among populations that are different yet also similar in terms of their shared behavior. Social variation in fashion has long been indigenous to complex societies of the Andes. This condition explains why some seriations have gone awry, and others may follow when they are assessed against adequate suites of radiometric constraints. However, the significance of synchronic variation has less to do with chronology than with culture. Scrutiny of the social axis will tell the discipline who was who, and transform archaeology into anthropology. Recognizing these neglected potentials of the prehistoric record now resides with scholars working in Bolivia and Tiwanaku. This is because their Peruvian counterparts are wedded to the faith-based interpretive structure of horizons and periods that Tiwanaku inspired more than a century ago.

Acknowledgments

Assuming responsibility for all errors, I am pleased to acknowledge highly constructive commentary from Juan Albarracin-Jordan, William Conklin, Susan deFrance, Tom Dillehay, Christopher Donnan, Carol Mackey, Joyce Marcus, Donna Nash, Joanne Pillsbury, Charles Stanish, and Alexei Vranich.

References Cited

Albarracin-Jordan, Juan
    1996 *Tiwanaku. Arqueología regional y dinámica segmentaria.* Editores Plural, La Paz.
    1999 *The Archaeology of Tiwanaku: The Myths, History and Science of an Ancient Andean Civilization.* Publicidad Arte Producciones, La Paz.
    2014 *Una reflexión histórica sobre Tiwanaku y el marco institucional indígena en Bolivia. Sus origenes civilizatorios y su posterior desarrollo.* Editores Plural, La Paz, in press.

Blom, D. E., B. Hallgrímsson, L. Keng, M. C. Lozada C., and J. E. Buikstra
    1998 Tiwanaku "Colonization": Bioarchaeological Implications for Migration in the Moquegua Valley, Peru. *World Archaeology* 30(2):238–261.

Burger, Richard (editor)
    2014 *The Writings of Julio C. Tello.* University of Iowa Press, Iowa City, in press.

Cieza de León, Pedro de
    1976 [1553–1554] *The Incas of Pedro Cieza de León.* University of Oklahoma Press, Norman.

Donnan, Christopher B.
    1965 Moche Ceramic Technology. *Ñawpa Pacha* 3: 115–138.

Ford, James A., and Gordon R. Willey
    1949 *Surface Survey of the Viru Valley, Peru.* Anthropological Papers of the American Museum of Natural History Vol. 43, Pt. 1. American Museum of Natural History, New York.

Goldstein, Paul
    1989 The Tiwanaku Occupation of Moquegua. In *Ecology, Settlement and History in the Osmore Drainage, Peru,* edited by Don S. Rice, Charles Stanish, and Phillip R. Scarr, pp. 219–255. BAR International Series Vol. 545, No. 2. British Archaeological Reports, Oxford.
    2004 *Andean Diaspora: The Tiwanaku Colonies and the Origins of South American Empire.* University Press of Florida, Gainesville.

Isbell, William
    1997 *Mummies and Mortuary Monuments: A Postprocessual Prehistory of Central Andean Social Organization.* University of Texas Press, Austin.

Kaulicke, Peter
    1998 *Max Uhle y El Perú Aantiguo.* Pontifica Universidad Católica del Perú, Lima.

Kembel, Silvia Rodriguez
    2001 Architectural Sequence and Chronology at Chavín de Huántar, Peru. Unpublished Ph.D. dissertation, Department of Anthropology, Stanford University, Stanford.

Kroeber, A. L.
    1925 The Uhle Pottery Collections from Moche. *University of California Publications in American Archaeology and Ethnology* 21(6):191–234. Berkeley.
    1944 *Peruvian Archaeology in 1942.* Viking Fund Publications in Anthropology No. 4. Viking Fund, New York.

1948 *Anthropology.* Harcourt, Brace and Company, New York.

1957 *Style and Civilization.* Cornell University, Ithaca.

Larco Hoyle, Rafael
1938–1939 *Los Mochicas.* Casa Editora "La Cronica" y "Variedades," Lima.

1948 *Cronologia arqueológica del norte del Perú.* Sociedad Geográfica Americana, Buenos Aires.

Lumbreras, L. G.
1974 *The Peoples and Culture of Ancient Peru.* Smithsonian Institution Press, Washington, D.C.

McClelland, Donna, D. McClelland, and C. B. Donnan
2007 *Moche Fineline Painting from San Jose de Moro.* Cotsen Institute of Archaeology Press, Los Angeles.

Menzel, Dorothy
1977 *The Archaeology of Ancient Peru and the Work of Max Uhle.* R. H. Lowie Museum, Berkeley.

2006 John Rowe's Archaeology. *Ñawpa Pacha* 28:229–231.

Menzel, Dorothy, John H. Rowe, and Lawrence E. Dawson
1964 *The Paracas Pottery of Ica: A Study in Style and Time.* University of California Publications in American Archaeology and Ethnology Vol. 50. University of California, Berkeley.

Morris, Craig
1995 Symbols to Power: Styles and Media in the Inka State. In *Style, Society, and Person: Archaeological and Ethnological Perspectives,* edited by C. Carr and J. Neitzel, pp. 419–433. Plenum Press, New York.

Moseley, Michael E.
2001 *The Incas and Their Ancestors: The Archaeology of Peru.* Revised ed. Thames and Hudson, London.

Moseley, M., R. Feldman, P. S. Goldstein, and L. Watanabe
1991 Colonies and Conquest: Tiahuanaco and Huari in Moquegua. In *Huari Administrative Structure: Prehistoric Monumental Architecture and State Government,* edited by W. H. Isbell and G. F. McEwan, pp. 21–40. Dumbarton Oaks, Washington, D.C.

Murra, John V.
1972 El "control vertical" de un máximo de pisos ecológicos en la economia de las sociedades andinas. In *Visita de la provincia de León de Huánuco en 1562 por Inigo Ortiz de Zuñiga. Documentos para la historia y etnología de Huanuco y la selva central,* Vol. 2, edited by John V. Murra, pp. 427–476. Universidad Nacional Hermilio Valdizán, Huánuco, Peru.

Owen, Bruce, and Paul Goldstein
2001 Tiwanaku en Moquegua: Interacciones regionales y colapso. In *Huari y Tiwanaku: Modelos vs. evidencias,* Pt. 2, edited by Peter Kaulicke and William H. Isbell, pp. 169–188. Boletín de Arqueología No. 5. Pontificia Universidad Católica del Perú, Lima.

Pillsbury, Joanne
1993 Sculpted Friezes of the Empire of Chimor. Unpublished Ph.D. dissertation, Columbia University, New York.

1996 The Thorny Oyster and the Origins of Empire: Implications of Recently Uncovered *Spondylus* Imagery from Chan Chan, Peru. *Latin American Antiquity* 7:313–340.

2009 Reading Art Without Writing: Interpreting Chimú Architectural Sculpture. In *Dialogues in Art History,* edited by Elizabeth Cropper. Center for Advanced Study in the Visual Arts, National Gallery of Art, Washington, D.C.

Rowe, John H.
1945 Absolute Chronology in the Andean area. *American Antiquity* 10(3):265–284.

1954 *Max Uhle, 1856–1944: A Memoir of the Father of Peruvian Archaeology.* University of California Publications in American Archaeology and Ethnology Vol. 46, No. 1. University of California, Berkeley.

1960 Cultural Unity and Diversification in Peruvian Archaeology. In *Men and Cultures,* edited by A. F. C. Wallace, pp. 627–631. University of Pennsylvania Press, Philadelphia.

1961 Stratigraphy and Seriation. *American Antiquity* 26(3):324–330.

1962a Alfred Louis Kroeber (1876–1969). *American Antiquity* 27(3):396–415.

1962b *Chavin Art: An Inquiry into Its Form and Meaning.* Museum of Primitive Art, New York.

1962c Stage and Periods in Archaeological Interpretation. *Southwestern Journal of Anthropology* 18(1):40–54.

1967 An Interpretation of Radiocarbon Measurements on Archaeological Samples from Peru. Reprinted in *Peruvian Archaeology: Selected Readings,* edited by John H. Rowe and Dorothy Menzel, pp. 16–30. Peek Publications, Palo Alto. Originally published 1966, *Proceedings of the Sixth International Conference, Radiocarbon and Tritium Dating.* U.S. Atomic Energy Commission, Springfield, Virginia.

Schreiber, Katharina
2006 In Memoriam: John Howland Rowe, 1918–2004. *Ñawpa Pacha* 28:195–202.

Stanish, Charles
2002 Tiwanaku Political Economy. In *Andean Archaeology.* Vol. 1, *Variations in Sociopolitical Organization,* edited by William H. Isbell and Helaine Silverman, pp. 169–198. Kluwer Academic/Plenum Publishers, New York.

Stübel, M., and M. Uhle
- 1892 *Die Ruinenstätte von Tiahuanaco im Hochlande des Alten Peru: Eine Kulturqueschichtliche Studie.* Verland von Karl W. Hiersemann, Leipzig.

Tello, J.
- 1960 *Chavín: Cultura matriz de las civilizaciónes andina.* Universidad Nacional San Marcos, Lima.

Uhle, Max
- 1903 *Pachacamac, Report of the William Pepper M.D., L.L.D. Peruvian Expedition of 1896.* University of Pennsylvania, Philadelphia.
- 1913 Ruinen von Moche. *Journal de la Société des Américanistes de Paris* 10:95–117.

Willey, Gordon R.,
- 1945 Horizon Styles and Pottery Traditions in Peruvian Archaeology. *American Antiquity* 11:49–56.
- 1948 Functional Analysis of "Horizon Styles" in Peruvian Archaeology. In *A Reappraisal of Peruvian Archaeology*, Memoir 4, edited by W. C. Bennett, pp. 8–15. Society for American Archaeology, Menasha, Wisconsin.
- 1951 The Chavin Problem: A Review and Critique. *Southwestern Journal of Anthropology* 7(2):103–144.

Willey, Gordon R., and Philip Phillips
- 1958 *Method and Theory in American Archaeology.* University of Chicago Press, Chicago.

Willey, Gordon R., John H. Rowe, Charles C. DiPeso, William A. Ritchie, Irving Rouse, and Donald W. Lathrap
- 1956 An Archaeological Classification of Culture Contact Situations. In *Seminars in Archaeology: 1955,* No. 11, edited by R. Wauchope, pp. 1–30. Memoirs of the Society for American Archaeology, Salt Lake City.

Zuidema, R. T.
- 1986 *La Civilisation Inca au Cuzco.* Presses Universitaires de France, College de France, Paris.

3

Tiwanaku: A Cult of the Masses

Patrick Ryan Williams

Over the years, archaeological perspectives on Tiwanaku have diverged substantially; it has been viewed as an autocratic state, a ceremonial center, and a collective of social groups. In this essay, I review the meaning of Tiwanaku from one of its most pronounced peripheries. Addressing what Tiwanaku was not in comparison to its peer polities of the period enhances this perspective.

Specifically, I compare and contrast Tiwanaku and Wari provincialism in the one place they both invested in heavily, the Moquegua Valley of southern Peru (Figure 3.1). Examining investments in monumental construction, agricultural systems, and access to exotic goods, I argue that the two polities were significantly different when confronted with a competing peer. I also assess distinctions in residential architecture and mortuary patterns between the two groups in their provincial setting. This latter distinction highlights drastically different social organization on their only known frontier.

Overall, I argue that Tiwanaku did not manifest a centralized authority in its provincial setting. Tiwanaku invested little in monumental construction and agrarian reclamation in comparison to the Wari state investment in the same valley (Figures 3.2, 3.3). In its provincial setting, Tiwanaku exhibits less diversity in rank and status in residential architecture than its peer. Both Wari and Tiwanaku peoples consumed exotic goods, but they were more restricted to certain elite groups in the Wari circles. Tiwanaku had more equity in access to status goods but also tended to have access to fewer goods than did Wari elites. Finally, Tiwanaku peoples in Moquegua show a higher degree of conformity to a cultural ideal than do Wari peoples, especially in terms of mortuary practice. That is, socioeconomically and culturally, Wari-related peoples were more diverse than Tiwanaku people in Moquegua. Thus, unlike Wari, the power of Tiwanaku ideology came from a group of shareholders whose common identity bound them together. In support of this assertion, I highlight the pertinent data from Moquegua.

Political Statements: Wari and Tiwanaku Infrastructure in Moquegua

Investments in monumental constructions and centralized agrarian works can be construed as political statements by their builders (Moore 1996). As such, the type of monumental architecture, its scale, and its emotive impact are all key variables in assessing how this class of construction may have served as political statements made by its creators and its users.

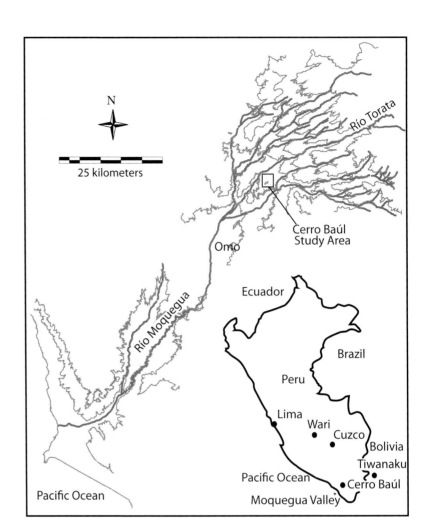

FIGURE 3.1. Moquegua Valley map.

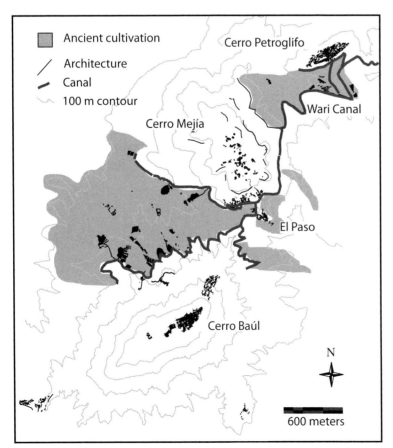

FIGURE 3.2. Plan of the Wari colony at Cerro Baúl.

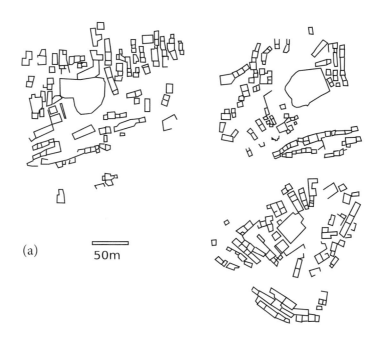

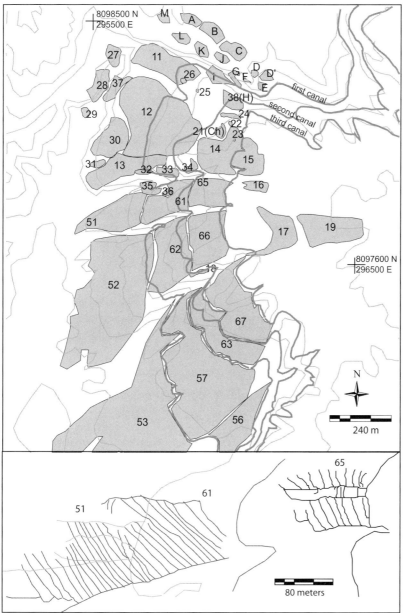

FIGURE 3.3. Plans of the Tiwanaku colonies at (a) Omo (Goldstein 2005); and (b) Chen Chen (Williams 2002).

Monumental Constructions

The principal Tiwanaku monumental construction in the valley is the temple at Omo (Goldstein 1993). It is a tripartite structure composed of three courts. The overall dimensions of the monument are approximately 120 m by 40 m (Figure 3.4). Constructed of a base of cut volcanic blocks and made of adobe bricks, it was certainly an impressive structure. It was, however, a unique monument in Moquegua and indeed in the Tiwanaku periphery generally.

The only other ostentatious Tiwanaku monumental structures that could be considered public statements are the several rustic tripartite plazas concentrated around the slopes of Cerro Baúl (Nash and Williams 2005; Owen 2005). Each complex measures between 70 m and 100 m long and 30 m and 50 m wide (Figure 3.4). The walls have a low fieldstone base less than 30 cm high. They were certainly austere compared to the Omo temple or any other class of monumental construction in the valley. Indeed, I have argued elsewhere (Nash and Williams 2005) that these were likely not constructed by a state entity but by leaders of small factions competing for followers.

Wari monumental construction, on the other hand, is both ubiquitous and extensive in Moquegua and bears the mark of a concerted centralized effort. The most conspicuous display is the summit of Cerro Baúl itself, which is composed of a series of cut-stone complexes over 250 m long and 100 m wide (Figure 3.5). This massive aggregate holds a palatial residence, two D-shaped temple structures, and a series of monumental plaza compounds. Two segregated tripartite temple complexes are separated from the main series of monumental compounds on the summit. The Picchu Picchu Temple (sector E) measures 60 m by 30 m and is oriented to the sacred mountain of the same name to the north. The Arundane Temple (sector D) measures 50 m by 30 m and is aligned with Arundane Peak to the east (Williams and Nash 2006). In terms of scale, the monumental structures on the summit of Baúl cover six times the area of the Omo Temple. Given its remote location, it required substantially more than six times the labor effort to build and maintain. Materials, water, and labor were all imported from the valley below and from surrounding mountainsides to construct the Baúl monuments.

Besides the monumental construction on its summit, the mountain of Cerro Baúl was artificially modified to become a monument itself. A 300-m-long staircase, which passes three massive walls that delimit the summit as restricted space, ascends the mountain. The massive walls of the palace compounds on the summit of the great mesa crowned the entire edifice. The emotive impact of the monumental construction of Cerro Baúl is equally dwarfing. The three massive perimeter walls, interspersed with small domestic constructions over a vertical distance of some 250 m, would have turned the north face of the mountain into a man-made facade mimicking a skyscraper. The summit architecture, plastered and painted in shades from white and blue-gray to red and orange, capped the monumental citadel, which could be seen from tens of miles away and from nearly every point in the valley.

Wari monumental construction was not confined to the summit of Cerro Baúl (Figure 3.2). A monumental wall, approximately 2 km in length, circumscribed the adjacent Wari site of Cerro Mejía and its summit of lavish residences, which was like-

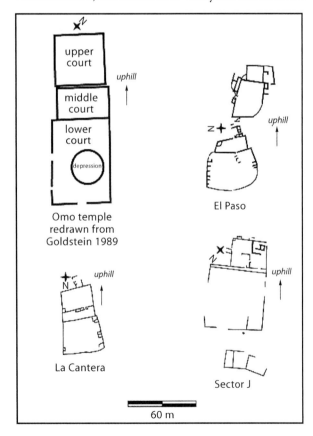

FIGURE 3.4. Comparative plans of Tiwanaku monumental architecture (Nash and Williams 2005).

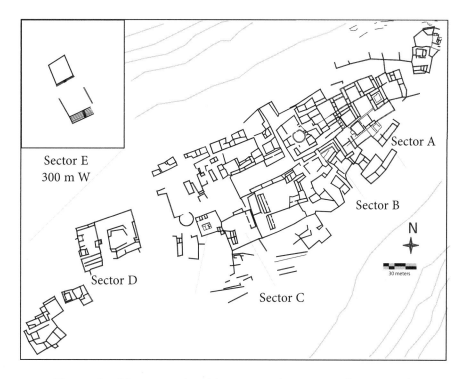

FIGURE 3.5. Monumental architecture on the summit of Cerro Baúl.

wise ascended via a set of monumental staircases (Nash 2002). Even the relatively austere settlement of Cerro Petroglifo had a dual monumental staircase that ascended from its base to its summit (Nash 1996). More than a decade of intensive archaeological survey and excavation has revealed no evidence for defensive projectiles amassed near walls, or anywhere for that matter.

Thus monumental architecture in the Tiwanaku realm in Moquegua was confined to what could be interpreted as religious temples. One of these temples was clearly in an architectural class of its own. The others were more austere and were likely built by small local communities. The Wari communities, on the other hand, housed several classes of monumental architecture that required extensive coordination to construct and maintain. An assessment of investment in agricultural infrastructure yields a similar perspective to that provided by an analysis of monumental architecture.

Agrarian Investments

The principal Wari agrarian investment in Moquegua was the massive canal system around Cerro Baúl (Figure 3.2). It drew water from a 14-km-long canal that carried some 400 liters of water per second at its midpoint. This likely translates to a 700- to 1,000-liter-per-second capacity at its source. It irrigated more than 300 ha of agricultural terracing, with more than 220,000 m of preserved terraced walls. Estimated construction costs for the preserved parts of the system are nearly 100,000 man-days (Williams 2006).

The largest Tiwanaku agricultural system in the valley was centered beside the population center at Chen Chen (Figure 3.3a). Here, a 10-km-long canal irrigated 93 ha of the flat plains behind the modern city of Moquegua. The midpoint capacity of this canal was circa 80 liters per second, a fifth the size of the Wari investment. Without any terraced infrastructure, the construction costs were significantly less per area cultivated than for the Wari system (Williams 2006). Despite a more massive population and arguably a higher demand for agricultural products of the fertile valleys for export back to the Tiwanaku capital, Moquegua's Tiwanaku province invested significantly less in agricultural infrastructure than its Wari counterpart. Besides, the Wari capital was probably too far away to take advantage of Moquegua's agricultural production, and most of the products that were grown in Moquegua could also have been grown around the Wari capital. Tiwanaku, thriving in a high-elevation plateau, had a much lower diversity of crops that could be grown in its heartland.

The legacy of Wari agricultural systems laid the foundations for all future indigenous agricultural pursuits in the western valleys of the south-central Andes. The economic success of later peoples during the great droughts of the twelfth through fifteenth centuries was predicated on Wari technology. And the ability of the Inca Empire to transform the Andean world through massive investment in terraced agriculture can be traced to Wari hydro-engineering precedents.

The Tiwanaku agricultural systems in Moquegua, extensive and innovative as they may have been, did not reflect the labor investment seen in the Wari systems in the same valley. These differences in monumental architecture and agrarian investments between Wari and Tiwanaku must reflect a distinctive modus operandi in how Wari and Tiwanaku societies were organized. Social organization in residential architecture and in access to exotic goods marks a different political economy between Wari colonists and their Tiwanaku counterparts.

Demographics

A complete systematic settlement survey (Owen 1996) documents the multiethnic Middle Horizon colony around Cerro Baúl. The colony was composed of sites with Ayacucho Wari–style ceramics, Arequipa Wari–style materials, local indigenous "Huaracane" materials, and, after A.D. 750, Tiwanaku-related materials (Figure 3.2). For the Cerro Baúl complex itself, I estimate a population of circa 2,000 individuals (Williams 2006), of which less than one-quarter were likely direct colonists from Ayacucho. With downstream populations in the Wari sphere in the Yaway and Trapiche areas and with upstream populations at the headwaters of the Wari canal, the total population of these upper valley settlements likely numbered around 4,000 inhabitants.

Using systematic survey data, Goldstein (this volume) estimates a middle valley population for Tiwanaku of 8,000 inhabitants, assuming complete occupation of all sites through the 200 years (A.D. 750–950) that I contend were Tiwanaku's demographic height in Moquegua (Figure 3.3). The later Tumilaca (A.D. 950–1150) components count 4,000 inhabitants after the abandonment of the earlier Tiwanaku towns. With a mortuary population of up to 20,000 individuals representing seven generations, the middle valley Tiwanaku mortuary component actually alive at any one time averaged 3,000 people. Likely, Tiwanaku population in the middle valley fluctuated between 4,000 and 8,000 during Tiwanaku hegemony. I do not agree with population estimates of up to 20,000 individuals in the middle valley Tiwanaku sites at a given time. This number conflates settlements of different time periods and combines mortuary populations across generations.

Rank and Status in Wari and Tiwanaku Residential Architecture

Differences in the classes of residential architecture between Wari and Tiwanaku settlements are distinctive. Within the Wari sphere, at least three classes of residential architecture can be distinguished based on construction technique, architectural configuration and elaboration, and habitation area (Figure 3.6). Within the Tiwanaku sphere in Moquegua, the residential hierarchy present in the altiplano capital (Couture 2002; Janusek 2008) is not present in the Moquegua colony. In fact, one could argue that there is only one class of residential architecture in Tiwanaku Moquegua (Figure 3.7).

The classic Tiwanaku residences in Moquegua's central Tiwanaku towns, such as Omo and Chen Chen, are wattle and daub structures based on cane architecture set upright in the ground (Figure 3.3). Goldstein (1993:30) describes them as "architecturally undifferentiated domestic units clustered around distinct open plazas." Of the approximately 100 residences at Omo M12, there is limited variability in house size, ranging from one to four rooms with an average floor surface area of 50 m^2 per house.

These Tiwanaku residential patterns have some commonalities with the simplest class of Wari residential architecture. These common features include a single cooking hearth, a floor area in the 30- to 50- m^2 range, and an appropriation of local materials for the construction of modest residences (Figures 3.6 and 3.7). Wari's simplest class of residential architecture in Moquegua was built on terraced hillsides, usually with at least two topographic levels. Foundations for walled structures were constructed of fieldstone walls around 50 cm high. We presume that vegetal superstructures with ichu-grass roofing

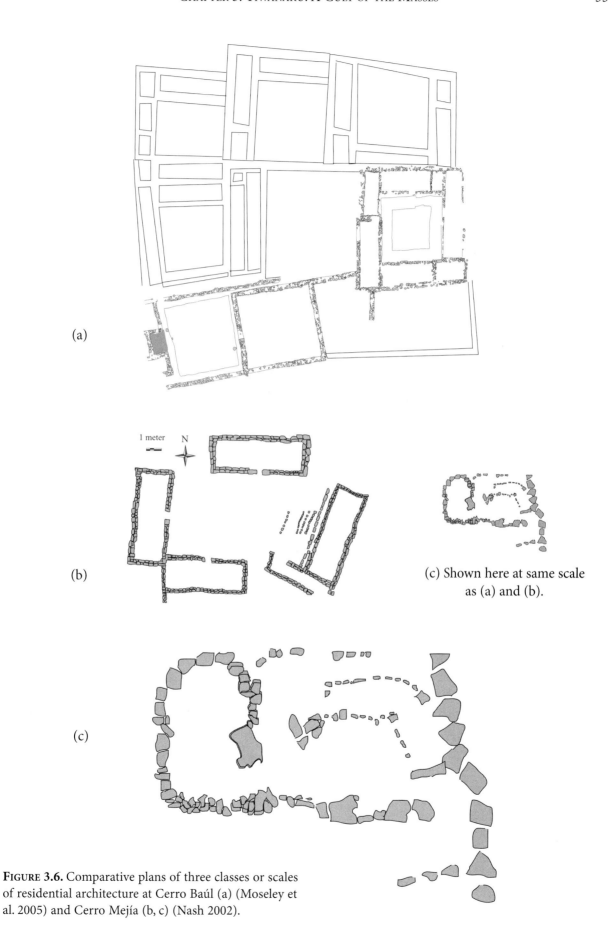

FIGURE 3.6. Comparative plans of three classes or scales of residential architecture at Cerro Baúl (a) (Moseley et al. 2005) and Cerro Mejía (b, c) (Nash 2002).

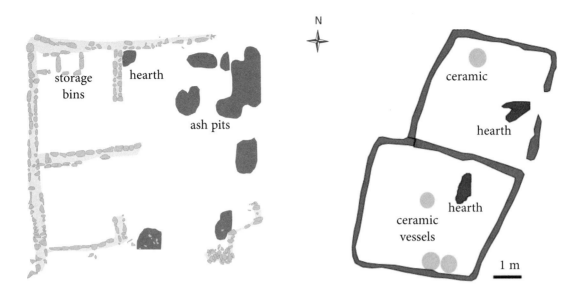

FIGURE 3.7. Examples of Tiwanaku residential architecture at (left) Tumilaca la Chimba (Williams et al. 2010) and (right) Omo (Goldstein 1993).

completed the structures, as is common in vernacular architecture in the Andean highlands today. No intact vegetal roofing material has been recovered from these residences, however.

The next class of Wari residential architecture is characterized by large compounds of several rooms built on flat hilltops surrounding a central patio (Figure 3.6). They vary greatly in scale, from 100 m^2 to 1,240 m^2. In Moquegua, these residences are found on the summit of Cerro Mejía and Cerro Petroglifo (Nash 2002) and on the slopes of Cerro Baúl at Pampa del Arrastrado. Rooms within these compounds tend to follow a Wari norm of being rectangular, with a width at a standard 2.45 m and lengths varying from 4 to 10 m on average. These rooms do not necessarily meet at standard right angles, as is characteristic of Ayacucho Wari elite residential architecture; nor do they form "orthogonal cellular architecture" with the walls of one room adjoining at right angles with the walls of adjacent rooms. Instead, adjacent rooms meet only at the corners or do not meet at all. This architectural pattern has been documented not only in Moquegua but also in Wari sites in Arequipa and thus represents a provincial Wari architectural pattern found in the far southern Wari realm (Cardona Rosas 2002).

The final class of Wari residential architecture is found only on the summit of Cerro Baúl (Figure 3.6a). It is characteristic of the "orthogonal cellular architectural form" found in Wari cities in the heartland. Rooms of 2.45 m width of one- and two-story stone construction surround a central patio and adjoin each other, sharing walls in every case. This Ayacucho Wari construction form is restricted to only sector A of the summit architecture, the area we have designated as "the palace" (Nash 2011). The central residential unit in this palace structure had a floor paved with flagstones and was composed of an 8-by-8-m central patio with six rooms flanking its four sides: two each on the east and south and one each on the north and west. At least nine other plaza complexes surround this central unit, with variations of the same architectural configuration. Evidence from excavations suggests that the walls of these compounds were plastered and painted in colors of purple, orange, and white. A monumental wall surrounded the entire compound, segregating it from the rest of the site.

Variation in Wari residential architecture delimits three distinct classes of residence based on scale, form, and elaboration. Tiwanaku residences do not exhibit this diversity of variation in the Moquegua hinterland, though palatial residences do exist in the Tiwanaku heartland (Couture 2002). It appears that Wari transplanted its social hierarchies to its hinterland colonies, whereas Tiwanaku did not. The lack of social hierarchies in Tiwanaku Moquegua is also reflected in access to exotic goods.

Economic Arrangements: Access to Exotic Goods by Wari and Tiwanaku Peoples

Within both the Wari and Tiwanaku spheres in Moquegua, access to exotic goods acquired through long-distance exchange was an important part of social life. Excavations indicate, however, that Wari access to these goods was more concentrated in elite-status households. Tiwanaku people in Moquegua had more equitable access to exotics but also overall had a lower density of exotic goods and more limited quantities of these goods than their Wari counterparts. Tiwanaku peoples also tended to have access to a higher diversity of metal artifacts than their Wari counterparts. In the Tiwanaku heartland itself, access to a wider range of obsidian sources complements this access to a diversity of metals (Giesso 2000). This access to diversity in limited quantities may represent a more diffuse and less centralized exchange network for Tiwanaku. Wari colonists, on the other hand, had more access to a restricted set of luxury goods, reflecting a more centralized distribution system.

Obsidian Exchange

Obsidian is a prime example of a resource that traveled long distances to arrive in Moquegua. It is rare, though present, in Tiwanaku sites in the valley (Paul Goldstein, personal communication 2006). It is much more ubiquitous in Wari sites, and obsidian tools are found in greater concentrations in Wari elite residential contexts than in non-elite contexts. For example, of four principal Wari elite residential contexts excavated on Cerro Baúl (units 2, 7, 9, and 24), all have an obsidian tool density in excess of .1 implements per square meter. On Cerro Mejía, the density of obsidian tools in residential contexts is below .05 implements per square meter in four of five residential contexts (units 4, 118, 136, and 145). Unit 6 had a high concentration of obsidian implements (.3 implements per square meter) despite being a modest residence (Nash 2002).

In Tiwanaku contexts in Moquegua, obsidian does not seem to be highly concentrated in particular contexts, as we see in Wari settlements. The density of obsidian tools in Tiwanaku contexts overall is very low. Of eight Tiwanaku houses excavated on the slopes of Cerro Baúl, half produced some obsidian retouch flakes, but only one had actual tools that were recovered in the excavations. More than 300 obsidian tools and thousands of flakes have been recovered in excavations in the Wari colony at Cerro Baúl. Only a handful of obsidian artifacts have been recovered from Tiwanaku contexts in the Moquegua Valley, and those that have been recovered come primarily from Wari, rather than Tiwanaku, sources (Burger et al. 2000).

Trade in Metals

Metal is also a good that traveled long distances to arrive in Moquegua. Within the Wari sphere in Moquegua, there are copper-arsenic bronzes, copper-tin bronzes, and copper-arsenic-nickel (ternary) bronzes. These alloys represent distinct regional sources of ores, from the altiplano to the circum-altiplano to the western cordillera of the Andes (Lechtman 2003). Lechtman argues that the tin bronzes and ternary bronzes are Tiwanaku metallurgical traditions, while arsenic bronzes characterize the Wari tradition. Moquegua is somewhat unique, however, in that access to the ternary and tin bronzes by Wari settlers is well established. Other Wari colonies, such as Pikillacta in the Cuzco area, are represented by a single dominant bronze source: arsenic bronzes from the western Andean cordillera (Lechtman 2003). The implication is that there was a significant exchange in metal products between Wari and Tiwanaku peoples in Moquegua. Who monopolized that exchange is documented in where metal objects are found.

Metal goods follow a similar pattern of elite access to larger quantities of exotics, especially adornments such as tupu pins (Moseley et al. 2005). Elite residences on Cerro Baúl (units 2, 7, 9, and 24) have a relatively high concentration of metal objects, with a range from .07 to .12 implements per square meter. Most intermediate elite and commoner residences on Cerro Mejía (units 4, 5, 118, and 145) have a much lower density of metal artifacts, with a range from .003 to .017 metal artifacts per square meter (Nash 2002). However, some small residences on Mejía (units 3, 6, and 8) have a disproportionately higher concentration of metal artifacts, closer to the range for the Baúl elite residences (from .08 to .16 per square meter). Yet in an overall count of metal objects, these latter commoner residences on Mejía have 4 to 5 objects per house, compared to 8 to 17 per residence on Baúl.

Metals from distant sources were also present, at Tiwanaku but not in the concentrations we have noted for the Wari colony, with upward of 10 to 20 artifacts in each house. As might be expected in Tiwanaku houses on the slopes of Cerro Baúl, altiplano ores (ternary bronze and tin bronze) are the most common bronzes, but copper-arsenic bronzes are present as well. One particular cemetery at the Tiwanaku site of Chen Chen contained a number of metal adornments (mostly rings) that were primarily silver or silver-gold alloys (Palacios 2005). For the most part, however, Tiwanaku metals are not concentrated in specific houses or cemeteries. The enigmatic cemetery excavated by Palacios is an exception. Overall, Tiwanaku access to metal goods is limited and diffuse. Only 8 of more than 100 metal objects from excavations by the Cerro Baúl Project come from the eight Tiwanaku houses excavated by the project.

Exotic goods procured via long-distance exchange indicate that Wari utilized a limited number of sources but had a centralized distribution network that favored their accumulation in elite households. Tiwanaku had access to a wider diversity of material sources, but there was no pattern of centralized distribution or centralized accumulation. Tiwanaku luxury goods were less common, though came from more diverse sources, than Wari goods obtained via long-distance exchange. This pattern is also present in the production of local luxury goods, as is evidenced by ceramic production by the two groups in the Moquegua Valley.

Ceramic Production and Distribution

Within the Tiwanaku sphere, Goldstein (1993:31) asserts that "a few specific households enjoyed a monopoly of access to elite ceramics" in the Tiwanaku colony at Omo M12. Despite this caveat, decorated ceramic wares were ubiquitous in Tiwanaku households on the slope of Cerro Baúl during the Late Middle Horizon (A.D. 800–1100). Many of these wares were made locally using diverse clay and temper materials, as evidenced by INAA and ICP-MS analysis of ceramic pastes. Even the most humble of Tiwanaku households on the slopes of Cerro Baúl had access to decorated ceramic *keros* (drinking vessels) and *tazones* (bowls), though they may have been of local manufacture.

The important aspect here is that Tiwanaku decorated wares were produced in a variety of locales, with some imported from the altiplano and with many small workshops throughout Moquegua itself producing a variety of local Tiwanaku ceramics. No centralized elite ceramic production facility has been documented in Moquegua in the Tiwanaku sphere. Like its social hierarchy, where individuals of an upper social class were resident only in the Tiwanaku heartland, "elite" ceramic vessels were manufactured elsewhere and may have "visited" once in a while. The limited evidence we have thus far for local Tiwanaku ceramic production in Moquegua suggests that it was an activity accessible to all and was not highly controlled or centralized.

Our compositional studies of Wari ceramics in Moquegua tell a different story, however. Wari elite ceramic production at the local level was highly specialized. Almost all the elite serving wares used in the palace residence and in brew houses on Cerro Baúl were produced from a single clay source with a stringent recipe for manufacture. The locale of this manufacture may have been on the summit of Cerro Baúl itself, as suggested by recent excavations (Nash 2011). Both INAA and ICP-MS data from these highly decorated ceramics indicate a more homogeneous production than other ceramic wares produced in Wari and Tiwanaku spheres in the valley at the time (Sharratt et al. 2009).

Wari ceramic production for local consumption in the modest residences on the slopes of the great mesa and on the slopes of Cerro Mejía drew from a variety of local clay sources in the valley, overlapping with some of the Tiwanaku clay chemistries. Two principal ceramic wares are distinguishable both on visible inspection and in the compositional data: a utilitarian plain ware, Mejía B, with a large amount of biotite temper; and a sometimes decorated serving ware, Mejía A, which is chemically heterogeneous and may represent several production loci in the upper valley. These wares are the predominant types found off the summit of Cerro Baúl.

It should not be surprising that exchange of ceramic wares between Wari and Tiwanaku was limited. Ceramics were central to identity, and their use in household contexts reflects adherence to a particular cultural identity. Ubiquitous exchange in ceramics between groups would likely be interpreted as evidence for acculturation, or at least incorporation into an elite political economy. I argue for neither here. I do, however, contend that the presence of at least a dozen Tiwanaku villages scattered around the slopes of Cerro Baúl and Cerro Mejía reflects an integration into the Wari colonial system. The rustic temple complexes on the slopes of the mountains also reflect an integration of Tiwanaku religious practice into Wari settlement space. Finally, the 2007 discovery in the Temple of Arundane on the summit of Cerro Baúl of a Tiwanaku ritual space containing fragments of six Tiwanaku *incensarios* and no Wari ceramics in the midst of the Wari citadel represents a clear nexus of contact.

Data from ceramic production and distribution suggest a high level of specialization in local ceramic production by Wari elites that was differentiated from production in Wari commoner contexts. Tiwanaku ceramic production, on the other hand, was more diffuse, and decorated wares were more accessible to the masses than in the Wari contexts in Moquegua. While certain elite households may have gained access to exotic vessels via long-distance exchange, they did not produce their own exotics as did the Wari lords at Cerro Baúl. This again suggests that Wari exported its social hierarchies to the colonial setting, along with the modes of production that supported them, while Tiwanaku did not.

Mortuary Patterns and Common Identity in Tiwanaku Moquegua

Despite the degree of variation in ceramic production and the apparent factionalist nature of Tiwanaku society in Moquegua in general, patterns in material culture, and especially in mortuary ritual, indicate a shared concept of treatment of the dead across broad temporal and cultural spectrums. The three macrosocial groups in Moquegua Tiwanaku were defined by Goldstein (1989) based on perceived chronological differences in ceramic style and settlement patterns. Goldstein (2005) revised the chronological differences while still maintaining the social distinctions among Omo, Chen Chen, and Tumilaca social groups within the Moquegua Tiwanaku sphere. Omo and Chen Chen were relatively contemporaneous, with Tumilaca overlapping with their terminal periods and continuing for a century later, according to the latest chronologies (Owen and Goldstein 2001).

Even though the social divides between these major factions may be distinctive, mortuary ritual was extremely conservative. People from all three groups were routinely interred in a flexed and seated position in individual small, cylindrical cists, some lined with stone and others not. In cemeteries from all periods and from all social groups, however, the pattern remains the same, and invariably the deceased are seated facing east. The eastern orientation was uncontested in a sample of over 60 tombs excavated at the Tiwanaku site of Tumilaca la Chimba (Sharratt et al. 2012), as well as from thousands of tombs excavated at the sites of Chen Chen and Omo (Goldstein 2005; Vargas 1988).

Grave inclusions in tombs from all three groups are also very similar, with flaring-sided bowls (*tazones*) and wooden spoons, ceramic drinking vessels (*keros*), and small jars the most common grave offerings. There are some interesting variations in grave offerings, with one cemetery sector at Chen Chen having a disproportional amount of metal jewelry (Palacios 2005). Only one cemetery sector at Tumilaca contained burials with camelid feet as part of the mortuary offerings (Sharratt et al. 2012). For the most part, however, Tiwanaku grave architecture, mortuary ritual, and funerary offerings were fairly standardized. Wari mortuary contexts in Moquegua show a great deal more variability, despite a much smaller sample (circa five tombs).

Most Wari mortuary contexts have been found in an extremely disturbed state in the Moquegua region. One burial from Cerro Mejía (Nash 2009, 2012) documents burial in closed rooms of residential contexts. In a couple cases on Cerro Baúl, we find disarticulated skeletons of adult individuals strewn across the floor of certain residential contexts. They likely were originally interred in subfloor cists that were subsequently looted in prehistory, or were housed in open wall niches within these rooms which have long since collapsed. Three infant burials and one juvenile burial have been recovered from intact contexts. One infant was buried in a stone cairn in the corner of a residential room. No grave goods accompanied this burial. One infant was interred in an unlined pit within a midden context. This individual was buried with a necklace of fine shell beads.

The juvenile was placed in a subfloor cist within a small 2-by-2-m mortuary building within a larger residential compound. No grave goods were in the cist, although four flaring-sided bowls and a Nazca 7 drum had been smashed on the floor above the cist.

In the corner of this same structure, the third intact juvenile burial was found in a small subfloor pit, buried in a ceramic urn covered with an upside-down flaring-sided bowl. The residential compound in which these burials were discovered was intimately related with one of the two D-shaped temples at Cerro Baúl and may not represent typical burial patterns for Wari juveniles. However, of the four intact burials recovered, and the several remains of adult burials scattered in domestic contexts, none conform to a "typical" pattern. While most interments were flexed, body position was nonstandard and grave goods varied drastically. Individuals could be buried in subfloor cists, in wall niches, in above-floor cairns, or in middens. The small sample of Wari burials prohibits a categorization of mortuary practices, but clearly they were far less standard than Tiwanaku rites in Moquegua.

Thus a real distinction in mortuary traditions existed between Wari and Tiwanaku burials in Moquegua. Tiwanaku featured discrete cemeteries with a highly patterned interment model; Wari had burials in residential and ceremonial areas with more variation in funerary ritual. These funerary patterns are extremely interesting, for political and economic data point to Wari centralization and Tiwanaku factionalism in these realms. Yet when it comes to worldview, Tiwanaku peoples were fundamentally more united in their common set of beliefs concerning the treatment of the dead. Centralization in one facet of society does not necessarily imply unity in others.

Tiwanaku Factionalism and Wari Incorporation

Interestingly, the Tiwanaku diaspora does not exhibit the full range of social classes found in the Tiwanaku heartland. It would seem the Tiwanaku diaspora focused on a single economic class who left their altiplano homelands to seek new economic opportunities or to escape economic turmoil at home. Their wealthier brethren did not accompany them to Moquegua. While escape from religious persecution or exodus for political reasons would likely result in a cross section of economic classes in the Moquegua colony, the lack of socioeconomic variability in Moquegua Tiwanaku suggests an economic diaspora, which Goldstein (2005) references in his seminal work on the subject.

I should be clear that I am arguing that Tiwanaku was a pluralistic expansive state. In its provincial setting, however, it lacked the political apparatus needed to run a multiethnic empire like Wari did. Tiwanaku's provincial homogeneity in Moquegua reflects its colonial concerns with resource extraction using an exported colonial population. Much like the Greek colonies in Italy or the English colonies in the Americas, Tiwanaku's focus was on land and resources and not indigenous labor. Wari, on the other hand, focused on multiethnic politics in its peripheries. Indigenous people from Moquegua (Costion 2009; Green and Goldstein 2010), from other Wari areas (Nash 2011), and even from Tiwanaku, as evidenced by the houses and temples on the slopes of Cerro Baúl, participated in Wari political interaction in Moquegua. Tiwanaku was not that kind of incorporative empire on the outskirts of its realm. I make no judgment as to the value of one kind of colonization versus the other. The influence of Tiwanaku lived on after Tiwanaku disappeared in derived coastal iconographic traditions and even perhaps in coastal domestic architecture. Wari influence endured in agricultural innovations and in the domestic architecture and settlement planning of the highland sierra groups that succeeded it.

What held Tiwanaku together was neither class consciousness nor political cohesion. Rather, it was a set of shared notions about common identity, and common perceptions about a shared experience in the world. Tiwanaku was a religious entity, while Wari was a political one. If Wari was the Rome of the Andean world, Tiwanaku was its Jerusalem. Tiwanaku united people not through manifestations of political centralization in its capital or in provincial centers but rather through a shared sense of origins and common cultural ideals as manifested through mortuary ritual and other cultural practices. Likewise, the distinction in wealth and status among Tiwanaku peoples in the provinces is unmarked when compared to the vast differences in residential architecture and access to exotics in the Wari populace. This is not the case in the capital of Tiwanaku, where status differences are pronounced in residential spaces (Couture 2002; Janusek 2008; Vranich 2006) and exotics are restricted to certain segments of the population. Wari exported its social hierarchies to its provinces, while Tiwanaku maintained its elites in the restricted ceremonial centers of greatest importance.

REFERENCES CITED

Burger, Richard, Karen Mohr Chávez, and Sergio Chávez
    2000   Through the Glass Darkly: Prehispanic Obsidian Procurement and Exchange in Southern Peru and Northern Bolivia. *Journal of World Prehistory* 14(3):267–362.
Cardona Rosas, Augusto
    2002   Arqueología de Arequipa: De sus albores a los Incas. El Centro de Investigaciones Arqueológicas de Arequipa, Arequipa, Peru.
Costion, Kirk
    2009   Huaracane Social Organization: Change over Time at the Prehispanic Community of Yahuay Alta, Peru. Unpublished Ph.D. dissertation, University of Pittsburgh, Pittsburgh.
Couture, Nicole C.
    2002   The Construction of Power: Monumental Space and Elite Residence at Tiwanaku, Bolivia. Unpublished Ph.D. dissertation, Department of Anthropology, University of Chicago, Chicago.
Giesso, Martin
    2000   The Impact of State Emergence and Expansion on Local Households. Unpublished Ph.D. dissertation, Department of Anthropology, University of Chicago, Chicago.
Goldstein, Paul S.
    1989   Omo, a Tiwanaku Provincial Center in Moquegua, Peru. Unpublished Ph.D. dissertation, University of Chicago, Chicago.
    1993   Tiwanaku Temples and State Expansion: A Tiwanaku Sunken-Court Temple in Moquegua, Peru. *Latin American Antiquity* 4(3): 22–47.
    2005   *Andean Diaspora: The Tiwanaku Colonies and the Origins of South American Empire.* University Press of Florida, Gainesville.
Green, Ulli M., and Paul S. Goldstein
    2010   The Nature of Wari Presence in the Mid-Moquegua Valley: Investigating Contact at Cerro Trapiche. In *Beyond Wari Walls: Regional Perspectives on Middle Horizon Peru,* edited by Justin Jennings, pp. 19–36. University of New Mexico Press, Albuquerque.
Janusek, John Wayne
    2008   *Ancient Tiwanaku.* Cambridge University Press, Cambridge.
Lechtman, Heather
    2003   Middle Horizon Bronze: Centers and Outliers. In *Patterns and Process: A Festschrift in Honor of Dr. Edward V. Sayre,* edited by L. van Zelst, pp. 168–248. Smithsonian Center for Materials Research and Education, Suitland, Maryland.
Moore, Jerry
    1996   *Architecture and Power in the Ancient Andes: The Archaeology of Public Buildings.* Cambridge University Press, Cambridge.
Moseley, Michael, Donna J. Nash, Patrick Ryan Williams, Susan deFrance, Ana Miranda, and Mario Ruales
    2005   Burning down the Brewery: Establishing and Evacuating an Ancient Imperial Colony at Cerro Baúl, Perú. *Proceedings of the National Academy of Sciences* 102(48):17264–17271. Washington, D.C.
Nash, Donna
    1996   Cerro Petroglifo: Settlement Pattern and Social Organization of a Residential Wari Community. Unpublished master's thesis, Department of Anthropology, University of Florida, Gainesville.
    2002   The Archaeology of Space: Places of Power in the Wari Empire. Unpublished Ph.D. dissertation, Department of Anthropology, University of Florida, Gainesville.
    2011   Fiestas y la economía politica Wari en Moquegua, Peru. *Chungara* 43(2):221–242.
    2012   El establecimiento de relaciones de poder a través del uso del espacio residencial en la provincia Wari de Moquegua. *Bulletin de l'Institut Français d'Études Andines* 41(1):1–34.
Nash, Donna, and R. Barrionuevo
    2009   Informe-proyecto arqueológico asentamientos en Cerro Mejía 2008. Instituto Nacional de Cultura, Lima.
Nash, Donna, and P. R. Williams
    2005   Architecture and Power on the Wari-Tiwanaku Frontier. *Archaeological Papers of the American Anthropological Association* 14(1):151–174.
Owen, Bruce
    1996   Inventario arqueológico del drenaje superior del Río Osmore: Informe del campo e informe final. Manuscript on file, Museo Contisuyo, Moquegua, Peru.
    2005   Distant Colonies and Explosive Collapse: The Two Stages of the Tiwanaku Diaspora in the Osmore Drainage. *Latin American Antiquity* 16(1): 45–80.
Owen, Bruce, and Paul Goldstein
    2001   Tiwanaku en Moquegua: Interacciones regionales y colapso. In *Huari y Tiwanaku: Modelos vs. evidencias,* Pt. 2, edited by Peter Kaulicke and William H. Isbell, pp. 169–188. Boletín de Arqueología No. 5. Pontificia Universidad Católica del Perú, Lima.
Palacios, Filinich Patricia
    2005   Proyecto de rescate arqueológico Chen Chen, Sectores 28 y 29, Moquegua. Informe presentado al Ministerio de Cultura, Lima.

Palacios, Filinich Patricia
   2005 Proyecto de Rescate Arqueológico Chen Chen, Sectores 28 y 29, Moquegua. Report submitted to the Ministerio de Cultura, Lima.

Sharratt, Nicola, Mark Golitko, Patrick Ryan Williams, and Laure Dussubieux
   2009 Ceramic Production during the Middle Horizon: Wari and Tiwanaku Clay Procurement in the Moquegua Valley, Peru. *Geoarchaeology* 24(6):792–820.

Sharratt, Nicola, Patrick Ryan Williams, Maria Cecelia Lozada, and Jennifer Starbird
   2012 Late Tiwanaku Mortuary Patterns in the Moquegua Drainage, Peru: Excavations at the Tumilaca la Chimba Cemetery. In *Advances in Titicaca Basin Archaeology 3*, edited by L. Klarich, C. Stanish, and A. Vranich, pp. 193–202. Museum of Anthropology, Ann Arbor.

Vargas, Bertha
   1988 Informe final del proyecto: Rescate arqueológico del cementerio de Chen Chen. Report submitted to the Instituto Nacional de Cultura, Moquegua.

Vranich, Alexei
   2006 The Construction and Reconstruction of Ritual Space at Tiwanaku, Bolivia (AD 500–1000). *Journal of Field Archaeology* 31(2):121–136.

Williams, P. R.
   2002 A Re-examination of Disaster Induced Collapse in the Case of the Andean Highland States: Wari and Tiwanaku. *World Archaeology* 33(3):361–374.
   2006 Agricultural Innovation, Intensification, and Sociopolitical Development: The Case of Highland Andean Agriculture on the Pacific Andean Watersheds. In *Agricultural Strategies*, edited by C. Stanish and J. Marcus, pp. 309–333. Cotsen Institute of Archaeology Press, Los Angeles.

Williams, P. R., and Donna Nash
   2006 Sighting the Apu: A GIS Analysis of Wari Imperialism and the Worship of Mountain Peaks. *World Archaeology* 38(3):455–468.

Williams, P. R., M. Lizzaraga, and N. Sharratt
   2010 Informe final: Proyecto arqueológico Cerro Baúl 2010. Report to the National Institute of Culture, Peru.

4

TIWANAKU AND WARI STATE EXPANSION:
DEMOGRAPHIC AND OUTPOST COLONIZATION COMPARED

PAUL GOLDSTEIN

What kind of state was Tiwanaku? Was Tiwanaku expansion "different" from that of other archaic proto-empires? And how did Tiwanaku expansion intersect with indigenous host populations and compare with the contemporary Wari expansion?

The transregional expansion of Tiwanaku peoples was not only simultaneous with but was also integral to the building of Tiwanaku civilization in the state's altiplano homeland. In this chapter, I will stress that Tiwanaku's version of state expansion, as a great popular migration, differs from the expansion of many agrarian archaic states worldwide and particularly from the neighboring but very distinct sphere of the Wari Empire. Tiwanaku civilization's long-lasting domination of annexed territory through corporate agropastoral migration contrasts with assumptions that effective expansive states must be centrally directed and militarily based, and contrasts particularly with the very different model of the Wari expansion of the Middle Horizon. In some quarters, an assumption that only centralized states can expand and compete effectively has led to an assumption of Wari supremacy, or at least hegemony, over Tiwanaku's colonial presence (e.g., Moseley et al. 2005; Williams this volume; Williams and Nash 2002). Such is the assumed competitive advantage of its colonialist imperial strategy that the Wari state is believed by some to have held sway even over the south-central Andes, a region well within the Tiwanaku demographic and cultural sphere and nearly three times farther away from the Wari core region than from Tiwanaku (Figure 4.1). In what follows, I will present new data from regional settlement history, household, and mortuary archaeology approaches to Tiwanaku and Wari colonization in the Moquegua region. I hope to temper some of our more hyperbolic assumptions about Middle Horizon imperialism with empiricism and to arrive at a better understanding of the contrast between these two highly effective contemporary, but very different, expansive state systems.

DIVERSITY, HETERARCHY, AND SEGMENTARY EXPANSIVE STATES

Territorially expansive states are usually associated with highly centralized forms of government and dominant core elites heading up class hierarchies. Permanent states are expected to comprise a territorially demarcated region (Goldstone and Haldon 2009:6), while comparativist anthropological models define archaic state societies by their transition from redundant kin-based social organizations to stratified

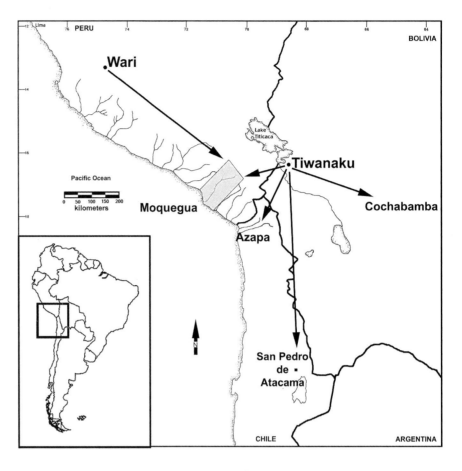

FIGURE 4.1. The south-central Andes, showing vectors of Tiwanaku colonization, Wari's southernmost outpost, and the Moquegua study area.

social hierarchies and centralized systems of control as the fundamental shift in regulatory principles and strategies (Marcus and Feinman 1998; Patterson and Gailey 1987; Spencer 1998:15). A key corollary of archaic state formation is that the authorities of component corporate groups are eliminated or eroded as the state asserts hierarchical control and authority through a bureaucratic chain of command. Typically, archaic states feature unitary rule in the form of facilities and instruments of authority, material and contextual evidence of exaggerated status differentiation for ruling elites in life and death, and ideology that stresses monopolized violence and highly hierarchical organization (Flannery 1998).

Yet classically centralized archaic states form a continuum with less centralized states organized as confederations of tribal or clan communities. Unencumbered by some of the permanent infrastructural furnishings of central control, these are often dismissed as primitive "proto-states," without institutional permanence, and are generally short-lived. A minority of scholars, however, accepts that states that combine hierarchy with a considerable range of heterarchy, factionalism, and shared corporate authority can be viable and even quite powerful in the long term (Blanton 1998; Blanton et al. 1996; Brumfiel 1994; Crumley 1987, 1995). One such conception for a unified yet less unitary early state is the "segmentary state," first proposed by Aiden Southall for the Alur (1956) as an intermediate political form between Western states and societies considered "tribal" by agents of European imperial powers. Southall conceived of segmentary states as large-scale polities in which diverse social entities retain a high degree of political autonomy and are only partially subsumed under the central authority of a king. These were dynamic confederations, integrated by structured oppositions between similar segments. Southall termed these polities "segmentary," not because of any particular kinship structure but "because there is complementary opposition between their component parts, the boundaries of political jurisdiction are differently perceived from different points of the system, and a central focus of ritual suzerainty is recognized over a wider area than effective political sovereignty" (Southall 1974, 1999).

A key element of segmentary states as applied in Africa is the limited ability of state centers to project unitary political power because the "spheres of ritual suzerainty and political sovereignty do not coincide" (Southall 1988:52). Most political action is articulated through horizontally arrayed assemblies or councils rather than a centralized hierarchy (McIntosh 1999:15, 77). Because segmentary states' social pluralism has concrete implications for political action, the resulting heterarchy is at odds with archaic state theory's focus on hierarchy and delegation (Crumley 1995). The largely ceremonial authority of the centers of segmentary states contrasts strongly with assumptions that archaic states enjoyed central authority, eliminated systemic redundancy, monopolized the use of force, and instituted powerfully hierarchical power structures through delegation (Table 4.1).

The segmentary state model has been adopted by some decentralist archaeologists of the pre-Columbian Maya, who emphasize the importance of lineage-based corporate descent groups or "house societies" as the keystone supra-household units of Maya social organization, as well as in other regions of Mesoamerica (Boorstein 2005; Fox 1988; Fox et al. 1996:797; Gillespie 2000, 2001; Houston 1993; Potter and King 1995:22). For larger states, the segmentary state model has gained particular traction among scholars of far larger South Asian states such as the Rajput of northern India and the Pallava, Chola, and Vijayanagara civilizations of southern India (Appadurai 1978; Fox 1971; Southall 1988; Stein 1980, 1985). B. Stein argues that the medieval Chola state of South India was a complex hybrid of centralization and segmentary pluralism. The king was a "raja of rajas" whose power was rooted in ritual suzerainty, a public acknowledgment of paramountcy in matters of worship, and a special relationship with cosmic forces. Chola kingship did not, however, confer absolute power in the economic and political realms, and distinct corporate segments maintained considerable autonomy both at home and abroad in matters of economic and political policy (Stein 1980). Among the Chola, the very concept of "state" was "not perceived as an administrative or coercive fact, as much as the expression of an idea of unity among many diverse peasant localities, as actualized in ritual linkages between kings and chiefs" (Stein 1985: 75). Segmentary descriptions or ritual suzerainty has been extended to South Asian polities of "imperial" scale and infrastructure such as Vijayanagara (Fritz 1986), which, despite its unparalleled achievement as city and empire, "cannot be easily incorporated into traditional models of imperial structure" (Sinopoli and Morrison 1995:85).

In the Andean region, the rich ethnographic and ethnohistoric record has contributed to an argument that pre-Columbian political structure in the Andes was segmentary and that salient units were defined along the structural model of *ayllus*. *Ayllus* are corporate groups that define social identities in a recursive hierarchy of nested segments, claim common

Table 4.1. A Continuum of Archaic State Traits

Centralized Archaic States	Segmentary Archaic States
Hierarchy dominates	Heterarchy dominates
Centralized political rule	Limited centralized rule
Class and state become salient social identities	Kin, clan, and caste persist as salient social identities
Corporate groups lose autonomy	Corporate groups retain autonomy
Institutional redundancy eliminated	Institutional redundancy between corporate groups
Unitary administrative hierarchy; delegated functions	Multiple authorities; functionally overlapping
King is king	King is first among equals
Royal power in the economic and political realms	Royal power in ritual suzerainty
Agrarian management from the top down	Agrarian management from the bottom up and community authorities
State expansion under central command	State expansion by corporate societal segments or communities
Frontier exploitative presence; mutual acculturation with locals	Frontier demographic presence; segregation from locals

ancestry, and worship landscape shrines of mythical shared origin (Platt 1986). Andean *ayllus* also function as "kin collectives" (Moseley 1999), supra-household communities, and (at their maximal level) ethnic corporate units capable of coordinating migration, landholding, labor management, and political action. The efficacy of segmentary community organization for effective local control of irrigation agriculture is an important part of this model, and canal management is a significant *ayllu* function in historical and ethnographic accounts (Mitchell and Guillet 1994; Netherly 1993). Archaeologically, similar patterns of autonomous, segmentary organization have been recognized as an effective and stable way to manage large-scale irrigation agriculture among the pre-Inca Huaylas and Sican state polities of the Late Intermediate period (Hayashida 2006; Lane 2009).

Could some Andean empires be considered segmentary? While acknowledging Inca infrastructural centralization, Gose suggests that the assertion of an Inca ideological supremacy was successful because it was structurally compatible with existing segmentary conceptions of nested hierarchy in Andean *ayllus* and their associated ritual systems. Because indigenous pre-Inca *ayllus* were the most effective corporate groups for agriculture and irrigation management, and because *ayllus* were unified through corporate worship of common origin places and water source shrines, the Inca developed an inclusive ideology that placed Inca ritual suzerainty above these existing systems without disrupting them. This was supported symbolically through control of the maximal water shrines—the Pacific and Lake Titicaca—making imperial control seem a natural concomitant of maximizing the water cycle, a "ritual suzerainty, expressed through symbolic manipulation and ritual" (Gose 1993:510).

Who Were the Tiwanaku?

The unique fascination of Tiwanaku studies in the twenty-first century is that we are beginning to understand this culture's internal diversity and the complex relations among its peoples as the state formed and expanded. Tiwanaku is a place-name of uncertain origin, yet scholars often fall into the semantic trap of empowering a single actor called Tiwanaku as an entity that built, farmed, fought, married, or migrated in lockstep unison. The challenge for Tiwanaku studies going forward is reconciling the tension between Tiwanaku's increasingly well-understood internal diversity and the comparativist assumption of unitary state action.

Increasingly sophisticated analyses of micro-affiliation within the Tiwanaku capital region are finding a cultural system that was enduringly heterogeneous and culturally and ethnically diverse. Early on, Kolata hypothesized that social pluralism within the Tiwanaku core region could correspond to several maximal *ayllus*—Aymara, Pukina, and Uru ethnic traditions—and that these ethnic groups may have been occupationally focused on herding, farming, and fishing, respectively (Kolata 1993, 2003). A first generation of household and settlement archaeology in the core region has confirmed not only social and economic diversity within the Tiwanaku phenomenon but also a variety of models of political pluralism in the Tiwanaku type site and altiplano core region. These visions of the Tiwanaku homeland include a nested hierarchy of confederated *ayllus* (Albarracin-Jordan 1996; Albarracin-Jordan and Mathews 1990), a vertically integrated system of otherwise autonomous localities (Bermann 1994, 1997; Isbell and Burkholder 2002), a cosmopolitan city of walled barrios with occupational specialties and some political action linked to persistent ethnic and foreign affiliations (Janusek 2003, 2004; Rivera Casanovas 2003), an iconographically complex diarchy (Berenguer 1998), or a collection of linked but autonomous settlement systems rather than a single integrated hierarchy (McAndrews et al. 1997). All these segmentary visions can and must coexist with the unifying reality of a shared Tiwanaku high culture funded by a complex political economy (Couture and Sampeck 2003; Janusek and Kolata 2004; Kolata 2003; Stanish 2002).

We are thus beginning to consider not only agency but also multiple, complex, and cross-cutting agencies within a diverse and pluralistic Tiwanaku cultural sphere. But does heterogeneity necessarily imply heterarchy? And if it does, was Tiwanaku a polity "governed by committee"? And if the Tiwanaku phenomenon is stacked up against the contemporary "Wari Empire," does Tiwanaku political pluralism imply weakness in the political arena of competitive expansive state systems? Pluralism and its implications can be difficult to isolate within the Tiwanaku capital region due to urban cosmopolitanism, cultural transformation, and the palimpsest effect of deep stratigraphy. In contrast, Tiwanaku's diaspora lowland settlements, where desert preservation is excellent and entire town plans are accessible, can offer powerful spatial insights on Tiwanaku's social and political diversity. Let us consider the implications of heterogeneity and heterarchy in the context of Tiwanaku expansion and the interregional relations between Tiwanaku peoples, Wari peoples, and others.

Tiwanaku as Expansive Segmentary State

As the papers in this volume demonstrate, the peoples we call the Tiwanaku created the largest and most cosmopolitan city yet seen in the Andes. However, Tiwanaku leaves an unusually light ground plan for the traits usually associated with expansive archaic state societies. Tiwanaku shows little iconographic, archaeological, or bioarchaeological evidence of military conquest and only limited evidence for kingship and the paramount social classes that would be expected in a unitary political and social hierarchy. Compared to societies like the Inca, it is difficult to identify the administrative infrastructure and hardware of state rule—storage facilities, provincial centers, or garrisons—consistently throughout the Tiwanaku sphere. We are yet to locate royal burials for Tiwanaku comparable to those of cultures like the Moche, and Tiwanaku left no conquest monuments extolling martial leaders or exemplary repression.

This is not to deny statehood to Tiwanaku but to recognize Tiwanaku as a socially diverse and politically confederative state, perhaps akin to the Chola and Vijayanagara civilizations of South India. Though these were states of awesome power and accomplishment, the state was "not perceived as an administrative or coercive fact, as much as the expression of an idea of unity among many diverse peasant localities, as actualized in ritual linkages between kings and chiefs" (Stein 1985:75). Tiwanaku's success as an expansive state was in a far-flung diaspora of new towns and ceremonial centers in outlying regions. Tiwanaku colonies constitute "diasporas" as expatriate communities that maintain a memory of an original homeland and see the ancestral home as a place of eventual return, and whose consciousness and solidarity are "importantly defined" by this continuing relationship with the homeland (Clifford 1994:304).

How Did Tiwanaku Expand? Tiwanaku Pluralism in Diaspora

Twenty-five years of regional research on the Middle Horizon occupation of the middle Moquegua Valley (Figure 4.2) has allowed us to move from discovering Tiwanaku influence to demonstrating Tiwanaku colonization to considering the component parts that distinguished Tiwanaku diasporic society. Early work established a baseline for Tiwanaku direct colonization by documenting and dating Tiwanaku settlement in Moquegua between the seventh and tenth centuries A.D. and rejecting scenarios of trade, conquest, or hegemonic acculturation. Initial household archaeology in the 1980s demonstrated the unalloyed highland Tiwanaku affiliation of the Omo site (Goldstein 1989, 1993a, 2005). In this first generation of problem-oriented Tiwanaku diasporic archaeology, it became apparent from vernacular architecture, domestic features, activities, and material assemblages that the Moquegua Tiwanaku colonies were peopled entirely by culturally Tiwanaku individuals in permanent residence. Tiwanaku colonists used not only Tiwanaku-style fine serving vessels such as *keros,* jars, and *tazones* in all domestic and mortuary contexts but also vast quantities of storage and cooking vessels identical to altiplano forms. Local styles are absent, and altiplano identity in the quotidian tools, toys, and furnishings of household contexts confirms that these items were made by Tiwanaku-trained craftspeople for the domestic usage of culturally Tiwanaku consumers. Uniquely Tiwanaku categories such as camelid mandible polishers (Webster and Janusek 2003), stone and wooden *trompos* or tops, cane and bone flutes, basketry, spoons, wooden vessels, and textiles dominated all household contexts. Tiwanaku forms of utilitarian plain pottery constituted 91 percent of the ceramics at the Moquegua Tiwanaku sites, indicating a culinary identity expressed in practice in every back kitchen.

The activity sets evident in the Tiwanaku colonies' ceramic assemblages can tell us much about the culture process of colonization beyond simple cultural affiliation. Significantly, even gender-linked private activities showed no acculturation to native

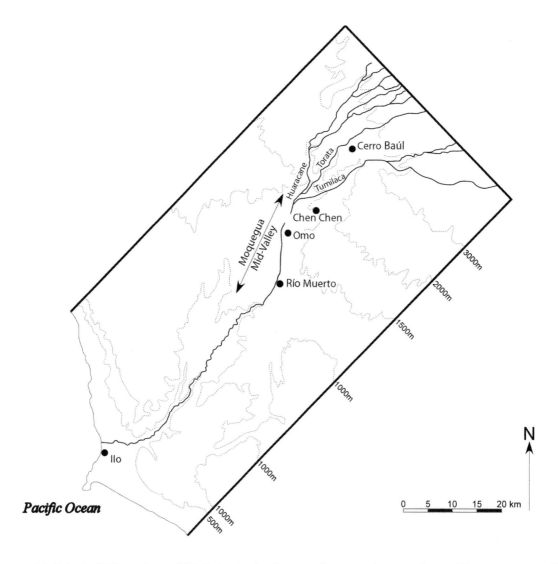

FIGURE 4.2. Principal Tiwanaku and Wari sites in the Osmore drainage, showing the middle Moquegua Valley.

culinary practice. In contrast to frontier regions like Spanish colonial Saint Augustine, where largely male frontiersmen took local spouses (Deagan 1973, 2004), the Tiwanaku colonies show little if any intermarriage between colonists and indigenous peoples. If we accept that cultural identity and social relationships are enacted through the repetitive actions of daily practice, these Tiwanaku colonists were entire families of altiplano origin who maintained their close affiliations to the core region for centuries of direct contact and beyond in the ethnogenesis of the region's post-expansive Tumilaca phase (A.D. 1000–1200) (Bawden 1989, 1993; Bermann et al. 1989; Goldstein 1989, 2005).

The full family settlement model is confirmed by gender balance in cemetery populations, with all interment and offering practices congruent with highland Tiwanaku burials (Buikstra 1995; Goldstein 2005; Korpisaari 2006). Independent bioarchaeological analyses of cranial deformation (Hoshower et al. 1995) and biological distance studies indicate close relationships between the Moquegua Tiwanaku and altiplano cemetery populations and little relationship to indigenous populations of Moquegua (Blom 1999, 2005; Blom et al. 1998). Most recently, oxygen and strontium isotope studies are confirming migration streams to Moquegua, with a mix of Moquegua-born Tiwanaku individuals and actual migrants from the altiplano Tiwanaku homeland (Knudson 2008; Knudson et al. 2004). At least one isotopic case indicates back-and-forth migration, suggesting a life history of transregionalism for some colonists. This pattern fits a long-term multigenerational settlement of families, with either return migration or the maintenance of multiple residences across extended families rather than a pioneer migration stream of single young males (Anthony 1990). Demographic profiles show a fully reproducing resident community, with the single exception of the underrepresentation of elderly adults in colonial cemeteries, suggesting return migration or repatriation of the deceased to the altiplano (Baitzel and Goldstein 2011), perhaps consistent with the transregional "expectation of return" of the diaspora model (Clifford 1994).

Perhaps most illuminating for understanding the internal workings of Tiwanaku's sociopolitical systems has been the results of systematic settlement survey. Since 1993 the Moquegua Archaeological Survey (MAS) has systematically surveyed the 150 km² area of the middle Moquegua Valley. The MAS research recorded a total of 531 pre-Columbian site components of all periods and adds three new dimensions to this assessment of a Tiwanaku colonial diaspora: scale, insularity, and diversity.

First, systematic survey, as the only way to accurately calculate settlement area, is the only reliable indicator of both indigenous presence and colonial scale. Prior to the Tiwanaku colonization, Moquegua was occupied by a formative agrarian tradition known as Huaracane (Goldstein 2000; Goldstein and Magilligan 2011) (Figure 4.3). In the middle Moquegua sector, Huaracane settlement was in small

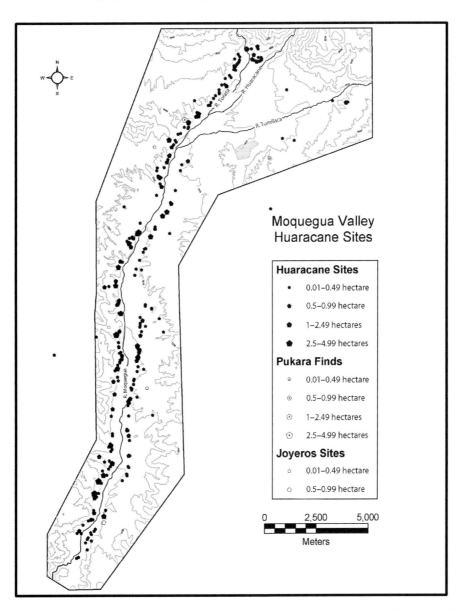

FIGURE 4.3. The indigenous setting. Map of Pre-Tiwanaku Huaracane settlements of the middle Moquegua Valley.

villages with a mean area of only .44 ha per domestic component, with only five settlements over 2 ha in area. Village sites did not show evidence of defensive walls or public architecture, and there is no evidence supporting a regional or primary center in the valley; thus a generally low-level political and economical integration is proposed. Huaracane subsistence consisted of a diverse diet and a nonspecialized agrarian strategy with habitation sites consistently located on bluffs very close to the floodplain of the river, indicating simple floodplain agriculture (Goldstein 2000:341; 2005). Recent dating of Huaracane contexts at the Los Joyeros, Cerro Trapiche, and Yaway sites (Costion and Green 2009; Green and Goldstein 2009) has extended late elements of the Huaracane tradition into the early Middle Horizon, supporting a continuous occupation by the Huaracane tradition and showing that the mid-valley was occupied contemporaraneously with the arrival of Tiwanaku and Wari colonists (Figure 4.4; Table 4.2).

The results of the MAS systematic survey indicate the true scale of the Tiwanaku demographic presence in Moquegua (Table 4.3). The Omo- and Chen Chen–style Tiwanaku settlements, which were indisputably associated only with altiplano migrant communities, account for 79 ha of settlement occupation area, with an additional 11 ha of cemeteries. Using a calculus of 100 people per ha for "moderate-density" settlements (Wilson 1988:79), this suggests a valley-wide population of 8,000. If we consider the entire three-century Tiwanaku settlement palimpsest by adding the post-expansive Tumilaca-phase sites, we bring the total demonstrated settlement area to 121 ha and an estimate of more than 12,000 Tiwanaku colonists.[1] Known Tiwanaku cemeteries in Moquegua produce an even higher estimate, with 10 ha of cemeteries with a typical density of tombs, suggesting a cemetery population between 10,000 and 20,000 (Goldstein 2005:123). One calculation indicates a cemetery population of 12,856 Tiwanaku individuals at the Chen Chen site alone (Owen and Goldstein 2001).

Second, Tiwanaku diaspora settlement demonstrates a remarkable insularity of colonial settlement. Systematic survey can demonstrate not only where settlement was but also where settlement was not. Contrary to expectations of a spatially hierarchical settlement system, few small Tiwanaku sites were found, with most settlement limited to residential sectors at four large site groups at Chen Chen/Los Cerrillos, Omo, Cerro Echenique, and Río Muerto (Figure 4.5). This suggests congregation in a specific niche, quite separate from indigenous Huaracane settlement locations adjacent to the floodplain. Tiwanaku settlement areas are all located some distance from the valley edge and are connected by

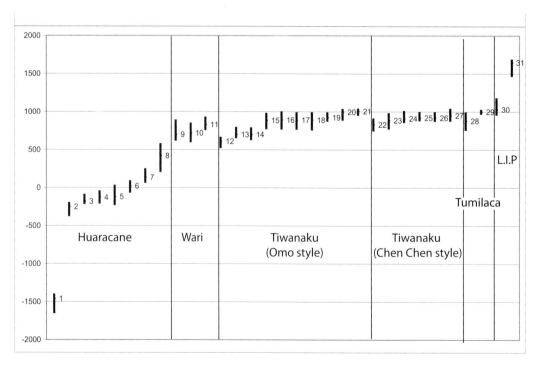

FIGURE 4.4. Moquegua Archaeological Survey, radiocarbon dates (1σ calibrated range).

Table 4.2. Radiocarbon Dates from the Moquegua Middle Valley

#	Lab No.	Specimen	Site	Material	Conventional Age	Affiliation	Context	Year Collected	Source
1	Beta-261514	M73=1264	Tres Quebradas	wood	3220 ± 60 BP	Huaracane	domestic sounding	2003	Goldstein and Magilligan 2011
2	AA-38030	M73=9999	Tres Quebradas	wood log	2220 ± 42 BP	Huaracane túmulo	túmulo 1	1998	Goldstein 2000b
3	Beta-120262	M17=1	Omo Bajo	wood post	2140 ± 50 BP	Huaracane túmulo	túmulo	1994	Goldstein 2000b
4	AA-38029	M73=1034	Tres Quebradas	wood branch	2112 ± 42 BP	Huaracane túmulo	túmulo 1	1998	Goldstein 2000b
5	Beta-212301	M103=1144	Montalvo	wood	2090 ± 60 BP	Huaracane habitation	domestic sounding	2003	Goldstein and Magilligan 2011
6	Beta-26651	M10=2197	Omo M10Y cemetery	wood, tomb roof	1990 ± 70 BP	Huaracane boot tomb	boot tomb 6, level 8	1987	Goldstein 1989a, 2000b
7	Beta-120263	M7=2	Trapiche M7	wood post	1860 ± 70 BP	Huaracane boot tomb	looted boot tomb	2003	Goldstein 2000b
8	Beta-212300	M76=1101	Los Joyeros	wood	1640 ± 70 BP	Huaracane Joyeros	looted cemetery	2003	Goldstein and Magilligan 2011
9	Beta-212298	M7=1053	Trapiche M7	charred material	1290 ± 60 BP	Wari	structure 3 patio group	2003	Goldstein 2005
10	Beta-212299	M7=1419	Trapiche M7	charred material	1320 ± 70 BP	Wari	structure 3 patio group	2003	Goldstein 2005
11	Beta-189445	M7=1248	Trapiche M7	organic material	1190 ± 40 BP	Wari	structure 3 patio group	2003	Goldstein 2005
12	Beta-36639	M12=1617	Omo M12	wood post	1470 ± 80 BP	Tiwanaku Omo	structure 2, domestic	1987	Goldstein 1993:31
13	Beta-129938	M16=5500	Omo M16	wood post	1290 ± 70 BP	Tiwanaku Omo	tomb 15	1999	Goldstein 2005
14	Beta-242273	M70=2996	Río Muerto M70	wood	1360 ± 40 BP	Tiwanaku Omo	cemetery, tomb R69	2006	Goldstein and Magilligan 2011
15	Beta-129939	M70=1509	Río Muerto M70	wood post	1160 ± 60 BP	Tiwanaku Omo	unit 6y, domestic	1998	Goldstein 2005
16	Beta-242272	M70=2943	Río Muerto M70	wood	1140 ± 50 BP	Tiwanaku Omo	cemetery, tomb R62	2006	Goldstein and Magilligan 2011
17	Beta-242274	M70=3466	Río Muerto M70	wood	1160 ± 40 BP	Tiwanaku Omo	cemetery, unit i	2006	Goldstein and Magilligan 2011
18	Beta-242271	M70=2296	Río Muerto M70	wood	1210 ± 50 BP	Tiwanaku Omo	cemetery, tomb R11	2006	Goldstein and Magilligan 2011
19	AA-38032	M70=1245	Río Muerto M70	wood	1132 ± 39 BP	Tiwanaku Omo	unit 4, domestic	1998	Goldstein 2005
20	Beta-120264	M12=3016	Omo M12	wood	1060 ± 70 BP	Tiwanaku Omo	structure 7, domestic	1987	Goldstein 2005
21	Beta-60762	M12=3388	Omo M12	wood post	1040 ± 70 BP	Tiwanaku Omo	structure 7, domestic	1987	Goldstein 2005
22	AA-44817	M10=3939	Omo M10	wood	1198 ± 47 BP	Tiwanaku Chen Chen	temple, unit 117	1990	Goldstein and Magilligan 2011
23	Beta-39679	M10=4014	Omo M10	wood	1160 ± 60 BP	Tiwanaku Chen Chen	temple, lintel, unit 113	1990	Goldstein 1993:34

Continued on the next page

Table 4.2 *(continued)*

#	Lab No.	Specimen	Site	Material	Conventional Age	Affiliation	Context	Year Collected	Source
24	Beta-26650	M10=1758	Omo M10	wood	1120 ± 70 BP	Tiwanaku Chen Chen	structure 13, domestic	1987	Goldstein 1989:69
25	AA-40628	M10=1121	Omo M10	wood	1101 ± 35 BP	Tiwanaku Chen Chen	structure 11, domestic	1987	Goldstein 2005
26	AA-38031	M43=1067	Río Muerto M43	wood	1122 ± 44 BP	Tiwanaku Chen Chen	unit 1, domestic	1998	Goldstein 2005
27	Beta-242270	M43=2497	Río Muerto M43	charred material	1060 ± 40 BP	Tiwanaku Chen Chen	unit 3, domestic	2007	Goldstein and Magilligan 2011
28	Beta-26649	M11=1406a	Omo M11	wood post	1170 ± 80 BP	Tiwanaku Tumilaca	structure 5	1987	Goldstein 1989:77
29	AA-40629	M11=1406b	Omo M11	wood post	1061 ± 37 BP	Tiwanaku Tumilaca	structure 5	1987	Goldstein 2005
30	Beta-261513	M59=1056	Ramadon M59	wood	990 ± 50 BP	Chiribaya	domestic sounding	2004	Goldstein and Magilligan 2011
31	Beta-261511	M21=1025	Bodega Grande M21	maize	250 ± 50 BP	Estuquina-Inka	domestic sounding	2004	Goldstein and Magilligan 2011

Table 4.3. Moquegua Mid-Valley Survey Results by Cultural Affiliation

Cultural Affiliation	Number of Habitation Components	Total Habitation Area (ha)	Number of Cemetery Components	Total Cemetery Area (ha)
Huaracane	169	73.5	70	20.2
Wari	3	4.2?	1	.1
Omo-style Tiwanaku sites	12	28.7	3	.1
Chen Chen–style Tiwanaku sites	31	50.5	39	10.4
Tumilaca Tiwanaku	45	42.0	10	.8
Chiribaya	21	11.6	13	1.2
Estuquiña	14	9.0	12	2.6
Other Late Intermediate	3	1.1	1	.1
Estuquiña-Inca	4	1.7	3	1.4

desert caravan trails to a series of llama geoglyphs still visible on hillsides near Chen Chen, Omo, and Río Muerto (Figure 4.6).

The third result from settlement pattern research is a spatially focused picture of Tiwanaku diversity in diaspora. At least two distinct Tiwanaku groups, both of entirely altiplano origin, colonized Moquegua between A.D. 600 and A.D. 1000. Fifteen site components with predominantly Omo-style Tiwanaku ceramics cover a total of 28.7 ha in the middle Moquegua Valley. Site components with predominant ceramic assemblages of the Chen Chen style cover 54.6 ha of domestic area, with an additional 10.4 ha of cemeteries. These two distinct varieties of Tiwa-

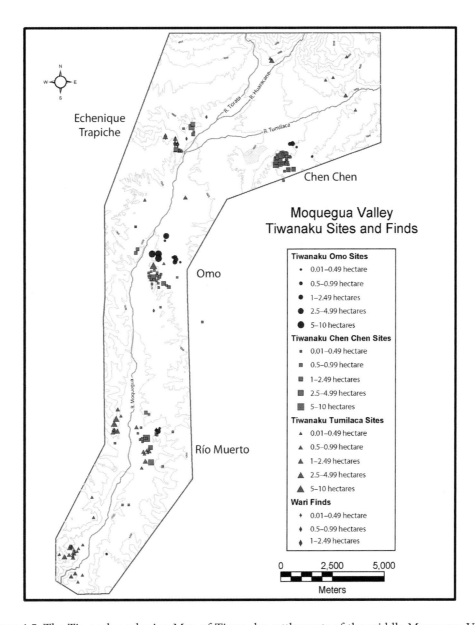

Figure 4.5. The Tiwanaku colonies. Map of Tiwanaku settlements of the middle Moquegua Valley.

naku culture overlapped in time but are represented at distinct residential components at each of the Tiwanaku site groups (Figure 4.7), with distinctive residential architecture and mortuary practice, as well as ceramic substyles. The two substyles are typical of Tiwanaku and some core region sites and suggest that migrant streams from two distinct parent communities migrated independently and maintained their segregation from one another in the colonial setting. These two distinct Tiwanaku "diasporas" coexisted in time and space yet remained separate, perhaps representing independent action by two Tiwaaku moieties, ethnic groups, or maximal *ayllus*.

What was the relationship between these two distinct colonial settlement systems? Between each and their respective segments in the altiplano homelands? At each of the three Moquegua Tiwanaku site groups, settlements of the two stylistic affiliations were arranged in a northeast/southwest opposition, with the Omo-style settlement sectors to the northeast. This suggests that segmentary identification may have been encoded in their relative positions, as is often the case in the directional opposition of moieties in Andean *ayllus*, which may anticipate Andean concepts of *tinku*, or the joining of complementary social opposites along ceremonial axes

Figure 4.6. Tiwanaku caravan route geoglyphs, including llamas and *keros*: (*a*) Chen Chen M1; (*b*) Omo M10.

(Platt 1986; Urton 1993). Thus it appears that the two Tiwanaku colonies replicated a structural division that originated in the social segmentation of distinct origins within the Tiwanaku homeland.

What were their parent communities? The prevalence of a characteristic variety of *kero* displaying Tiwanaku's "front face god," polished black *keros* and other serving wares, continuous volute motifs, and other ceramic types in the Omo-style assemblage suggests affiliations with parent communities on the southwestern shore and islands of Lake Titicaca (Figures 4.8, 4.9) and perhaps another colony at the Piñami site in the distant Cochabamba Valley of Bolivia (Anderson 2009). This extends this particular subgroup's technological style, its separate exchange network, and perhaps its shared corporate

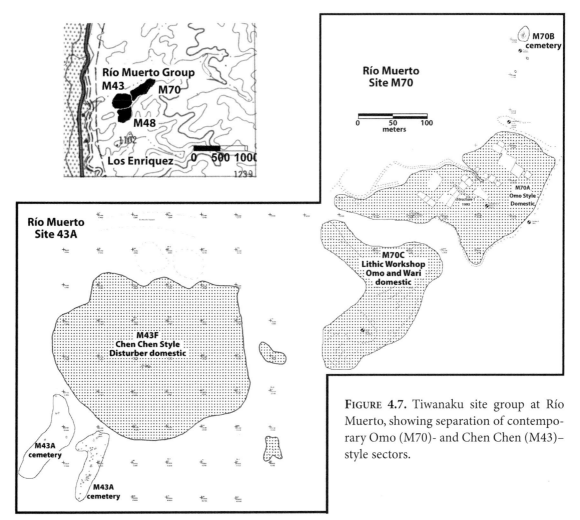

FIGURE 4.7. Tiwanaku site group at Río Muerto, showing separation of contemporary Omo (M70)- and Chen Chen (M43)–style sectors.

identity from the shores of Lake Titicaca to both the Omo-style colonies of Moquegua and to a mirror colony of the same micro-affiliation sent to the eastern slopes of the Andes. Conversely, the Chen Chen ceramic style appears to have more in common with a subset of the assemblages from the Tiwanaku site itself.

It is plausible that the structured sharing of colonial space between Omo-style and Chen Chen–style colonists may reflect the transplantation of distinct diasporas from two autonomous segments of Tiwanaku society that joined to form a shared high culture. Ethnohistory in the Titicaca core region suggests that maximal ethnic

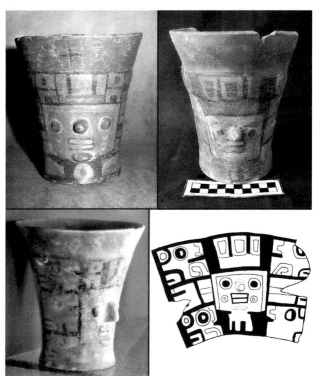

FIGURE 4.8. Tiwanaku red-slipped serving ware: front-face god *keros* from (upper left) Isla del Sol (AMNH Bandelier Collection), (lower left) Copacabana (Copacabana Museo del Sitio), and (right) Omo M12.

FIGURE 4.9A. Tiwanaku black polished vessels in the form of reclining llamas, Ciriapata cemetery, Island of the Sun (AMNH Bandelier Collection) (top) and Omo M12, Moquegua (bottom).

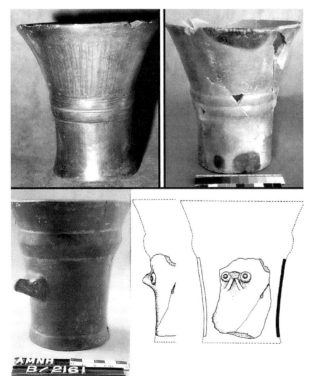

FIGURE 4.9B. Tiwanaku black polished serving ware: (left) Titin Uuayani and Ciriapata cemeteries, Island of the Sun (AMNH Bandelier Collection; (right) Omo style, Omo M12, Moquegua.

and linguistic groups aligned into two great moieties of Urco and Umasuyu, opposed along the spatial axis formed by Lake Titicaca (Bouysse-Cassagne 1986:207). Kolata argues that these same dualistic dynamics underlay an earlier Tiwanaku cosmology that also expressed itself in the division of ritual space within Tiwanaku, a site also known as Taypicala, or "the stone in the middle of the world" (Kolata 1993:101). If the Omo and Chen Chen settlements were affiliated with specific societal segments in the altiplano, the two settlement diasporas appear to have operated autonomously, and their sharing of the Moquegua Valley would suggest the "multiethnic coexistence" by outlier settlements of two social segments sharing a colonial context (Murra 1972).

Summing up, these parallel lines of inquiry verify that corporate popular migration was the motor of Tiwanaku state expansion. How would this internally diverse yet externally cohesive phenomenon of Tiwanaku demographic growth compare and compete with the Wari expansion?

TIWANAKU AND WARI EXPANSION: DEMOGRAPHIC AND OUTPOST COLONIZATION COMPARED

The interaction or codevelopment of the Tiwanaku and Wari cultures is a key issue in Andean archaeology, and particularly so in the Moquegua region, where the two spheres of influence intersect. The Tiwanaku and Wari cultures' fundamentally different approaches to regional expansion permitted their enclaves a segregated coexistence in adjacent and occasionally overlapping territories on their frontier in Moquegua. I believe this "multiethnic coexistence" writ large was only possible because of the marked contrast between Tiwanaku and Wari approaches to colonization. This contrast can be tested empirically by considering: (1) systematic settlement patterns and demography, (2) quantitative data on household architecture, activities, and assemblages, (3) systematic mortuary archaeology and bioarchaeology, and (4) comparison of architectural context.

From a regional settlement perspective, Wari and Tiwanaku sites are arrayed in distinct sectors of the Osmore drainage (Goldstein and Magilligan 2011). These patterns correspond to a Wari preference for up-valley (more than 2,000 m above sea level) terrace agriculture, versus the Tiwanaku reclamation of relatively flat lower-elevation (less than 1,500 m above sea level) desert lands without terracing. As discussed above, systematic survey data based on settlement and mortuary sites in the middle Moquegua Valley indicate a valley-wide Tiwanaku population of 10,000 to 20,000 colonists.

Wari scholars differ on the degree to which Wari imposed a substantial settlement hierarchy in its hinterland colonies (Jennings 2006; Williams and Nash 2002). Despite suggestions to the contrary, and despite the Moquegua Wari sites' evident investment in stone architecture, walls, and agricultural terracing, it is difficult to find Wari settlement hierarchy in Moquegua—or indeed very much Wari settlement at all. Systematic survey data for the Wari settlement zone are as yet incomplete, but only seven Wari sites have been reported in the Osmore drainage (Nash and Williams 2005:163). Considering the three published upper Osmore Wari sites (Cerros Baúl, Mejía, and Petroglifo), plus Cerro Trapiche in the middle Moquegua Valley, Wari habitation covered less than 20 ha in the drainage. Even if all of these sites' inhabitants were colonists of Wari origin, this suggests a total Wari-affiliated population of fewer than 2,000 people. If these Wari sites were built, serviced, and maintained by a population that included a significant input of indigenous people, as surely appears to be the case at multicultural Cerro Trapiche (Green and Goldstein 2009), the number of actual foreign colonists would have been minuscule indeed.

Turning to household and mortuary archaeology, two clear trends are evident: (1) a phenomenal degree of segregation between the Wari- and Tiwanaku-affiliated settlements and (2) very different domestic frontier relationships between each group of state colonists and indigenous peoples. First, despite their proximity, Wari and Tiwanaku settlers never occupied the same habitation sites, and sites of each affiliation maintained utterly different traditions in architectural construction and plan and in domestic activities and assemblages. Some have taken a "glass 1/100 full" position on Wari–Tiwanaku interaction, citing the rare examples of items exchanged between Wari and Tiwanaku sites to imply significant interaction between the two societies (Nash and Williams 2005; Williams 2001; Williams and Nash 2002; Williams et al. 2001). I take a "glass 99/100 empty" position. When assemblages are compared quantitatively, the frequency of Wari ceramics in Tiwanaku contexts in Moquegua is microscopic, at a level that would be minimal even for cases of exotic trade let alone for prolonged interaction. A review of Coscopa Wari-style vessels reported in Tiwanaku tombs in the Chen Chen Tiwanaku cemetery in Moquegua, for example (García Marquez 1990), reveals that this amounted to fewer than a dozen vessel offerings out of 1,200 excavated tombs. Most importantly, assemblage-wide analysis of large-household unit excavations and systematic surface collections from the Chen Chen, Omo, and Río Muerto Tiwanaku domestic town sites, totaling well over 100,000 sherds, have found fewer than two dozen Wari sherds in Tiwanaku domestic contexts (Goldstein 2005; Boswell and Goldstein 2009). Even at the very foot of Cerro Baúl, at the small Omo-style Tiwanaku site of La Cantera, a systematic collection of more than 7,500 sherds from surface collections and test pits included only 4 Wari sherds (Owen and Goldstein 2001).[2] At Tiwanaku itself, it is also notable that while a variety of exotic trade ceramics are present in quantifiable frequencies, Wari exotics are not reported (Janusek 2003). The frequency of obsidian from Wari-controlled sources at Moquegua Tiwanaku sites, as in the altiplano, is also minuscule, and it could be due to scavenging or plunder as much as trade. There is a marked distinction between Wari's heavy use of obsidian and the Tiwanaku settlements' overwhelming reliance on other lithic materials. In sum, in domestic, mortuary, and monumental settings of both cultures, there is remarkably little evidence of trade, co-residence, intermarriage, or other interaction between Wari and Tiwanaku at large. These data indicate a remarkable segregation between the cultures and populations at contemporary sites less than 10 km apart in Moquegua.

The second key to understanding the coexistence of Wari and Tiwanaku on their mutual frontier is acknowledging the two expansive systems' very different modes of frontier interaction with *indigenous* peoples. Household assemblages can be instructive in illustrating variable forms of frontier relations between colonies and host populations, often with a gendered dimension. Seventeenth-century Dutch colonists in New Amsterdam, for example, strongly maintained ethnic identity at a family level, as expressed in the ubiquity and dogged persistence of Dutch material culture in domestic assemblages.

Notably, the Dutch West India Company colonized women as well as men, and Dutch intermarriage with Native Americans was minimal. Dutch colonial material culture thus included not only the Dutch-style architecture, pipes, and fancy serving wares that were characteristic for male realms of activity but also kitchen assemblages replete with characteristic Dutch food preparation vessels, such as three-footed *grapen* pots, *steelpanen* skillets, and colanders, indicating that traditional Dutch culinary practice was maintained by Dutch women (Cantwell and Wall 2001). In contrast, seventeenth-century Spanish colonialism sent males for conquest and occupation, and European women rarely came to Spanish America in the initial stages. *Mestizaje* with indigenous populations was commonplace in settlements like Saint Augustine, producing a characteristic mestizo pattern of gendered ethnicity in domestic contexts. Like Dutch colonization, Spanish colonization brought European-style activities to the male-related domestic sphere, as evident in architectural styles and construction techniques, military-political items, hunting weapons, and prestige items like serving majolica. However, in contrast to Dutch New Amsterdam, European *utilitarian* pottery was virtually absent from colonial Saint Augustine households. Instead, all utilitarian wares were of aboriginal manufacture, indicating a food preparation technology run by "Indian women in Spanish or mestizo household units within a predominantly male-oriented cultural milieu" (Deagan 1973:62; 2004).

The household archaeology suggests a similar distinction between Tiwanaku colonization and Wari colonialism. As discussed above, Moquegua Tiwanaku sites have *entirely* Tiwanaku domestic assemblages, including a vast "back kitchen" array of food preparation and cooking vessels, much as was the case in Dutch colonial households. In contrast, recent household archaeology at the Wari-Huaracane site of Cerro Trapiche in the middle Moquegua Valley has found a mixture of Wari-style stone structures, including a patio group that served as a *chicheria* for hosting local guests (Figure 4.10), along with more modest residential structures of local construction types. To varying degrees, all of the Wari-contemporary occupation was furnished with a mix-

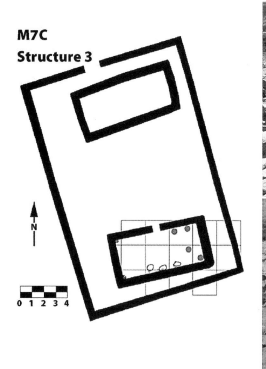 

FIGURE 4.10. Wari *chicheria* patio group, Trapiche M7, structure 3.

ture of Wari polychrome serving vessels, with the majority of food storage and preparation vessels made of the local Huaracane style (Figures 4.11, 4.12) (Green and Goldstein 2009). This suggests significant *mestizaje* in the Wari-Huaracane domestic sphere, following the Spanish pattern of food preparation techniques and crafts that reflects indigenous patterns brought by indigenous women (Deagan 1973). Wari colonizers in Moquegua, few in numbers and 600 km from that culture's core region, must have chosen local spouses or retainers for domestic reproduction and, most importantly, must have sought local labor to staff their agricultural and construction projects. The Wari-Huaracane households of the Cerro Trapiche settlement demonstrate that these communities could not have been self-sustaining without significant local input into the domestic facts of daily life.

Comparing mortuary evidence for the enclaves, we also find a stark contrast between Tiwanaku's

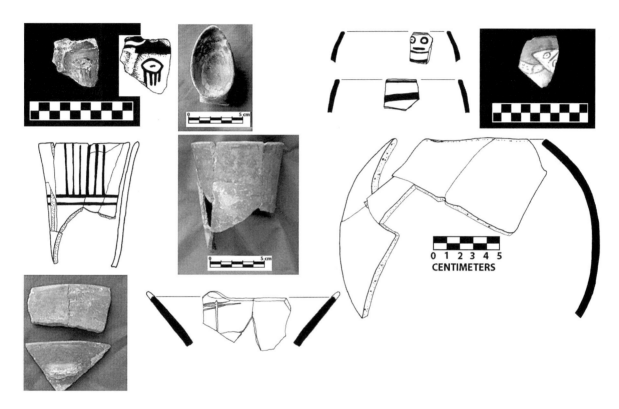

FIGURE 4.11. Wari serving ceramics, Trapiche M7, Huaracane neckless olla utilitarian vessel.

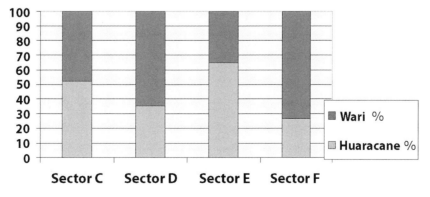

FIGURE 4.12. Relative surface frequencies of Wari and Huaracane ceramics, Middle Horizon sectors, Trapiche M7 (after Green et al. 2009).

massive colonial demographic presence and Wari's sparsely peopled frontier. Simply put, there are a lot of Tiwanaku people buried in Moquegua and virtually no Wari burials. The 10 ha of Tiwanaku cemeteries in Moquegua indicate a cemetery population between 10,000 and 20,000 (Goldstein 2005:123), with one calculation indicating a cemetery population of 12,856 Tiwanaku individuals at the Chen Chen site alone (Owen and Goldstein 2001). Additional Tumilaca-style Tiwanaku cemeteries in the middle Moquegua Valley, as well as in the upper drainages and the coastal Osmore Valley, add to the picture, indicating the strength of Tiwanaku cultural identity in continuity of mortuary practice after the collapse of state interaction dissolved political bonds to altiplano parent communities and Tiwanaku colonists dispersed to new site locations (Bawden 1993; Bermann et al. 1989; Owen 2005). In contrast, despite two decades of research, only five Wari burials have yet been excavated in Moquegua, no Wari cemeteries have been located in survey, and Wari vessels do not appear in local private collections (as compared to thousands of vessels looted from Tiwanaku cemeteries). One needn't apply advanced statistics to intuit an enormous disjuncture in both scale and permanence of settlement between these two populations.

Finally, Wari hegemonists focus on provincial Wari monumental architecture as "both ubiquitous and extensive in Moquegua" and as bearing "the mark of a concerted centralized effort" (Williams this volume). Cerro Baúl's fieldstone patio groups are elegantly named "palaces" with an élan worthy of Bingham's Machu Picchu districts, while Tiwanaku's 10,000 to 20,000 inhabitants are dismissed as living in "wattle and daub," similar to "the simplest class of Wari residential architecture." Wari's small colony, it is implied, must have inspired hegemonic awe as an "embassy" (Moseley et al. 2005).

In fact, the Wari and Tiwanaku domestic architectural traditions are distinguished more by cultural than status distinctions. Wari peoples everywhere built homes in stone, while Tiwanaku peoples, even in fine neighborhoods of the type site, preferred adobe, instead focusing their labor investment in cut stone and plastered surfaces on elaborate Tiwanaku temple architecture, both in the altiplano homeland and at the Omo M10 site in Moquegua (Goldstein 1993b). Considering the two cultures' almost antithetical architectural traditions (Conklin 1991), any "my palace is bigger than your temple" argument is moot in the absence of a quantification of invested labor time and association of that labor time with real people who *did* the labor.

A final, telling comparison of architectural context comes back to each culture's choice of settlement location. The Wari mountaintop sites of Cerro Baúl and its supporting enclaves may have been chosen for defensibility as much as grandeur. Like Cerro Trapiche, the Wari or Wari-Huaracane outposts were further defended by stone walls and stockpiles of sling stones. In sharp contrast, the great Tiwanaku towns built in the era of state colonization were built on open plateaus and utterly undefended.[3] Their only fortified site contemporary with the Tiwanaku state is the M2 sector of Cerro Echenique, a partially walled mountain site that could have been built in response to the highly fortified Cerro Trapiche settlement at a distance of less than 2 km. Thus, while the Wari sites were tense frontier outposts in a strange land, Moquegua's Tiwanaku settlers appear to have felt secure in their numbers and their proximity to home.

Conclusion: A Vision of Tiwanaku from the Provinces

In their vast collective project of transregional migration to lowland areas, peoples of the Tiwanaku civilization enjoyed annexing important resources and peopling them with migrant communities that replicated the segmentary social structure of their homeland in new regions. That Tiwanaku society was an intense and enduring pluralism of distinct group identities is evident in multiple contemporary diasporas of Tiwanaku peoples who inhabited the colonial periphery (Goldstein 2005). The distinct migration patterns of the two groups suggest that each pertained to extended communities that acted with a degree of political autonomy throughout the Tiwanaku sphere of broader cultural unity. As proposed for the medieval South Indian states, the boundaries of any Tiwanaku political jurisdiction over this mélange may have been perceived very differently from different points of the system. A Tiwanaku king or kings may have enjoyed sovereignty that was more ritual than secular, and many aspects of daily decision making, including the day-to-day workings of their colonies, originated in Tiwanaku's component corporate groups. Only as the sum of such agencies can we understand Tiwanaku civilization as a set of shared identities that crosscut the Tiwanaku homeland and periphery.

Some might argue that Tiwanaku's internal diversity marks factionalism and hence a primitive or weak state, and that unitary centralization and hierarchical administration, like those sometimes proposed for Wari, are the true marks of state power. I differ. A state that is pluralistic and heterarchical is still a state, and the sum of Tiwanaku's corporate communities equaled a full-fledged regional power, with a remarkably enduring grip on the Andean imagination. Tiwanaku domination of the southern Andes by large transregional colonies in Moquegua and by mass acculturation of local cultures to Tiwanaku culture in Azapa and Cochabamba is indisputable.

Tiwanaku colonization left a far more lasting impact than the wide but shallow influence of small Wari colonies that attempted to build colonialism on the backs of indigenous peoples and ultimately disappeared into the populations they attempted to dominate. Wari colonists in Moquegua, and perhaps elsewhere, were scarce on the ground and had no choice but to beseech local labor through a complex colonialist dialectic with indigenous people. It has been noted that someone's "frontier" is usually somebody else's homeland (Lightfoot and Martinez 1995: 473). Wari frontiersmen, always few on the ground and far from home, needed land, labor, and above all, tolerance and assistance from indigenous peoples to reproduce even a small colony of their homeland culture. Regardless of any esteem their enclave achieved as a military or pilgrimage phenomenon, Wari's outpost never became the massive and demographically transformative presence of foreign culture that was Tiwanaku colonization.

When Tiwanaku culture expanded to new lands, it did so in familiar territory and in great numbers. In their own backyard, Tiwanaku colonists used the altiplano's greatest resources—demographic expansion, agropastoral mobility, and a unifying popular ideology—as an engine of "people power." The proof of the fitness of Tiwanaku's confederative and demographic route to state expansion was its four centuries of popular dominion over the south-central Andes, a cultural hegemony that endured in the ethnogenesis of local cultures even long after the political unity of the Tiwanaku state withered. For Tiwanaku expansion, pluralism simply worked better than politically monolithic expansion—a "popular" phenomenon in both senses of the word. Tiwanaku colonists always found their strength within, confederating a kaleidoscope of transregionally extended communities into a powerful and enduring civilization. Tiwanaku was always more than the sum of its parts.

Notes

[1] The Tumilaca style in the middle Moquegua Valley overlaps temporally with both the previous Chen Chen Tiwanaku style and the subsequent Chiribaya tradition. Tumilaca-phase sites demonstrate strong cultural continuity from prior Tiwanaku settlement but decreased contact with the altiplano and a rapid political balkanization in the tenth and eleventh centuries. As Tumilaca-style occupations persist well after the Tiwanaku state collapse, we can refer to these as post-expansive Tiwanaku settlements (Bawden 1993; Bermann et al. 1989; Goldstein 1989, 2005; Owen 2005; Owen and Goldstein 2001).

[2] La Cantera produced three fragments of one Ocros vessel and one Chakipampa sherd.

[3] Tumilaca-style sites, which postdate the Tiwanaku collapse, are usually defensibly located and walled.

References Cited

Albarracin-Jordan, Juan
   1996 *Tiwanaku. Arqueología regional y dinámica segmentaria*. Editores Plural, La Paz.

Albarracin-Jordan, J. V., and J. E. Mathews
   1990 *Asentamientos prehispánicos del Valle de Tiwanaku*, Vol. 1. Producciones CIMA, La Paz.

Anderson, Karen
   2009 Tiwanaku Influence on Local Drinking Patterns in Cochabamba, Bolivia. In D*rink, Power and Society in the Andes*, edited by Justin Jennings and Brenda Bowser, pp. 167–199. University Press of Florida, Gainesville.

Anthony, D. W.
   1990 Migration in Archaeology: The Baby and the Bathwater. *American Anthropologist* 92(3):895–914.

Appadurai, A.
   1978 Kings, Sects and Temples in South India 1350–1700 A.D. In *South Indian Temples: An Analytical Reconsideration*, edited by Burton Stein, pp. 47–73. Vikas, New Delhi.

Baitzel, S. I., and P. S. Goldstein
   2011 Manifesting Ethnic Identity in an Ancient Society: Evidence from a Tiwanaku Cemetery in

Moquegua, Peru. In *Ethnicity from Various Angles and through Varied Lenses*, edited by C. Hunefeldt and L. Zamosc, pp 30-44. Sussex Academic Press, Sussex.

Bawden, G.
- 1989 The Tumilaca Site and Post-Tiahuanaco Occupational Stratigraphy in the Moquegua Drainage. In *Settlement, History and Ecology in the Osmore Drainage, Southern Peru*, edited by D. S. Rice, C. Stanish, and P. Scarr, pp. 287–302. British Archaeological Reports Vol. 545, No. 2. British Archaeological Reports, Oxford.
- 1993 An Archaeological Study of Social Structure and Ethnic Replacement in Residential Architecture of the Tumilaca Valley. In *Domestic Architecture, Ethnicity, and Complementarity in the South-Central Andes*, edited by M. Aldenderfer, pp. 42–54. University of Iowa Press, Iowa City.

Berenguer, J. R.
- 1998 La iconografía del poder en Tiwanaku y su rol en la integración de zonas de frontera. *Boletín, Museo Chileno de Arte Precolombino* 7:19–37.

Bermann, M. P.
- 1994 *Lukurmata: Household Archaeology in Prehispanic Bolivia.* Princeton University Press, Princeton, New Jersey.
- 1997 Domestic Life and Vertical Integration in the Tiwanaku Heartland. *Latin American Antiquity* 8(2):93–112.

Bermann, Marc, Paul Goldstein, Charles Stanish, and Louis Watanabe
- 1989 The Collapse of the Tiwanaku State: A View from the Osmore Drainage. *In Settlement, History and Ecology in the Osmore Drainage, Southern Peru,* edited by D. S. Rice, C. Stanish, and P. Scarr, pp. 269–286. British Archaeological Reports Vol. 545, No. 2. British Archaeological Reports, Oxford.

Blanton, Richard E.
- 1998 Beyond Centralization: Steps Toward a Theory of Egalitarian Behavior in Archaic States. In *Archaic States*, edited by Gary M. Feinman and Joyce Marcus, pp. 135–172. School of American Research Press, Santa Fe.

Blanton, Richard, Gary Feinman, Stephen A. Kowalewski, and Peter Peregrine
- 1996 Agency, Ideology and Power in Archaeological Theory: A Dual Processual Theory of the Evolution of Mesoamerican Civilization. *Current Anthropology* 37(1):1–14.

Blom, D. E.
- 1999 Tiwanaku and the Moquegua Settlements: A Bioarchaeological Approach. Ph.D. dissertation, Department of Anthropology, University of Chicago, Chicago.
- 2005 Embodying Borders: Human Body Modification and Diversity in Tiwanaku Society. *Journal of Anthropological Archaeology* 24(1):1–24.

Blom, D., B. Hallgrímsson, L. Keng, M. C. Lozada C., and J. E. Buikstra
- 1998 Tiwanaku "Colonization": Bioarchaeological Implications for Migration in the Moquegua Valley, Peru. *World Archaeology* 30(2):238–261.

Boorstein, J. A.
- 2005 Epiclassic Political Organization in Southern Veracruz, Mexico: Segmentary versus Centralized Integration. *Ancient Mesoamerica* 16:11–21.

Boswell, A. M. and P. S. Goldstein
- 2011 Daily Maintenance of Ethnic Identity away from the Homeland: Tiwanaku Domestic Practices of the Moquegua Valley, Peru. In *Ethnicity from Various Angles and Through Varied Lenses*, edited by C. Hunefeldt and L. Zamosc, pp 45–58. Sussex Academic Press, Sussex.

Bouysse-Cassagne, T.
- 1986 Urco and Uma: Aymara Concepts of Space. In *Anthropological History of Andean Polities*, edited by J. V. Murra, N. Wachtel, and J. Revel, pp. 201–227. Cambridge University Press, Cambridge.

Brumfiel, E.
- 1994 Factional Competition and Political Development in the New World, an Introduction. In *Factional Competition and Political Development in the New World*, edited by E. Brumfiel and J. Fox, pp. 3–13. Cambridge University Press, Cambridge.

Buikstra, J. E.
- 1995 Tombs for the Living … or … for the Dead: The Osmore Ancestors. In *Tombs for the Living: Andean Mortuary Practices*, edited by T. D. Dillehay, pp. 229–280. Dumbarton Oaks, Washington, D.C.

Cantwell, Ann-Marie, and Diana diZarega Wall
- 2001 *Unearthing Gotham: The Archaeology of New York City.* Yale University Press, New Haven.

Clifford, J.
- 1994 Diasporas. *Cultural Anthropology* 9(3):302–338.

Conklin, W.
- 1991 Tiwanaku and Huari: Architectural Comparisons and Interpretations. In *Huari Administrative Structure: Prehistoric Monumental Architecture and State Government*, edited by W. Isbell and G. McEwan, pp. 281–292. Dumbarton Oaks, Washington, D.C.

Costion, K. E., and U. M. Green
- 2009 Responding to the Colonization of the Moquegua Valley: The Changing of Huaracane Identity through the Selective Adoption of Colonial Traditions. Paper presented at the 74th Annual Society for American Archaeology Meeting, Atlanta.

Couture, N., and K. Sampeck
2003 Putuni: A History of Palace Architecture at Tiwanaku. In *Tiwanaku and Its Hinterland: Archaeology and Paleoecology of an Andean Civilization.* Vol. 2, *Urban and Rural Archaeology,* edited by Alan L. Kolata, pp. 226–263. Smithsonian Institution Press, Washington, D.C.

Crumley, C. L.
1987 Dialectical Critique of Hierarchy. In *Power Relations and State Formation*, edited by T. C. Patterson and C. W. Gailey, pp. 155–168. American Anthropological Association, Washington, D.C.
1995 Heterarchy and the Analysis of Complex Societies. In *Heterarchy and the Analysis of Complex Societies*, edited by R. M. Ehrenreich, C. L. Crumley, and J. E. Levy, pp. 1–5. Archeological Papers of the American Anthropological Association No. 6. American Anthropological Association, Washington, D.C.

Deagan, K. A.
1973 Mestizaje in Colonial St. Augustine. *Ethnohistory* 20(1):55–65.
2004 Reconsidering Taíno Social Dynamics after Spanish Conquest: Gender and Class in Culture Contact Studies. *American Antiquity* 69(4):597–626.

Flannery, K. V.
1998 The Ground Plans of Archaic States. In *Archaic States*, edited by G. M. Feinman and J. Marcus, pp. 15–58. School of American Research, Santa Fe.

Fox, J. W.
1988 *Maya Postclassic State Formation: Segmentary Lineage Migration in Advancing Frontiers.* Cambridge University Press, Cambridge.

Fox, John W., Garrett W. Cook, Arlen F. Chase, and Diane Z. Chase
1996 Questions of Political and Economic Integration: Segmentary versus Centralized States among the Ancient Maya. In *The Maya State: Centralized or Segmentary?* Special section, *Current Anthropology* 37(5):795–801.

Fox, R. G.
1971 *Kin, Clan, Raja, and Rule: State-Hinterland Relations in Preindustrial India.* University of California Press, Berkeley.

Fritz, J. M.
1986 Vijayanagara: Authority and Meaning in a South Indian Imperial Capital. *American Anthropologist* 88(1):44–55.

García Marquez, M.
1990 *Excavación en el cementerio de Chen Chen, Moquegua, una interaccion de contextos funerarios Tiwanaku/Wari.* Universidad Católica de Santa María, Arequipa.

Gillespie, S. D.
2000 Rethinking Ancient Maya Social Organization: Replacing "Lineage" with "House." *American Anthropologist* 102(3):467–484.
2001 Personhood, Agency, and Mortuary Ritual: A Case Study from the Ancient Maya. *Journal of Anthropological Archaeology* 20(1):73–112.

Goldstein, P. S.
1989 Omo: A Tiwanaku Provincial Center in Moquegua, Peru. Unpublished Ph.D. dissertation, Department of Anthropology, University of Chicago, Chicago.
1993a House, Community and State in the Earliest Tiwanaku Colony: Domestic Patterns and State Integration at Omo M12, Moquegua. In *Domestic Architecture, Ethnicity, and Complementarity in the South-Central Andes*, edited by M. Aldenderfer, pp. 25–41. University of Iowa Press, Iowa City.
1993b Tiwanaku Temples and State Expansion: A Tiwanaku Sunken-Court Temple in Moquegua, Peru. *Latin American Antiquity* 4(3):22–47.
2000 Exotic Goods and Everyday Chiefs: Long Distance Exchange and Indigenous Sociopolitical Development in the South Central Andes. *Latin American Antiquity* 11(4):1–27.
2005 *Andean Diaspora: The Tiwanaku Colonies and the Origins of Andean Empire.* University Press of Florida, Gainesville.

Goldstone, J. A., and J. F. Haldon
2009 Ancient States, Empires and Exploitation. In *The Dynamics of Ancient Empires: State Power from Assyria to Byzantium*, edited by I. Morris and W. Scheidel, pp. 1–29. Oxford University Press, Oxford.

Goldstein, P. S. and F. J. Magilligan
2011 Hazard, Risk and Agrarian Adaptations in a Hyperarid Watershed: El Niño Floods, Streambank Erosion, and the Cultural Bounds of Vulnerability in the Andean Middle Horizon. *Catena* 85 (2011): 155–167

Gose, P.
1993 Segmentary State Formation and the Ritual Control of Water under the Incas. *Comparative Studies in Society and History* 35:480–514.

Green, U. M., and P. S. Goldstein
2009 The Nature of Wari Presence in the Mid-Moquegua Valley: Investigating Contact at Cerro Trapiche. In *Beyond Wari Walls: Regional Perspectives on Middle Horizon Peru*, edited by J. Jennings, pp. 19–36. University of New Mexico Press, Albuquerque.

Hayashida, F. M.
2006 The Pampa de Chaparri: Water, Land, and Politics on the North Coast of Peru. *Latin American Antiquity* 17(3):243–263.

Hoshower, Lisa M., Jane E. Buikstra, Paul S. Goldstein, and Ann D. Webster
    1995 Artificial Cranial Deformation at the Omo M10 Site: A Tiwanaku Complex from the Moquegua Valley, Peru. *Latin American Antiquity* 6(2): 145–164.

Houston, S. D.
    1993 *Hieroglyphs and History at Dos Pilas: Dynastic Politics of the Classic Maya.* University of Texas Press, Austin.

Isbell, William, and Jo Ellen Burkholder
    2002 Iwawi and Tiwanaku. In *Andean Archaeology.* Vol. 1, *Variations in Sociopolitical Organization*, edited by William H. Isbell and Helaine Silverman, pp. 199–241. Kluwer Academic/Plenum Publishers, New York.

Janusek, J. W.
    2003 The Changing Face of Tiwanaku Residential Life: State and Local Identity in an Andean City. In *Tiwanaku and Its Hinterland: Archaeology and Paleoecology of an Andean Civilization.* Vol. 2, *Urban and Rural Archaeology*, edited by Alan L. Kolata, pp. 264–295. Smithsonian Institution Press, Washington, D.C.
    2004 *Identity and Power in the Ancient Andes: Tiwanaku Cities through Time.* Routledge, New York.

Janusek, J. W., and A. L. Kolata
    2004 Top-Down or Bottom-Up: Rural Settlement and Raised Field Agriculture in the Lake Titicaca Basin, Bolivia. *Journal of Anthropological Archaeology* 23(4):404–430.

Jennings, J.
    2006 Understanding Middle Horizon Peru: Hermeneutic Spirals, Interpretative Traditions, and Wari Administrative Centers. *Latin American Antiquity* 17(3):265–285.

Knudson, K. J.
    2008 Tiwanaku Influence in the South Central Andes: Strontium Isotope Analysis and Middle Horizon Migration. *Latin American Antiquity* 19(1): 3–23.

Knudson, K. J., T. D. Price, J. E. Buikstra, and D. E. Blom
    2004 The Use of Strontium Isotope Analysis to Investigate Tiwanaku Migration and Mortuary Ritual in Boliva and Peru. *Archaeometry* 46(1):5–18.

Kolata, A. L.
    1993 *The Tiwanaku: Portrait of an Andean Civilization.* Blackwell, Cambridge, Massachusetts.
    2003 The Social Production of Tiwanaku: Political Economy and Authority in a Native Andean State. In *Tiwanaku and Its Hinterland: Archaeology and Paleoecology of an Andean Civilization.* Vol. 2, *Urban and Rural Archaeology*, edited by A. L. Kolata, pp. 449–472. Smithsonian Institution Press, Washington, D.C.

Korpisaari, Antti
    2006 *Death in the Bolivian High Plateau: Burials and Tiwanaku Society.* BAR International Series 1536. British Archaeological Reports, Oxford.

Lane, K.
    2009 Engineered Highlands: The Social Organization of Water in the Ancient North-Central Andes (AD 1000–1480). *World Archaeology* 41(1):169–190.

Lightfoot, K.G., and A. Martinez
    1995 Frontiers and Boundaries in Archaeological Perspective. *Annual Review of Anthropology* 24: 471–492.

Marcus, J., and G. Feinman (editors)
    1998 *Archaic States.* School of American Research, Santa Fe.

McAndrews, T., J. Albarracin-Jordan, and M. Bermann
    1997 Regional Settlement Patterns in the Tiwanaku Valley of Bolivia. *Journal of Field Archaeology* 24:7–84.

McIntosh, S. K. (editor)
    1999 *Beyond Chiefdoms: Pathways to Complexity in Africa.* Cambridge University Press, New York.

Mitchell, W. P., and D. Guillet
    1994 *Irrigation at High Altitudes: The Social Organization of Water Control Systems in the Andes.* American Anthropological Association, Washington, D.C.

Moseley, M. E.
    1999 Convergent Catastrophes: Past Patterns and Future Implications of Collateral Natural Disasters in the Andes. In *The Angry Earth: Disasters in Anthropological Perspective*, edited by A. Oliver-Smith and S. Hoffman, 59–71. Routledge, London.

Moseley, Michael, Donna Nash, Patrick Ryan Williams, Susan deFrance, Ana Miranda, and Mario Ruales
    2005 Burning Down the Brewery: Establishing and Evacuating an Ancient Imperial Colony at Cerro Baúl, Perú. *Proceedings of the National Academy of Sciences* 102(48):17264–17271. Washington, D.C.

Murra, John V.
    1972 El "control vertical" de un máximo de pisos ecológicos en la economía de las sociedades andinas. In *Visita de la Provincia de León de Huánuco en 1562 por Iñigo Ortiz de Zuñiga*, edited by John V. Murra, pp. 427–476. Universidad Nacional Hermilio Valdizan, Huánuco, Peru.

Nash, Donna J., and P. R. Williams
    2005 Architecture and Power on the Wari-Tiwanaku Frontier. *Archeological Papers of the American Anthropological Association* 14(1):151–174.

Netherly, P. J.
    1993 The Nature of the Andean State. In *Configurations of Power: Holistic Anthropology in Theory*

and Practice, edited by J. S. Henderson and P. J. Netherly, pp. 11–35. Cornell University Press, Ithaca.

Owen, Bruce
   2005   Distant Colonies and Explosive Collapse: The Two Stages of the Tiwanaku Diaspora in the Osmore Drainage. *Latin American Antiquity* 16(1):45–80.

Owen, Bruce, and Paul Goldstein
   2001   Tiwanaku en Moquegua: Interacciones regionales y colapso. In *Huari y Tiwanaku: Modelos vs. evidencias,* edited by Peter Kaulicke and William H. Isbell, pp. 169–188. Boletín de Arqueología PUCP No. 5, pt. 2. Pontificia Universidad Católica del Perú, Lima.

Patterson, T., and C. W. Gailey
   1987   Power Relations and State Formation. In *Power Relations and State Formation,* edited by T. Patterson and C. Gailey, pp. 1–27. American Anthropological Association, Washington, D.C.

Platt, T.
   1986   Mirrors and Maize: The Concept of Yanantin among the Macha of Bolivia. In *Anthropological History of Andean Polities,* edited by J. Murra, N. Wachtel, and J. Reve, pp. 228–259. Cambridge University Press, Cambridge.

Potter, D. R., and E. M. King
   1995   A Heterarchical Approach to Lowland Maya Socioeconomics. In *Heterarchy and the Analysis of Complex Societies,* edited by R. M. Ehrenreich, C. L. Crumley, and J. E. Levy, pp. 17–32. Archeological Papers of the American Anthropological Association, No. 6. American Anthropological Association, Washington, D.C.

Rivera Casanovas, Claudia
   2003   Ch'iji Jawira: A Case of Ceramic Specialization in the Tiwanaku Urban Periphery. In *Tiwanaku and Its Hinterland: Archaeology and Paleoecology of an Andean Civilization.* Vol. 2, *Urban and Rural Archaeology,* edited by Alan L. Kolata, pp. 296–315. Smithsonian Institution Press, Washington, D.C.

Sinopoli, Carla, and Kathleen Morrison
   1995   Dimensions of Imperial Control: The Vijayanagara Capital. *American Anthropologist* 97(1):83–96.

Southall, A.
   1974   State Formation in Africa. *Annual Review of Anthropology* 3:153–165.
   1988   The Segmentary State in Africa and Asia. Comparative *Studies in Society and History* 30(1):52–82.
   1999   The Segmentary State and the Ritual Phase in Political Economy. In *Beyond Chiefdoms: Pathways to Complexity in Africa,* edited by S. K. McIntosh, pp. 32–38. Cambridge University Press, New York.

Spencer, C. S.
   1998   A Mathematical Model of Primary State Formation. *Cultural Dynamics* 10(1):5–20.

Stanish, C.
   2002   Tiwanaku Political Economy. In *Andean Archaeology.* Vol. 1, *Variations in Sociopolitical Organization,* edited by William Isbell and Helaine Silverman, pp. 169–198. Kluwer Academic/Plenum Publishers, New York.

Stein, B.
   1980   *Peasant, State and Society in Medieval South India.* Oxford University Press, New Delhi.
   1985   Politics, Peasants and the Deconstruction of Feudalism in Medieval India. *Journal of Peasant Studies* 12:54–86.

Urton, G.
   1993   Moieties and Ceremonialism in the Andes: The Ritual Battles of the Carnival Season in Southern Peru. In *El mundo ceremonial andino,* edited by L. Millones and Y. Onuki, pp. 117–142. National Museum of Ethnology, Osaka.

Webster, A. D., and J. W. Janusek
   2003   Tiwanaku Camelids: Subsistence, Sacrifice and Social Reproduction. In *Tiwanaku and Its Hinterland: Archaeology and Paleoecology of an Andean Civilization.* Vol. 2, *Urban and Rural Archaeology,* edited by Alan L. Kolata, pp. 343–362. Smithsonian Institution Press, Washington, D.C.

Williams, P. R.
   2001   Cerro Baúl: A Wari Center on the Tiwanaku Frontier. *Latin American Antiquity* 12(1):67–83.

Williams, Patrick Ryan, and Donna J. Nash
   2002   Imperial Interaction in the Andes: Huari and Tiwanaku at Cerro Baúl. In *Andean Archaeology.* Vol. 1, *Variations in Sociopolitical Organization,* edited by William H. Isbell and Helaine Silverman, pp. 243–265. Kluwer Academic/Plenum Publishers, New York.

Williams, P. R., J. A. Isla, and D. Nash
   2001   Cerro Baúl: A Wari Enclave Interacting with Tiwanaku. *Boletiín de Arqueología PUCP* 5:69–87.

Wilson, D. J.
   1988   *Prehispanic Settlement Patterns in the Lower Santa Valley, Peru.* Smithsonian Institution Press, Washington, D.C.

5

THE CULTURAL IMPLICATIONS OF TIWANAKU AND HUARI TEXTILES

WILLIAM J CONKLIN

Andean textiles, displayed on the sparkling white walls of modern museums, have throughout the last century been considered amazing examples of the textile arts. The fineness of their construction and their brilliant graphics create awe in the modern mind. They even played a role in our own culture when, along with other "primitive" arts, they influenced the early evolution of modernism. This paper, however, examines Tiwanaku tunics and related tunics from Huari from a different point of view—as expressions of their own cultures—by examining them as clothing created and worn by significant individuals in the two related cultures. Where it has been preserved, the textile evidence generally coincides with other archaeological evidence defining the textiles' geographic and chronological boundaries. Specifically, this paper examines, via a comparative study of both the art and technology of the two cultures, their apparently deeply interactive relationship and the apparently performative role of textiles in public events. It is hoped that this examination will cast light on the larger question "What was Tiwanaku?"—the subject of the spring 2006 conference.

THE TUNIC

The major textile form for the two cultures was the tunic, which, since it offers virtually no environmental protection, must have been somewhat akin to a flag worn over the shoulders, with its primary purpose apparently being display and identification—probably the *societal* identification of the wearer and without doubt also the *sexual* identification.

Tunics were not cut out of other rectangular textiles but were created as special pieces of cloth, intended for a body but worn hanging over the shoulders, somewhat like a sandwich board. It is tempting to think of these culture-identifying, nonindividualistic textiles as uniforms, but with their featherweight nature and brilliant colors, they seem to be closer in concept to church robes and to negate all utilitarian connotations. Tiwanaku itself was not a war-prone culture, so militaristic implications derived from the term *uniform* would also be misleading. However, Tiwanaku culture *can* be clearly seen as performance oriented (Vranich 2006), so a stage analogy, with the garments seen as costumes, may provide a more likely association. Perhaps we can then think of these Tiwanaku textiles, and their counterparts in Huari, as a form of stagecraft, with the tunics worn as identification of the players in a public drama. Following that analysis we can compare the textiles from the two cultures in an attempt to discover the nature of their relationship.

Interestingly, there is little evidence of cultural hierarchies in the tunics of either culture. Although the presence or absence of a tunic itself must surely represent a cultural difference, the tunics that do exist seem to be, broadly speaking, equally elegant. Although the design patterns on the tunics differ, suggesting both a chronological changing of styles (Sawyer 1963) and the probable role differentiation through motif variation and weaving fineness, no king-size or bejeweled Huari or Tiwanaku tunic has been discovered; nor have royal tombs or even royal burials been identified in either culture. Hundreds of surviving tunics are all almost exactly the same size. Does such standardization suggest an egalitarian culture or does it suggest a culture with a single invisible but nevertheless all-powerful ruler? The massive concentration of effort on central pyramid construction in Tiwanaku would seem to have required an authority-driven culture, but there is no costume evidence for such authorities. Perhaps our customary Western models of societal structures simply provide no answers to this question concerning the structure of a culture that seems either to have been self-directing and cooperative or to have had some form of invisible leadership.

Early Highland Andean Textiles

To understand the evolution of these amazing garments and the societal role they seem to have played, we must briefly examine their chronological evolution. Since the Huari and Tiwanaku cultures show such little evidence of an interest in clothing as bodily protection, it should not be surprising to find evidence for a similar disregard for rain and weather in their predecessor highland cultures. However, because of the very limited textile-preservation conditions of the highlands, we have only scant evidence of body coverings used in the highland cultures that preceded Tiwanaku. Hundreds of fragments of textiles from the highland Chavín culture (of more than a millennium earlier) exist, although they were found not in the highlands but where they had been buried in the dry coastal deserts, and among them there are no actual fragments of *body-covering* clothes at all.

The representations or images that we have of Chavín clothing (Figure 5.1) tell us the same story: that clothing for both low-status and high-status individuals in Chavín times consisted of only belts, headbands, wristlets, and anklets.

The succeeding highland culture of Pucará has attributed to it several human representations, in sculptural form, that generally show figures wearing, like their Chavín predecessors, only body-banding items such as belts, wristlets, and anklets.

An exception would be the breechcloth shown on one sculpture (Figure 5.2), which seems to be the most extensive Pucará covering clothing represented

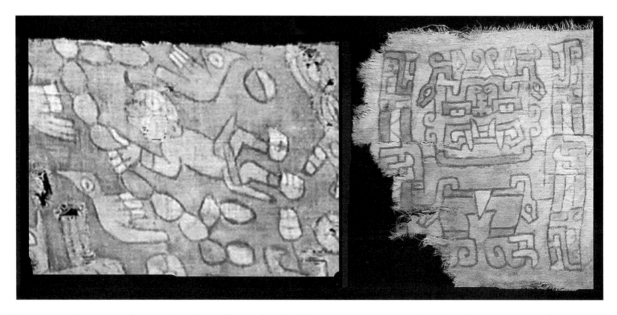

Figure 5.1. Portions of two painted textiles, each of which contains an example of a Chavín figure: left, an apparently low-status Chavín figure (Textile Museum, TM 1981.36.1); right, a high-status figure. Neither of these figures wears covering clothing; they have only body bands of various sorts, such as wristlets, anklets, headbands, neckbands, and belts (private collection).

FIGURE 5.2. A breechcloth is shown on this Pucara sculptural figure. More characteristically, only body banding is shown on Pucara figures (private collection. Photo courtesy Denver Art Museum).

in their sculpture. Curiously, however, the construction technology involved in weaving was highly developed in Pucará, but such construction was used only to create art and ceremonial textile forms and not for actual clothing. (See Conklin 1983 for an example of a nonclothing Pucará textile.) But this Pucará idea of using weaving to create art and signs that were then carried around must have been the inspiration for the Tiwanaku concept of clothing as essentially cultural costume.

Early Pre-Tiwanaku Apparel

It seems quite possible that there were multiple inspirations for the sudden emergence in Tiwanaku of iconic clothing. One of these might have been Wankarani, but no surviving textiles from this site have been discovered. Another source might have been the pre-Tiwanaku Chilean coastal culture named Alto Ramirez and studied by Mario Rivera (Rivera 1985).

A leading example of a post-Pucará but still slightly pre-Tiwanaku culture is Khonkho (Janusek 2004). We have no surviving textiles from Khonkho, but several stelae (Figure 5.3) found at the complex temple site show as clothing only body-banding items

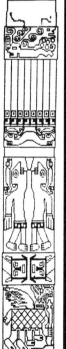

FIGURE 5.3. A sculptural stela found at Khonkho. The human figure in this stela is unclothed except for body banding. However, surprisingly, at the bottom of this stela is a mythical flying llama that seems to be wearing a patterned coat (photo F. K. Paddock; drawing by author).

FIGURE 5.4. The two-dimensional figures incised onto the Kantatayita stone architrave wear body banding similar to figures in Chavín and Pucara art but have very different headdresses and ritual paraphernalia.

such as wristlets, anklets, belts, and headbands, as with the other early highland cultures. All the Khonko body-banding items, however, carry iconic imprints of the culture, thus setting precedence (Ohnstad 2013) for the more complete statements of clothing with iconography in the Tiwanaku stelae that followed.

At the site of Tiwanaku, there is no local textile preservation, although there is textile preservation in the high, dry outer areas of Tiwanaku influence. However, *tupus* (the pins that Andean women characteristically used to secure their clothing) have been found at Tiwanaku desert graves (Goldstein 2005). Some *tupus* show imprints of textiles. Some textile fragments of shawls are also reported. So we can be fairly certain that local Tiwanaku women wore something like the wrap that local women now wear.

At the site of Tiwanaku, because there is no local textile preservation, the only evidence for early clothing is that found carved in stone in the preclassic architecture found on the site, such as the lightly clothed figures carved on the Kantatayita Architrave (see Figure 5.4). The figures carved on this stone lintel from the collapsed Kantatayita Temple seem to be attired much as figures were in the figural representations in Chavín, Pucará, and Khonkho. The individual figures, presumably representations of deities, are shown flying horizontally through the air, wearing belts, wristlets, anklets, and headbands and carrying ritual paraphernalia, but there is no evidence of covering clothing. They fly toward the center in a composition similar to the still-earlier architrave called the Calle Linares Lintel.

Similar to the Kantatayita figures, but probably somewhat later, are figures on a textile fragment from a scattered Tiwanaku burial found in Quebrada Vitoria in Chile (Figure 5.5). For a study of these figures, see Conklin 1983.

Representation of Clothing on Tiwanaku Stelae

As we proceed into classic Tiwanaku times, stone carving seems to become an increasingly important form of art, with the well-preserved vertical stone

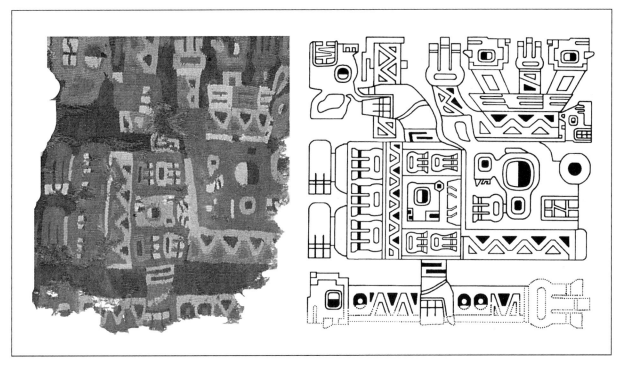

FIGURE 5.5. A fragment of a Tiwanaku textile from a burial on Quebrada Vitoria, Chile. The flying figure, wearing a belt and suspenders, was in this horizontal position in the loom, but alternate figures were vertical, standing figures (*private collection*).

stelae the most impressive art at the site. In these stelae, the complex carved textile patterns are contained within representations of the garments worn by the figures, as has been understood since their discovery. According to Betanzos[1] (who saw these figures while they were still standing, shortly after the Spanish conquest, and then talked to locals about them), the carved stone figures did not represent *ancestral* figures; nor did they represent *deities*. They were *didactic models*, whose purpose was to teach people how to dress (Conklin 2004b).

Since the carving of the clothing is much more carefully done than the representation of the human bodies, this amazing interpretation seems convincing. So the *basic* subject matter of these stelae was the clothing itself, with its iconography, and not the anonymous supporting bodies inside. The care and detail of the carving of the clothing representations stands in sharp contrast to the standardized facial and bodily representations on the figures, who, though wearing the new-style clothing, seem to have been essentially mannequins.

As a group, these colossal costumed but silent stone figures must then have been thought of as permanent actors on the complex display platforms of Tiwanaku temples. Although we do not know the actual placement of the Bennett Stela, it seems probable that it would have been associated with a comparably large platform-stage.

WARI STONE ART

At the counterpart site of Wari, stone carving seems to have been only a minor art form, with the recovered stone figures (Figure 5.6) having belts and headbands but no engraved iconic representations. Painted representations on these stone figures may have existed, however. So although Wari, the capital, and its cultural manifestation, Huari, were certainly Tiwanaku's equal if not its superior in textile design and production, Wari seems never to have been the home of any carved stone images of those textiles. The announcement of the idea of icon-laden garments remained a capital expression only at Tiwanaku. Should Huari, then, perhaps be seen as a kind of audience for these Tiwanaku-focused events? A close analysis of the textiles of the two cultures can provide clues to their very interesting relationship.

FIGURE 5.6 A group of Huari statues photographed after their discovery and assembly but before they were transferred to the local museum.

THE ARCHITECTURE OF TIWANAKU

Tiwanaku architecture (Conklin 1991) differs profoundly from Western concepts of architecture in that it essentially has no interior rooms (although there were some on-top "rooms"—probably built later) but uses solid forms that consist predominantly of stepped pyramids. Tiwanaku architecture thus has no inside function that the outside expresses, as does most of the world's architecture. Perhaps in Egyptian thought, Egyptian pyramids, apparently having no utilitarian role, were closer to our concept of sculpture or monument than to our concept of architecture.

The human action associated with Tiwanaku architecture must then have taken place where it would have been visible—on the repeated terraces and steps that cover the surfaces of the pyramids (Figure 5.7). So in Tiwanaku, the life of the temples occurred on their outsides—on their many kilometers of terraces, on their summits, and on their associated plazas. So

we can to some extent understand, to some extent, the setting of the rituals and dramas that must have justified the construction. Also, because we know something about the costumes that were worn, we can perhaps envision the pageantry. The clothing that was worn, assuming that it consisted of the Tiwanaku clothing that has been recovered, also played an important role in the event, not only because of its high visibility but because of its special nature. In a previous study (Conklin 2007b), I have shown that the second dimension was the sacred dimension in Tiwanaku art and thought. Tiwanaku *mythological* figures were always represented in two-dimensional form, in wood or stone bas-relief or in textiles. But real-world people were represented in realistic three-dimensional sculptural form. Thus the participants, in wearing their mythically dimensioned garments, must have thought of themselves as participants in a quasi-cosmic event.

Because we also know something of the highly developed nature of Tiwanaku astronomical obser-

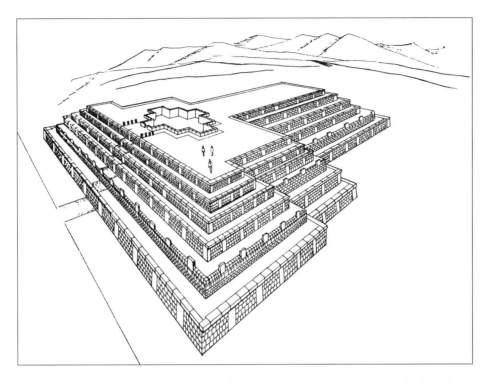

FIGURE 5.7. Reconstruction drawing of the Akapana pyramid as it would have been viewed from the northeast (courtesy of Javier Escalante, INAR, La Paz, Bolivia.)

vations (Benitez 2007), the mythological importance of the distant mountains visible from the site and therefore from the terraces of the pyramids (Benitez 2007), and that the oft-represented deities were well-organized, flying, cosmic ones (as are most world deities) (Conklin 1986), we can reasonably speculate that the costumed events that occurred on the stepped pyramids, beneath the overarching cosmic sky, were concerned with understanding Tiwanaku society's place within both the visible and invisible cosmos.

Wari Architecture

Neither in Wari, the capital of the empire, nor in its provincial centers are there any stepped pyramids like those in Tiwanaku. Highly developed *residential* forms characterize Huari cities such as Pikillacta and Cerro Baúl. Occasional public plazas and inward-focused, almost circular walled compounds, apparently for civic or religious use, occur in Huari cities, but there are no Huari sky-oriented ceremonial structures comparable to those in Tiwanaku. Although the costumes in Huari closely parallel those in Tiwanaku, the relationship between costume and local civic architecture in the Huari Empire could not have paralleled the pattern suggested here for Tiwanaku.

The Role of the Tiwanaku Stelae

Statuary is a familiar accompaniment to the rituals associated with civic architecture throughout the world, but the special roles of these then-painted stone actors in the Tiwanaku civic drama in being *didactic* rather than simply *beatific* make them unlike statuary in classic Western architecture. The ivory and gilded statue of Athena in the Parthenon was not conceived of as a teacher but was to be worshiped as an important deity. At 12 m, she was the largest known Greek statue (Chris Conklin, scholar of Greek mythology, personal communication, 2006), significantly larger than the largest known Tiwanaku statue, the Bennett Stela (7.4 m).

The Bennett Stela (Bennett 1934) (Figure 5.8) was no doubt painted (as was much Greek art and architecture), and although there are now no traces of paint remaining on the Bennett Stela, there are traces of paint on several other carved stone works at Tiwanaku, and the colors of the clothing representations on the stelae can be approximated by comparison with surviving real Tiwanaku clothing. The imagery on the stelae is similar to the imagery found on actual Tiwanaku clothing, although the real Tiwanaku clothing that we have recovered was undoubtedly created later than the stelae.

The tunic represented on the Bennett Stela is one with short sleeves. No such short-sleeved tunics have been found among the surviving Tiwanaku tunics, but short-sleeved Huari tunics, including miniatures, do exist and would thus seem to show a closer relationship to the Tiwanaku stelae than do the surviving Tiwanaku tunics.

So the Tiwanaku clothing memorialized on the stela seems to represent the first use in the Andean highlands of icon-laden, covering clothing. The announcement by the statues in the capital of the Tiwanaku world must have been a sensation and, to use a modern term, a *fashion statement* on the then most important stage in the Andes, whose effect is still felt today. Clothing in the Andes remains the most important form of cultural identification, be it in a village or a region. The drama of these probably painted stelae must have added considerably to the theatrical power of this Tiwanaku site.

FIGURE 5.8. The Bennett Stela, the largest and perhaps best preserved of the many Tiwanaku stelae, was recovered by American archaeologist Wendell Bennett. The figure is shown elaborately clothed, wearing a short-sleeved tunic, a belt, and a headband—all covered with representations of mythical figures (photo by the author; drawing by Arturo Posnansky).

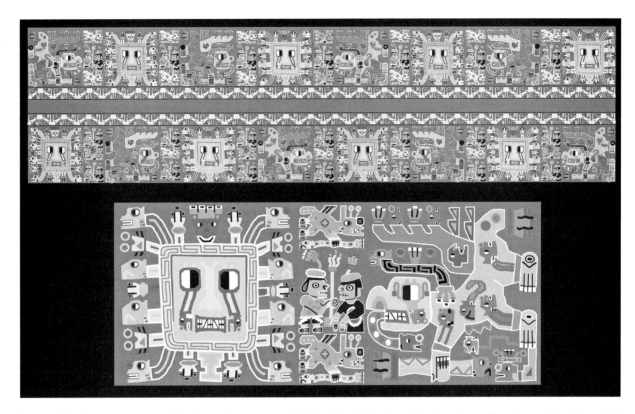

FIGURE 5.9. A reconstruction drawing of a ceremonial Huari textile believed to have been found near Ica, Peru, but now in the Textile Museum's collection. It is technically closer to a Huari textile than a Tiwanaku one, although the iconography is closely associated with Tiwanaku (drawing and detail of Textile Museum 2002.20.1 by the author).

Early Huari Textiles

Seemingly the earliest recovered *Huari* textiles are not clothing at all but are long,- rectangular ceremonial textiles whose iconography is clearly derived from Tiwanaku sources. In the Huari ceremonial textile illustrated (Figure 5.9), the iconographic details associated with the 16 major deity figures shown are closely related to Tiwanaku carved stone images (Conklin 2004b). So the probable movement of the icon-laden textile idea from Tiwanaku to Huari was perhaps first accomplished in ceremonial textiles and only later in clothing. But the actual use in Huari of these purely rectangular ceremonial textiles is unknown. Their size and two-dimensional nature suggest a religious use and probably a horizontal placement, perhaps reminiscent of the horizontal placement of the earlier large Chavín textiles (Conklin 2007a) and of the subsequent horizontal sand iconography found in the Nazca deserts. The dimensions of these textiles suggest a function like the Christian use of altar cloths or the Muslim use of rugs, though no form of related evidence is known from Wari. But following the beginnings of these textile arts in Tiwanaku and the creation of the early rectangular Huari textiles, the evolution of Huari and Tiwanaku tunics seems elaborately interactive.

Tiwanaku and Huari Tunics: Comparisons

Although there are *hundreds* of Huari tunics around the world, very few have scientific provenience. Fragments of only *a few dozen* Tiwanaku textiles exist, but many of these Tiwanaku textiles do have provenience. Initial study and comparisons of such tunics were begun by Amy Oakland (Oakland 1986; Oakland and Fernández 2000).

To engage in a comparison of the textiles of the two cultures, a prototype tunic has been selected from each culture (Figure 5.10), with the knowledge, however, that each created tunic was to some extent an individual work of art and that no single example can fully represent the full repertoire of tunics. But

FIGURE 5.10. Left, a digital reconstruction of a Tiwanaku tunic from a burial excavated by Padre Gustavo LePaige in San Pedro de Atacama, Chile. The tunic was conserved and analyzed by the author (Coyo Oriente 5382). Right, a Huari tunic (private collection).

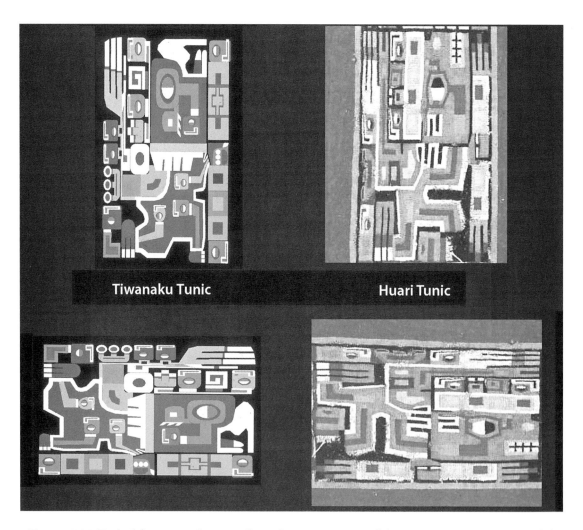

FIGURE 5.11. Typical figures used repeatedly in the compositions of the two tunics in Figure 5.10; left, Tiwanaku; right, Huari.

within the group of textiles identified as belonging to each of the two cultures, the technical construction of the tunics does seem to be consistent.

These two representative tunics will be compared in five ways:

1. By the prototypical figures used in the tunic compositions
2. By the textile structures utilized by each tunic
3. By the loomsmanship for each, or arrangement for the textile construction on the loom
4. By the materials used in the construction of each tunic
5. By the design concepts, or the significance of the arrangement of the individual design elements

The Prototypical Tunic Figures

The upper images in the illustration (Figure 5.11) are samples of the prototypical figures as they appear in the two tunics. They are shown as standing figures as they would have appeared to a viewer on a tunic being worn. Their legs seem to be floating, and they have wings. The two figures are remarkably alike for two such geographically separated cultures.

The lower images are the same figures but are shown horizontally, as they were both designed and woven in the loom, permitting us to see them as horizontally flying figures, as they were created. Their design concept, in the eye of their creator, was very similar to the earlier Kantatayita flying figures (see Figure 5.4).

Analysis of the Two Textile Structures

A comparison of the two tunic textile structures indicates that the tunics of both cultures were created with structurally identical interlocked tapestry, with interlocking joins at every change in color (Figures 5.12, 5.13).

Analysis of the Loomsmanship of the Two Tunics

However, the construction methodology, or loomsmanship, for such look-a-like tunics is strangely different. Given the warp and weft directions, we can reconstruct what the looms probably looked like.

The Tiwanaku method (Figure 5.14), presumably the older of the two, involves the creation of a

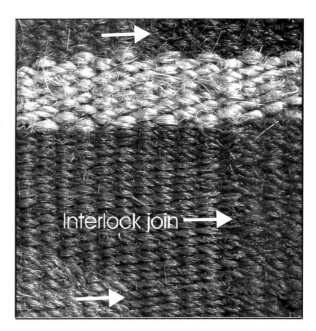

FIGURE 5.12. The weft interlocking creates sharp demarcations between colors in this detail of a Huari tunic. Cotton warp (vertical), camelid weft (horizontal) (private collection; photo by author).

FIGURE 5.13. A Tiwanaku tunic textile fragment from a Tiwanaku site west of Moquegua, collected by Gary Vescelius, displays camelid weft interlocking but also uses camelid fiber warp (courtesy of American Museum of Natural History).

one-piece rectangular textile constructed of very fine interlocked tapestry. After completion of the weaving, with a neck slot provided in the center, the

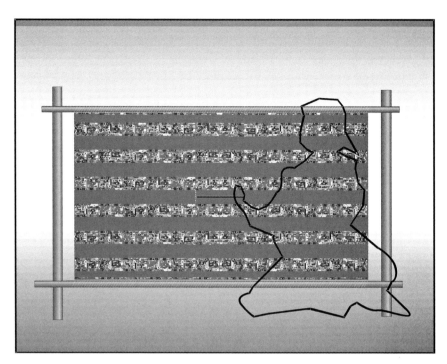

FIGURE 5.14. A Tiwanaku loom. A reconstruction drawing is used to illustrate how a Tiwanaku tunic from the Coyo Oriente burial grounds in San Pedro de Atacama, Chile, would have appeared in a Tiwanaku loom.

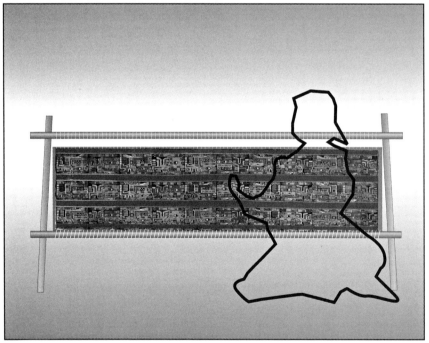

FIGURE 5.15. A Huari loom. A Huari tunic is created in two equal, symmetrical, but separate parts, which were later joined together to create the same type of tunic as those that have a Tiwanaku parentage. The drawing shows how one part of the tunic would have looked in its loom.

textile was then folded and seamed down the two sides, leaving arm holes, but there was no seam down the center. The Tiwanaku tunic has six major columns of figures as well as two minor ones, making 48 figures in all—the same general design plan (six major and two minor columns of vertically repeated figures) used in many Huari tunics, but the Tiwanaku construction used entirely different loomsmanship. Possibly the lower half of the tunic was woven first and compacted against the lower selvedge, and then the whole frame and textile was turned upside down and again woven from the bottom up, leaving the neck slot that had been created with looped warps around a common temporary scaffold thread, which was then removed (Fig. 5.15).

The different loomsmanship used by the two cultures is totally consistent within each culture, with no known exceptions. So although we might choose one or the other method to follow our own perception of utility, it seems highly probable that these differences in the making of the tunics were primarily of cultural significance.

Camelid Fiber or Cotton

Another difference between the tunics of Tiwanaku and those of Huari is in their construction materials. Both Huari and Tiwanaku used readily dyeable camelid fiber for weft. But for warp, Tiwanaku weavers used camelid fiber whereas Huari weavers, characteristically but not always, used cotton. This can seemingly be explained on the basis of resource availability, since Tiwanaku had no ready access to cotton but Huari did. Among the many known Huari tunics, a few have camelid fiber warp or used camelid fiber along with cotton for warp (Bird and Skinner 1974), but *no* known Tiwanaku textile used cotton warp. As to the characteristics of the structures of the threads themselves, both cultures used only two-ply, S-spun, Z-plied materials, with no known exceptions.

Design Concepts

For our final area of comparison, the *design concepts* used in the creation of Tiwanaku and Huari tunics, we will begin with a reference to the Tiwanaku Sun Gate, a stone portal probably relocated from the Pumapunku Temple.[2] It may be best to think of this iconic portal as a record of popularly held design concepts rather than as a *source* of those ideas, since it is considered to be so late in the Tiwanaku sequence.

Three parts of the Sun Gate design will be considered:

- The so-called attendants on either side of the central figure
- The reverse face of the portal
- The undulating bottom band

The Sun Gate Attendant Figures. The 24 figures carved on either side of the central figure are mythical figures, not of this world, because they are polymorphic. That is, they have human bodies but also have wings or beaks. They are carved in bas-relief, a two-dimensional format reserved exclusively in Tiwanaku art and architecture for the representation of such mythical beings (Conklin 2007b). We can compare three examples of these typological figures, the most common figures found in Tiwanaku and Huari iconography.

The attendant figures from both the Tiwanaku and the Huari textiles in Figure 5.16 are oriented as seen by a viewer of the textile. The figures on the

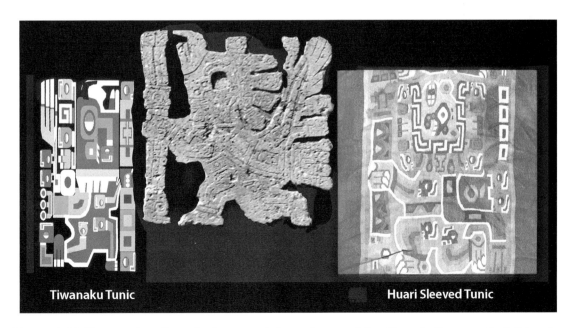

FIGURE 5.16. The attendant figure in the center is from the carved Sun Gate; the figure on the left is a detail from the Tiwanaku tunic shown in Figure 10; the figure on the right is from the early Huari sleeved tunic shown in Figure 10 (private collection). Although such short sleeves are shown on Tiwanaku stelae, no Tiwanaku sleeved tunics have yet been identified.

Tiwanaku tunic are a polymorphic condor, as is the Sun Gate carved-stone two-dimensional figure in the center. The figures shown on the Huari tunic are puma faced, but both polymorphic images are commonly represented in the art of both cultures. The differences between the stone and textile figures are largely proportional ones, so the two cultures, in spite of their geographical separation, spoke in the same iconic language in their art.

A Numerical Analysis of the Tunic Design Plans. If we count up the attendant figures shown to the right and left of the central figure of the Gate of the Sun image (Figure 5.17; note that some seem unfinished and that the apparently intended gold background was never installed) and then count up the same attendant figures shown on the right and left of the Tiwanaku tunic as worn, we discover that they are exactly the same: 24 on each side; 48 in total. This suggests that tunics brought status to their wearers, established a resonance with a central cultural iconic concept, and performed a role perhaps somewhat like the role of epaulets on a uniform, establishing a connection between the wearer and the larger construct of which he is a part. In this consideration, the term *uniform*, discussed earlier for the tunics of the cultures under consideration, does have some relevance because uniforms do relate wearers to a larger entity in nonmilitary as well as military contexts.

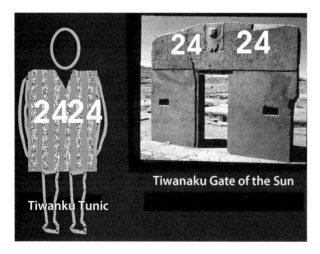

FIGURE 5.17. A diagram showing an image of a Tiwanaku tunic on a human figure and an image of the Gate of the Sun. The number of attendant figures on each is identified.

The Design Image of the Figures. This numerical analysis of the figures establishes broad resonance between the tunic wearer and his culture, but it is complemented and refined by the significance of their geometric arrangement.

Especially in Huari tunic conventions, multiple bands of figures that vary in size are used, with the smallest on the lateral sides of the tunic and the largest in the center of the tunic (Figure 5.18). These bands of figures seem to be organized into vanishing horizons in a logarithmic-like progression of horizontally flying figures.[3] Individual iconic figures were repeated indefinitely in the ceramic and other art forms of the two cultures, but apparently the whole cosmic assemblage was represented or hinted at only in carved stone and textiles, both of which were of course present in the outdoor ceremonies under consideration.

This mental image—the image in the mind—is independent of the actual orientation of the textile—just as the mental image of the American flag with its "horizontal" stripes is independent of the temporary orientation of the flag. When an American flag is draped over the shoulder, the image of the flag as one with horizontal stripes remains in the minds of all concerned as a mental image as opposed to a visual image.

This concept of a mental image of lines receding is highly developed in Huari textiles but only slightly evident in Tiwanaku textiles, seeming to show Huari influence on Tiwanaku textile art. But we do not have enough examples or dates yet to really prove out that idea. The geometry of the idea, however, is carved in stone on the Tiwanaku Sun Gate.

If we think of the wearer as being encompassed by the tunic (Figure 5.19) that hangs around him, he conceives of it as a formation of flying figures extending out from him, specifically out from his head-centered body. Remembering that the condensation toward the horizon occurs on the outside of the tunic, he would then perceive the figures as flying horizontally on either side of him but receding toward the surrounding horizon. His tunic then becomes a kind of cosmic carpet in which he is the central participant. If we consider the tunic wearer to have been a participant in a Tiwanaku ceremony, then this image from his tunic would seem to be resonant with his image of the cosmos surrounding him.

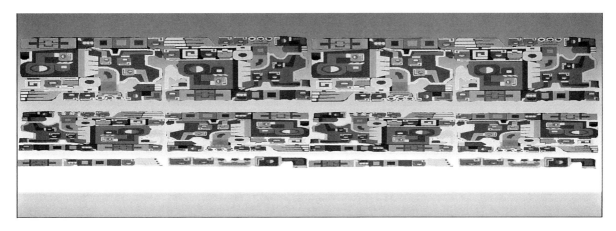

FIGURE 5.18. The mythological figures on Tiwanaku and Huari tunics seem to represent an image that must have been common to the mind's eye of ancient weavers of the tunics, wearers of the tunics, and viewers of the tunics. It is an image of horizontally flying mythological figures that recede in size and into the apparent distance.

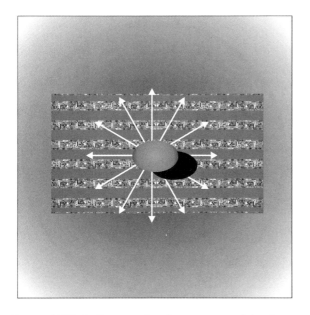

FIGURE 5.19. A diagram showing an array of the figures characteristic of the arrangement of Tiwanaku and Huari tunics as perceived from the wearer's point of view. Note that the figures seem to recede toward the left and right distant horizons.

Perhaps what would have come into this Huari tunic wearer's mind, then, is not at all our museum image of these tunics as colorful abstractions but instead the iconic content of the image that he knew so well: the horizontally flying mythical figures who seem to occupy the cosmos, fly horizontally from the left and right toward a center line, and seem to recede in rows toward the horizon. This image might have seemed to the wearer to be a guide to the world around him, suggesting that he was a part of a cosmos-wide event.

The Reverse Face of the Sun Gate. A confirmation of this logarithmic-like geometric concept found on Huari and Tiwanaku textiles is found carved in stone on the so-called back side of the Sun Gate, which seems to be something of a summary of Tiwanaku cosmic geometry (Figure 5.20). The several sets of multiple lines that surround the portal seem to emanate upward from a baseline. Each set is arranged in a logarithmic-like geometry that appears to replicate the spacing concept of the horizontal rows of figures found portrayed on the tunics of Huari and slightly evident on the tunics of Tiwanaku.

Sometimes in Huari textile art, the geometry of the cosmic horizons receding from the tunic wearer in the center seems to be the exclusive subject matter of the art, as if the geometry itself carried the full meaning without its inhabiting polymorphic flying figures (Figure 5.21). If indeed these many geometric images are of the cosmos, then they perhaps imply that the two cosmic axes differ, with perhaps the north–south axis of that cosmos differing distinctly from the east–west axis. The north–south axis of the inhabitants' cosmic grid had terminal points, perhaps since their sun, broadly associated with heat and life, is associated with their northern direction and their southern direction is associated with cold and death. But the east–west axis in these Tiwanaku graphics proceeded continuously and regularly like the days and nights and like time in general.

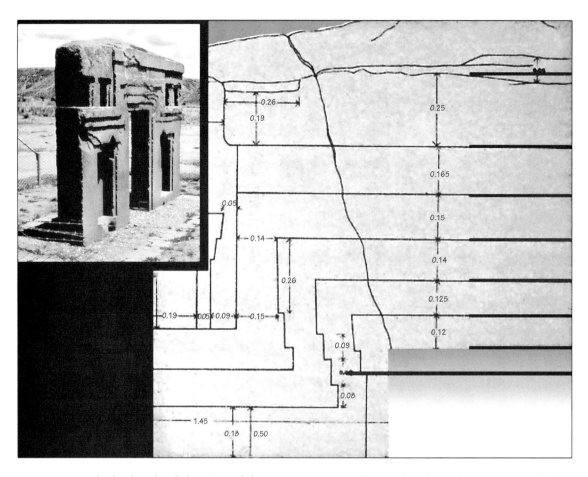

FIGURE 5.20. The back side of the Gate of the Sun portal. The diagram by the author was created from drawings made by Stübel and Uhle in 1893.

FIGURE 5.21. A checkerboard Huari tunic. The vanishing horizon lines seem to emanate from the wearer of the tunic and proceed toward the sides of the tunic (north–south?), with regular or arithmetic spacing in the opposite direction (east–west?), suggesting the geometric nature of the Huari cosmos. However, the color pattern is diagonal, with the wearer in the center seeming to be encompassed by the design (private collection).

Like the tunic in Figure 5.21, Inca checkerboard tunics (Figure 5.28) also omit the polymorphic iconic figures of Tiwanaku and Huari art. However, they undoubtedly had their basic design and geometric idea derived from the Tiwanaku/Huari geometric concept. Presumably, since there is such extensive evidence of Lake Titicaca (and Tiwanaku) being the mythical homeland of the Inca, seeing Inca geometric/cosmic ideas as being derived from Tiwanaku/Huari ideas is a wholly appropriate deduction.

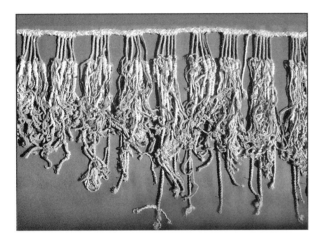

FIGURE 5.22. This *khipu*, which is quite unlike Inca *khipu* and is attributed to Huari, makes extensive use of multicolor wrapping. It uses single overhand knots for counting without the use of the long knot—the long knot presumably being a shorthand *khipu* technique invented by the Inca to represent numbers between 5 and 9 (private collection).

Khipu and Mathematics. The interest in mathematics that seems evident in the elaborately developed geometry of Tiwanaku stonework is not found in Huari stonework but is most certainly apparent in the geometry found in Huari textiles, as noted above, and that interest in mathematics is also highly evident in Middle Horizon *khipu*.

The illustrated *khipu* (Figure 5.22), although constructed of complex cotton threads with extensive patterned wrapping, is structurally quite unlike Inca *khipu* but is like other fragmentary *khipu* that were associated with Huari ceramics (Conklin 1982). This *khipu* with wrapped threads has been AMS dated to adjusted A.D. 779–981.[4] Other *khipu* with structural characteristics like the dated *khipu*, but without provenience, are characteristically attributed to Huari. As yet, no *khipu* have been directly attributed to Tiwanaku, but the extreme paucity of surviving Tiwanaku textiles and the extensive commonality of the textile traditions of the two cultures make appropriate the broad identification of this *khipu* as one from the Middle Horizon.

The Sun Gate Undulating Band. In addition to the distribution of the attendant figures, the Sun Gate has another design feature that provides insight into the significance of textile patterning and hence probably into deep-seated Tiwanaku and Huari concepts. Along the bottom of the front of the Sun Gate is an undulating band (Figure 5.23) whose numeri-

FIGURE 5.23. Sun Gate undulating band. The central channel, which seems to be carrying the connecting energy to the attached lively mythical heads, has been graphically emphasized (based on photo by the author).

design of the tunics make simple personal use of the tunics seem improbable.

One possible answer is that there was much more travel than we commonly think likely, and Huari celebrants felt at home when participating in cultural events in Tiwanaku. We also know that they were proximate neighbors in the Moquegua Valley. However, no Huari textiles or other Huari objects have, to this author's knowledge, ever been found within the vicinity of urban Tiwanaku. One suspects strongly that excavations in Mecca would reveal ceramic sherds from many cultures, although probably not textiles. But also consider the following:

- This possible postulate of traveling participants could also explain the detailed knowledge that Huari weavers obviously had of the theological and astronomical information found on Tiwanaku stonework.

- Clear evidence exists for the long-distance transport across Lake Titicaca of massive stones used in the construction of Tiwanaku temples—a much more unlikely travel event than long-distance pilgrimages of people.

- One small collapsed monument in Wari (Figure 5.27) seems to have stone workmanship not found elsewhere in Wari but characteristic of Tiwanaku masons, suggesting work interchange between the two centers.

We have been asked to go beyond our usual attempts at scientific certainty and to provide some food for thought for readers with our best guess as to "What was Tiwanaku?"

Earlier Andean archaeologists called the archaeological site and its associated evidence that we now call Wari and Huari simply "coastal Tiwanaku." The name *Huari* is not found in any Spanish records but was the word used by local inhabitants of the site (when it was found in the twentieth century) as a reference to the "ancient ones." The word *Tiwanaku* was also applied by archaeologists to the Bolivian site because of local usage, but it is found in Spanish sources. Since we cannot be certain that any of the names for the two sites were actually in use in ancient times, it is better to base our tentative conclusions on actual artifactual evidence, and the available textile evidence is extensive and most certainly more reliable than the verbal evidence.

My conclusions are as follows:

The combo culture now called Tiwanaku/Huari was the Mecca of the Middle Horizon and also was, in its day, the leading Andean intellectual and cultural center in art, textiles, architecture, mathematics, and astronomy. The two sites were both foci in a cooperative, peaceful, and far-flung culture in which the site now called Wari was undoubtedly the leading light in the field of textiles. Textiles, their most portable and highest form of art, probably performed an important idea/communication function within the culture and especially between the two foci, where Tiwanaku must have been famous for its seemingly eternal stone icons. Together they formed a uniquely Andean dualistic entity that later became the precedent for the Inca, whose clothing very clearly followed this precedent (Figure 5.28), whose cosmic representation did likewise, and whose em-

FIGURE 5.27. A group of cut stones in the site of Wari whose geometry and workmanship seem remarkably like those found in Tiwanaku. They were apparently once part of a larger structure.

pire map follows the combined maps of their great predecessor, the Tiwanaku/Huari interactive and dualistic culture.

FIGURE 5.28. A reconstruction drawing of a typical Inca checkerboard tunic as it would have appeared during its creation on the loom. Note the condensation of the checkerboard pattern on the outer lateral edges of the tunic.

NOTES

[1] Betanzos, in a translation of Narration by Frank Salomon for this author, says in part: "Then he [Viracocha] came out of Lake Titicaca, the second time and in that same hour as we have already said, they say he made the sun and day and moon and stars, and that this done, that in that site of Tiaguanaco he made out of stone certain people and a sort of model of the people whom later he would bring forth [According to Salomon, the sixteenth-century sense of the Spanish word used, dechado, clearly implies a prototype to be copied, not a model of something existing. So the Tiwanaku stone images were prototypes to be copied.]—making in this way what he made of stone a certain number of people and a leader who used to govern them and rule over them [However, no single figure stands out as the leader.] and many pregnant women and others delivered [There are a few Tiwanaku stone sculptures that can possibly be identified as female, but no evident sculptures of children.]—and that they used to have the babies in acunas according to their custom, all of which were made of stone [acunas refers to babies in Andean bundle board cradles. However, no such sculptures have been found.]—which he used to remove to a certain place, and that then he made another province of people ... by forming them of stone in the manner already mentioned. And as soon as he had finished making them he ordered all his people to depart, all those that he had with him there, leaving only two in his company—whom he told to watch those forms [that is, the models mentioned above] just as I have them painted and made of stone here."

So the stone stelae and their garments seem to have been created as conceptual prototypes for later Andean peoples. They were not deities; nor were they images of ancestors. They were didactic, exemplary, and even futuristic in intention.

[2] The reference to the central Sun Gate figure being female is not based upon any visual evidence in the sculpture itself but purely upon what seem to be her most evident predecessors: Pucará stone representations of similar figures that are clearly female, and Chavín painted textile representations of similar figures that are also clearly female.

[3] See Conklin 1986 for an earlier interpretation of the graphics of these mythical horizon concepts. At the time, I was impressed by their similarity to Renaissance perspective. However, Renaissance perspective used the surface of the world as a ground plane. The flying figures of Tiwanaku have a sky or cosmic reference plane, a fact now recorded (I hope correctly) in the current illustrations.

[4] NSF Arizona AMS lab AA56794, Middle Horizon khipu - 24.1 1,151 ± 33 calibrated (2σ), A.D. 779 to 981.

REFERENCES CITED

Allen, Catherine J.
1988 *The Hold Life Has*. Smithsonian Institution Press, Washington, D.C.

Benitez, Leonardo R.
2007 Pre-Inca Calendar at Tiwanaku, Bolivia. In *Proceedings of the Tiwanaku Symposium*, edited by Margaret Young-Sánchez, pp. 47–81. Denver Art Museum, Denver.

Bennett, Wendell
1934 Excavations at Tiahuanaco. *Anthropological Papers of the American Museum of Natural History* 34 (3):339–494.

Bird, Junius B., and Milica D. Skinner
1974 The Technical Features of a Middle Horizon Tapestry Shirt from Peru. *Textile Museum Journal* 4(1):5–11.

Conklin, William J
1982 The Information System of Middle Horizon Quipus. In *Ethnoastronomy and Archaeoastronomy in the American Tropics*, edited by Anthony F. Aveni and Gary Urton, pp. 261–281. Annals of the New York Academy of Sciences Vol. 385. New York Academy of Sciences, New York.
1983 Pucara and Tiahuanaco Tapestry: Time and Style in a Sierra Weaving Tradition. *Ñawpa Pacha* 21:1–44.
1986 The Mythic Geometry of the Ancient Southern Sierra. In *The Junius B. Bird Conference on Andean Textiles*, edited by Anne Rowe, pp. 123–135. Textile Museum, Washington, D.C.
1996 Huari Tunics. In *Andean Art at Dumbarton Oaks*, Vol. 2., edited by Elizabeth Boone, pp. 375–398. Dumbarton Oaks, Washington, D.C.
2004a The Fire Textile. *Hali* 133:94–102.
2004b Las piedras textiles de Tiwanaku. In *Tiwanaku: Approximaciones a sus contextos historicos y*

sociales, edited by Mario A. Rivera and Alan L. Kolata, pp. 235–262. Editorial Universidad Bolivariana, Colección, Estudios Regionales, Santiago.

2005 Tecnologia de tejidos durante el formative en Ramiditas. In *Arquelogia del desierto de Atacama*, edited by Mario A. Rivera, pp. 173–194. Editorial Universidad Bolivariana, Santiago.

2007a The Culture of Chavín Textiles. In *Chavín: Art, Architecture and Culture*, edited by William J. Conklin and Jeffrey Quilter. Cotsen Institute of Archaeology Press, Los Angeles.

2007b The Iconic Dimension in Tiwanaku Art. In *Proceedings of the Tiwanaku Symposium*, edited by Margaret Young-Sánchez, pp. 115–132. Denver Art Museum, Denver.

Cook, Anita G.
1994 *Wari y Tiwanaku: Entre el estilo y la image*n. Pontifica Universidad Católica del Perú, Fondo Editorial, Lima.

Frame, Mary
1990 *Andean Four Cornered Hats*. Metropolitan Museum of Art, New York.

Goldstein, P.
2005 *Andean Diaspora: The Tiwanaku Colonies and the Origins of South American Imperialism*. University of Florida, Gainesville.

Isbell, William H., and Alexei Vranich
2004 Experiencing the Cities of Wari and Tiwanaku. In *Andean Archaeology*, edited by Helaine Silverman, pp. 167–182. Blackwell, Oxford.

Janusek, John Wayne
2004 *Identity and Power in the Ancient Andes: Tiwanaku Cities through Time*. Routledge, New York.

Murúa, Martin de
2004 *Codice Murúa: Historia y geneaologia de los reyes incas del Peru del padre mercenario Fray Martin de Murúa: Codice Galvin/studio de Juan Ossio*. Testimonio Compania Editorial, Madrid.

Oakland, Amy
1986 Tiahuanaco Tapestry Tunics and Mantles from San Pedro de Atacama, Chile. In *The Junius B. Bird Conference on Andean Textiles*, edited by Anne Rowe, pp. 101–122. Textile Museum, Washington, D.C.

Oakland, Amy, and Arabel Fernández
2000 Los tejidos Huari y Tiwanaku: Comparaciones y contextos. In *Huari y Tiwanaku: Modelos vs. evidencia*, Pt. 1, edited by Peter Kaulicke and William H. Isbell, pp. 119–130. Boletín de Arqueología PUCP No. 4. Pontificia Universidad Católica del Perú, Lima.

Ohnstad, Arik
2013 The Stone Stelae of Khonkho Wankane: Inventory, Brief Description, and Seriation. In *Advances in Titicaca Basin Archaeology 2*, edited by Alexei Vranich and Charles Stanish. Cotsen Institute of Archaeology Press, Los Angeles.

Rivera, Mario A.
1985 Alto Ramirez y Tiwanaku. In *La problematica Tiwanaku Huari en el contexto pan andino del desarrollo cultural*, edited by M. A. Rivera, pp. 39–58. Dialogo Andino Vol. 4. Universidad de Tarapacá, Arica.

2002 *Historias del desierto: Arqueologia del norte de Chile*. Editorial del Norte, La Serena, Chile.

Rowe, Anne Pollard
1977 *Warp Patterned Weaves of the Andes*. Textile Museum, Washington, D.C.

Rowe, John Howland
1979 Standardization in Inca Tapestry Tunics. In *The Junius B. Bird Pre-Columbian Textile Conference, May 19-20, 1973*, edited by Anne P. Rowe, Elizabeth P. Benson, and Louise Schaffer, pp. 239–264. Textile Museum and Dumbarton Oaks, Washington, D.C.

Sawyer, Alan. R.
1963 *Tiahuanaco Tapestry Desig*n. Museum of Primitive Art, New York.

Schreiber, Katharina
2001 The Wari Empire of Middle Horizon Peru: The Epistemological Challenge of Documenting an Empire without Documentary Evidence. In *Empires: Perspectives from Archaeology and History*, edited by Susan E. Alcock, Terence D'Altroy, Kathleen Morrison, and Carla Sinopoli, pp. 70–90. Cambridge University Press, Cambridge.

Vranich, Alexei
2006 The Construction and Reconstruction of Ritual Space at Tiwanaku, Bolivia (A.D. 500–1000). *Journal of Field Archaeology* 31(2):121–136.

Willey, Gordon R.
1974 *Das Alte America*. Propyläen Verlag, Berlin.

Williams, Patrick Ryan, and Donna J. Nash
2002 Imperial Interaction in the Andes: Huari and Tiwanaku at Cerro Baúl. In *Andean Archaeology. Vol. 1, Variations in Sociopolitical Organization*, edited by William H. Isbell and Helaine Silverman, pp. 243–265. Kluwer Academic/Plenum Publishers, New York.

Young-Sánchez, Margaret
2004a Envoltorios de Tipo Nuevo y los tejidos de la transición Pucarará—Tiwanaku. In *Tiwanaku: Aproximaciones a sus contextos historicos y sociales*, edited by Mario A. Rivera and Alan L. Kolata, pp. 221–234. Editorial Universidad Bolivariana, Coleccion Estudios Regionales, Santiago.

2004b *Tiwanaku: Ancestors of the Inca*. Denver Art Museum, Denver.

Young-Sánchez, Margaret (editor)
2007 *Proceedings of the Tiwanaku Symposium*. Denver Art Museum, Denver.

6

TIWANAKU INFLUENCE ON THE CENTRAL VALLEY OF COCHABAMBA

KAREN ANDERSON

Core-periphery theorists have long asserted the importance of studying peripheries not only for understanding the nature of regional interaction networks but also to better understand the nature of the core polities themselves. By examining the nature of core influence, how it spreads, and what characteristics of local identity remain intact or change, periphery studies provide new insight into the organization, values, and sources of power of the core as well as into the extent and limits of its influence and control (Chase-Dunn and Hall 1991; Schortman and Urban 1994; Stein 1998).

For Tiwanaku, a key periphery is the valley region of Cochabamba, 260 to 460 km to the southwest of the capital city (Figure 6.1). That Cochabamba, particularly western Cochabamba, had significant interaction with Tiwanaku has long been evident (Anderson and Céspedes Paz 1998; Bennett 1936; Byrne de Caballero 1984; Céspedes Paz 2000; Céspedes Paz et al. 1994, 1998; Rydén 1959; Walter 1966) based on the widespread, abundant presence of Tiwanaku-style ceramics throughout the Cochabamba valleys, but efforts to examine diachronic change have been limited by a lack of detailed stratigraphic excavations. This paper presents domestic and mortuary data covering the entirety of the Middle Horizon. It speaks not only to Tiwanaku expansionary strategies but the nature of state power and its strength.

CORPORATE VERSUS EXCLUSIONARY STATES

While there are a variety of models available for examining archaic states, in this paper I want to focus on a model put forward by Blanton and colleagues that I feel is particularly useful for Tiwanaku. In this model, states range along a continuum of exclusionary to corporate modes based on the ideological framework employed as a basis for hierarchical relationships and state power. (Blanton 1998; Blanton et al. 1996)

In exclusionary states, "power wielders have few restrictions on their exercise of power" (Blanton 1998:147). Power is centered in the hands of individuals who dominate networks of subordinates or a bureaucracy. These states often have a cult of personality such that images of the ruler and his or her name, conquests, and power are displayed overtly as state propaganda, with rulers buried in ostentatious royal tombs. Also common in exclusionary states is that elites gain power by proximity to the person of the ruler and by acquiring prestige goods that are rigorously restricted to elites and not available to commoners. Exclusionary states are found archaeologically rather easily due to their showy use of royal burials, palaces, elite compounds, restricted access to prestige goods, and limited local production of state

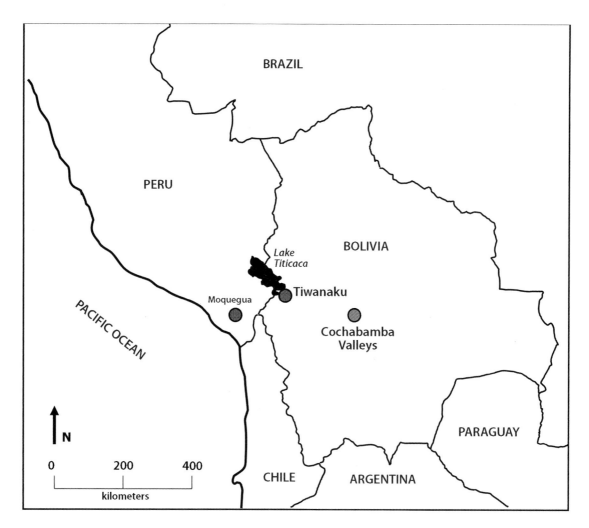

FIGURE 6.1. Map of the south-central Andes showing Tiwanaku and relative distances to peripheries Cochabamba and Moquegua.

styles. In exclusionary states, indirect control of a periphery by making alliances through local elites would provide status and access to state prestige goods. However, access to prestige goods would not be available to the general population.

On the other end of the continuum is the corporate state. In these states, the ruler or governing body has power but is constrained by ritual obligations, laws, or bureaucracy. There are seldom images of a specific ruler or ostentatious royal tombs, and specialty goods tend to be widely distributed and available throughout the population. A corporate state often rules by assembly rather than despotically, with greater emphasis on "soft power" via attraction and use of inclusive rituals. Personal status is increased through moral and ritual performance rather than by acquiring prestige goods, which can involve "ex-

tending important ritual practices to *households* of all social statuses" (Blanton 1998:160; emphasis added). In corporate states, semi-autonomous rule is the norm, and at the household level, semi-autonomous rule can be expressed via larger, more differentiated family compounds or by encoding more complex symbolism in living spaces via household alignment to cosmic symmetries, use of household shrines, or use of more extensive ritual paraphernalia (Blanton 1998: 168). State-style artifacts and rituals are often widespread due to inclusive rituals. Semi-autonomy would also include decentralized local production of symbolic artifacts resulting in some degree of local variability in expression of the state style and often widespread availability of the state style. Indirect rule by a corporate state would include more widespread access to state rituals and artifacts as an inclusive strategy to tie a colonized area to the core.

Blanton et al. (1996) point to another axis of variability in that both exclusionary and corporate states can be powerful and enduring, or limited in power and extent. However, they note that powerful corporate states can be harder to identify due to the lack of palaces, elite goods, royal burials, and the like, which can lead to their archaeological signature being interpreted as that of a weak or fragmented state. Indeed, Blanton argues that corporate societies may be highly integrated, powerful, and long lasting.

As noted above, exclusionary and corporate states are not mutually exclusive but rather on the opposite ends of a continuum, with a dynamic dialectic between individuals and groups pushing for greater exclusionary power and others pushing back toward more decentralized corporate power. As a result, corporate states can over time swing more toward exclusionary modes and back again. This model gives us a framework for evaluating changing power relations and ideological and political shifts over time in the state.

WHICH COCHABAMBA? ADDRESSING VARIABILITY IN THE COCHABAMBA REGION

While there has been a variety of research addressing Tiwanaku expansion in the Cochabamba, to date there has been no consensus on the type or intensity of Tiwanaku state investment or the political implications of Tiwanaku-style artifacts. Models run the gamut from direct imperial control to hegemonic control, trade enclaves, or very little social impact (Browman 1984, 1997; Céspedes Paz 2000; Higueras-Hare 1996; Kolata 1993; Oakland 1986; O'Brien 2003; Stanish 2003).

Much of the disparity of interpretation is due to geographical ambiguity about what is meant by Cochabamba. The name *Cochabamba* can signify the department of Cochabamba, the city of Cochabamba, or the loosely connected intermontane valleys. Even if we focus on the Cochabamba valleys, these valleys form an enormous system extending over an east-to-west distance of almost 200 km and ranging in altitude from 2,650 m above sea level to 1,600 m above sea level (Figure 6.2). Such a large area, with many of the valleys somewhat isolated

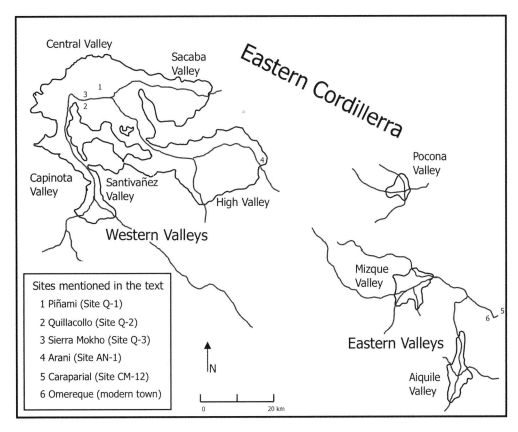

FIGURE 6.2. Map of Cochabamba's valleys and sites mentioned in the text.

from each other, should not be assumed to be a single political or cultural region. Subregional variation ought to be expected, and failure to take this into account can grossly affect how we interpret our data.

To address the geographic variation, I divide the Cochabamba region into three major zones. Closest to Tiwanaku are the western valleys: the Central, High, Sacaba, Capinota, and Santivañez; around 120 km farther east are the eastern valleys of Mizque, Pocona, and Aiquile, and, finally, 60 to 80 km farther east are the far valleys: narrow river valleys along the Río Mizque and other small rivers.

Studies from the far valleys region suggest only limited Tiwanaku influence in the area. My analysis of ceramics from the site of Caraparial (Figure 6.2) along the Río Mizque (originally excavated by Céspedes Paz) found that less than 10 percent of the decorated ware was Tiwanaku style. Other studies from the zone showed similar results. Textile specialist Amy Oakland investigated Middle Horizon textiles from far valley cave sites and found that the majority used local rather than Tiwanaku techniques, which she felt indicated Tiwanaku influence via trade, not colonization (Oakland 1986). Physical anthropologist Tyler O'Brien analyzed Middle Horizon skeletal collections from the Mojocoya region of Cochabamba, also part of the far valleys region, and found that the majority of skulls showed no highland traits and concluded that there was little genetic impact from Tiwanaku (O'Brien 2003). Their conclusions of low Tiwanaku influence are completely consistent with the ceramic data for those regions but I feel are misinterpreted if the results are applied to Cochabamba as a whole.

Moving closer to Tiwanaku, ceramics from site survey in the Miqzue Valley found that 70 percent of the Middle Horizon decorated ware was Tiwanaku style (Higueras-Hare 1996: Appendix X)—a significant jump in Tiwanaku ceramics from the far valleys. Finally, the area with the greatest Tiwanaku influence was the westernmost Cochabamba valleys, where Tiwanaku ceramics were about 90 percent of the Middle Horizon decorated ware (Céspedes Paz 2000; Céspedes Paz et al. 1994; Higueras-Hare 1996).[1]

THE STUDY AREA: COCHABAMBA CENTRAL VALLEY

Based on the above, it is clear that the best place to examine strong Tiwanaku influence would be in the western valleys, and of these the Central Valley is the best candidate. The Central Valley is the most agriculturally productive and was the valley most directly controlled by the later Inca and Spanish empires. Even today, the Central Valley is the most productive in the region (Honorable Municipalidad de Cochabamba 2005). In addition, the Central Valley is one of the largest of the Cochabamba valleys, similar in size to the Tiwanaku Valley and substantially larger than other Tiwanaku peripheries (Table 6.1).

MIDDLE HORIZON CHRONOLOGY AND PHASES

The Central Valley Middle Horizon is defined by Tiwanaku contact and subdivided into two major subphases: Illataco and Piñami (Céspedes Paz 2000). The Illataco phase is a short transitional period beginning with the first appearance of Tiwanaku ceramics amid local assemblages. The Piñami phase is a longer period when the local version of the Tiwanaku ceramic style was dominant, replacing all other decorated styles. I further subdivided the Piñami phase into early and late components based on changes in the ceramics, habitation density, and mortuary patterns found at Piñami.

The dates for the Middle Horizon are typically placed at A.D. 600 to 1100 based mostly on comparison with the highlands as well as on a couple of radiocarbon dates with very wide error ranges (Brockington et al. 1985; see Table 6.2).[2] However, comparison of Tiwanaku ceramics at Piñami with the few time-sensitive highland ceramics such as *incensarios* (Janusek 2003b:61, 63, 71) suggests that Tiwanaku presence had begun in the western valleys by at least the second half of Late Tiwanaku IV (about A.D. 750), with extensive occupations during Tiwanaku V (A.D. 800 to 1100) (Figure 6.3).

We as yet have no radiocarbon dates for the subphases, but based on ceramics, it would appear that the Illataco phase corresponds to Late Tiwanaku IV, with the Early Piñami phase corresponding to the end of Late Tiwanaku IV through Early Tiwanaku V and the Late Piñami phase corresponding to Tiwanaku V.

PIÑAMI AND QUILLACOLLO EXCAVATION RESULTS

The following presents excavation results from two long-term habitation mounds in the Central Valley

Table 6.1. Cochabamba Western, Eastern, and Far Valleys, Compared with Moquegua and Tiwanaku Valleys

Region	Specific Valleys	Distance from Tiwanaku (km*)	Approx. Valley Area (km²)**	Ha Under Cultivation Today	% of Tiwanaku-Style Sherds at Middle Horizon Sites	Data from Survey (S) or Excavation (E)	Source
Cochabamba western valleys	Central	270	340	29,000 ha[a]	~ 90–95%	(E)	Anderson and Céspedes 1998; Higueras-Hare 1996
	Capinota	280	80	–	~ 90%	(S)	
	Santivañez	280	60	–	–	–	
	Sacaba	292	50	–	–	–	
	High	315	350	–	–	–	
Cochabamba eastern valleys	Aiquile	372	40	–	~ 60%	(S)	Higueras-Hare 1996
	Mizque	385	75	–	–	–	
	Pocona	413	70	–	–	–	
Cochabamba far valleys	Omereque	440	< 20	–	~ 10%	(E)	Anderson 2007
	Saipina	470	50	–	–	–	
Moquegua	Middle Moquegua	255	85	3,300 ha[b]	~ 95%	(E) and (S)	Goldstein 2005
Tiwanaku	Tiwanaku Valley	0	350		~ 95%	(E)	Janusek 2004

[a] Data from Honorable Municipalidad de Cochabamba 2005.
[b] Data from Goldstein 2005.
* Distances are from the site of Tiwanaku to the center of the named valley based on Google Earth measurements.
** Valley sizes are also based on Google Earth measurements of the valley flatlands in each valley. The area measurements were done for the sake of consistency.

Table 6.2. ^{14}C Dates for Central Valley Sites for the Beginning of the Middle Horizon

Lab ID Number	Central Valley Site	Excavation Location	Uncalibrated Date B.P.	Uncalibrated Date A.D.	Calibrated Date Intercept	1σ Error	2σ Error	Type of Material	Date
GX-10760	Sierra Mokho	pit 1 levels 7–8	1280 ± 115	690 ± 115	A.D. 690	A.D. 650–890	A.D. 550–1025	animal bone	1984
GX-12136	Sierra Mokho	pit 0 levels 9–13	1355 ± 190	667 ± 190	A.D. 660	A.D. 540–880	A.D. 260–290 and 325–1025	animal bone	1985
Beta-068750	Quillacollo	north pit, floor 5	1160 ± 40	790 ± 40	A.D. 890	A.D. 810–900 and 920–950	A.D. 775–980	charcoal	1993

Note: The dates from Sierra Mokho are taken from Döllerer 2004; the dates from Quillacollo are from Céspedes et al. 1994; all calibrations done by Beta Analytic 2007. The Sierra Mokho excavations used arbitrary levels, and the samples are roughly at or slightly before the advent of Tiwanaku (Brockington et al. 1985, 1995; Döllerer 2004). The Quillacollo excavations followed stratigraphic layers, and the sample was from the earliest stratigraphic layer with clear Tiwanaku associations (Céspedes et al. 1994).

flatlands, Piñami (Q-1) and Quillacollo (Q-2) (Figure 6.2). Piñami provides the majority of the data based on stratigraphic horizontal and vertical excavations I conducted at Piñami from 2002 to 2005. The site of Piñami was approximately 3 ha in size. (It is now reduced to .5 ha due to urbanization.) It was lightly occupied starting in the Late Formative but intensively occupied in the Middle Horizon and Late Intermediate.

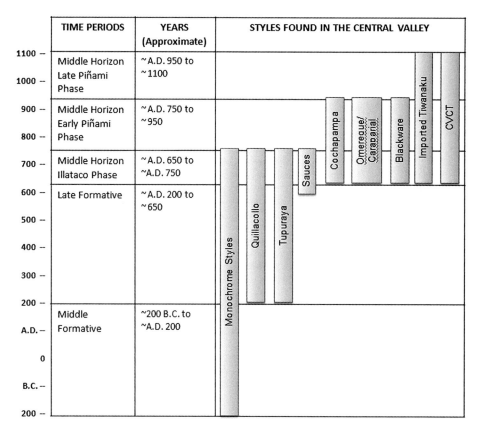

FIGURE 6.3. Cochabamba Central Valley chronology and ceramic styles. Dates are based on limited ^{14}C data and stylistic comparison with highland ceramics. Chronology for ceramic styles reflects their presence in the Cochabamba Central Valley, not their beginnings and endings regionally. Styles are considered to be discontinued (or not yet begun) if their frequency in the assemblage is .2 percent or less.

Piñami data are supplemented by stratigraphic evidence from a small salvage excavation at Quillacollo (Figure 6.2). Quillacollo is a large mound, originally over 10 ha and now covered by the city of Quillacollo. It was occupied from the Early Formative to the present, but the salvage excavation in the mound covered only the Middle Formative through the beginning of the Piñami phase (Céspedes Paz et al. 1994).

Fineware Ceramics

As noted previously, decorated fineware ceramics have been the key indicator used for decades to show Tiwanaku influence in the region. The new detailed diachronic ceramic data from Piñami and Quillacollo enable us to see more fine-grained changes in ceramics that have social implications. (Figures 6.4, 6.5)

In the pre-Tiwanaku Late Formative at both Quillacollo and Piñami, the serving ware styles were either Quillacollo painted ware or Monochrome ware. This pattern was not the case in all Central Valley sites. The nearby Sierra Mokho used a different Monochrome style during the earlier Formative, and Tupuraya style was the dominant painted style, suggesting that there was not a single, unified people in the area when Tiwanaku arrived but distinct ethnic units.

In the Illataco phase, one of the most striking changes at both Quillacollo and Piñami was the rapid increase in the *variety* of fineware styles found together. Up to eight decorated styles could be found in a single context. These styles included imported Tiwanaku styles,[3] the Central Valley styles Monochrome, Quillacollo, and Tupuraya, and the Cochabamba eastern and far valley styles Sauces, Mojocoya, Omereque, and Caraparial. Also present were new

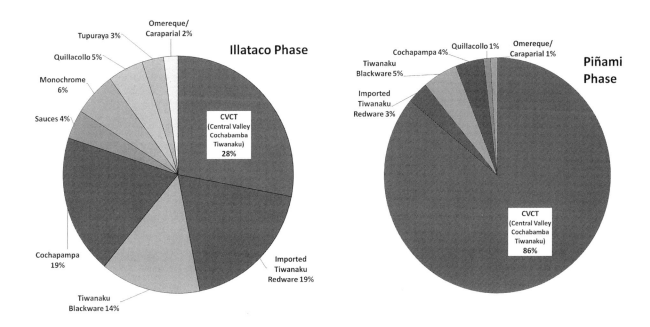

FIGURE 6.4. Comparison of Illataco- and Piñami-phase decorated style frequencies as a percentage of decorated sherds from Piñami. The chart shows the change from stylistic variety in the early Middle Horizon Illataco phase to dominance of the CVCT style in the later Middle Horizon Piñami phase.

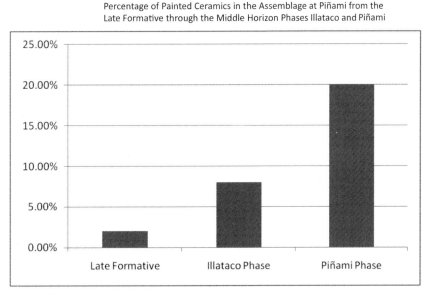

FIGURE 6.5. Increasing frequency of decorated ceramics from the Late Formative through the Middle Horizon.

local Tiwanaku or Tiwanaku-influenced styles. The sudden presence of multiple styles indicates greatly increased interregional trade and possibly movement of people within the larger Cochabamba region.

And it is not just variety in regional Cochabamba styles alongside a single imported Tiwanaku style. Instead, the imported Tiwanaku vessels appear to come from a variety of regions within the Tiwanaku sphere. For example, at both Piñami and Quillacollo we found a number of vessels that had diagnostic Katari Basin traits, such as *tazones* with continuous volutes ending in faces, red rim bands on *tazones,* and star patterns (Bermann 1994; Janusek 2003b), as well as *incensarios,* also reportedly more common in the Katari Basin (Janusek 2003b:71). We also found that the frequency of Tiwanaku blackware (2.7 percent of the Illataco assemblage) slightly exceeded the imported redware (2.3 percent of the assemblage). This is a higher proportion of blackware to redware than at Tiwanaku and may indicate contact with people from areas with a consistent blackware tradition, such as Moquegua or the western lake region (Goldstein 2005). It is interesting that the various Tiwanaku substyles are found together, a situation unlike that at Moquegua, where the Tiwanaku substyles Omo and Chen Chen were segregated and are presumed to represent distinct communities of Tiwanaku immigrants that had limited interaction (Goldstein 2005).

Two locally produced Tiwanaku styles developed during the Illataco phase. One of these is the Cochapampa FN4 style,[4] which has clear similarities to Late Formative styles but includes some Tiwanaku influence in form and iconography (Céspedes Paz 2000).[5] The second is the Central Valley Cochabamba Tiwanaku style (CVCT), a highly accurate version of Tiwanaku redware in terms of color scheme, iconography, forms, and production technology, with local variation evident in slight alterations in vessel form or hue.[6]

The two most common serving ware forms during the Illataco phase were the *tazón* and *kero* (Figure 6.6). Bowls were common in the Formative, though in the Quillacollo style they were round bottomed rather than flaring. Dedicated drinking vessels were rare in the Formative. This substantial increase suggests that new drinking traditions were an integral part of early Tiwanaku influence. (See Anderson 2009 for a detailed discussion of this issue.)

The Early Piñami phase is defined by two major changes in the fineware. First is a stark transition from multiple styles to one dominant style. By the beginning of the Early Piñami phase, CVCT jumped

FIGURE 6.6. Examples of common CVCT-style drinking vessels from Piñami, including variations on *kero* forms and *challadores* (funnel-shaped cups).

to 80 percent of all decorated fineware, and by the Late Piñami phase it had increased to over 90 percent. Imported blackware and redware continued but were diminished greatly, and the Late Formative local styles had disappeared by the end of the Early Piñami phase (Figure 6.7).

A second critical change is a sudden and sustained increase in the *quantity* of serving ware. In the Illataco phase, 8 percent of the sherds were decorated and 14 percent were serving ware. In the Piñami phase, the numbers jumped to 20 percent decorated sherds and 29 percent total serving ware (Figure 6.5). This high level of decorated ceramics in the Piñami phase does not appear to be restricted to the Piñami site, as the limited evidence from the Early Piñami phase at Quillacollo shows a similar pattern of increasing levels of fineware and a predominance of the CVCT style.

High percentages of decorated Tiwanaku serving ware are consistent with sites in the Tiwanaku heartland that ranged from 7 to 35 percent (Janusek 2004:130), and widespread use of Tiwanaku fineware in household contexts is a hallmark of all Tiwanaku communities (Bermann 2003; Burkholder 1997; Goldstein 2005; Janusek 2003b, 2004:130; Rivera Casanovas 1994, 2003), with only a few ceramic vessel types or motifs restricted to elites (Couture 2002; Couture and Sampeck 2003; Janusek 2003b).

During the Piñami phase, *keros*, and *tazones* continued to be the dominant serving ware forms, though also common were *challadores, vasijas*, and *jarras*.

Utilitarian Ceramics

Substantial changes in utilitarian ware, including new forms, paste preferences, and manufacturing technologies showing both highland and local influences, began in the Illataco phase. The clearest

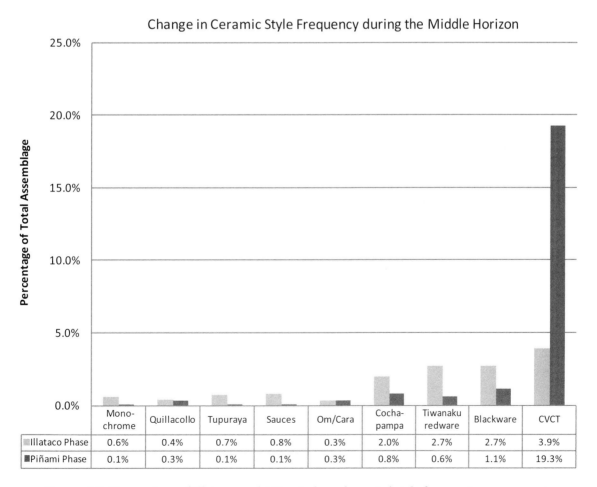

FIGURE 6.7. Comparison of Illataco- and Piñami-phase decorated style frequencies as a percentage of the total ceramic assemblage at Piñami.

example of highland influence is in new utilitarian vessel forms, such as the Tiwanaku pear-shaped olla and the globular olla. Yet there were other changes in paste and temper for utilitarian ware that tracks neither the highlands nor the prior Central Valley Formative styles. Instead, some of the changes in paste and temper appear to be more closely aligned with other Cochabamba local styles such as Sauces. Since change in utilitarian ware tends to be conservative, these patterns possibly reflect movement of colonists not only from Tiwanaku areas but also from other areas of Cochabamba to the Central Valley.

In addition to changes in utilitarian vessels, there is evidence of change in cooking practices as well. During the Formative, utilitarian vessels at both Quillacollo and Piñami showed no evidence of carbon on the exterior. The lack of carbon on the Formative vessels suggests that cooking did not take place over open flames and that hot rock cooking was likely used instead (Hastorf et al. 2006). This changed in the Illataco phase and became significant in the Piñami phase, when on average 10 to 30 percent of *all* utilitarian sherds had carbon on them.[7] Carbon on cooking pots was common at Tiwanaku, where Janusek found that 70 to 90 percent of sherds from *cookware* were encrusted with carbon (Janusek 2003b:58). While the presence of carbon on sherds starting in the Middle Horizon suggests that Tiwanaku influenced Central Valley cooking practices, the variance in percentages of vessels with carbon between Tiwanaku and Piñami could also be a sign that many local Formative food preparation techniques were retained as well.

Domestic Architecture and Features

Domestic architecture and related features and artifacts can be telling evidence of changes in household organization and activities. My Piñami excavation revealed the first domestic architecture for the Middle Horizon in the Cochabamba region, providing us with completely new kinds of data about the Cochabamba Middle Horizon.

No Formative architecture was recovered at Piñami or Quillacollo, but other research on the Early and Middle Formative sites in various western valleys shows a preference for round, single-room dwellings (Brockington et al. 1985, 1995; Döllerer 2004; Gabelmann 2005). However, there may have been some change away from round structures starting in the Late Formative, as Döllerer does report some limited Late Formative rectilinear walls in the Mizque Valley (Döllerer 2004).

All Middle Horizon architecture at Piñami was rectilinear. The only Illataco-phase architecture found was the base of one wall. This early wall was rectilinear and was constructed from layered mud (*tapia*) and connected to a small platform. The wall did not have any foundations, was approximately 50 cm in width, and was oriented about 10 degrees east of north.

We did not find any Early Piñami architecture but encountered significant Late Piñami architecture. The best example is compound 1, which filled most of a 10-by-12-m excavation unit. Compound 1 was rectilinear, with agglutinated rooms and a patio area to the south (Figure 6.8), and is similar to compound architecture found at Tiwanaku (Janusek 1994, 2004) and Lukurmata (Bermann 1990, 2003). The building had at least three major reconstruction episodes, when rooms were expanded and walls removed or added, with numerous patching and reflooring events. Walls were made of *tapia* construction and were approximately 50 cm wide and without foundations.

Tapia walls were the most commonly used throughout the Middle Horizon at Piñami and were typically about 50 cm wide, with straight walls and with roughly 90-degree corners. The *tapia* layers were formed of variable colors of clay, and the layers ranged from 5 to 10 cm thick. Almost none of the *tapia* walls had foundation stones, and little preparation was done before the walls were laid down. Indeed, only one short section of a *tapia* wall had a double-course cobble foundation. *Tapia* construction has not been previously identified for the Cochabamba Middle Horizon but was found in various sectors at Tiwanaku, primarily outside the ceremonial core (Couture 2003; Janusek 2003a; Rivera Casanovas 2003). *Tapia* walls without foundations, similar to those at Piñami, have been found in the distant Ch'iji Jawira sector of Tiwanaku, significantly to the east of the ceremonial core (Rivera Casanovas 2003:299).

Formed adobe bricks were used at Piñami, but in the examples we found, they were used only to form low platforms rather than walls.

(a)

FIGURE 6.8. Late Piñami rectilinear domestic architecture from Piñami. Walls were typically made of *tapia* (layers of mud) with no foundation stones.

(b)

Ideological Symbolism in Architecture

Orientation. All rectilinear architecture found from the Illataco phase through the Late Piñami phase was oriented 10 to 15 degrees east of north. This alignment influenced mortuary customs as well, as rectangular and oval burials had the long axis set to this same alignment. This orientation is very consistent with alignments of domestic architecture for Tiwanaku. Janusek reports that outside the ceremonial core, domestic architecture had a consistent directional orientation of 6 to 8 degrees east of north and, at the secondary site of Lukurmata, slightly more variable orientation, up to 12 degrees east of north (Bermann 2003; Janusek 2004). Thus the orientation at Piñami fits within the range of variation found at the heartland. Janusek feels that this consistent directional orientation of domestic architecture implies a "formal urban design that reified a single ... spatial cosmology" (Janusek 2004:150). The surprisingly early and consistent use of essentially the same orientation for both domestic and mortuary architecture suggests the adoption of a likely Tiwanaku spatial cosmology in the western valleys during the Middle Horizon.

Clean Room. The Late Piñami-phase compound 1 mentioned above contained a room that possibly had specialized ritual functions. The room was unusual in that it was the only room that was clean of any artifacts or debris. It had an unusual thick, whitish clay floor. The room was disturbed by later occupations and remodeling events but measured at least 2 by 4 m in size. The clay used for the floor was whiter than that of other floors found at the site and had a particularly smooth surface. The room was refloored once in the same manner using the same unusually white clay over a thin layer of ashes. Similar "clean rooms" have been found in various areas at Tiwanaku and are considered ceremonial spaces (Janusek 2004:110–112).

Diagnostic Tiwanaku Nonceramic Artifacts

A number of nonceramic artifacts found at Tiwanaku sites are considered to be particularly diagnostic of Tiwanaku occupations. These include camelid mandible scrapers, stone *trompos*, and hallucinogenic bone snuff spoons (Bermann 1990, 1994, 2003; Goldstein 1989, 2005; Janusek 1994, 2003a, 2004; Rivera Casanovas 1994, 2003; Webster and Janusek 2003).

At Piñami, camelid mandible scrapers were found in Early to Late Piñami phases in household and midden contexts. These included scrapers that used the upper jaw bone as the scraping surface, considered characteristic of Tiwanaku IV and V domestic contexts (Bermann 1994:188–189; 2003:335; Goldstein 2005:199–200; Janusek 1994, 2004; Webster and Janusek 2003), as well as a type not reported as characteristic of Tiwanaku that used the lower jaw (Figure 6.9).

Various bone ritual items were found, including various small spoons and other tools characteristic of Tiwanaku hallucinogenic snuff rituals (See Figure 6.10). Also present were bone flutes made of camelid long bones with a single set of holes similar to those found at Tiwanaku. (Webster and Janusek 2003:358).

A stone artifact considered diagnostic of Tiwanaku occupations is the trompo, a small conical object of unknown function (Bermann 1994, 2003; Goldstein 1989, 2005; Janusek 1994). At Piñami we found 18 examples, ranging from 3 to 5.5 cm in length (Figure 6.11). They were found throughout the Middle Horizon but not before, during the Formative, or after, during the Late Intermediate.

Projectile points were rare at Piñami's Middle Horizon household contexts and were slightly more common in the Late Intermediate. The Middle Horizon examples were triangular and stemmed but do not have the pronounced tang seen in many Tiwanaku projectile points (Giesso 2003:378). In general, however, household implements considered unique in Tiwanaku occupations in the heartland and key peripheries were present at Piñami.

Evidence of Intensification

One of the key lines of evidence necessary to evaluate the extent to which Cochabamba was pulled into the greater Tiwanaku political economy is that showing the intensification of production of goods desired by Tiwanaku. The following sections present some evidence of possible intensification of production from plant and animal remains and storage features.

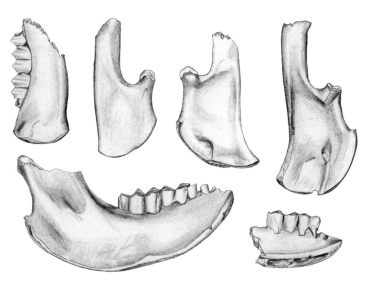

Figure 6.9. Camelid jaw scraper tools from Middle Horizon contexts at Piñami. The examples show variation in the part of the bone used as the scraping surface. Drawings by Oscar Valencia.

FIGURE 6.10. A Tiwanaku-style snuff spoon from a Late Piñami context.

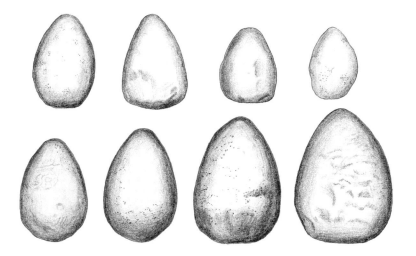

FIGURE 6.11. Stone *trompos* from Middle Horizon contexts at Piñami. Lengths range from 3 cm to 5.5 cm. Drawings by Oscar Valencia.

Maize. Access to maize has long been considered a reason for Tiwanaku expansion to the Cochabamba region, and our evidence does suggest intensification of production. During the Middle Horizon at Piñami, subsistence was dominated by maize consumption. Maize was the dominant macro-botanical, and isotope analysis of Middle Horizon Piñami burials by Kellner (2010) shows that maize comprised more than 80 percent of the diet throughout the Middle Horizon—more than in the maize-growing regions of the American Southwest.

This high level of maize does appear to be a substantive increase in local maize consumption, certainly from the Early and Middle Formative. At the Early Formative site of Yuroq Molino in the Mizque Valley, the macro-botanical specimens were almost entirely *tarwi*, and maize was only inferred by the presence of some tools *possibly* used to remove kernels from the cobs (Pereira Herrera et al. 2001:173). Upcoming analysis of flotation samples from Late Formative contexts in the Santivañez Valley by Vetters (Marianne Vetters, personal communication 2007) and from Middle Formative contexts by Terceros Céspedes, along with isotope analysis of Formative burials by Kellner and colleagues, will greatly add to our discussion of this issue. However, the available data show a marked dependence on maize in the Middle Horizon with as yet no documented equivalent in the Formative.

Comparative analysis of maize by Hastorf and colleagues (Hastorf et al. 2006) suggests that Cochabamba did produce surplus maize for export. The researchers examined maize from Tiwanaku, Moquegua, and Piñami and found that three varieties of maize were present at Tiwanaku: one consistent with the variety at Piñami, one consistent with the Moquegua variety, and one as yet unidentified. The authors concluded that maize from Cochabamba and Moquegua had been imported to the highlands.

Camelids. Preliminary faunal analysis from Piñami identified a broad range of animal food sources, including camelids, guinea pigs (*cuy*) and other small rodents, deer, small fish, birds, and bird eggs. Also present was evidence of imports from the tropical lowlands to the east, such as larger river fish. Camelids were the dominant meat source and constituted over 70 percent of the faunal remains. MNI determinations have yet to be conducted, but high camelid bone counts suggest a similar percentage to those found at Tiwanaku and Lukurmata, where camelids ranged between 77 and 94 percent of the total faunal assemblage (Webster and Janusek 2003). The majority of the camelid bones found at Piñami were fragmented, and up to 25 percent showed signs of being burned or carbonized. Whether the custom of fragmenting bones was common in the western valleys prior to the Middle Horizon is unknown at this time. However, fragmented camelid bones, likely broken to obtain fat and marrow, were commonly found at Tiwanaku during the Formative and Tiwanaku periods (Webster and Janusek 2003:355–356).

Comparative evidence from the Cochabamba Formative is limited, but it is clear that while camelids were present and used as food during the Formative, hunting was more important than herding in Early and Middle Formative sites (Brockington et al. 1995; Gabelmann 2005; Pereira et al. 2001).

Storage Pits. Increased storage capacity is a common indicator of intensified production. At Tiwanaku, increased storage was seen via larger and more frequent storage pits—either bell shaped or cylindrical—in domestic spaces (Bermann 2003:333; Janusek 2003a:275).

At Piñami, bell-shaped and cylindrical pits were present throughout the Middle Horizon. These pits were likely used for storage, though almost all of them ended their use lives as refuse pits. The frequency and size of household storage pits does appear to increase, as at Tiwanaku. In the Early Piñami phases, we excavated a few bell-shaped and cylindrical pits, typically no more than 70 cm deep. By the Late Piñami phase, storage pits were more frequent and larger, reaching 1.5 m deep for bell-shaped pits and up to 2 m deep for a cylindrical pit. It is difficult to determine the increase in storage capacity over time since significantly more Late Piñami contexts were excavated than earlier ones and occupation density also increased during the Late Piñami phase. However, review of the large profiles left by a previous salvage excavation at Piñami confirms an increase in household storage. In the profiles there were at least six large bell-shaped pits from Late Piñami contexts, compared with two or three smaller pits in the Early Piñami occupations.

During the Late Piñami phase, co-occurring with larger storage pits, occupation density also increased. Previously, during the Illataco and Early Piñami phases, occupations had wider strata with more fill between occupation surfaces, but sitewide, Late Piñami occupations had very dense and narrow strata, usually not more than 5 cm thick, with little space between occupation layers and numerous repeated reflooring and remodeling events. This may be part of a similar process of intensification that reached its height during the Late Piñami phase.

Mortuary Evidence

Mortuary rituals are an important way to examine social change, as burials are important indicators of social identity, ideology, and worldview. A crucial advantage of mortuary data is the chance to see individual choice rather than a palimpsest of evidence from many individuals spanning months, years, or decades, as is typical for domestic contexts. While tending toward conservative traditions, burials are public events and provide opportunities for the living to express and renegotiate the social order while remembering and celebrating the dead. New customs from the highlands would have increased the local choices available for expressing social identities and affiliations during these ceremonies.

As a basis for comparison between Tiwanaku and the Central Valley, the following are some salient points of Tiwanaku-style burial patterns. (For a detailed presentation of Tiwanaku burial patterns, see Korpisaari 2006.) Middle Horizon burials in the Tiwanaku core were commonly in belowground pits or chambers, with the body placed in a flexed position, usually seated flexed, though on-the-side flexed was also found in the Katari Basin and the Taraco Peninsula (Bermann 1994; Blom and Bandy 1999; Korpisaari 2006). This pattern did not begin in the Middle Horizon; both seated flexed and on-the-side flexed burials were present in Late Formative contexts in the highlands (Blom and Bandy 1999). Construction techniques included simple pits, cists with stone collars, and fully stone-lined and stone-covered round or rectangular chambers (Bermann 1990,

1994; Burkholder 1997; Janusek 2004; Korpisaari 2006). Urn burials were present in the Formative and Middle Horizon but were very rare and contained only children (Bermann 1990:94; Korpisaari 2006). Ceramic offerings in highland Tiwanaku tombs were frequent but limited in quantity and usually averaged only one or two vessels per tomb, typically including at least one decorated Tiwanaku vessel (Korpisaari 2006:157). Middle Horizon burial contexts at Tiwanaku and environs could be found in or near habitation areas or in discrete cemeteries (Bermann 1994; Janusek 2004; Korpisaari 2006; Rivera Casanovas 2003).

Pre-Tiwanaku burial patterns in the Cochabamba valleys were quite distinct from those of the highlands. The predominant burial methods were urn burials, extended face-up burials, and haphazard extended burials. Of these, urn burials were the most common in the Central Valley Late Formative (Bennett 1936; Gabelmann 2005; Pereira Herrera et al. 1992, 2001). The only flexed burial reported in the western valleys is from the Middle Formative site of Santa Lucia in the High Valley. The individual was placed on-the-side flexed under a large overturned ceramic basin (Gabelmann 2005). To date, no Formative belowground seated flexed burials or stone-lined or stone-collared cists have been encountered in the western valleys.

Middle Horizon Burials from Piñami

At Piñami we have 42 Middle Horizon burials. These burials are divided into an early group of 29 burials that correspond to the end of the Illataco phase through the Early Piñami phase[8] and a late group of 13 burials that correspond to the Late Piñami phase.

Types of Burials Found at Piñami. A variety of burial traditions was present at Piñami, including seated flexed, on-the-side flexed, urn burials, and secondary burials. All of these burial types were present in the early group and were intermixed both temporally and spatially, with no evidence of changing preferences over time. In the late group, on-the-side flexed burials were more common, and the late group seated flexed burials and a single urn burial were found outside the cemetery cluster.

The most common Middle Horizon burial style was flexed position, comprising 84 percent of all burials. For the early burials, seated flexed and on-the-side flexed burials were almost equally represented, with 40 percent on the side and 44 percent seated flexed. In the early group, various construction techniques employed for flexed burial tombs are consistent with local Formative traditions, such as irregular pits with and without cover/marker stones. However, the stone-lined and stone-collared tombs likely represent new traditions from Tiwanaku. Stone-lined and -collared tombs comprised 36 percent of all early burials and were found in both rectangular (with on-the-side individuals) and round (with seated flexed individuals) forms (Table 6.3). The most complex Early tombs had stone facades, stone covers, and floor slabs (Figure 6.12).

For the late group, on-the-side flexed burials were more common and comprised 70 percent of all burials. There was a big change in construction materials in the late burials, as all stone disappeared and

Table 6.3. Tomb Construction Techniques for Seated-Flexed and on-the-Side Flexed Burials by Middle Horizon Phase at Piñami

	Round Seated Flexed		Rectangular/Oval on-the-Side Flexed		Totals		
	Early	Late	Early	Late	Early	Late	Total
Stone/adobe-lined and roofed	1 (stone)	0	5 (stone)	2 (adobe)	6	2	8
Cover stones with collar	2	0	1	0	3	0	3
Cover stones only	5	0	1	0	6	0	6
Formal cut pit	2	0	0	2	2	2	4
Irregular pit	3	2	5	5	8	7	15
Total	13	2	12	9	25	11	36

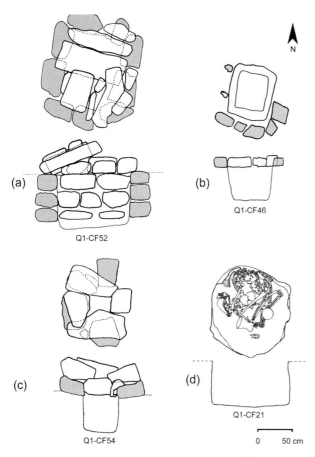

FIGURE 6.12. Diagram of various early Middle Horizon tomb types at Piñami: (a) rectangular stone-lined and stone-covered tomb; (b) rectangular cut pit tomb with a stone rim; (c) round cut pit tomb with a stone rim and cover; (d) circular cut-walled tomb. Drawings by Gori Tumi Echevarría Lopez.

was replaced by clay. However, the size and dimensions of the interior space of rectangular tombs remained the same.[9]

A few urn burials, typical of the Cochabamba valleys, were present throughout the Middle Horizon—three from the early group and one from the late group. The early urn burials were similar to Formative burials reported by Bennett (1936) at the Central Valley site of Colcapirhua: the body was placed in an olla or *tinaja,* and at times a second large utilitarian vessel was placed on top. The urn itself was placed in a belowground pit. All four urn burials contained the remains of children. Ceramic offerings in the three early urn burials were few, up to two vessels each, and all were local-style serving ware, though in one case the urn itself was highland olla. The late urn burial was quite different. It had four offering vessels, the most of any late burial, including two decorated CVCT-style vessels; with the urn was an imported Tiwanaku *tinaja.*

Context. Burials occurred in two main social contexts: cemetery clusters and isolated in domestic contexts. Our two cemetery clusters each contained multiple burials placed close together in roughly similar stratigraphic levels. Both clusters were placed in abandoned domestic areas. The isolated burials, all from Late Piñami contexts, were placed within domestic areas still in use, such as under room floors or in patio areas, with no more than one burial found in any particular context.

Orientation. As noted previously, the presumably Tiwanaku orientation of architecture applied to burials as well. Beginning in the early group burials, all but one of the oval or rectangular burials had the same orientation as the architecture, with the long axis approximately 10 to 15 degrees east of north. The only anomalous burial seems to reinforce the rule. This oval burial pit was directly perpendicular to the normal orientation, and it was unusual in other ways. It included the body of a child placed on its face, with its arms down to the sides and its legs bent up behind. This is the only burial at Piñami in this body position. The body was found under fill directly beneath the possible ceremonial "clean room" mentioned above, and the burial and its orientation may have related ritual functions.

OFFERINGS

A variety of offerings were included in the burials. Ceramic offerings included serving ware, including drinking vessels (*keros* and *challadores*), bowls (*tazones*), small vessels and pitchers (*vasijas* and *jarras*), and ritual vessels (*incensarios* and effigy vessels), and a few utilitarian vessels such as small cooking pots (*ollitas*). Other types of offerings included unfired clay vessels, beads, camelid feet and crania, metal disks, and basketry.

The quantity and type of ceramic offerings changed over time. The quantity of ceramic offerings per burial ranged from 0 to 12 for the early group burials and from 0 to 4 for the late group burials. In the early burials, decorated fineware vessels predominated, comprising about 80 percent of offerings, and included a wide variety of styles: imported Tiwanaku redware, imported Tiwanaku blackware, CVCT, Cochapampa, Sauces, Omereque, Caraparial, and Formative Monochrome. Surprisingly, the Central Valley Late Formative styles Quillacollo and Tupuraya were not present as offerings. In the late group, fineware was only about 45 percent of the offerings and only the CVCT style was present.

The quantity of vessels for early burials most closely correlates with burial type rather than tomb construction method. Urn burials averaged 1.3 vessels, seated flexed burials averaged 2.6 vessels, and on-the-side burials averaged 5.6 vessels per burial. There is little correlation between the construction type of the tomb and the number of offerings (aside from the two higher-status burials described below). Indeed, some of the simple pit burials contained more offerings than those in stone chamber tombs.

It might be expected that if burial types were expressive of different local and Tiwanaku traditions, there would be a correlation between offerings and style. However, only the urn burials show a clear correlation, as early group urn burials contained only local-style offerings. The flexed traditions—seated flexed and on-the-side flexed—included both local and Tiwanaku-styles vessels. In these burials it appears that vessel form was most correlated with style (Table 6.4). That is, *keros* and ritual vessels were predominantly in the Tiwanaku style: 85 percent of early group *keros* and 100 percent of ritual vessels were either imported Tiwanaku or CVCT. This contrasts with *tazones*, of which only 48 percent were Tiwanaku style, or the *vasija/jarras* at only 36 percent.

Imported Tiwanaku Vessel Offerings. An exclusionary prestige goods model would predict that imported Tiwanaku fineware would be restricted to higher-status individuals, but that is not the case. Of the total 119 vessels in the early burials, 21 vessels (18 percent) could be clearly identified as imports from Tiwanaku (based on paste, temper, and technological and iconographic factors). Of early burials that contained offerings, 54 percent had at least one imported vessel. These burials included children through adults and both males and females, and simple pit burials through stone-lined tombs. Thus access to imported Tiwanaku goods was not restricted

Table 6.4. Vessel Forms by Style in Early and Late Burials at Piñami

STYLE	DRINKING VESSELS		OTHER VESSEL TYPES				TOTAL
Early burials	*kero*	*vaso embudo*	ritual	*tazón*	jar or pitcher	utilitarian	vessels by style
Tiwanaku style (imported and CVCT)	17 (85%)	11 (73%)	3 (100%)	13 (48%)	13 (36%)		57 (48% of early burial vessels)
Hybrid style (Cochapampa)	1 (5%)			2 (7%)	12 (33%)		15 (13%)
Local style	2 (10%)	4 (27%)		7 (26%)	5 (14%)		18 (15%)
Style cannot be determined				5 (19%)	6 (17%)	17 (100%)	28 (24%)
Total early vessels by form	20	15	3	27	36	17	118
Late burials							
Tiwanaku style (all CVCT)	4 (100%)			3 (75%)			7 (44% of late burial vessels)
Style cannot be determined				1 (25%)		8 (100%)	9
Total early vessels	4			4		8	16

to elites. Instead the goods might have been brought as personal items by highland colonists.

Age. Age was ascertained for 40 individuals: 22 adults, six adolescents, seven children, and five infants (Yoshida 2005) and patterned to some extent by burial type. All urn burials, both early and late, contained children or infants. The two secondary burials were both adults. Flexed burials included all age groups. For early and late groups, all age categories could be accompanied by ceramic offerings, although adults averaged more.

Gender. Analysis produced 17 burials where sex could be determined: eight males and nine females (Yoshida 2005). All were from flexed burials—both seated flexed and on-the-side flexed. Overall, there are no clear gender distinctions in burial patterns.

For tomb construction types, we can say that both men and women were buried in pit and stone-collared tombs. Unfortunately, bone preservation in the stone-lined tombs was particularly poor, so we have no information on the sex of the individuals in tombs with higher construction costs in the early group burials. However, for the late group, the structurally equivalent burials that were lined with clay blocks or walls instead of stone contained both men and women .

For offerings, there was no distinction between the sexes in frequency or styles of grave goods. In addition, there was no gender distinction in vessel forms, as both men and women were buried with all vessel types, including drinking vessels, ritual vessels, and small cooking pots. In contrast, in Tiwanaku areas there does appear to have been gender differentiation in some vessel types. For instance, *keros* were not found in female burials at the Tiwanaku sites Moquegua (Goldstein 2005) or Iwawi (Jo Ellen Burkholder, personal communication 2007). In addition, Goldstein (2005) reports that small cooking pots (*ollitas*) were found only in burials of women and children. This is one aspect of Tiwanaku practice that was not adopted at Piñami throughout the Middle Horizon.

Ethnicity. Cranial deformation is one of the clearest markers of ethnic identity in the Andes (Blom and Bandy 1999). At Piñami, few of the crania were in good enough condition for us to state whether cranial deformation was present. However, four crania—three from the early group and one in the late group—clearly had cranial deformation. In the early group, two kinds of deformation were present: annual and fronto-occipital, with some crania showing no deformation. The variety further supports the likelihood that the people coexisting at Piñami during the early Middle Horizon were from a variety of areas or ethnic groups. The only late group cranial deformation was annular, and a few nondeformed crania were also identified.

Higher-Status Burials. Two of the burials appear to be higher status than the rest based on the quantity and variety of offerings. Both are early burials but were encountered outside the main excavation units, so their full context is unknown. Both tombs were rectangular, with stone walls, floors, and covers. One contained a single flexed adult, and the other contained two individuals, an adult and an adolescent—the only burial found with two individuals. Each had a variety of offerings, including substantially higher than average ceramic vessels (12 each of mixed imported Tiwanaku, CVCT, and local styles). In addition, both had offerings that were not found in other burials, both had sets of small green sodalite beads, and one had a couple of silver plaques.

These burials were also unique in that each had four identical ceramic drinking vessels placed in pairs. One tomb had pairs of *challadores,* and the other had small *kero* shapes with Caraparial iconography. Pairs of cups have been found in various Andean archaeological sites (Bray 2003:104–105; Cook and Glowacki 2003:195–196; Pärssinen 2005; Rydén 1959) and are still used in the Andes today as part of feasting events where the host retains one cup and provides the other to each guest in turn (Cook and Glowacki 2003). These cups may be evidence of particular ritual obligations. Overall, these burials give a picture of higher-status individuals expressing both Tiwanaku and local identities, possibly serving as intermediaries or bridging the various groups present at Piñami.

Post-Tiwanaku—The Late Intermediate Period (about A.D. 1100 to 1450)

There was considerable modification in the western valleys during the Late Intermediate period. Site sur-

Figure 6.13. Comparison of changes in pitcher and cup forms from the Middle Horizon (right) and the Late Intermediate period (left). All vessels are from Piñami.

vey by Gyarmati and Varga of the western Central Valley showed a continuation of valley flatland sites, along with many new, small sites in defensive locations at higher elevations around the valley perimeter (Gyarmati and Varga 1999), suggesting marked shifts in valley politics and intersite social interactions.

The change in ceramic styles was also notable. Material culture that heavily referenced Tiwanaku was abandoned and replaced by a variety of new styles, all using geometric iconography, including Ciaco, Chojnacollo, Batracios, and various styles that have yet to be named (Céspedes Paz 1982; Ibarra Grasso 1965; Ibarra Grasso and Querejazu Lewis 1986; Muñoz Collazos 1993). The variety of styles found together is reminiscent of the variety found in the Illataco phase. Manufacturing techniques for ceramics became less labor intensive, as less time and energy were expended on vessel hardness, evenness, wall thinness, smoothing, and burnishing.

Serving ware forms changed. *Challadores* disappeared, and although *kero*-like forms continued, they were greatly reduced in size, did not have a torus, and often had a single protruding handle (Figure 6.13). Pitchers were more common than in the Piñami phase and much larger, with capacities up to 5 liters.

Both *tapia* and stone walls were used in Late Intermediate–period architecture, though Late Intermediate–period stone walls typically used sharp-angled stone. This type of stone architecture is common throughout the Cochabamba valleys during the Late Intermediate.

Thus during the Late Intermediate, the Central Valley discontinued its strong connection to the highlands. Although many Middle Horizon traditions remained, they were modified in ways that set them apart from the earlier time period.

Summary and Discussion

Tiwanaku Influence in the Central Valley

From the perspective of the Central Valley, we can see waves of change during the Middle Horizon. First, during the Illataco phase, we see greatly increased interregional contact and access to goods from a variety of areas outside the Central Valley. While there is evidence that some interregional trade occurred during the Formative, the abrupt change from the Late Formative to the Illataco phase from few styles to many suggests that two things occurred with early Tiwanaku contact: greatly increased interregional trade *and* a breakdown of preexisting stylistic/ethnic distinctions within and between sites. The Tiwanaku contact likely came from various areas, possibly at the hands of independent traders or lineage groups looking to establish lower-elevation footholds.

² It is critical to be able to compare what was happening in Cochabamba and Tiwanaku to have a good handle on the comparative chronologies of the regions. Unfortunately, for Cochabamba there are few ¹⁴C dates available, and the four that pertain to the Middle Horizon (Table 6.2) are problematic. For example, based on an unpublished ¹⁴C date, Céspedes Paz suggests the Middle Horizon began in A.D. 350 and feels that first contact between Tiwanaku and Cochabamba possibly began before Tiwanaku IV (Céspedes Paz et al. 1998]). Brockington and colleagues set the beginning of the Cochabamba Middle Horizon at A.D. 600 based on two 14C dates from the Central Valley site of Sierra Mokho (Brockington et. al 1985:14). These dates have calibrated intercepts of A.D. 660 and 690 (Late Tiwanaku IV), but they have very broad error ranges (2σ ranges A.D. 550–1025, A.D. 260–290, and A.D. 325–1025). Another 14C date for the beginning of the Middle Horizon comes from the site of Quillacollo (Céspedes Paz et al. 1994). This date has a narrow range of error +/- 40 but produced a calibrated intercept date that is significantly later—A.D. 890 (2σ range A.D. 775–980)—and that corresponds almost entirely to Early Tiwanaku V. These dates leave the inception of the Middle Horizon in Cochabamba very ambiguous and open to interpretation. The end date for the Middle Horizon in Cochabamba for most models has been set at around A.D. 1100, but this is entirely based on highland dates and has not been confirmed directly in the Central Valley.

³ Imported Tiwanaku redware sherds were identified based on highland temper (in particular, gold mica not used in local wares) and subtle aspects of color and iconography. Imported Tiwanaku redware made up a sizable portion of the Illataco assemblage, forming 18 percent of the total decorated ware. Blackware, at 19 percent, was also an important component. Though I believe the blackware was imported, this is less certain because it did not share the same easily discerned foreign paste or temper as the redware did.

⁴ The style has also been called the Parotani style by Döllerer (2004), as he found numerous examples near Parotani in the Capinota Valley.

⁵ It was earlier thought that the local production of a Tiwanaku style began as the Cochapampa style during the Illataco phase and grew over time into the Central Valley Cochabamba Tiwanaku style during the Piñami phase (Céspedes Paz 2000). I feel the best explanation for the co-occurrence is that the Cochapampa style represents western valley potters being influenced by Tiwanaku, whereas the early and exceedingly accurate Central Valley Cochabamba Tiwanaku style indicates the arrival of Tiwanaku potters.

⁶ For a more detailed examination of Cochabamba ceramic styles, including the CVCT style, see Anderson n.d.

⁷ In Cochabamba there is no easy distinction in paste type between cooking and storage vessels, so it is impossible to state with any precision what percentage of nondiagnostic utilitarian sherds corresponded to cooking versus storage vessels.

⁸ While our team recorded the burials, the early group burials were excavated by a salvage team that was excavating in 20-cm arbitrary units. Thus we do not have complete context information on the burials. Based on comparison with our stratigraphic excavations from the Illataco and Early Piñami phases, only the earliest burials in the group were from the Illataco phase, with the majority corresponding to the first half of the Piñami phase.

⁹ One of the late burials has a below-ground freestanding rectangular construction made of clay. This is the only burial with freestanding walls rather than using clay or stone to form an interior façade. In prior excavations at Piñami, Céspedes Paz has noted that these may be an early form of chullpa (aboveground burial tower that became common during the Late Intermediate. (Céspedes Paz 2000).

References Cited

Albarracin-Jordan, Juan
   1992 Prehispanic and Early Colonial Settlement Patterns in the Lower Tiwanaku Valley, Bolivia. Unpublished Ph.D. dissertation, Department of Anthropology, Southern Methodist University, Dallas.
   2003 Tiwanaku: A Pre-Inka, Segmentary State in the Andes. In *Tiwanaku and Its Hinterland: Archaeology and Paleoecology of an Andean Civilization*. Vol. 2, *Urban and Rural Archaeology*, edited by Alan Kolata, pp. 95–111. Smithsonian Institution Press, Washington, D.C.

Alconini Mujíca, Sonia
   1993 La cerámica de la pirámide Akapana y su contexto social en el estado de Tiwanaku. Unpublished licenciatura thesis, Department of Anthropology-Archaeology, Universidad Mayor de San Andrés, La Paz.

Anderson, Karen
   2006 Tiwanaku Impact on the Cochabamba Region: Household Evidence from Piñami. Paper presented at the 71st Annual Meetings of the Society for American Archaeology, San Juan, Puerto Rico.
   2007 The Cochabamba Tiwanaku Style: How "Derived" Was It? Paper presented at the Southern Andean Iconographic Series Colloquium in Pre-Columbian Art and Archaeology, Universidad de Chile, Santiago.
   2009 Tiwanaku Influence on Local Drinking Patterns in Cochabamba, Bolivia. In *Drink, Power and Society in the Andes*, edited by Justin Jennings and Brenda Bowser, pp. 167–199. University Press of Florida, Gainesville.

n.d. The Tiwanaku Style in Cochabamba: How "Derived" Was It? Manuscript in the possession of the author.

Anderson, Karen, and Ricardo Céspedes Paz
1998 Tiwanaku and the Local Effects of Contact: The Late Formative to Middle Horizon Transition in Cochabamba, Bolivia. Paper presented at the 63rd Annual Meeting of the Society for American Archaeology, Seattle.

Bennett, Wendell C.
1936 Excavations in Bolivia. *Anthropological Papers of the American Museum of Natural History* 35(4):329–507.

Bermann, Marc
1990 Prehispanic Household and Empire at Lukurmata, Bolivia. Unpublished Ph.D. dissertation, University of Michigan, Ann Arbor.
1994 *Lukurmata: Household Archaeology in Prehispanic Bolivia*. Princeton University Press, Princeton, New Jersey.
2003 The Archaeology of Households in Lukurmata. In *Tiwanaku and Its Hinterland: Archaeology and Paleoecology of an Andean Civilization*. Vol. 2, *Urban and Rural Archaeology*, edited by Alan L. Kolata, pp. 327–340. Smithsonian Institution Press, Washington, D.C.

Blanton, Richard E.
1998 Beyond Centralization: Steps Toward a Theory of Egalitarian Behavior in Archaic States. In *Archaic States*, edited by Gary M. Feinman and Joyce Marcus, pp. 135–172. School of American Research Press, Santa Fe.

Blanton, Richard E., S. A. Kowalewski, G. M. Feinman, and P. N. Peregrine
1996 A Dual-Processual Theory for the Evolution of Mesoamerican Civilization. *Current Anthropology* 37:1–14.

Blom, D. E., and M. S. Bandy
1999 Human Remains and Mortuary Analysis. In *Early Settlement at Chiripa, Bolivia: Research of the Taraco Archaeological Project*, edited by C. A. Hastorf, pp. 117–122. Contributions of the University of California Archaeological Research Facility No. 57. University of California Archaeological Facility, Berkeley.

Bowser, Brenda
2002 The Perceptive Potter: An Ethnoarchaeological Study of Pottery, Ethnicity, and Political Action in Amazonia. Unpublished Ph.D. dissertation, University of California, Santa Barbara.

Bray, Tamara
2003 Imperial Pottery, Commensal Politics, and the Inca State. In *The Archaeology and Politics of Food and Feasting in Early States and Empires*, edited by Tamara L. Bray, pp. 93–142. Kluwer Academic/Plenum Publishers, New York.

Browman, David
1984 Tiwanaku: Development of Interzonal Trade and Economic Expansion in the Altiplano. In *Social and Economic Organization in the Prehispanic Andes*, edited by David Browman, Richard Burger, and Mario Rivera, pp. 117–142. British Archaeological Reports, International Series 194. British Archaeological Reports, Oxford.
1997 Political Institutional Factors Contributing to the Integration of the Tiwanaku State. In *Emergence and Change in Early Urban Societies*, edited by Linda Manzanilla, pp. 229–243. Plenum, New York.

Brockington, Donald L., David. M. Pereira Herrera, Ramón Sanzetenea Rocha, Ricardo Céspedes Paz, and Carlos Perez L.
1985 *Informe preliminar de las excavaciones arqueológicas en: Sierra Mokho y Chullpa Pata (Período Formativo)*. Cuaderno de Investigación, Serie Arqueología 5. Instituto de Investigaciones Antropológicas y Museo Arqueológico, Universidad Mayor de San Simón, Cochabamba, Bolivia.

Brockington, Donald L., David M. Pereira Herrera, Ramón Sanzetenea Rocha, and Maria de los Angeles Muñoz Collazos
1995 *Estudios arqueológicos del período Formativo en el sur-este de Cochabamba*. Cuaderno de Investigación, Serie Arqueología 8. Instituto de Investigaciones Antropológicas y Museo Arqueológico, Universidad Mayor de San Simón, Cochabamba, Bolivia.

Burkholder, Jo Ellen
1997 Tiwanaku and the Anatomy of Time: A New Ceramic Chronology from the Iwawi Site, Department of La Paz, Bolivia. Unpublished Ph.D. dissertation, State University of New York, Binghamton.

Byrne de Caballero, Geraldine
1984 El Tiwanaku en Cochabamba. *Arqueología boliviana* 1:67–72.

Céspedes Paz, Ricardo
1982 *La cerámica incaica en Cochabamba*. Cuaderno de Investigación, Serie Arqueología 1. Instituto de Investigaciones Antropológicas y Museo Arqueológico, University Mayor de San Simón, Cochabamba, Bolivia.
2000 Excavaciones arqueológicas en Piñami. *Boletín de INIAN—Museo Arqueología UMSS* 9:1–14.
2001 Les vallées de Cochabamba sous la domination de Tiahuanacu. *Dossiers d'archaeologie* 262:42–49.

Céspedes Paz, Ricardo, Karen Anderson, and Ramón Sanzetenea
  1994 Report on the Excavation at the Parochial Building, Quillacollo, Bolivia. Museo Arqueológico de la Universidad Mayor de San Simón, Cochabamba. Manuscript on file, Instituto Antropológico y Museo Arqueológico de la Universidad Mayor de San Simón, Cochabamba, Bolivia.

Céspedes Paz, Ricardo, M. d. l. A. Muñoz, and S. Ramon
  1998 Excavations at Piñami: Chronological Sequences and Regional Development for the Valle Central in Cochabamba, Bolivia during the Development of Tiwanaku. Paper presented at the 63rd Annual Meetings for the Society for American Archaeology, Seattle, Washington.

Chase-Dunn, C., and T. Hall (editors)
  1991 *Core/Periphery Relations in Precapitalist Worlds.* Westview Press, Boulder.

Cook, Anita G., and Mary Glowacki
  2003 Pots, Politics, and Power: Huari Ceramic Assemblages and Imperial Administration. In *The Archaeology and Politics of Food and Feasting in Early States and Empires*, edited by Tamara L. Bray, pp. 173–202. Kluwer Academic/Plenum Publishers, New York.

Couture, Nicole
  2002 The Construction of Power: Monumental Space and an Elite Residence at Tiwanaku, Bolivia. Unpublished Ph.D. dissertation, Department of Anthropology, University of Chicago, Chicago.
  2003 Ritual, Monumentalism, and Residence at Mollo Kontu, Tiwanaku. In *Tiwanaku and Its Hinterland: Archaeology and Paleoecology of an Andean Civilization.* Vol. 2, *Urban and Rural Archaeology*, edited by Alan L. Kolata, pp. 202–225. Smithsonian Institution Press, Washington, D.C.

Couture, Nicole, and Kathryn Sampeck
  2003 Putini: A History of Palace Architecture at Tiwanaku. In *Tiwanaku and Its Hinterland: Archaeology and Paleoecology of an Andean Civilization.* Vol. 2, *Urban and Rural Archaeology*, edited by Alan L. Kolata, pp. 226–263. Smithsonian Institution Press, Washington, D.C.

Dietler, Michael
  1990 Driven by Drink: The Role of Drinking in the Political Economy and the Case of Early Iron Age France. *Journal of Archaeological Anthropology* 9:352–406.
  2003 Clearing the Table: Some Concluding Reflections on Commensal Politics and Imperial States. In *The Archaeology and Politics of Food and Feasting in Early States and Empires*, edited by Tamara Bray, pp. 271–282. Kluwer Academic/Plenum Publishers, New York.

Döllerer, Cristof
  2004 *Proyecto Tupuraya: Informe preliminar sobre los trabajos arqueológicos y documentación de los estilos cerámicos Tupuraya y Sauces como los dos desarrollos tránsitos entre el Formativo y la epoca Tiwanaku en Cochabamba, Bolivia.* Universidad Mayor de San Simón, Instituto de Investigaciones Antropológicas y Museo Arqueológico, Cochabamba, Bolivia.

Gabelmann, Olga
  2001 Choroqollo—Producción de cerámica e intercambio de bienes durante el Período Formativo, Un ejemplo del valle Santivañez, Cochabamba. *Textos antropológicos* 13(1–2):197–229.
  2005 Proyecto Santa Lucía 2003/04: Organización social, producción de cerámica e intercambio en el Período Formativo en el valle alto de Cochabamba. In *Jornadas arqueológicas* 2004, edited by V. E. Salinas Camacho, pp. 51–73. Centro de Investigación Arqueológicas y Museo Arqueológico, Universidad Mayor de San Francisco Xavier, Sucre, Bolivia.

Giesso, M.
  2003 Stone Tool Production in the Tiwanaku Heartland. In *Tiwanaku and Its Hinterland: Archaeology and Paleoecology of an Andean Civilization.* Vol. 2, *Urban and Rural Archaeology*, edited by Alan L. Kolata, pp. 363–383. Smithsonian Institution Press, Washington, D.C.

Goldstein, Paul S.
  1989 Omo, A Tiwanaku Provincial Center in Moquegua, Peru. Unpublished Ph.D. dissertation, Department of Anthropology, University of Chicago, Chicago.
  2003 From Stew-Eaters to Maize-Drinkers: The Chicha Economy and the Tiwanaku Expansion. In *The Archaeology and Politics of Food and Feasting in Early States and Empires*, edited by Tamara L. Bray, pp. 143–172. Kluwer Academic/Plenum Publishers, New York.
  2005 *Andean Diaspora: The Tiwanaku Colonies and the Origins of South American Empire.* University Press of Florida, Gainesville.

Gyarmati, Janos, and A. Varga
  1999 *The Chacaras of War: An Inka State Estate in the Cochabamba Valley, Bolivia.* Museum of Ethnography, Budapest.

Hastorf, Christine A.
  1991 Gender, Space and Food in Prehistory. In *Engendering Archaeology*, edited by Joan Gero and Margaret Conkey, pp. 132–159. Basil Blackwell, Oxford.

Hastorf, Christine A., William T. Whitehead, Maria C. Bruno, and Melanie Wright
  2006 The Movements of Maize into Middle Horizon Tiwanaku, Bolivia. In *Histories of Maize: Multi-*

disciplinary Approaches to the Prehistory, Linguistics, Biogeography, Domestication and Evolution of Maize, edited by John Staller, John Tykot, and Bruce Benz, pp. 429–448. Elsevier, Oxford.

Higueras-Hare, Alvaro
- 1996 Prehispanic Settlement and Land Use in Cochabamba, Bolivia. Unpublished Ph.D. dissertation, Department of Anthropology, University of Pittsburgh, Pittsburgh.

Honorable Municipalidad de Cochabamba
- 2005 *Plan de Ordenamiento Territorial del Municipio Cercado de Cochabamba—Diagnostico*. Honorable Municipalidad de Cochabamba, Cochabamba, Bolivia.

Ibarra Grasso, Dick Edgar
- 1965 *Prehistoria de Bolivia*. Los Amigos del Libro, La Paz.

Ibarra Grasso, Dick Edgar, and Roy Querejazu Lewis
- 1986 *30,000 años de Prehistoria en Bolivia*. Los Amigos del Libro, La Paz.

Janusek, John Wayne
- 1994 State and Local Power in a Prehispanic Polity: Changing Patterns of Urban Residence in Tiwanaku and Lukurmata, Bolivia. Unpublished Ph.D. dissertation, Department of Anthropology, University of Chicago, Chicago.
- 2002 Out of Many, One: Style and Social Boundaries in Tiwanaku. *Latin American Antiquity* 13(1): 35–61.
- 2003a The Changing Face of Tiwanaku Residential Life: State and Local Identity in an Andean City. In *Tiwanaku and Its Hinterland: Archaeology and Paleoecology of an Andean Civilization*. Vol. 2, *Urban and Rural Archaeology*, edited by Alan L. Kolata, pp. 264–295. Smithsonian Institution Press, Washington, D.C.
- 2003b Vessels, Time, and Society: Toward a Ceramic Chronology in the Tiwanaku Heartland. In *Tiwanaku and Its Hinterland: Archaeology and Paleoecology of an Andean Civilization*. Vol. 2, *Urban and Rural Archaeology*, edited by Alan L. Kolata, pp. 30–89. Smithsonian Institution Press, Washington, D.C.
- 2004 *Identity and Power in the Ancient Andes: Tiwanaku Cities through Time*. Routledge, New York.

Janusek, J., and A. Kolata
- 2003 Prehispanic Rural History in the Katari Valley. In *Tiwanaku and Its Hinterland: Archaeology and Paleoecology of an Andean Civilization*. Vol. 2, *Urban and Rural Archaeology*, edited by Alan L. Kolata, pp. 129–171. Smithsonian Institution Press, Washington, D.C.

Kellner, Corina
- 2010 Dietary Analysis of Cochabamba Individuals from the Early and Late Middle Horizon Using Stable Isotope Analysis of Bone Collagen. Manuscript on file, Northern Arizona University, Flagstaff, Arizona.

Kolata, Alan
- 1993 *The Tiwanaku: Portrait of an Andean Civilization*. Blackwell, Cambridge, Massachusetts.
- 2003 The Proyecto Wila Jawira Research Program. In *Tiwanaku and Its Hinterland: Archaeology and Paleoecology of an Andean Civilization*. Vol. 2, *Urban and Rural Archaeology*, edited by Alan L. Kolata, pp. 3–17. Smithsonian Institution Press, Washington, D.C.

Korpisaari, Antti
- 2006 *Death in the Bolivian High Plateau: Burials and Tiwanaku Society*. BAR International Series 1536. Archaeopress, Oxford.

Korpisaari, A., J. Sagarnaga Meneses, R. Kesseli, and J. Bustamante
- 2003 Informe de las investigaciones arqueológicas realizadas en los cementerios Tiwanakotas de Tiraska y Qiwaya, Departamento de La Paz, en la temporada de Campo del 2002. In *Reports of the Finnish-Bolivian Archaeological Project in the Bolivian Amazon*, Vol. 2, edited by A. Siiriäinen and A. Korpisaari, pp. 73–95. Department of Archaeology, University of Helsinki, Helsinki.

Money, Mary
- 1993 El tesoro de San Sebastian: Una tumba importante de la cultura Tiwanaku. *Beiträge zur allgemeinen und vergleichenden Archäologie* 11:682–695.

Muñoz Collazos, Maria de los Angeles
- 1993 *El Intermedio Tardío en Cochabamba: Arqueología y etnohistoria*. Escuela Nacional de Antropología e Historia, INAH, Mexico City.

Oakland, Amy Sue
- 1986 Tiwanaku Textile Style from the South Central Andes, Bolivia and North Chile. Unpublished Ph.D. dissertation, Department of Art History, University of Texas, Austin.

O'Brien, Tyler G.
- 2003 Cranial Microvariation in Prehistoric South Central Andean Populations: An Assessment of Morphology in the Cochabamba Collection, Bolivia. Unpublished Ph.D. dissertation, Department of Anthropology, Binghamton University, Binghamton.

Pärssinen, Martti
- 2005 Tiwanaku: Una Cultura y un Estado Andino. In *Pariti: Isla, misterio y poder. El tesoro cerámico de la cultura Tiwanaku*, edited by Antti Korpissari and Martti Pärssinen, pp. 17–37. Producciones CIMA, La Paz.

Pereira Herrera, David M., and Donald L. Brockington
- 2005 *Mojocoya y greyware: Interacción e intercambios entre la Amazonia, Chaco y Andes*. Cuaderno de

Investigación, Serie Arqueología 10. Instituto de Investigaciones Antropologicas y Museo Arqueológico, Universidad Mayor de San Simón, Cochabamba, Bolivia.

Pereira Herrera, David M., and Donald L. Brockington (editors)
  2000 *Investigaciones Arqueológicas en Las Tierras Tropicales del Departamento de Cochabamba, Bolivia.* Universidad Mayor de San Simón, Cochabamba, Bolivia.

Pereira Herrera, David M., Maria de los Angeles Muñoz Collazos, Ramón Sanzetenea Rocha, and Donald L. Brockington
  1992 *Conchupata: Un Panteón Formativo Temprano en el Valle de Mizque.* Cuaderno de Investigación, Serie Arqueología 7. Instituto de Investigaciones Antropológicas y Museo Arqueológico, Universidad Mayor de San Simón, Cochabamba, Bolivia.

Pereira Herrera, David M., Ramón Sanzetenea Rocha, and Donald L. Brockington
  2001 Investigaciones del Proyecto Arqueológico Formativo en Cochabamba, Bolivia. *Textos Antropológicos* 13(1–2):167–182.

Ponce Sanginés, Carlos
  1981 *Tiwanaku: Espacio, tiempo y cultura: Ensayo de síntesis arqueológica.* Los Amigos del Libro, La Paz.

Rivera Casanovas, Claudia
  1994 Ch'iji Jawira: Evidencias sobre la producción de cerámica en Tiwanaku. Unpublished licenciatura thesis, Universidad Mayor de San Andrés, La Paz, Bolivia.
  2003 Ch'iji Jawira: A Case of Ceramic Specialization in the Tiwanaku Urban Periphery. In *Tiwanaku and Its Hinterland: Archaeological and Paleoecological Investigations of an Andean Civilization.* Vol. 2, *Urban and Rural Archaeology,* edited by Alan L. Kolata, pp. 296–315. Smithsonian Institution Press, Washington, D.C.

Rydén, Stig
  1959 *Andean Excavations.* Vol. 2, *Tupuraya and Cayhuasi: Two Tiahuanaco Sites.* Monograph Series No. 6. Ethnographical Museum of Sweden, Stockholm.

Sanchez Canedo, W., and R. Sanzetenea Rocha
  2003 Un vaso keru sonajero Tiwanaku. *Boletín de INIAN—Museo Arqueológico UMSS* 5(30):1–18.

Seddon, Matthew Thomas
  1998 Ritual, Power and the Development of a Complex Society: The Island of the Sun and the Tiwanaku State. Unpublished Ph.D. dissertation, University of Chicago, Chicago.

Schortman, E., and P. Urban
  1994 Living on the Edge: Core-Periphery Relations in Ancient Southeastern Mesoamerica. *Current Anthropology* 35:401–430.

Stanish, Charles
  2003 *Ancient Titicaca: The Evolution of Complex Society in Southern Peru and Northern Bolivia.* University of California Press, Berkeley.

Stein, G. J.
  1998 World System Theory and Alternative Modes of Interaction in the Archaeology of Culture Contact. In *Studies in Culture Contact: Interaction, Culture Change, and Archaeology,* edited by J. G. Cusick, pp. 220–255. Center for Archaeological Investigations Occasional Paper No. 25. Southern Illinois University, Carbondale.

Wachtel, Nathan
  1982 The Mitimas of Cochabamba Valley: The Colonization Policy of Huayna Capac. In *The Inca and Aztec States, 1400–1800,* edited by George A. Collier, R. I. Rosaldo, and J. D. Wirth, pp. 199–235. Academic Press, New York.

Walter, Heinz
  1966 *Beiträge zur Archäologie Boliviens.* Baessler Archiv, Neue Folge 4. Verlag Dietrich Reimer, Berlin.

Webster, A. D., and J. W. Janusek
  2003 Tiwanaku Camelids: Subsistence, Sacrifice and Social Reproduction. In *Tiwanaku and Its Hinterland: Archaeology and Paleoecology of an Andean Civilization.* Vol. 2, *Urban and Rural Archaeology,* edited by Alan L. Kolata, pp. 343–362. Smithsonian Institution Press, Washington, D.C.

Wright, Melanie F., Christine A. Hastorf, and Heidi A. Lennstrom
  2003 Pre-Hispanic Agriculture and Plant Use at Tiwanaku: Social and Political Implications. In *Tiwanaku and Its Hinterland: Archaeology and Paleoecology of an Andean Civilization.* Vol. 2, *Urban and Rural Archaeology,* edited by Alan L. Kolata, pp. 384–403. Smithsonian Institution Press, Washington, D.C.

Yoshida, Bonnie
  2005 Preliminary Results of Anatomical Analyses of the Burials from Piñami, Bolivia. 2005 Field Season Report. Manuscript on file, Grossmont College, El Cajon, California.

7

TIWANAKU RITUAL AND POLITICAL TRANFORMATIONS IN THE CORE AND PERIPHERIES

MATTHEW T. SEDDON

Archaeologists recognize Tiwanaku primarily through the material remains of long-forgotten state, local, and private rituals. The most easily recognized Tiwanaku artifacts are fragments of *keros* that were largely, if not entirely, utilized in feasting events that had ceremonial components (Alconini 1993; Janusek 2004:86). The aspect of the site of Tiwanaku itself that has longest held the most power and allure for visitors and archaeologists is the central complex of ritual structures—Akapana, Pumapunku, Kalasasaya, Putuni, and the Sunken Temple (Escalante Moscoso 1993; Kolata 1993; Ponce Sanginés 1981)—astounding constructions that were the first to catch the eye of Western visitors to the region (Cobo 1990 [1653]; Posnansky 1945; Squier 1878). These types of structures are repeated at other areas within the extent of the state. Indeed, the hallmark of Tiwanaku centers is the architecture of state ritual: sunken and raised temples, monumental earthen platforms, and pyramids (Goldstein 1993; Kolata 1993; Protzen and Nair 2002; Stanish 2003:203; Vranich 1999)—all undoubtedly used as stages for the performance of ritual. State ritual was a crucial component of Tiwanaku state practices, as ritual is for all complex polities. To understand the development and expansion of the Tiwanaku polity, we need to understand the role of ritual in the development of this polity.

Although we are long past an understanding of Tiwanaku as an empty ceremonial center of a widespread but politically meaningless south-Andean cult, we are only beginning to understand the role of ritual in the formation of the Tiwanaku polity (Goldstein 1993; Janusek 2004; Kolata 1993; Seddon 1998). Tiwanaku was an archaic state (cf. Feinman and Marcus 1998), with the site of Tiwanaku as its capital (although the exact role, function, and development of this "capital" is a matter of ongoing investigation). However, recent definitions of archaic states encompass almost any polity with some degree of social stratification and surplus production (cf. Marcus and Feinman 1998:7–10). Thus the simple characterization of Tiwanaku as an archaic state, while important in particular contexts (such as comparative studies), is neither interesting nor informative of anthropological questions regarding the development of power and complex social organizations. The more interesting question is how what we recognize as Tiwanaku came to be found outside the core of the state area, which, in agreement with Stanish et al. (2005) and Janusek (2004), I define as the Tiwanaku, Katari, and possibly the Desaguadero valleys.

I argue that although the presence of Tiwanaku ritual architecture and artifacts throughout the Titicaca Basin and beyond is not simply the result of an expanding cult, with no political component, ritual did in fact play a key role in political transformations in the many peripheries of Tiwanaku—the periphery of the core valleys, the periphery of the Titicaca Basin "core," and possibly the far peripheries of the south-central Andes. Indeed, I believe there is good evidence that one of the mechanisms by which Tiwanaku ideology and political control expanded was through transformations of rituals by Tiwanaku and local elites. While undoubtedly not the only factor in the success and spread of Tiwanaku, political transformation within ritual contexts was certainly a major factor. The precise manner in which this occurred, moreover, has numerous implications regarding the nature and development of the Tiwanaku polity as it became manifested in material culture and architecture outside its core valley.

To support my argument, and to develop further testable hypotheses, I will examine the evidence for Tiwanaku political ritual—communal rituals in non-domestic contexts—in three areas of the altiplano heartland of Tiwanaku: the core of the state, the periphery of this core on the Island of the Sun, and the periphery of the altiplano core. I will argue that a key transformation in political ritual occurred at the Tiwanaku IV–V transition. This transformation, which was undoubtedly a process rather than an event, appears to have occurred sometime around A.D. 700–800. This transformation involved rituals utilized to establish reciprocal relationships with deities. Prior to the Tiwanaku IV–V transition, these rituals were predominantly open and accessible to all. After the Tiwanaku IV–V transition, these rituals were predominantly restricted to elites. Rituals that previously established and maintained reciprocal relationships between people and deities became rituals conducted solely by and for elites. Previous feasting that established relationships between peoples also became the sole provenience of elites. From an activity where non-elites related directly in ritual to the deities and in feasting to emergent elites, now only elites related to deities in ritual, and non-elites related to elites in feasting. This subtle transformation in ritual is visible at the core and at the periphery of the core and appears to be becoming visible in the periphery of the periphery in the altiplano.

I will first briefly summarize theories of ritual and political formation as well as provide a short overview of Andean concepts of reciprocity and social order, as expressed in ritual contexts. I will then focus on three aspects of Tiwanaku and Tiwanaku political ritual across the Tiwanaku IV–V transformation: developing exclusivity of state ritual practices in the core of the state, restriction of access to state ritual at the periphery of the core on the Island of the Sun, and the limited evidence for Tiwanaku ritual at the far periphery of the altiplano core.

RITUAL AND STATE FORMATION

Ritual (as defined by Bell 1992, 1997) has been long viewed by anthropologists and political theorists as the means to maintain social order and the status quo (Durkheim 1964 [1915]; see also summaries in Apter 1992:5, 93–94; Comaroff and Comaroff 1993:xv; Combs-Schilling 1989:31–37). Recently, however, ritual is increasingly understood as a venue and locus for the development of social change (for summaries see Bell 1992, 1997; Comaroff and Comaroff 1993; Kelly and Kaplan 1990). As ritual can support political orders, it can be constructive and even transformative. In many ways, a simple functionalist approach to ritual flies in the face of common sense. It is in the potential of ritual to change and negotiate that the transformative power of ritual is revealed.

This is not to deny that there is a repetitive aspect to ritual or to say that ritual does not in some sense act to order the world. Very frequently this is the action of ritual, particularly state or officially directed ritual. Ritual aims, through claims to timelessness and "sacred propositions" that are "unfalsifiable" (Rappaport 1971:31), at a construction of the cosmological order. Rituals, with their differences from the continuum of ordinary duties and claims to the eternal, directly address the order of the world as it is understood in each culture. Simultaneously, rituals often address, directly or indirectly, the social order. "Ritual communication makes the social world appear organized in a fixed order which recurs without beginning and without end. As a result the social is like the natural, even a part of nature, and so ritual communication projects the political, the social, the discontinuous, the cultural and the arbitrary into the image and realm of repetitive nature" (Bloch 1978: 328).

Royal or state-sponsored rituals in particular often have as their most explicit purpose an ordering of the cosmology that is favorable to the ruling elite. For example, Helms has argued that ancient Panamanian chiefly rituals "not only established contact and communication between supernatural powers of the wider universe and the sacred-secular ruling elite of human society, but also offered verification to the populace at large of the truth of their beliefs and of the *legitimacy of their ruler's authority*" (Helms 1979: 119; emphasis mine). Combs-Schilling describes in great detail the ways in which royally sponsored rituals in Morocco supported the royal lineage's claims of right to rule. "Great collective performances that emphasized the power of blood became the blood-legitimated monarchy's most reliable means of reproduction, the mechanism for its continual reinsertion into popular practice and consciousness. The performances drove the monarchy ever deeper into the population's ultimate longings and essential concerns" (Combs-Schilling 1989:10).

However, while it is necessary to recognize that ritual can, at a minimum, attempt a cosmological and social ordering of the world, in a manner that reinforces particular social organizations at a particular time, it is important to recognize that ritual also has the potential to be transformative. "One does not become a vulgar functionalist by recognizing that, *from an official point of view*, royal ritual maintains political authority. Only when one claims that this perspective subsumes and explains all others does the reductionist epithet apply" (Apter 1992:5; emphasis in original). On the outside, a strict functionalist reading may find that ritual often functions to maintain a particular social order. However, rituals can also be the locus and medium for contestation of social orders. As argued by Comaroff, "the power of ritual may come to be used, under certain conditions, to objectify conflict in the everyday world, and to attempt to transcend it" (Comaroff 1985:119; see also Apter 1992, 1993; Braithwaite 1984:94; Masquelier 1993).

In state-level societies, state-sponsored rituals can be seen as an attempt to configure the political order of the state itself. The degree to which this works or is subverted by the ritual itself is a matter of local history. Nonetheless, ritual here is clearly one of the major arenas in which elites can attempt to deploy ideological strategies that support their own hegemonies. I argue that successful states will often link state ritual to local strategies.

Combs-Shilling provides an excellent example in her discussion of Moroccan marriage ceremonies (Combs-Schilling 1989:188–220). These rituals were created during a moment of crisis in the Moroccan rulership in the seventeenth century, when a new lineage, the Alawi, took over rule (Combs-Schilling 1989:175–189). In the early stages of wedding ceremonies, the bridegroom is transformed into the figure of the monarch. "To become an adult male, the boy first becomes the quintessential male, the Moroccan king, the blood descendant of Muhammad who reigns from Morocco's throne. The transformation is dramatic. The young man takes on the ruler's persona, embodies his postures, affects his attitudes, adopts his authority, and becomes central and pivotal to all that transpires" (Combs-Schilling 1989:190). At a local level, the transformation of the bridegroom into the ruler, along with other aspects of the ritual, serves to bring the boy into the world of men. Within this world he gains power and prestige, and through participation in the patriarchy he gains direct power over his wife and by extension all women (Combs-Schilling 1989:205, 211). "The ritual of first marriage makes men the conduit between God's power of reproduction and life on earth, and of all men makes the Moroccan ruler the most worthy link" (Combs-Schilling 1989:220). The latter part of this equation is particularly noteworthy. With the young man adopting the role of the ruler, even to the extent of dressing and acting like him, the ritual constantly reaffirms the primacy of the ruling elite in the realm of social relations. Thus, while from a local perspective participation in the ritual serves local strategies, from a wider perspective it serves to perpetuate the state political system. "During the Alawi era, local marriage ceremonies renewed the monarchy. They made it seem ineffable, part of the very structure of being, linking the population to it through passionate longing, sexual identity, and procreative hopes" (Combs-Schilling 1989:189).

Ritual, then, is a mechanism within which power relationships can be established, supported, contested, or transformed. Notably, ritual practices often attempt to configure social orders. Participants in rituals, how they are related to one another within the order and practice of the ritual, how cosmological principles of social relationships are expressed symbolically—all serve to provide a venue for establishing and negotiating social arrangements.

While I have concentrated here on ritual, I do not by any means wish to argue that ritual always and in all cases drives social change. Ritual is only one of a number of strategic practices that could be chosen by participants in any cultural system at any historical moment (Bell 1992:176). The economy, politics, and many other factors influence cultural development. Nonetheless, it is also clear that ritual is now understood to be far from a simple static model of belief; it is also a locus for social change and social negotiation.

Furthermore, in emerging state societies, ritual practices—along with their form, locale, encoded social norms, and so on—can become a venue in which local and state identities can be negotiated and linked. By using commonly held beliefs and idioms, rituals can become a medium for linking distant, state-sponsored goals and social ideals within local contexts. In the case of Tiwanaku, I argue that through gradual appropriation of commonly accepted rituals of reciprocity, Tiwanaku elites and local elites were able to increase and solidify emerging social hierarchies and help link previously disparate communities into a common, and hierarchical, whole.

RITUAL, RECIPROCITY, AND POWER IN THE ANDES

To understand this hypothesis, it is first necessary to examine the role of reciprocity in traditional Andean ritual practices. In the interest of focusing on specific archaeological data and models, I will not dwell extensively on the role of ritual and reciprocity in the pre-Hispanic and premodern Andes, a topic of considerable complexity. Nonetheless, it is possible to argue that anthropological and historical evidence for ritual practices among the Inca and the early Aymara can serve as models for the types of ritual practices and the relationship between ritual and politics seen in the core of the state (Seddon 1998). I do want to emphasize that by using ethnographic and historical models of ritual and politics, I am not uncritically extending necessarily contingent practices onto the past (Isbell 1997). I would agree with many that the precise meanings and many of the practices seen in the past differ from those seen today and in the recent historical past. Nonetheless, I do believe in what MacCormack (1991:13) has called "guiding religious ideas": general, broad aspects of belief and practice that can be extended into the past, even over several millennia, particularly if the archaeological evidence suggests that such interpretations are reasonable.

The salient point of what we do know ethnographically and historically about Andean ritual and politics is that rituals of reciprocity—direct exchange offerings between people and deities—formed a key part of political ritual. Modern and historical Aymara practices, and historical evidence for Inca state ritual, indicate that ritual has focused on establishing and maintaining reciprocal relationships between humans and deities while sometimes establishing, negotiating, and changing relationships between individuals, social classes, and groups.

A number of general principles tend to guide or structure traditional Andean religious beliefs, though the emphasis on and expression of these principles vary over space and time. The concept of reciprocity is a noted key cosmological belief in contemporary Aymara religious thought. Through *pagos* or, in Aymara, *ch'allas* (Abercrombie 1986, 1993; Bastien 1978; Fernández Juárez 1995), relations between humans and deities are ordered through ritual offerings expressing reciprocity. *Ch'alla* offerings can be simple libations or can be *mesas,* or intricate constructions. Aymara *mesas* generally consist of a number of "ingredients" (coca, herbs, llama fat, animal skin, white rocks, miniature figures in tin and lead, candy, colored wool, incense, alcohol, wine, paper, and occasionally a llama fetus), which are constructed in a specific manner and offered to a deity or deities through burial or burning (Fernández Juárez 1995:231–251). The construction is carried out by a ritual specialist, a *yatiri* ("one who knows"), who selects and configures the ingredients in the proper manner to satisfy the "taste" of the deities being called upon through the ritual (Fernández Juárez 1995:402). The offerings are made typically in the form of a request to the deities—for good harvest, for good planting, for health, for luck, and so on—and it is expected that the deities will respond in a reciprocal manner.

On the one hand, the offerings are encapsulations of cosmological beliefs and serve as a means of ordering the cosmos (Abercrombie 1993:156). Simultaneously, they can embody concepts of social ordering, as "an offering to a god is made via an exchange among men, or conversely exchange among men is understood as a form of exchange between men and gods" (Abercrombie 1986:164). When the offering is public, the power of the ritual to organize society can become more explicit. Bouysse-Cassagne relates a harvest ritual and offering that occurred in the early part of the sixteenth century in Lampaz, northwest of Lake Titicaca (Bouysse-Cassagne 1987: 265–267). Social ranking was explicit in the ritual. "El diagrama del ritual era el reflejo de la organización del pueblo. Cada cacique se sentaba en el lugar que le correspondía" (The diagram of the ritual was a reflection of the organization of the pueblo. Each chief was seated in the place that corresponded to him) (Bouysse-Cassagne 1987:267). In addition, the *yatiri* effecting the exchange is in a position of power, for it is only he or she who has the proper knowledge and is able to effect the exchange. While in theory *yatiris* are not allowed to utilize their knowledge to their own ends (Bastien 1978:64), in practice they gain a great deal of prestige in the community, and the simple fact that they must be paid for their services often enhances their economic and social positions.

To extend this concept further back in time, the Inca can be seen as a well-documented case study of the relationship in the Andes between ritual, politics, and power. Inca state religion encapsulated many of the basic Andean religious principles mentioned above while utilizing these principles in the construction of a state. Here I will discuss Inca state religion (for overall summaries of the Inca Empire, see Kolata 1991a; Rowe 1946, 1982) as distinguished from the myriad of more local religious practices that the Inca would leave intact or incorporate (MacCormack 1991; Rowe 1946). This discussion of Inca state religion will not attempt to be systematic, for the primary and secondary literature on Inca religion is extensive (see Bouysse-Cassagne 1987, 1988; Cobo 1990 [1953]; Conrad and Demarest 1984; MacCormack 1984, 1991; Rostworowski de Diez Canseco 1983; Salles-Reese 1997; Sullivan 1985). Rather, the focus is on Inca imperial religion and the ritual practices utilized by the Inca in the construction of their empire.

Although an uncritical extension of contemporary and recent historical Andean belief systems to the past is problematic, it can be argued that broad patterns of effecting relationships to deities through rituals of reciprocity were present during the reign of the Inca Empire. For the Inca, communication with deities, *huacas*, and ancestors was effected through offerings in a manner similar to *ch'alla* offerings.

These offerings could take place in the context of grand and public state-sponsored rituals or in more localized contexts. Interestingly, offerings of drink, like the *ch'alla* offerings of alcohol today, were a common means of communication with the deities. In Guaman Poma's representation of an offering to the sun during the fiesta of Inti Raymi, *chicha*, or maize beer, is poured and drunk by the Inca king as a libation to the sun (Figure 7.1). The sun receives his portion in Guaman Poma's Christianized version from a demon, but the conception of a reciprocal drinking ceremony, between gods as between humans, is clearly represented.

Reciprocity was also an important aspect of Inca religious belief. Guaman Poma depicts an Inca king consulting with a collection of *huacas* (Figure 7.2). The king asks the *huacas*, "Huacas, huacas! Which of you has said 'Do not rain, do not snow, do not hail'?" (my translation from Murra et al.'s Spanish translation of the Quechua in Ayala 1987 [1615]:252). Here, relations between humans and deities are formulated in terms of reciprocity, and humans may demand a response when they have properly offered and petitioned the deity. Rituals establishing relationships between humans and humans and between humans and gods were pervasive throughout the Inca Empire.

These rituals could be and apparently were also utilized to establish aspects of the social order. The festival of Inti Raymi is a salient example. Inti Raymi occurred on or near June 21, the winter solstice (for descriptions, see Cobo 1990 [1653]:142–143; Molina 1988 [1553]:67–71). The fiesta was explicitly dedicated to the Inca high god of the sun and included llama sacrifices at key points around Cuzco, as well as offerings of coca, maize, and seashells. Molina states that, following the major ceremonies in the Cuzco region, a group would undertake a journey from Cuzco through a series of surrounding valleys, visiting certain peaks and offering llama sacrifices to each (Molina 1988 [1553]:68–69). Every peak had a different meaning within imperial history. Some were aligned with the origin of the sun; others with mythical origins (see Molina 1988 [1553]:note 35, p. 69). Through this ritual, the Inca linked their imperial and mythical history to the sun itself, the forces of the cosmos, and the sources of agricultural production. An eyewitness observation of the Inti Raymi ceremony by a clergyman in the mid-sixteenth century related the following details:

FIGURE 7.1. Inca *ch'alla* offerings (from Ayala 1987: 239)

FIGURE 7.2. An Inca king consults with *huacas* (from Ayala 1987:240)

They were all orejones, very richly dressed in cloaks and tunics woven with silver. They wore bracelets, and the disks on their heads were of fine gold and very resplendent. They stood in two rows, each of which was made up of over three hundred lords . . . they stood very silent, waiting for sunrise. When the sun had not yet fully risen, they began slowly and in great order and harmony to intone a chant . . . and as the sun went on rising so their song intensified. The Inca had his awning in an enclosure with a very fine seat. . . . And when the singing began, he rose to his feet with great authority and stood at the head of all, and he was the first to begin the chant; and when he began, so did all the others. (MacCormack 1991:75–76)

In this event, the Inca king ritually establishes his preeminence over all other lords and the kingdom while symbolically linking his person and actions to the rising of the sun at the beginning of the new year. He, like the sun, rises out of darkness (his enclosure) and through his actions begins the new year. Interestingly, this same cleric noted that soon after the conclusion of the Inti Raymi ceremony, at the time of field preparation and planting in the early spring, the Inca king would ceremoniously plow the first field: "Without the Inca inaugurating [the plowing season], there was no one who would have ventured to break the earth, nor would they have thought that the earth would produce [a harvest] unless the Inca were the first to break it" (MacCormack 1991:77). Ritual established the Inca king as the necessary source of production and wealth. Other ceremonies, such as Capac Raymi and the Citua rites, also encoded aspects of social order (Seddon 1998:79–83).

From state-sponsored Inca ceremonies to more localized Aymara *ch'alla* offerings, key aspects of Andean belief in the importance of reciprocal offerings between humans and deities were and are continually enacted. Importantly, each of these rituals also encodes and develops social and political arguments about the human order. The individuals performing the offering, the ranked access of people to witness the offering, and other aspects of the ritual indicate that political ritual was commonly a staged event designed to ensure the functioning of both the natural and the social and political worlds. Ritual both reflected and created power.

The relationship between political ritual and power is visible in both the core and the peripheries of the core of the Tiwanaku polity. There is good evidence for ritual practices that appear to have involved reciprocal exchange between humans and deities and for feasting events that served to establish relationships between various subgroups within the overall Tiwanaku polity. Key changes in the location of, and access of people to, these ritual practices indicate that these rituals were transformed and that this transformation is closely related to the expansion of what archaeologists recognize as the Tiwanaku state.

THE APPROPRIATION OF RITUAL AND THE TIWANAKU CORE

Political ritual in the Tiwanaku core is best known from the site of Tiwanaku itself. The Tiwanaku central core, consisting of the Akapana, Kalasasaya, Pumapunku, and other structures, is arguably a gigantic stage for the presentation and observation of political ritual. Significantly, there is good evidence that such rituals included the performance of reciprocal offerings between humans and deities. Architectural evidence suggests that there was always an element of restrictiveness to the performance and observation of these rituals. Mounting evidence suggests that the exclusiveness of these rituals increased over time.

Multiple dramatic features identified in the central civic/ceremonial core of Tiwanaku provide evidence for rituals of reciprocity. Features identified on terraces of the Akapana indicate the deliberate destruction of huge numbers of fine ceramic drinking vessels, or *keros* (Alconini Mujica 1993; 1995:75–114, 166–176; Manzanilla 1992:91–102). In addition, in other areas at the base of the Akapana, offerings of humans possibly in wrapped bundles and of whole and disarticulated camelids were recovered (Alconini Mujica 1995; Blom et al. 2003; Janusek 1994: 105; Manzanilla 1992; Manzanilla and Woodard 1990). There is also evidence for similar types of activities in Lukurmata's ceremonial core at this time (Bermann 1994:195–199).

The large kero smashes on the Akapana are reminiscent of *ch'alla* offerings in contemporary communities where libations are offered to Pachamama. Based on the iconographic content of these offerings, Alconini Mujica has argued that the Akapana functioned as an earth shrine during the Tiwanaku IV period, dedicated to the forces of *manqha pacha* or their Tiwanaku equivalent (Alconini Mujica 1995: 213–219). Minimally, these offerings indicate the deliberate destruction or offering, in a nondomestic and undoubtedly ritual context, of objects in a way that provides strong inferential evidence for rituals of reciprocity.

These rituals occurred on and around architecture that seems to have been designed to both allow and restrict the performance and visibility of these rituals. Tiwanaku monumental architecture, while undoubtedly encoding a multiplicity of symbolic meanings, does appear to have functioned, at least in part, to provide space and stage for the performance of ritual practices. The Akapana, the Sunken Temple, Kalasasaya, Pumapunku, and possibly sections of the Putuni and Kherikala are all architectural spaces that combine areas for public visibility from around the structure with areas for smaller-scale ritual performances with more restricted viewing spaces. Each of these monuments includes (or likely included) a smaller interior court, often sunken, that is (or was) surrounded by terrace areas. Additionally, in many cases it may also have been possible to view performances of ritual from around and outside these monuments.

Sunken temple spaces, found at the Sunken Temple itself and atop the Akapana and Pumapunku, are spaces where a limited subset of the population can perform rituals, but a larger subset can view the ritual performance and possibly participate vicariously or in some other, indirect way. The temples within the Akapana and Pumapunku allow for more restricted access to viewed rituals in the central temples of these monuments. Notably, each of these structures, with their stairways and gates, indicates that restriction of access to ceremonies that may originally have been more open (such as at the Sunken Temple) was a crucial consideration of the designers of the structures. It is the case that the Akapana and Pumapunku exterior terraces would have allowed for more broad-scale viewing of rituals of reciprocity by larger populaces. Nonetheless, the evidence suggests that even by the early Tiwanaku IV period, when the Akapana and Pumapunku were built (Janusek 2004:132; Vranich 1999), the architecture was designed to accommodate both public and private viewing and participation in ritual events.

The combination of small and intimate spaces with increasingly larger viewing platforms is particularly suggestive that the monumental constructions were designed to allow a hierarchy of access to ritual performances. As described by proxemics analysis, the immediacy of a ritual or performance—the access of observers to the words, facial expressions, and so forth of the ritual specialists conducting the ritual—is limited by physical distance (Hall 1966; Moore 1996; Inomata and Coben 2006). The sunken courts within Tiwanaku monumental architecture are comparable in size to the larger sunken circular courts analyzed by Moore (1996:149). By his estimation, these courts could have held a maximum of 50 to 100 people. Those individuals would have been the only observers with direct access to the intimate aspects of the ritual performances; they would have been the only participant/observers with clear access to words, expressions, and subtle details. In other words, they would have been the only "public-near/participants" (Moore 1996:166). Other people, arranged on platforms and/or more distant, would have been "public-distant" and primarily observers (cf. Moore 1996:166–167). These distinctions in access create, reflect, and maintain distinctions within the society conducting the ritual.

Examining these monuments from a diachronic perspective, then, reveals changes in access to rituals. Across the Tiwanaku IV and V periods, there appears to be an increasing restriction of access to the rituals of reciprocity occurring in the core of the state. The Sunken Temple, built in the Late Formative and probably one of the first constructions in the area, would have accommodated large numbers of people with relatively unrestricted views and access on the surrounding ground. By Late Formative 2, the Kalasasaya had been constructed (Janusek 2004: 108). Shortly thereafter, this structure formed a unit with the Sunken Temple and notably allowed for possibly the first restricted access to rituals (though the interior court or courts of the Kalasasaya are very large). The Kalasasaya itself, which appears from good evidence to have been built in stages (Janusek 2004:108–109), probably underwent a transformation wherein an open interior platform became enclosed to form a restricted sanctuary during Tiwanaku IV times (Janusek 2004:109). This structure appears to have included architectural features designed to allow for viewing solar and astronomical events (Posnansky 1945; Benitez 2009). Notably, however, the ability to view these events in precise or generalized ways was restricted by the form of the architecture, with interior participants able to observe the events closely and exterior participants witnessing a more generalized, though nonetheless spectacular, event (Vranich and Benitez in press).

As time passed and the structures were modified further, architecture continued to encode restriction of access to and intimacy with ritual performances and performers/specialists. The later additions of the Kalasasaya and Pumapunku, as described above, further restricted access to rituals of reciprocity with their nested entryways, stairs, and secluded temples with more limited viewing spaces. Although evidence from wear patterns on the stairways does suggest long use and possibly large numbers of people (Janusek 2004:135), it is clear that, at least at any one time, intimate, public-near viewing of ritual performances was restricted to a smaller subset of the population by the architecture of these structures.

The construction of the possible Tiwanaku moat may have been related to this increasing restriction of access to ritual. As well summarized by Janusek (2004:130–131), we have no unambiguous evidence of the timing of construction of this feature. Janusek (2004:131) provides a reasonable hypothesis that it was constructed in stages, perhaps originating simply as borrow areas for soil for the monumental constructions. I am willing to hypothesize that the moat reached its final form at or around the Tiwanaku IV–V transition and provided one of the final restrictions to ritual performance. It may well have also served, among other functions and symbolic meanings (see Kolata 1993), to further restrict access to key rituals at the core, helping further define social hierarchy through ritual performances. Nonetheless, until an intrepid researcher or graduate student systematically profiles and dates the moat, these ideas will remain testable hypotheses.

The overall trend in public ritual in the center of the Tiwanaku capital, then, is for increasing restriction of access to rituals of reciprocity. While the exact nature and meaning of all the undoubtedly wonderfully rich, varied, and changing rituals that occurred within this space are only beginning to be known, it is clear from the many offerings and sacrifices that rituals of reciprocity that were at least broadly analogous to similar rituals known from the historical and recent periods did occur and were key components of the practices. The Sunken Temple, as the first construction, provides evidence that while performance of such rituals was always at least somewhat restricted, viewing the rituals was not necessarily restricted. This feature was then joined to what was first a large, open platform, the Kalasasaya, which was then closed in what would have been the first architectural manifestation of restricted access to ritual performances. Over time, even viewing became increasingly restricted, as sunken temples were brought inside structures such as the Akapana and Pumapunku, with controlled access, smaller viewing areas, and an overall hierarchy of access to the performance and even intimacy with the ritual itself. By Tiwanaku V, it is possible that the entire central area of the site was restricted by a moat.

In short, political ritual at the core of Tiwanaku appears to have involved key rituals of reciprocity between people and deities. Importantly, however, after Tiwanaku IV, these rituals were placed within architectural settings that were seemingly designed to keep at least the performance of these rituals under the near exclusive control of a small group of elites. At this time, the group rituals establishing relationships between people and deities were thus formally appropriated by the elite.

The Appropriation of Ritual on the Periphery of the Core

A similar transformation appears to have occurred at the periphery of the core on the Island of the Sun. Excavations at the site of Chucaripupata, a large ceremonial and elite habitation at the north end of the island, adjacent to the later Inca ritual center (Seddon 1998, 2004, 2005), have indicated that a major transformation occurred at the site at the Tiwanaku IV–V transition.

During the later Inca occupation of the Titicaca Basin, the Island of the Sun was a significant shrine and pilgrimage area, known throughout the Inca Empire (Bauer and Stanish 2001; Cieza 1959 [1553]; Cobo 1983 [1653], 1990 [1653]; Garcilaso 1961 [1609]:189–191; Ramos Gavilán 1988 [1621]). During the Tiwanaku IV period, the island contained major occupations associated with Tiwanaku artifacts and architecture and underwent significant settlement reorganization (Bauer and Stanish 2001: 149). Chucaripupata was one of two major settlements on the island in the Tiwanaku IV period, and while the site was undoubtedly occupied at a small scale during the Formative period, the first large-scale occupation was during this period. The Tiwanaku IV and V occupations at the site indicate both significant ritual activity and significant transformations in these activities.

During the Tiwanaku IV occupation of Chucaripupata, the central area of the site, which forms the highest and most prominent portion of the occupation area, was the focus of rituals and feasting that appear to have been relatively open and public. Radiocarbon samples from this occupation provide calibrated 2σ age ranges of A.D. 560–670 and A.D. 620–691 (Seddon 2004:107–108). The site at this time appears to have consisted of a small platform or upper terrace area demarcated by a low, simple wall (Seddon 1998, 2004:102). The remaining wall foundations were simple and would probably not have supported much more than a low adobe superstructure. Two small, 10-cm-wide canals were located in the central portion of this platform or terrace area (Figure 7.3). Although the canals were somewhat disturbed, enough was present to indicate that both were constructed of small, thin slabs. The canals would not have served for utilitarian irrigation or drainage functions; they appear to have served primarily to either manipulate ritual offerings or to serve as mechanisms for ritual manipulation of rainwater (Seddon 1998, 2004:102–103). They indicate that at least a major activity, if not *the* major activity, that occurred on the central portion of the site was ritual performances involving the manipulation of liquids.

Specialized trash deposits and storage features indicate that feasting activities were also common. A complex of circular pits and features was identified in another portion of the central site area (Figure 7.4). Three of the features contained significant quantities of ceramics, charcoal, and camelid and *cuy* (guinea pig) bone remains (Seddon 2004:99–100). The ceramic vessels included storage and cooking vessels typical of domestic assemblages, but they also contained notably high frequencies of decorated

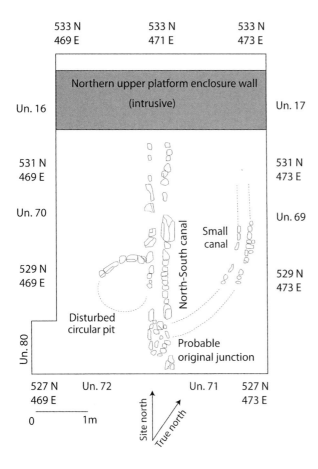

FIGURE 7.3. Small canals located in the Tiwanaku IV–period occupation of Chucaripupata.

serving wares such as *keros* (Figure 7.5) and several *sahumador* (incense burner) fragments (Seddon 2004:108–115). The proportion of serving vessels in these features was higher than that for domestic components at the site. These data, along with the other remains indicative of cooking, drinking, and eating, indicate that the features contain debris that appears to be from feasting events (Seddon 2004: 113–114). Numerous rock-lined storage features, all found devoid of their original contents, indicate that preparation for and storage of items to be used in feasting events were significant foci of activities in the central portion of the site (Figure 7.6).

All of these vessels were clearly within the Tiwanaku stylistic canon for ceramics, both in form and decoration. However, they were nearly entirely locally made, with only a very small proportion of imported vessels (Seddon 2004:113). Interestingly, a number of fragments of *tinajas,* vessels intended for storage of liquids (possibly *chicha* or other alcoholic beverages used in feasting events), were manufactured with pastes that indicated they were imported from Tiwanaku. The ceramic assemblage indicates a close affinity, at least in the use of vessels in ritual and feasting contexts, with Tiwanaku. The presence of imported *tinajas,* ordinarily common storage vessels, raises the distinct possibility that such feasting occurred between local inhabitants and representatives

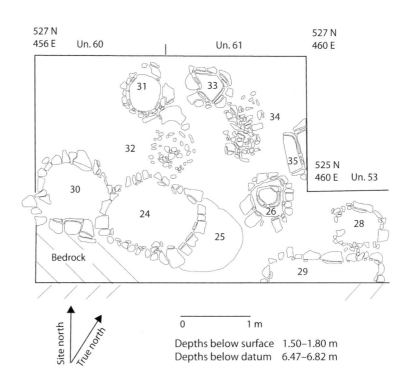

FIGURE 7.4. A complex of circular pits located in the Tiwanaku IV–period occupation of Chucaripupata.

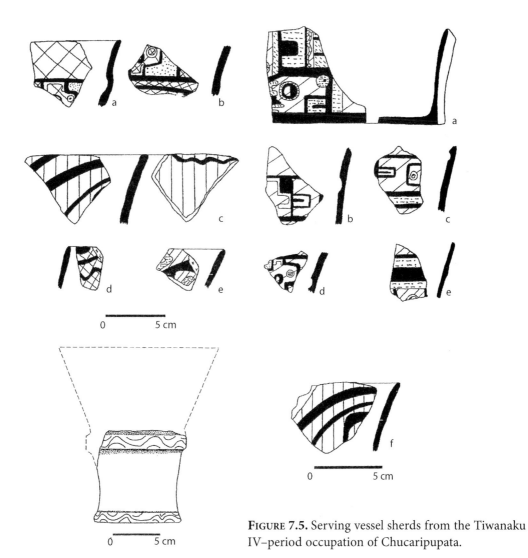

FIGURE 7.5. Serving vessel sherds from the Tiwanaku IV–period occupation of Chucaripupata.

FIGURE 7.6. Circular pits in the Tiwanaku IV–period occupation of Chucaripupata, post-excavation.

of populations from the core area. It appears unlikely that populations would have obtained ordinary storage vessels through trade with Tiwanaku, particularly when they were obviously capable of manufacturing local copies of elaborate serving vessels. Rather, it seems possible, even probable, that the imported tinajas indicate that feasting involved peoples from Tiwanaku itself, who brought beverages as part of the reciprocal feasting event.

At a final phase of the Tiwanaku IV occupation, the area was used for burial. Fifteen tombs were identified in the excavations (Seddon 2004:103–107). Many of these tombs crosscut earlier features, and no later features crosscut the tombs. Thus it is clear that the last use of the area was for formal interment activities. The tombs were slab-lined cist tombs, generally 75 to 100 cm in diameter and 50 cm deep, capped with large circular and oblong single slabs. Notably, a few smaller cists, probably containing infants or children, were present, but overall bone preservation was poor, making identification of age, gender, and other individual attributes nearly impossible. Nonetheless, the available osteological remains, and particularly the dental remains, indicate that males and females, as well as adults and children, were present.

The tombs were particularly noteworthy for their grave furniture. Five of the tombs contained grave goods (Seddon 2004:104–106). Two of these tombs contained locally manufactured vessels—a *vasija* and an olla base similar to an offering from a tomb at Wakuyu on the southern end of the island (Perrin Pando 1957:194, Figure 49)—and the others contained elaborate serving vessels imported from Tiwanaku itself. Two of these were *keros,* one decorated with a front-face god motif (Figure 7.7); the third was an elaborately decorated *vasija.*

Overall, while domestic occupations were undoubtedly also present on lower terraces of the site during the Tiwanaku IV period (Seddon 1998), evidence from the central and highest portion of the site indicates that a central activity at the site included open, public rituals and feasting. It seems that the central area was demarcated by a low wall, its identified foundations being small and suggestive of a wall that would not have been significantly tall. This wall, then, helped to define the area rather than to exclude participants. Small canals indicate that liquids were manipulated in a nondomestic, nonutilitarian manner, undoubtedly associated with ritual events in the open, central area of the site. Feasting was also a significant, and planned, activity. Specialized storage pits were placed on the upper platform for storing feasting paraphernalia, food, and drink. Trash pits provide direct evidence for feasting activities. Finally, the area was utilized as a cemetery, continuing the role of the site in nondomestic, ritual activities.

Two aspects of the site at this time are particularly salient. One is the close affiliation of the site with the growing Tiwanaku polity, but an affiliation that retained a distinctively local character. The ceramic assemblage, while clearly within the Tiwanaku canon, is almost entirely locally manufactured (Seddon 2004:115). The tombs, while not unusual for the region, are most similar to tombs on the rest of the island and in nearby regions and are distinct from tombs at Tiwanaku and Lukurmata in the core area of the state (Seddon 2004:115). While undoubtedly the result of a long—perhaps centuries-long—process, the sudden and dramatic increase in Tiwanaku vessels at the site and island indicates that by the Tiwanaku IV period, the periphery of the core of the state was closely affiliated with the state. However, the imported vessels, along with their nature and contexts, indicate that direct contacts with individuals from the Tiwanaku state were not broad-based. Small numbers of *tinajas* from Tiwanaku suggest that limited numbers of individuals from Tiwanaku participated in the feasting events. Limited distribution of Tiwanaku import vessels in tombs suggests that close personal ties with individuals or groups from Chucaripupata were frequent but not common. Overall, the evidence seems to indicate that the Chucaripupata populace was affiliated with the emerging Tiwanaku state mainly through interpersonal contacts with limited

FIGURE 7.7. *Keros* from tombs, late Tiwanaku IV–period occupation of Chucaripupata.

numbers of persons from Tiwanaku itself. These contacts were certainly facilitated by feasting and probably joint ritual activities as well.

Whatever the long-lost details of these contacts, feasts, and rituals, it is clear that they were generally open and public. The area for these activities, while demarcated by a low wall, was open, with few other restrictions to participation. Indeed, the density of feasting storage features and trash pits appears to indicate that large numbers of people would have packed into and directly participated in activities on the upper platform area during the Tiwanaku IV period at the site. The activities are analogous to the public rituals at Tiwanaku in that they occur on specially demarcated and elevated areas where participation can be had by large numbers of individuals and where viewing by larger numbers is possible. Notably, however, the activities appear even more communal in that there is no sunken temple, raised central temple, or other restricted area (such as the Tiwanaku sunken courts and Kalasasaya features) at Chucaripupata. Ritual activities are distinctly communal in nature during the Tiwanaku IV period at the site.

After approximately A.D. 750, this architectural, ritual, and communal pattern would change significantly. The formerly open area was walled in by a massive retaining wall (Figure 7.8). The wall was placed just to the outside of the original outer platform wall and ran around the entire boundary of the upper platform. The wall was 90 cm thick, and in places remains of the wall were extended a total of 1.5 m in height. The wall was double-faced and filled, with fitted sandstone blocks forming the exterior faces and large sandstone rubble in the interior of the wall, making it a substantial construction. Cut-stone andesite blocks associated with the wall indicate that the remaining wall was merely a large and substantial foundation for a taller wall, one that undoubtedly consisted of cut-stone blocks mimicking monumental constructions at Tiwanaku itself (Seddon 1998, 2004:117–118). Within this wall, a layer of sterile sand and then fill sediments brought from site midden deposits covered the earlier features and cemetery and formed a large level platform interior to the wall.

On this platform was a ceremonial structure modeled on the Kalasasaya structure at Tiwanaku. Close to the center of the platform was a row of large upright stone slabs, interspersed with smaller stones (Seddon 2004:120). The construction of this wall, with alternating large standing stones filled by smaller stones, is clearly reminiscent of the exterior wall construction of the Kalasasaya at Tiwanaku (Figure 7.9). Inside, or continuing toward the center of the now-walled upper platform, were pairs of large stone-lined rectangular structures (Figure 7.10). These features are reminiscent of the large internal rectangular structures at the Kalasasaya at Tiwanaku. While the

FIGURE 7.8. View of portion of massive outer retaining wall, Tiwanaku V–period occupation of Chucaripupata.

FIGURE 7.9. Overview of possible Kalasasaya structure at Chucaripupata. Note the large upright slabs at the left of the picture.

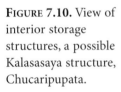

FIGURE 7.10. View of interior storage structures, a possible Kalasasaya structure, Chucaripupata.

latter structures are now reconstructed aboveground, evidence suggests that they were originally belowground structures (Escalante Moscoso 1993:187) or part of a wall or platform surrounding an interior courtyard (Alexei Vranich, personal communication 2007). Thus the Chucaripupata structures are at least analogous and possibly identical to the structures at the Kalasasaya at Tiwanaku.

On the exterior, or toward the edge of the upper platform, were a pair of thin walls, closely linked and crossing in places. Between these walls and the large slabs was a clean, prepared floor of green clay. The interior surfaces of these walls are not finely faced; the exterior surfaces are faced, though not particularly finely. It is possible that they functioned as retaining walls for small platforms exterior to the main, large Kalasasaya-like wall. Recent investigations and reexaminations of excavation notes from 1960s excavations of the Kalasasaya at Tiwanaku have revealed the presence of similar small walls and/or platforms outside the Kalasasaya at Tiwanaku (Alexei Vranich, personal communication 2007; Tony Chapa, personal communication 2007). In at least one area, a green floor was located between the small walls and the main Kalasasaya wall (Alexei Vranich, personal communication 2007). Thus the structure at Chucaripupata may be even more similar to the Kalasasaya structure at Tiwanaku than originally thought (Seddon 2004:122–123). Minimally, there is no doubt that overall the form of the structure appears to strongly emulate the Kalasasaya structure at Tiwanaku (Figure 7.11).

There were few artifacts clearly and directly associated with this Tiwanaku V–period construction. The floor within the structure was clean, perhaps emulating ritually clean spaces at Tiwanaku itself (Janusek 1994; 2004:111). The storage structures had been emptied after final abandonment and were filled with debris from later site destruction and trash disposal activities. However, because the structure is minimally nondomestic (Seddon 2004:122) and most likely a copy of the Kalasasaya temple at Tiwanaku, it is entirely reasonable to infer that ritual activities and perhaps ritual feasting occurred within the confines of the structure that now entirely covered the earlier ritual area. In the associated domestic oc-cupation, ceramics are almost entirely locally manufactured copies of Tiwanaku-style vessels.

While ritual activities were still a focus of social behavior on the Chucaripupata upper platform, it is highly significant that these activities, previously open, were now closed. The open and communal area was now surrounded by a large wall. The only potential location for a gated entrance was found in the middle of the eastern portion of the site. While near-surface bedrock has resulted in poor preservation of remains in this area, remnants of foundations suggest the presence of a gated entryway, common to Tiwanaku temple structures (Protzen and Nair 2000). While the interior could support a fairly large number of people at a given time, perhaps as many as 50 to 100 (depending on ritual and social spacing conventions), the area was now clearly restricted, with even visibility of events restricted to a select few. Entrance was gated and controlled, and the thin interior walls outside the Kalasasaya slab walls raise the possibility that even once a participant reached the interior of the platform, there may have been further restrictions to entry into other spaces within the overall temple. Ritual activities had become both highly linked to Tiwanaku architectural and ritual forms and restricted to a select few.

The appropriation of ritual activities and restriction to a limited subset of the population mimics what is seen at the heartland. Just as at Tiwanaku, where previously open rituals became increasingly restricted, perhaps even with various levels of restriction, ritual activities at Chucaripupata went from open and communal to closed and restricted. Indeed, in some ways the changes in access to ritual are even more dramatic at Chucaripupata than at Tiwanaku. At Tiwanaku it appears that even though performance of rituals was restricted, many architectural forms allowed for the viewing of rituals by larger numbers of people. It is likely, for instance, that rituals on the Akapana could have been viewed by large portions of the populace, even those outside the probable moated area. At Chucaripupata, ritual activities went from being extremely communal to being highly restricted, accessible to and visible by only a small populace. Regardless of the details, however, a key aspect of the spread of Tiwanaku as seen by the transformations at the site of Tiwanaku itself is the restriction of ritual to a probably elite portion of the populace. I hypothesize that it was the

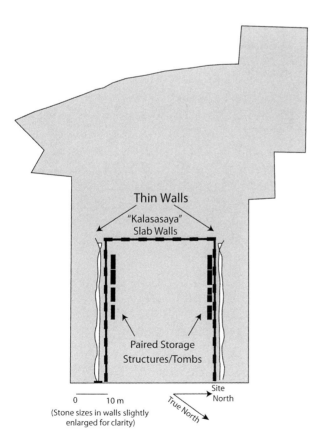

FIGURE 7.11. Plan of a possible Kalasasaya structure at Chucaripupata. Note the thin walls on the north.

very individuals or kin groups who initially had the closest ties to Tiwanaku (as expressed by receipt of imported grave goods) who became the individuals/kinship groups allowed into the later temple.

Incipient Ritual Appropriation at the Far Periphery

Our understanding of the nature of Tiwanaku state expansion, Tiwanaku ritual activities, and Tiwanaku architecture at the periphery of the periphery, the northern Titicaca Basin, remains preliminary. Nonetheless, it is minimally apparent that generally similar forms of Tiwanaku architecture and artifact patterning are present, and I am willing to predict that we should see evidence for ritual and political transformations similar to those seen at the heartland and periphery of the heartland. What we do know from various systematic and reconnaissance surveys (cf. Stanish 2003:186–189) and from only recently emerging data is that Tiwanaku has a relatively limited expression in the far northern Titicaca Basin. With one possible exception, Tiwanaku occupation in the area is identified by the presence of Tiwanaku-style artifacts on sites with what appears to be corporate architecture that can be associated with Tiwanaku. At present, known Tiwanaku artifacts are limited to particular key sites such as Isla Esteves, Paucarcolla-Santa Barbara, and Maravillas. At these sites there is some limited suggestion that particular, restrictive forms of Tiwanaku architecture, such as the Sunken Temple and the Kalasasaya, are replicated. For example, a possible Kalasasaya structure has been identified on Isla Esteves by de la Vega and Chávez (Stanish 2003:187). A possible platform mound with a potential sunken court has been identified across from Isla Esteves at Huajje (Stanish 2003:187). Another potential raised ceremonial area has been identified at Maravillas (Stanish 2003:187). The architectural styles and layout of these sites strongly suggest that they are elite occupations, and there is the possibility that a Tiwanaku "presence" in these areas is predominantly the presence of inter-elite interactions.

However, our knowledge of these key areas is only in preliminary stages, with most of our inferences based on surface ceramics rather than careful excavations. I would note that we have limited understanding of the presence and contexts of Tiwanaku artifacts at non-elite centers. Stanish notes that some smaller sites with Tiwanaku artifacts have been recorded, particularly in the Puno Bay area or close to the lake in the Omasuyu/Escoma area (Stanish 2003:187, 189). The site of Punanave is particularly intriguing, as it appears to have high densities of Tiwanaku domestic architecture and debris but no clear corporate architecture (Stanish 2003:187). It may represent a non-elite, specialized Tiwanaku occupation. However, I would hesitate to derive too much from what are predominantly surface observations from Punanave or any other site. We desperately need more systematic excavation in these areas to understand whether the processes seen at Tiwanaku sites in the core, such as Chucaripupata, are replicated in the peripheries. Notably, a Tiwanaku temple at the site of Omo on the Pacific coast does have architectural features suggestive of restricted access to ritual (Goldstein 1993). I would predict that since a major Tiwanaku transformation involves elite appropriation of ritual, one that began with inter-elite interaction, the predominant manifestation of Tiwanaku in the far periphery will be predominantly found in elite contexts.

However, the presence of corporate architecture, at least at several sites known to date, does raise the distinct possibility that restriction of previously open ritual activities was an aspect of the Tiwanaku expansion in this area. I hypothesize that ritual activities in the far periphery should be open in nature and not yet closed (if the state had not yet fully consolidated in the northern periphery prior to collapse), or that sites should show evidence of transformation from open to closed areas. I do not expect that previously closed areas will become open or that transformation in ritual will involve increasing access or visibility to ritual activities.

Political Transformation of Ritual and the Spread of Tiwanaku Ideology and Elite Power

Today we recognize the remains of the Tiwanaku state through the material culture and architecture of Tiwanaku ritual, and I believe that particular political transformations that occurred in ritual formed one key aspect of the expansion of Tiwanaku material culture through the Titicaca Basin. Solid evidence from the core of the state and the periphery of the core, along with tantalizing suggestions from the far periphery, indicates that the time of greatest expansion of Tiwanaku, the Tiwanaku IV–V transition, was associated with a significant transformation in the communal nature of ritual activities. Previously, during the Tiwanaku IV period, social and divine relationships had been expressed through feasting between people and rituals of reciprocity between everyone and the gods. Early feasting events were open and communal. Rituals establishing reciprocal relationships between humans and deities are evidenced at multiple localities in Tiwanaku and at Chucaripupata. These ritual activities were minimally viewed by large numbers of people. At Tiwanaku they may have been performed by a limited subset of the populace in the central district, but viewing was possible by large numbers of people, and private rituals were also occurring in the residential barrios at the site. At Chucaripupata, an area for feasting and ritual was very open and highly communal.

After the Tiwanaku IV–V transition, such activities became feasting between unequals and elite reciprocity with gods. Access to ritual and feasting areas was restricted. Architectural forms were established to limit the number of people who could view a ritual and to control access to the ritual and any associated feasting. Clear hierarchies in behavior, food reception, and other aspects of ritual mark the architecture and archaeology of Tiwanaku political ritual in the Tiwanaku V period.

This transformation presents us with a key for understanding the transition from a more egalitarian set of relationships within Tiwanaku and between Tiwanaku and peripheral settlements to the establishment and adoption of Tiwanaku forms and identities throughout the region. Ritual establishes both divine and social relationships. The key transformation in ritual accomplished at the Tiwanaku IV–V transition enabled emerging elites—for example, the subset of the Chucaripupata populace who received direct goods from Tiwanaku—to further extend their control over their local populace. Now, it appears, only a small subset of the Chucaripupata populace (and possibly of the larger island) was allowed access to the rituals of reciprocity that established beneficial relationships between humans and deities. Access to these rituals, and access to feasts with key individuals, was now controllable through the gate at the center of the temple wall. I argue that although the spread of Tiwanaku throughout the Titicaca Basin was undoubtedly complex and involved multiple factors, one component of the success of Tiwanaku was to export its model of restricted ritual and to enable emergent local elites to take advantage of this model to support their own local ends.

INTIMATE RITUALS, DIVERSITY, AND THE NATURE OF THE TIWANAKU POLITY

Such a strategy of ritual and power enhances our ability to model the nature of the Tiwanaku polity itself. Researchers attempting to model the Tiwanaku polity (see summary in Janusek 2004:53–95) have long been challenged by the simultaneous evidence for centralization and diversity within the polity. On the one hand, the presence of a recognizable Tiwanaku stylistic canon in ceramics, textiles, jewelry, and architectural forms has contributed to the arguments of those who see Tiwanaku as a highly centralized polity. On the other hand, the recognition of diversity within this canon (cf. Blom 2005:155), a recognition that has continued to increase as the data have accumulated, has contributed to the models of those who argue for a more loosely affiliated state, even a type of segmentary polity (cf. Janusek 2004:70–73). Recently, Janusek has bravely attempted to unify these concepts through his argument that Tiwanaku was somehow both a collection of independent groups and an integrated polity; that its integration was achieved through the coalescence of ties between independent groups (Janusek 2004:279–280; 2005:49–50).

While I am sympathetic to this emerging model, I do believe we have a long way to go in terms of fleshing out potential details of what such a centralized yet segmentary state might look like. I do think that we can make a confident argument that much of what united the diverse populations within the "Tiwanaku sphere" or polity were tightly crafted and carefully maintained interpersonal relationships. We now have good evidence for feasting, the importance of intimate contacts in ritual settings, and the maintenance of local identities within the polity itself at a variety of levels. We see the negotiation of local *and* state identities between house compounds at Tiwanaku itself, between Tiwanaku and peripheral occupations such as Lukurmata, between Tiwanaku core and periphery occupations in the altiplano such as the Island of the

Sun, and between Tiwanaku core and far periphery in places like Moquegua. All of these factors strongly suggest that Tiwanaku political integration entailed the creation and maintenance of contacts and relationships between various kin groups and between various elites.

The architecture and nature of ritual that I have discussed also imply that these relationships required constant maintenance at all levels. Within Tiwanaku itself, particularly by the later Tiwanaku V period, there is a multiplicity of spaces designated for ritual performances and feasting. Multiple sunken temples abound, and domestic spaces also indicate opportunities for interpersonal feasting and contact in intimate settings (cf. Couture 2002). As I have argued with direct evidence from the Island of the Sun and inferred from emerging evidence elsewhere in the Titicaca Basin, such activities were also integral to the integration of other populations into the Tiwanaku polity outside the core. Tiwanaku can appear segmentary or nested precisely because the polity did consist of networks of different kin and/or ethnic groups tied together through common ritual, feasting, and other group practices.

I believe that the limited tantalizing data we have to date suggest that the glue that held these groups together was a common desire on the part of emerging and competing elites to cement their own local control. To make this argument more explicit, we must recall from the discussion at the beginning of this paper that power is most often rooted in a multiplicity of local strategies. Individuals pursue strategies to enhance their position in the world. The most successful powers will be able to link the success of the central elites to the local strategy of other members of the polity. I believe the spread of Tiwanaku material culture can be explained by the successful manner in which Tiwanaku elites were able to tie their "successes" in creating and maintaining hierarchy to more local successes of their connected partners throughout the region. Emerging elites in the peripheries of the state participated in the "global" phenomenon of Tiwanaku because it was locally advantageous for them to do so.

A significant venue in which this occurred, I have argued here, is the arena of ritual practices. The spread of Tiwanaku appears in large part to have been closely related to a major change in the access of people to rituals of reciprocity, a change that placed local elites in a new position in relation to both cosmological and social power. This transformation in ritual indicates that the Tiwanaku polity, rightly argued to be a new creation in the region (Janusek 2002), did grow out of and was carefully formed through a multiplicity of personal and intimate relationships between elites at a variety of levels.

The importance of close interpersonal ties may be a reason for the social diversity and cosmopolitan nature of the populace of Tiwanaku itself. Growing bioarchaeological and artifactual evidence indicates that Tiwanaku housed a highly diverse population, with inhabitants from many parts of the region, even far-flung areas, living at Tiwanaku itself (Blom 2005; Janusek 2004, 2005). The need for the individuals to be close and present for rituals and other network-forming activities at the core may have driven this diversity. External groups, kin associations, and other elites may have needed close contact with Tiwanaku elites to continually maintain the ties that bound them to Tiwanaku elites and supported their local rule at home.

Restated, then, under this model, much of what we recognize as Tiwanaku is the result of a complex inter-elite network. A deficiency in this model of Tiwanaku is that we are currently unable to define the exact nature of inter-elite relationships within the larger polity. At best we can currently argue from the diversity seen in the developing archaeological record that the relationships between Tiwanaku elites and more local elites probably employed a multiplicity of forms; patron–client relationships, direct reciprocity, dependency, and perhaps even conquest are all possible relationships at this point, given the paucity of data outside the core itself. In particular, we currently suffer from a lack of data on non-elite domestic occupations in the Titicaca Basin but outside the core itself. Until we have more data regarding how non-elites related to local elites outside the polity, and more data on relationships between local elites and Tiwanaku elites, I predict that we will continue to see a diversity of "Tiwanakus."

Nonetheless, the model of the polity that I have posed here, and particularly the model of ritual within Tiwanaku, has a number of testable implications. Outside the core, under this model what we recognize as Tiwanaku is primarily an inter-elite phenomenon. While we are still investigating this issue, and sites such as Pununave may contradict this simplistic extension of the model, I predict that the frequency and use of Tiwanaku artifacts at nonceremonial domestic hamlets and habitations will decrease with distance from the core. I expect that there will be Tiwanaku artifacts in non-elite domestic contexts. However, I also expect that these artifacts will be low in proportion to all serving wares in such contexts and less elaborate or finely decorated than those in feasting contexts. This proportion should decrease over time, particularly across the Tiwanaku IV–V transition. Non-elite participation in Tiwanaku ceremonies, while common early in the sequence, should decrease as emerging Tiwanaku-affiliated elites increase restriction of access to key rituals and feasting events.

Corporate architecture should also replicate this pattern. I predict that at many, if not most, of the sites in the northern periphery of the Titicaca Basin, Tiwanaku architectural forms, such as Kalasasaya temples, platform pyramids and mounds, and sunken temples, should overlie or enclose previously open areas that were used for feasting and ritual. This is the pattern seen clearly in the core and near periphery of the Tiwanaku heartland, and I expect it is a likely strategy elsewhere. However, if this implication is not borne out, if Tiwanaku corporate architecture at the northern periphery is installed in areas that previously lacked ritual, the implication is equally interesting. Such a pattern would suggest that the development and spread of Tiwanaku employed multiple strategies, with implications for the historical course of the polity.

There were many aspects to the spread of Tiwanaku. Notably, however, many things that are often aspects of state expansion—warfare, control of trade, control of elite good/craft production—were not present. So far our best, and meager, direct evidence of warfare is a single broken statue (Chávez 1975; Kolata 1993:248–249). Craft production was decentralized (Janusek 1999, 2004:194). Although trade clearly occurred, we have no unambiguous evidence that Tiwanaku monopolized trade routes through direct control. However, we do have good evidence that much of what we recognize as Tiwanaku is ritual artifacts and architecture and that a key transformation in control of rituals of reciprocity appears to be always associated with the arrival of what we recognize as the Tiwanaku state. Although it would be simplistic to attribute all of the success of the Tiwanaku polity to ritual, and I do not believe that power served pomp in this case, I would argue that the power of pomp was a key aspect of the Tiwanaku expansion.

References Cited

Abercrombie, Thomas
1986 The Politics of Sacrifice: An Aymara Cosmology in Action. Unpublished Ph.D. dissertation, Department of Anthropology, University of Chicago, Chicago.
1993 Caminos de la memoria en un cosmos colonizado: Poética de la bebida y la conciencia histórica in K'ulta. In *Borrachera y memoria: La experienceia de lo sagrado en los Andes*, edited by T. Saignes, pp. 139–170. Hisbol, La Paz.

Alconini Mujica, Sonia
1993 La cerámica de la pirámide Akapana y su contexto social en el estado de Tiwanaku. Unpublished licenciatura thesis, Department of Anthropology-Archaeology, Universidad Mayor de San Andrés, La Paz.
1995 *Rito, símbolo e historia en la Pirámide de Akapana, Tiwanaku: Un análisis de cerámica ceremonial prehispánica*. Editorial Acción, La Paz.

Apter, A.
1992 *Black Critics and Kings: The Hermeneutics of Power in Yoruba Society*. University of Chicago Press, Chicago.
1993 Atinga Revisited: Yoruba Witchcraft and the Cocoa Economy, 1950–1951. In *Modernity and Its Malcontents: Ritual and Power in Postcolonial Africa*, edited by J. Comaroff and J. Comaroff, pp. 111–128. University of Chicago Press, Chicago.

Ayala, F. G. P. de
1987 [1615] *Nueva crónica y buen gobierno*. Edited by John V. Murra, Rolena Adorno, and Jorge L. Urioste. Historia 16, Vol. 29. Madrid.

Bastien, Joseph
1978 *Mountain of the Condor: Metaphor and Ritual in an Andean Ayllu*. West Publishing, Saint Paul.

Bauer, B., and C. Stanish
2001 *Power and Pilgrimage in the Ancient Andes: The Lake Titicaca Basin Sanctuary on the Islands of the Sun and Moon*. University of Texas Press, Austin.

Bell, C.
1992 *Ritual Theory, Ritual Practice*. Oxford University Press, Oxford.
1997 *Ritual: Perspectives and Dimensions*. Oxford University Press, Oxford.

Benitez, L.
2009 Descendants of the Sun: Calendars, Myth, and the Tiwanaku State. In *Tiwanaku: Papers from the 2005 Mayer Center Symposium at the Denver*

Art Museum, edited by Margaret Young-Sánchez, pp. 49–81. Denver Art Museum, Denver.

Bermann, M.
1994 *Lukurmata: Household Archaeology in Prehispanic Bolivia*. Princeton University Press, Princeton, New Jersey.

Bloch, M.
1978 The Disconnection between Power and Rank as a Process: An Outline of the Development of Kingdoms in Central Madagascar. In *The Evolution of Social Systems*, edited by J. Friedman and M. J. Rowlands, pp. 303–340. University of Pittsburgh Press, Pittsburgh.

Blom, Deborah E.
2005 Embodying Borders: Human Body Modification and Diversity in Tiwanaku Society. *Journal of Anthropological Archaeology* 24(1):1–24.

Blom, D. E., J. W. Janusek, and J. E. Buikstra
2003 A Reevaluation of Human Remains from Tiwanaku. In *Tiwanaku and Its Hinterland: Archaeological and Paleoecological Investigations of an Andean Civilization*. Vol. 2, *Urban and Rural Archaeology*, edited by Alan L. Kolata, pp. 435–448. Smithsonian Institution Press, Washington, D.C.

Bouysse-Cassagne, T.
1987 *La identidad Aymara: Aproximación histórica (siglo XV, siglo XVI)*. Hisbol, La Paz.
1988 *Lluvias y cenizas: Dos Pachacuti en la historia*. Hisbol, La Paz.

Braithwaite, M.
1984 Ritual and Prestige in the Prehistory of Wessex c. 2200–1400 BC: A New Dimension to the Archaeological Evidence. In *Ideology, Power and Prehistory*, edited by D. Miller and C. Tilley, pp. 93–110. Cambridge University Press, Cambridge.

Chávez, Sergio J.
1975 The Arapa and Thunderbolt Stelae: A Case of Stylistic Identity with Implications for Pucara Influences in the Area of Tihuanaco. *Ñawpa Pacha* 13:3–24.

Cieza de León, P.
1959 [1533] *The Incas*. Translated by Harriet de Onis. University of Oklahoma Press, Norman.

Cobo, B.
1983 [1653] *History of the Inca Empire*. Translated by Roland Hamilton. University of Texas Press, Austin.
1990 [1653] *Inca Religion and Customs*. Translated and edited by Roland Hamilton. University of Texas Press, Austin.

Comaroff, J.
1985 *Body of Power, Spirit of Resistance: The Culture and History of a South African People*. University of Chicago Press, Chicago.

Comaroff, J., and J. Comaroff
1993 Introduction. In *Modernity and Its Malcontents: Ritual and Power in Postcolonial Africa*, edited by J. Comaroff and J. Comaroff, pp. xi–xxxvii. University of Chicago Press, Chicago.

Combs-Schilling, M. E.
1989 *Sacred Performances: Islam, Sexuality, and Sacrifice*. Columbia University Press, New York.

Conrad, G. W., and A. A. Demarest
1984 *Religion and Empire: The Dynamics of Aztec and Inca Expansionism*. Cambridge University Press, Cambridge.

Couture, N. C.
2002 Elite Residence at Tiwanaku, Bolivia. Unpublished Ph.D. dissertation, Department of Anthropology, University of Chicago, Chicago.

Durkheim, E.
1964 [1915] *The Elementary Forms of the Religious Life*. Free Press, New York.

Escalante Moscoso, Javier
1993 *Arquitectura prehispánica en los Andes Bolivianos*. Producciones CIMA, La Paz.

Feinman, Gary, and Joyce Marcus (editors)
1998 *Archaic States*. School of American Research Press, Santa Fe

Fernández Juárez, G.
1995 *El banquete Aymara: Mesas y yatiris*. Hisbol, La Paz.

Garcilaso de la Vega
1961 [1609] *Royal Commentaries of the Incas and General History of Peru*. Translated by Maria Jolas. Orion Press, New York.

Goldstein, P.
1993 Tiwanaku Temples and State Expansion: A Tiwanaku Sunken-Court Temple in Moquegua, Peru. *Latin American Antiquity* 4(3):22–47.

Hall, E. T.
1966 *The Hidden Dimension*. Doubleday, New York.

Helms, M. W.
1979 *Ancient Panama: Chiefs in Search of Power*. University of Texas Press, Austin.

Inomata, Takeshi, and Larry Coben
2006 *Archaeology of Performance*. Altamira Press, Lanham, Maryland.

Isbell, William
1997 *Mummies and Mortuary Monuments: A Postprocessual Prehistory of Central Andean Social Organization*. University of Texas Press, Austin.

Janusek, John Wayne
1994 State and Local Power in a Prehispanic Andean Polity: Changing Patterns of Urban Residence in Tiwanaku and Lukurmata, Bolivia. Unpublished Ph.D. dissertation, Department of Anthropology, University of Chicago, Chicago.

2002 Out of Many, One: Style and Social Boundaries in *Tiwanaku*. *Latin American Antiquity* 13(1):35–61.

2004 *Identity and Power in the Ancient Andes: Tiwanaku Cities through Time*. Routledge, New York.

Kelly, J. D., and M. Kaplan
  1990 History, Structure, and Ritual. *Annual Review of Anthropology* 19:119–150.

Kolata, A.
  1991a In the Realm of the Four Quarters. In *America in 1492: The World of the Indian Peoples before the Arrival of Columbus*, edited by Alvin Josephy, pp. 214–247. Alfred A. Knopf, New York.
  1991b The Technology and Organization of Agricultural Production in the Tiwanaku State. *Latin American Antiquity* 2:99–125.
  1993 *The Tiwanaku: Portrait of an Andean Civilization*. Blackwell, Cambridge.

MacCormack, Sabine
  1984 From the Sun of the Incas to the Virgin of Copacabana. *Representations* 8:30–60.
  1991 *Religion in the Andes: Vision and Imagination in Early Colonial Peru*. Princeton University Press, Princeton, New Jersey.

Manzanilla, L.
  1992 *Akapana: Una Pirámide en el Centro del Mundo*. Instituto de Investigaciones Antropológicas, Universidad Nacional Autónoma de México, Mexico City.

Manzanilla, L., and E. Woodard
  1990 Restos humanos asociados a la Pirámide de Akapana (Tiwanaku, Bolivia). *Latin American Antiquity* 1(2):133–149.

Marcus, Joyce, and Gary Feinman
  1998 Introduction. In *Archaic States*, edited by Gary Feinman and Joyce Marcus, pp. 3–14. School of American Research Press, Santa Fe

Masquelier, A.
  1993 Narratives of Power, Images of Wealth: The Ritual Economy of Bori in the Market. In *Modernity and Its Malcontents: Ritual and Power in Postcolonial Africa*, edited by J. Comaroff and J. Comaroff, pp. 3–33. University of Chicago Press, Chicago.

Molina, Cristóbal de
  1988 [1553] Relación de las Fábulas i Ritos de los Ingas. In *Fábulas y Mitos de los Incas*, edited by H. Urbano and P. Duviols, pp. 49–134. Historia 16. Madrid.

Moore, Jerry
  1996 *Architecture and Power in the Prehispanic Andes: The Archaeology of Public Buildings*. Cambridge University Press, Cambridge.

Murra, John V., Rolena Adorno, and Jorge I. Urioste (eds.)
  1987 *Nueva crónica y buen gobierno*. Crónicas de América 29a–c. Historia-16. Madrid.

Perrin Pando, A.
  1957 Las tumbas subterraneos de Wakuyo. In *Arqueologia boliviana (Primera Mesa Redonda)*, edited by C. Ponce Sanginés, pp. 172–205. Biblioteca Paceña, La Paz.

Ponce Sanginés, Carlos
  1981 *Tiwanaku: Espacio, tiempo y cultura*. Academia Nacional de Ciencias de Bolivia Publicación No. 30. Academia Nacional de Ciencias de Bolivia, La Paz.

Posnansky, A.
  1945 *Tihuanacu: The Cradle of American Man*. Vols. 1 and 2. J. J. Augustin Publisher, New York.

Protzen, Jean-Pierre, and Stella Nair
  2000 On Reconstructing Tiwanaku Architecture. *Journal of the Society of Architectural Historians* 59: 358–371.

Ramos Gavilán, A.
  1988 [1621] *Historia del Santuario de Nuestra Señora de Copacabana*. Edited by Ignacio Prado Pastor. Gráfico P.L. Villanueva S.A., Lima.

Rappaport, R. A.
  1971 The Sacred in Human Evolution. *Annual Review of Ecology and Systematics* 2:23–44.

Rostworowski de Diez Canseco, M.
  1983 *Estructuras andinas del poder: Ideología religiosa y política*. Instituto de Estudios Peruanos, Lima.

Rowe, J. H.
  1946 Inca Culture at the Time of the Spanish Conquest. In *The Andean Civilizations*, edited by J. H. Steward, pp. 183–330. Handbook of South American Indians, Vol. 2. Smithsonian Institution, Washington, D.C.
  1982 Inca Policies and Institutions Relating to the Cultural Unification of the Empire. In *The Inca and Aztec States, 1400–1800*, edited by George Allen Collier, Renato Rosaldo, and John D. Wirth, pp. 93–118. Academic Press, New York.

Salles-Reese, V.
  1997 *From Viracocha to the Virgin of Copacabana: Representation of the Sacred at Lake Titicaca*. University of Texas Press, Austin.

Seddon, M. T.
  1998 Ritual, Power, and the Development of a Complex Society: The Island of the Sun and the Tiwanaku State. Ph.D dissertation. Department of Anthropology, University of Chicago.
  2004 Excavations at the Site of Chucariputata: A Tiwanaku IV and V Temple and Domestic Occupation. In *Archaeological Research on the Islands of the Sun and Moon, Lake Titicaca Bolivia: Final Results from the Proyecto Tiksi Kjarka*. 93–137. Cotsen Institute of Archaeology Press, Los Angeles.

2005 The Tiwanaku Period Occupation on the Island of the Sun. In *Advances in the Archaeology of the Titicaca Basin-I*, edited by Stanish, Charles, Amanda B. Cohen, and Mark S. Aldenderfer, pp. 135–142. Cotsen Institute of Archaeology Press, Los Angeles.

Squier, E. George
1877 *Peru: Incidents of Travel and Exploration in the Land of the Incas*. Harper and Brothers, New York.

Stanish, C.
2003 *Ancient Titicaca: The Evolution of Complex Society in Southern Peru and Northern Bolivia*. University of California Press, Berkeley.

Stanish, Charles, Kirk Lawrence Frye, Edmundo de la Vega, and Matthew T. Seddon
2005 Tiwanaku Expansion into the Western Titicaca Basin, Peru. In *Advances in the Archaeology of the Titicaca Basin-I*, edited Charles Stanish, Amanda B. Cohen, and Mark S. Aldenderfer. Cotsen Institute of Archaeology Press, Los Angeles.

Sullivan, L. E.
1985 Above, Below, or Far Away: Andean Cosmogony and Ethical Order. In *Cosmogony and Ethical Order: New Studies in Ethics*, edited by R. W. Lovin and F. E. Reynolds, pp. 98–129. University of Chicago Press, Chicago.

Vranich, A.
1999 Interpreting the Meaning of Ritual Spaces: The Temple Complex of Pumapunku, Tiwanaku, Bolivia. Unpublished Ph.D. Dissertation, University of Pennsylvania.

8

Tiwanaku Origins and Early Development:
The Political and Moral Economy of a Hospitality State

Matthew Bandy

It is becoming increasingly recognized that the Tiwanaku polity does not fit comfortably within standard models of the centralized archaic state. As Marc Bermann wrote more than 15 years ago:

> Little is known about the manner in which the Tiwanaku political formation was integrated.... Tiwanaku lacks many features of ... administrative infrastructure that are present in many other prehispanic Andean states, suggesting that the Tiwanaku polity was either quite small ... not tightly integrated in terms of decision making and administrative control, or integrated in very different ways than other prehispanic Andean states. (Bermann 1994:36)

Features such as royal mausoleums, palace complexes sprawling over many hectares, massive warehouse facilities, and Inca-style highways and *tambos* are at present entirely unknown for Tiwanaku's altiplano heartland. This contrasts strikingly with the case of the contemporaneous Wari Empire, for which these and other features have been amply documented (Isbell 2004; Isbell and Schreiber 1978; McEwan 1989, 2005; Schreiber 1987, 1991, 1992, 2001; Williams 2001).

Given this lacuna in the material record of the Tiwanaku polity, how are we to reconstruct its structure, institutions, and political economy? Models of Tiwanaku as a centralized archaic state (Kolata 1986, 1993, 2003; Stanish 2002, 2003) have not adequately accounted for the missing features that are expected to accompany that form of social organization and political economy. The challenge posed by Bermann in the quotation that opens this chapter has not been met. In this chapter I will make a series of observations that are pertinent to this question. Some of these will be rather obvious to students of Tiwanaku, but others relate to recent discoveries. Throughout I will pursue two lines of inquiry. The first is a diachronic focus on Tiwanaku development. It is my contention that the initial formation and early development of the Tiwanaku state, city, and polity have a particular importance for our models of the mature state. Data relevant to these early periods of Tiwanaku history have to date played only a minor role in interpretations of Tiwanaku society. One of the goals of this paper is to present those data, as far as they are known, and to assess their significance for reconstructing the Tiwanaku political economy.

My second line of inquiry will be a close and narrowly focused reading of a limited corpus of stone sculptural compositions dating to the Middle Horizon. The iconography produced by the Tiwanaku state provides the richest record of how its leaders viewed the world, their society, and relations between the people and groups of which it was composed. Though no final and authoritative reading of these texts will ever be possible, a consideration of certain elements of the iconography can illuminate the way in which relations between the state and the individual were structured in determinate architectural and social contexts. Combined with diachronic data relevant to Tiwanaku's antecedent social forms and its initial urbanization, this reading of the iconography produces a novel and compelling picture of the political and moral economy of the Tiwanaku polity and of the process by which it developed.

Modularity and Commensality in the Tiwanaku Monumental Core

Accounts of Tiwanaku as a centralized, hierarchical state have tended to emphasize the significance of the two most salient monuments of the Tiwanaku ceremonial core: the Akapana and the Pumapunku. This is especially clear in Kolata's (1993) formulation of his model of Tiwanaku as a sacred city, an "exemplary ceremonial center" (Couture 2002:11–16) at the pivot of a vast empire. Kolata's emphasis on the major platform mounds downplays the fact that the majority of the structures in Tiwanaku's monumental core are of an entirely different nature. These are the multiple platform/courtyard complexes: the Putuni, Kantatayita, and Kherikala, as well as several unexcavated examples. These structures appear to be Middle Horizon reinterpretations of the sunken court complex: the paradigmatic public space of the Middle and Late Formative periods. Like earlier sunken courts, they seem to be spaces designed and constructed for the hosting of public gatherings and festivities, often understood to involve the consumption of food and drink. In the case of the Putuni, the best known of these structures, Couture (2002) has demonstrated that during the Tiwanaku V period, it comprised a monumental courtyard attached to a large kitchen and a residential complex that she interprets as the palace of an elite lineage or ruling dynasty. The Putuni may therefore be regarded as a hospitality facility: an architectural locus in which social relations were enacted and reproduced through the medium of commensal activity. "Substantial feasting events" (Couture 2002:332) took place in the Putuni courtyard, presumably under the sponsorship of the elite household that occupied the attached residential quarters. The probable storage of ancestral mummy bundles in niches surrounding the Putuni courtyard (Couture 2002; Janusek 2004; Kolata 1993) may have further emphasized the relationship between the feasting events that took place there and the elite group that occupied the palace.

The chronology of the construction and remodeling of the various structures that comprise Tiwanaku's monumental core is not well understood, despite Vranich's (2005, 2006) recent advances in that direction. Currently the best understood of the structures are the Akapana and the Pumapunku (Protzen and Nair 2000, 2002; Vranich 1999, 2001, 2006) and the Putuni (Couture 2002; Couture and Sampeck 2003). The numerous other platform/courtyard groups within the monumental core are poorly known, and some remain untouched by excavation. It is therefore impossible to say when exactly they were built and occupied and which of them may have been in simultaneous use. Couture (2002) tentatively suggests that they may have been constructed sequentially, like the royal palace compounds in Cuzco and Chan Chan, pursuant to customs governing succession. It is equally plausible, however, that many of these structures were in use at the same time and that the core of Tiwanaku was inhabited, at least during the Tiwanaku V phase, by multiple elite residential groups, each with an attached hospitality facility and mortuary complex.

The possibility that multiple structures of this type were in simultaneous use suggests that the activity of hospitality in Tiwanaku may not have been organized exclusively by a unitary state administrative apparatus but may rather have been conducted independently by multiple elite social groups in a heterarchical configuration. The hosting of pilgrims and visitors to the city may therefore not have been an activity of the polity itself, at least not exclusively, but of the multiple segments of which its elite social stratum was composed. This hypothesis is impossible to evaluate with the data that are currently available. If this were the case, however, the organization of the Tiwanaku polity's leadership would appear to have been segmentary. I am in substantial agreement with Couture's statement that the core of Tiwanaku was occupied by "competing elite groups" (Couture 2002:303) and that "the patronage and hosting of large feasts served as critical avenues for expressing elite power and identity" (Couture 2002:304).

Commensal Politics in Tiwanaku Iconography

Tiwanaku art includes many representations of high-status individuals engaged in the act of hospitality. The most important depictions of this activity are the class of stone sculptures I refer to as presentation stelae. This is a class of anthropomorphic stone sculpture depicting a standing person holding a *kero* in the left hand and another object, less securely identified, in the right. Three examples of this class of sculpture—the Bennett, Ponce, and El Fraile monoliths—are preserved intact. Numerous other examples exist in fragmentary or eroded form.

These sculptures display a number of common features that assist us in producing a reading. First of all, they depict a standing individual with both hands held in front of the body (Figure 8.1). The left hand always holds a Tiwanaku drinking cup, or *kero* (Figure 8.2). Rays emanating from the mouth of the *kero* depict the foam and bubbles of *chicha*. The fact that the *kero* is invariably held in the left hand is a detail of great importance. In Inca society a rigid protocol governed the use of the right and left hands in feasting contexts. According to Classen (1993:59), Inca custom dictated that using the left hand "one would offer the cup of *chicha* to an inferior, and with one's right hand to an equal or superior." The reverse also held true: one would receive a cup of *chicha* from an inferior with the left hand and from a superior or equal with the right hand. If the inhabitants of Tiwanaku adhered to a similar protocol, the form of the presentation stelae inscribes a relation of social inequality. The fact that the stela figures hold the *kero* in the left hand automatically places the viewer in a subordinate social position within the social protocol of the feast. It is important to emphasize that this relation of inequality is established through an idiom of commensality; through the act of hospitality, the figures represented in the presentation stelae are constituted as socially superior to the viewer/guest.

The object held in the figure's right hand (Figure 8.3) is less securely identified but is often interpreted as a snuff tablet (Berenguer 1985; Janusek 2006). What is more interesting than the identification of the object itself, however, is the depiction of the hand. The palm side of the left hand is depicted, complete with fingernails and the fleshy ridge (the palm heel) near the wrist. However, the position depicted is clearly anatomically impossible. Holding the right hand in front of the body and oriented palm outward would not only be exceedingly awkward but would position the thumb facing downward, not upward as shown. This is a very curious detail of these sculptures that is present on every preserved example. What does it mean?

The palm of the hand and the thumb would appear in the configuration depicted if the hand were placed behind the body and viewed from the rear. What is being portrayed by the presentation stelae, then (and I owe this insight to Amanda Cohen), is an elite personage standing with the left hand grasping a *chicha*-filled *kero* in front of the body and with the

Figure 8.1. The Ponce Monolith.

FIGURE 8.2. Left hand of the Ponce Monolith.

FIGURE 8.3. Right hand of the Ponce Monolith.

right hand grasping a snuff tablet—or an unidentified object—behind the back. These stelae were apparently designed to be viewed from the front, and the bizarre configuration of the hand was meant to convey the position of the right hand behind the back to viewers standing in front of the sculpture. In other words, multiple perspectives are represented in a single dimension.

If we extend our earlier insight about the protocol of the use of the right and left hands in feasting contexts, a fuller reading of the presentation stelae can be produced. The figure is represented as simultaneously receiving some object or quality from a superior source located to its rear and offering a *kero* filled with *chicha* to a social inferior, or a group of social inferiors, that it is facing. What might be called "the flow of the gift" therefore has a linear structure: a vector progressing from the divine realm (presumably to the west if these figures were placed facing the primary entrances of platform/courtyard complexes such as the Kalasasaya), passing through the body of the elite personage, and finally arriving in the hands of the socially inferior guest in the form of a *kero* of *chicha*. The figure represented in the sculpture is cast as an intermediary between what might be interpreted as the divine and the temporal worlds, between the realm of the supernatural to its rear and the mundane humans assembled before it. Importantly, again, this position of intermediation is cast in terms of commensal relations. The figure represented is constituted as an intermediary by virtue of his or her role as a host. The practice of hospitality—feasting—is therefore implicated at the very core of the production of social inequality in the Tiwanaku polity.

A Reconfiguration of Commensality in the Late Formative

The relation expressed by the presentation stelae—the elite individual constituted as an intermediary figure in a feasting context—represents a dramatic shift from earlier modes of commensality in the southern Titicaca Basin. This shift is documented by a change in the form of the ceramic bowls used to serve food and drink in public contexts. In her analysis of Middle and Late Formative ceramics from the site of Kala Uyuni, Lee Steadman (2007) makes an observation that I think will prove critical to our understanding of early forms of social inequality in the southern Titicaca Basin. Among the many changes in the ceramic assemblage at the Middle–Late Formative transition (around 200 B.C.), changes in the portion of the assemblage dedicated to serving activities were the most pronounced. In the Middle Formative the serving assemblage had been dominated by very large bowls, in some cases more than 30 cm in diameter. The portions associated with serving vessels of this size, employed in contexts of public commensality, would appear to have been larger than an individual serving. Steadman suggests that food may have been served in a communal or "potluck" manner, with multiple individuals helping themselves to food or drink contained in these large bowls. The roles of host and guest would therefore have been distributed widely within any particular assembly. The general mode of commensality in the Middle Formative could be called many-to-many (Figure 8.4a).

At the beginning of the Late Formative 1 period, sometime during the first two centuries B.C., bowls became smaller and more common. A new form replaced the large communal serving bowls of the earlier period: smaller bowls appropriate for the serving of individual portions. These are the buff-paste, red-banded, hemispherical vessels often referred to as Kalasasaya bowls (Figure 8.5), and they are one of the most distinctive diagnostic artifacts of the Late Formative 1 period. Steadman proposes that this

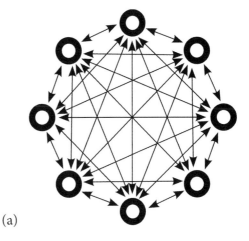
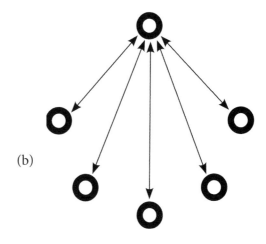

FIGURE 8.4. Modes of commensality inferred from serving vessels: (*a*) Middle Formative; (*b*) Late Formative and Middle Horizon.

FIGURE 8.5. Kalasasaya-style serving bowl, characteristic of the Late Formative 1.

marked change in the character of the serving assemblage can be attributed to a change in the mode of commensality in the context of public hospitality. The old communal serving pattern was replaced, in the Late Formative 1, by a pattern of participants being served individual portions in individually owned ceramic bowls. This change is consistent with the emergence of a better-defined status of "host" and a mode of commensality that can be described as one-to-many (Figure 8.4b). It is precisely this one-to-many mode of commensality that is expressed in the presentation stelae. The small, individual serving bowls of the Late Formative 1 were the conceptual precursors of *keros* and *tazones*, the diagnostic and superabundant individual serving vessels of the Middle Horizon. *Keros* and *tazones* seem to have had a strong association with their owners, and a high percentage of burials are accompanied by one or more vessels of these types. This Middle Horizon mortuary practice was anticipated by the frequent use of red-banded Kalasasaya bowls as mortuary goods during the Late Formative 1 period. Interestingly, ceramic bowls are virtually unknown as grave goods in the Middle Formative, suggesting that serving vessels at this earlier time had not yet acquired a strong identification with their owners.

The fact that this shift—from a many-to-many to a one-to-many mode of commensality in feasting events, combined with the strong cultural identification of an individual with his or her serving vessel—took place at the same time that we see the first appearance of complex, multicommunity political organization (Bandy 2001, 2006, 2007; Bandy and Hastorf 2007a) cannot be fortuitous. I believe that this reconfiguration of the institutions and practices of commensality was profoundly related to the rise of the Late Formative polities of the southern Titicaca Basin, to the attendant increase in the degree of social inequality and scale of political integration, and ultimately to the origins of the Tiwanaku state. The origin of the kind of commensal politics expressed in the presentation stelae is to be found early in the Late Formative.

Tiwanaku Was Not a Marka

The emphasis I have placed on the segmentary organization of the Tiwanaku elite and on the importance of ritual and feasting in the constitution of social difference and hierarchy is compatible with the most influential alternative model of Tiwanaku urbanism and social organization. Juan Albarracin-Jordan (1996) has argued persuasively that Tiwanaku represents a social phenomenon similar to ethnohistorically known Aymara towns, or *markas*. Aspects of this model have also been embraced by other investigators, notably by Janusek (2004). In this model, the city of Tiwanaku was an arena in which the various communities of the Tiwanaku Valley interacted, competed, and negotiated their social relationships within a framework of nested hierarchies. The segmentary nature of Tiwanaku would, in this model, therefore relate to the various constituent communities, each building and operating its own platform/courtyard complex. This is an attractive model, but it is false.

With Carlos Lémuz, I have recently completed a reanalysis of the settlement data from the Tiwanaku heartland: the Katari and Tiwanaku valleys and the Taraco Peninsula. We revisited a large number of sites and applied the current Formative-period ceramic chronology that was not available to Albarracin-Jordan and Mathews when they completed their original Tiwanaku Valley survey. As a result, we now have detailed settlement data for the Formative period in this entire 550-km^2 region and are able to evaluate demographic processes through time in a way that was previously not possible. Some preliminary results of this study have already been presented elsewhere in this volume.

One of the significant results of this restudy has been the realization that the Tiwanaku Valley was largely unpopulated prior to the Middle Horizon. Population levels in the Tiwanaku Valley in the Late Formative period were very low outside of Tiwanaku itself. That is to say that Tiwanaku's foundation (sometime in the first or second century B.C.) and initial growth to urban proportions (probably beginning around A.D. 200) preceded the establishment of the Tiwanaku Valley communities documented by Albarracin-Jordan. Tiwanaku therefore could not have been a product of the nested hierarchies of the Tiwanaku Valley settlement system, as Albarracin-Jordan proposes. Quite the reverse: the nested hierarchies of the Tiwanaku Valley settlement system were a creation of Tiwanaku and came into being only after Tiwanaku had already become a city. An alternative model of Tiwanaku urbanism and political economy is necessary.

Raised-Field Agriculture and Tiwanaku Urban Origins

Cities, argues Yoffee, "are the transformative social environments in which states were themselves created" (2005:45). It is impossible to speak of the origins of Tiwanaku as a state without also considering the origins of Tiwanaku as a city. Tiwanaku rapidly grew to urban proportions beginning sometime late in the Late Formative 1 period, possibly around A.D. 200. Growth was very rapid through the beginning of the Middle Horizon, around A.D. 500. During this 200-to-300-year interval, the occupied area of the site grew from something less than 20 ha to 100 ha or more, well in excess of plausible rates of intrinsic population growth. There can be no doubt that the bulk of the initial urban growth of Tiwanaku was a product of immigration. At the same time that Tiwanaku was experiencing this rapid growth, the nearby Taraco Peninsula, an area densely packed with large, ancient villages already more than 1,000 years old, experienced a pronounced population decline for the first time in its long history of human occupation (Bandy 2001, 2006). These two processes were linked. A compelling argument can be made that a large percentage of the immigrants to Tiwanaku during the Late Formative came from the Taraco Peninsula.

The estimated population of the Taraco Peninsula was reduced from a Late Formative 1 value of about 5,580 to a Late Formative 2 value of 4,380, a growth rate of –0.12 percent annually. Details concerning the calculation of these and subsequent estimates are provided in my dissertation (Bandy 2001). Assuming a rate of intrinsic population growth comparable to that of the Middle Formative, the Taraco Peninsula lost approximately 2,430 estimated inhabitants over the 200-year span of the Late Formative 2. I have estimated elsewhere that this figure represents half (Bandy 2001) or more (Bandy 2007) of the total number of immigrants received by Tiwanaku during its initial period of rapid urban expansion.

Why did thousands of people, whose ancestors had continuously occupied the Taraco Peninsula villages for more than 40 generations, choose, in the space of a few centuries, to relocate their homes and their families to Tiwanaku? What possible enticements could have been offered by the civic leaders of Tiwanaku? The great Middle Horizon florescence of Tiwanaku was the product of this early period of migration. Explaining it is crucial for understanding the evolution of Tiwanaku as a city and as a polity. This question is especially crucial because it requires us to formulate models for how the Tiwanaku elite attracted and retained followers and retainers; for how wealth was created, circulated, and consumed; and for how agricultural surpluses were generated and disposed of. It requires us to create explicit models of the Tiwanaku political economy as it operated in the heartland of the polity.

I believe that the key to explaining this critical event in Andean prehistory is raised-field agriculture. At some point during the Late Formative 1, probably late in the period, a new form of political economy was developed in the small-scale polities of the southern Titicaca Basin. Raised-field agriculture was its central technological element. This new set of strategies for surplus production and appropriation changed the way authority was constituted in these polities and, importantly, transformed the competitive dynamic between these polities. Tiwanaku urbanism, and later Tiwanaku state formation, was the result.

In the Middle Formative, I have argued, status competition in the Taraco Peninsula villages, and in other substantial settlements of the southern Titicaca Basin, centered on the accumulation and distribution of trade goods, including exotic lithic materials (Bandy 2004). Limited wealth accumulation was made possible by tolls from passing caravans linking the western Titicaca Basin with the eastern lowlands: the *yungas* and the *selva*. The southern Titicaca Basin villages constituted what I term decentralized transit communities. Influential personages in these villages established enduring relationships with itinerant traders, essentially exchanging passage through the community territory for preferential access to trade items. These wealth items could then be used as gifts to engender debt and to establish relations of patronage within the community itself. In this way prominent persons in these villages were able to build up dedicated factions of followers that enhanced their local prestige and therefore their bargaining position with the traders. This process is an example of what Dietler and Herbich (2001) call a growth spiral and what might in another idiom be called deviation-amplifying feedback (Maruyama 1963).

This spiraling process of political-capital accumulation in combination with competition between neighboring communities led, by the beginning of the Late Formative 1, to the formation of a number of small-scale polities integrating areas of perhaps several hundred square kilometers under the leadership of a series of central communities. These newly constituted central places included Kala Uyuni on the Taraco Peninsula (Bandy 2001, 2006; Bandy and Hastorf 2007b), Tiwanaku itself in the middle and upper Tiwanaku Valley (Janusek 2004), perhaps Lukurmata in the Katari Valley (Bermann 1994), Kanamarka/Lakaya in the southern Capia area (Bandy 2001; Stanish et al. 1997), Khonkho Wankane to the south of the Quisachata Mountains (Janusek 2006; Janusek et al. 2003), and perhaps Similake and/or Iruhito on the Río Desaguadero and Kallamarka in the upper Tiwanaku Valley (Albarracin-Jordan et al. 1993; Lémuz and Paz 2001). A regional landscape of competing small-scale polities was therefore in place from around 100–200 B.C.

Though we know very little about most of these centers (Tiwanaku, Kala Uyuni, and Khonkho Wankane are the only ones to have been intensively investigated), the peer polity system appears to have been relatively stable for at least 300 years, until the final century of the Late Formative 1 period. It was at approximately this time that Tiwanaku began to grow rapidly, as I argued earlier, and it was at this time also that Kala Uyuni was abandoned and a massive migration episode began. This process would, in the course of three centuries, reduce the population of the Taraco Peninsula by about 20 percent and produce the explosive expansion of Tiwanaku into an urban settlement by A.D. 500 (Bandy 2001, 2006).

Stanish (1994) argues on the basis of settlement evidence from the Juli-Pomata area that raised fields were a crucial component of the complex political economies of Late Formative polities. This cannot have been the case for all of the southern Titicaca Basin Late Formative polities, however. In particular, it is clear that raised-field agriculture played no significant role in the economy of the Taraco Peninsula polity or of Kala Uyuni. There are only 12.7 ha of ancient raised fields located within the Taraco Peninsula survey area, and of these only 2 ha are located within the reconstructed borders of the Taraco Peninsula polity (Bandy 2001). The Taraco Peninsula, unlike the neighboring Katari and Tiwanaku valleys, is entirely unsuited to raised-field agriculture, containing very few areas of high groundwater and virtually no large permanent watercourses. The political economy of Kala Uyuni and of the Taraco Peninsula polity was certainly not based on intensive agricultural production in raised-field systems. It may instead have been an elaborated form of the kind of exchange-based growth spiral that I have described for the Middle Formative, with the leaders of Kala Uyuni, possibly hereditary, monopolizing relations with passing caravans and other foreign parties.

The large-scale transfer of population from the Taraco Peninsula to Tiwanaku that began late in the Late Formative 1 reflects an increase in the importance of raised-field agriculture and a transformation in the nature of interpolity competition in what was later to become the Tiwanaku heartland. A new political economy in the Tiwanaku polity, incorporating raised fields, was inducing residents of the adjacent Taraco Peninsula polity to move to Tiwanaku. Prior to this time, again, these two polities had existed in a state of rough competitive equilibrium, neither gaining an enduring advantage over the other. Raised fields, however, were a technological device unavailable to the leaders of the Taraco Peninsula polity. They were unable to duplicate the innovations of the Tiwanaku polity and were therefore at a competitive disadvantage.

I have argued elsewhere (Bandy 2005) that raised-field agriculture made possible a strategy of staggered production cycles in the southern Titicaca Basin, an area characterized by a tightly circumscribed annual agricultural cycle. This strategy would have made possible the agricultural use of labor during times of the year that were otherwise relatively idle. It therefore permitted an increased overall level of annual surplus production without conflicting with the labor necessary for the subsistence and reproduction of tributary households and communities. The leaders of Tiwanaku constructed raised fields and used the resulting surplus to fund, through the mechanism of "work feasts" (Dietler and Herbich 2001), the construction of more agricultural infrastructure, as well as to build monuments and support permanent retainers. In this way, they created an entirely new kind of growth spiral and an entirely new political economy—one that again could not be reproduced on the Taraco Peninsula. The result was the gradual but inexorable shift of population into the growing settlement of Tiwanaku. This process, probably so slow as to be imperceptible to most of the persons involved, transformed the entire political and cultural landscape of the southern Titicaca Basin in the course of the Late Formative 2.

In any migration, the order of arrival and the length of residence are strong factors determining the relative status of the persons involved. In the case at hand, the kin groups that resided in Tiwanaku prior to its rapid growth formed what Van Gijseghem (2005:124) calls apex families. These kin groups, including but not limited to the leaders of the Tiwanaku polity, controlled the territory of the Tiwanaku Valley and the right to cultivate those raised-field groups that had already been constructed. Newcomers were therefore incorporated into the polity on a subordinate basis. Van Gijseghem (2006) calls this the pioneer effect. They were unable to construct and operate raised fields in the same manner and on the same scale as the longer-term residents. In the work feasts and the festivals, these newcomers were always guests, never hosts; they benefited from the largesse of the established families and may have been given fields and pastures for their own support, but they were unable to compete on an equal basis. Through time, as the new political economy of raised-field work feasts continued to develop, the old families of Tiwanaku expanded their holdings and their wealth, the size of their factions, and the number of their retainers. By the end of the Late Formative 2, the wealth of the apex families of Tiwanaku had grown to the point where they could sponsor the construction of substantial monuments like the Kalasasaya, and the raised-field work feast political economy became increasingly codified, formalized, and institutionalized. I suggest that the beginning of the Middle Horizon marks the point at which this developing relation was crystallized into a class system. The apex families of Tiwanaku had become an aristocratic class presiding over the labor of a vast city of immigrants and the descendants of immigrants.

Quite apart from its causes, the movement of population from the Taraco Peninsula to Tiwanaku had very important long-term effects on interpolity competition in the region. As a result of this migration process, Tiwanaku rapidly grew to a much larger size than any of its erstwhile competitors. In the Late Formative 1, Tiwanaku had been one of many roughly equal political centers in the southern Titicaca Basin. In fact, in terms of population it was considerably smaller than the Taraco Peninsula polity. By the end of the Late Formative 2, Tiwanaku had far outgrown any conceivable rivals and was finally in a position to expand its influence through military means, though whether it did so remains debatable. In any case, Tiwanaku's disproportionate size, by the beginning of the Middle Horizon, left its macro-regional expansion unchecked by any potential rival. The result was the rapid colonization and political incorporation of certain areas within the Titicaca Basin and more distant regions like Moquegua and possibly parts of the Cochabamba Valley (Stanish 2002, 2003).

The city is the mother of the state. This statement converts Yoffee's observation, with which this section began, into a useful aphorism. Tiwanaku as a city resulted from a voluntary and gradual migration of people from an adjacent polity. This migration predictably created and progressively exacerbated a distinction between the original families and the descendants of immigrants. Tiwanaku as a state resulted from the progression of a growth spiral that continually strengthened the difference between these two segments of the city's population, and from the codification, formalization, and naturalization of this distinction. The process of Tiwanaku state formation as I have reconstructed it is therefore radically different from that of, for example, the southern Moche state (Billman 1999, 2002), in which military conquest and force played a primary role. Tiwanaku was a very different city than the roughly contemporary Cerro Oreja and was a very different state than the southern Moche one.

The Tiwanaku Moral Economy

So far I have argued that the elite of Tiwanaku resided in the monumental core of Tiwanaku and were organized segmentally. These segments, the "competing elite groups" Couture mentions, were descended predominantly from the apex families of the Late Formative 2 city and ultimately from the inhabitants of the settlement before it began its rapid growth. The raised-field work feast growth spiral formed the basis of the Tiwanaku political economy. The naturalization and universalization of that institution, and of the role of the various groups and factions of Tiwanaku in relation to it, formed the basis of the

Tiwanaku moral economy. Elite status at Tiwanaku was formulated in a commensal idiom, as illustrated by the presentation stelae. The aristocracy was constituted as a body of permanent hosts, and their subjects as eternal guests.

As I argued earlier, the basic armature of this relationship probably dates to the beginnings of multicommunity political organization in the Late Formative 1, when the predominant mode of commensality, at least on public occasions, shifted from a many-to-many to a one-to-many configuration. It became progressively formalized and codified through the course of the Late Formative 1 and the early Middle Horizon. There are some indications that during the Middle Horizon the social relations underpinning the Tiwanaku political economy as I have described it came to be intertwined with notions of natural and social order to such an extent that we may speak of an integrated moral economy of the Tiwanaku state.

The transaction that takes place between guest and host, sponsor and attendant—this relation that lies at the center of the raised-field work feast growth spiral and is materialized in the presentation stelae—is intimately related to key themes of modern and ethnohistoric Andean cosmology. Reciprocity, says Allen (1988:93), "is like a pump at the heart of Andean life." The reciprocal exchange of labor serves as the cornerstone of the traditional Andean economy and social relations. The concept of balanced reciprocity applies well beyond the economic sphere, however. Reciprocal obligation "extends to domesticated animals and plants, to *pacha*, to the many animated places on the landscape itself, even to the saints" (Allen 1988:93). This concept of universal reciprocal exchange is tied up with the metaphor of the body. In Inca and more recent Andean cultures, the cosmos is conceptualized metaphorically as a human body. This body, human and cosmic, comprises "a structure animated and integrated into a whole by an exchange of fluids" (Classen 1993:25; see also Bastien 1978). Disruption in the orderly flow of these fluids is a cause of illness (in humans) and of more general malaise on the scale of the world and the cosmos. Human relations with the natural and supernatural worlds, then, are a part of the larger life process of the cosmic body and are critical to the continued well-being of the world.

According to Allen, the general energy principle that circulates through the body and the world is called *sami* in Quechua, which she renders in English as "animating essence" (Allen 1988:49). *Sami* should be understood as a general sort of life energy. It is what accounts for the skill of gifted musicians, diviners, and weavers. It is present in the smoke of burning coca leaves, in the foam of beer and carbonated beverages, and in the aroma of cooking foods. The wind, the rainbow, and lightning are all related to the flow of *sami*. However, "the most tangible manifestations of *sami*, without which the earth would lie dormant and unproductive, are water and light" (Allen 1988:51). Water and light, then, are the forms in which *sami* circulates in the world. Rivers and streams are "conceptualized in terms of a vast circulatory system that distributes water throughout the cosmos" (Allen 1988:52). Through the flow of *sami*, the whole of creation is tied together in a web of reciprocal exchange.

The intermediary position of the elite host as expressed in the presentation stelae therefore has a cosmological dimension; the act of offering *chicha* is cast as a component of the circulation of *sami* in the world. This dimension of commensal relations also has ethnographic parallels. Abercrombie (1986) has made an ethnographic study of the *cha'lla* (libation) ritual in a modern Bolivian Aymara community. He claims that the ceremony's sponsor or host situates himself in the role of the *wak'as* (supernatural figures, ancestral or otherwise) in distributing largesse. This activity, "in which relations among men are objectified in the cosmos at large . . . is not mere mystification, as it . . . makes expressible the cultural ordering which gives specific form to the relations of social production" (Abercrombie 1986:146). In other words, the distribution of *chicha* represents half of a cycle of reciprocal exchange, which is properly completed, in this case, by service rendered to the ritual's sponsor. Moreover, this relationship between guest and host is metaphorically equated to that between human beings and the divine.

It is when viewed in this frame that certain elements of Tiwanaku iconography become particularly suggestive. Rays terminating in zoomorphic heads or geometrical figures are common features of Tiwanaku sculptural, ceramic, and textile art. I will refer to them by the generic term directional indicators. The rays emerging from the Ponce Monolith's *kero* (Figures 8.2 and 8.6) are examples of this, in this case terminating in avian heads. These seem to be intended to represent

FIGURE 8.6. The Ponce Monolith left hand; directional indicators marked by arrows.

this to be a reasonable reading in light of the undeniably solar aspect of the figure's visage. In other representations of the Gateway God, other elements are substituted for the feline heads and disks, including rays terminating in avian heads or in outward-facing arrows, which further emphasizes their structural role as directional indicators. These elements seem to be more or less interchangeable, suggesting that what is significant is not the specific figure employed as a distal terminator but rather the fact that all represent flow and circulation.

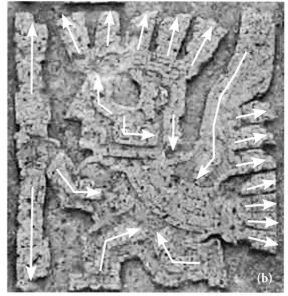

FIGURE 8.7. Details of the Gateway of the Sun; directional indicators marked by arrows: (*a*) central figure; (*b*) attendant figure, lower row.

the presence of a fermented beverage, probably a form of *chicha*. Allen has noted that in modern Cuzco it is understood that "the sami of beer passes spontaneously through its bubbles and foam" (Allen 1988: 50). The use of directional indicators to represent foam and bubbles in this way suggests that these iconographic elements may perhaps be generally interpreted as representing dynamic flows of energy, something akin to the Quechua concept of *sami*.

An examination of the iconography of the Gateway of the Sun's sculpted frieze reveals a proliferation of directional indicators. The most conspicuous examples of these elements are the lines radiating from the face of the Gateway God figure itself (Figure 8.7a). These take the form of linear arrangements of parallel lines terminating in outward-facing feline heads or disks. These have commonly been interpreted as representing rays of the sun, and I consider

Other directional indicators are also present in the figure of the Gateway God (Figure 8.7a). Avian heads emanate from the top and bottom of its staves and from the diagonal bands on its chest, and the "tear bands" around its eyes, rendered as stylized birds, radiate downward-projecting feline heads. In this one figure, then, we can discern indications of the flow of both water (the tear bands) and light (the solar rays), according to Allen the most important manifestations of the cosmic circulation of *sami*. What is perhaps most significant in this image, however, is the uniform orientation of these directional indicators. In the figure of the Gateway God, all of these elements emerge from the body of the deity; there are no examples of inward-facing directional indicators. This is nearly universal in depictions of the deity; I am aware of only one exception to this rule, on a wooden snuff tray from the provincial area of San Pedro de Atacama (Torres 1987: Figure 1).

Representations of the Attendant Figures, by way of contrast, invariably include both inward- and outward-facing directional indicators (Figure 8.7b). In depictions of these beings, there are generally four directional elements oriented inward, into their bodies. Two of these are initiated from the feet, one from the forward-projecting hand, and another from the wing. Outward-projecting elements include a tear band and elements emanating from the wings, headdress, and staves and from the bags the figures carry suspended from their shoulders. What is notable about the outward-projecting directional indicators in the Attendant Figures is that they invariably are oriented either vertically or posterior to the figures. Therefore, in the main panel of the Gateway Frieze there are no directional indicators that face the central figure of the Gateway God. The overall flow of energy represented in the panel is a concentric or centrifugal one (Figure 8.8). *Sami* emanates from the body of the Gateway God, in part being absorbed and circulated through the bodies of the Attendant Figures. But what is most striking in this tableau, when it is viewed from the standpoint of the ideal of balanced reciprocity and uninterrupted circulation, is its lack of balance. The circulatory system that is represented is not a complete one. I contend that this lack of balance represents the central rhetorical strategy of the Gateway Frieze and the foundation of the Tiwanaku moral economy.

When interpreted in this fashion, and in light of more recent Andean notions of cosmology and social order, the Gateway of the Sun and the presentation stelae employ the same rhetorical strategy. Each can be seen to portray the flow of *sami*, or its conceptual equivalent, from a central figure. In the case of the presentation stelae, the central figure is an elite individual or deified ancestor depicted as a host in the act of offering *chicha* to a guest or to an assembly of guests. In the case of the Gateway Frieze, the central figure is portrayed as the divine source of energy that subsequently circulates through the bodies of various secondary or intermediary figures while always progressing outward according to a centrifugal logic. Most importantly, though, each of these compositions is essentially incomplete: energy flows in one direction only, outward from the central figure. The reciprocal motion, completing the cycle of *sami* in the world, remains unrepresented and is effected only by the actions of the viewer. The rhetoric employed involves the individual viewer intimately and directly in maintaining the balance of the cosmos.

The iconography of the Gateway of the Sun, then, when experienced in contexts of elite-sponsored hos-

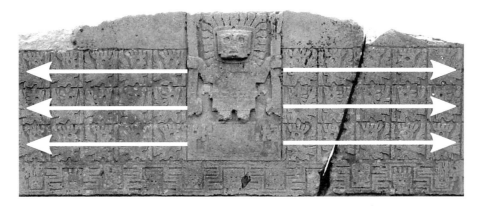

FIGURE 8.8. The flow of *sami* in the gateway frieze

pitality, seems to have been designed to evoke a sense of obligation on the part of its viewers and to attach this obligation to the sponsor of the event or to the state. When considered alone, the iconography presents a system out of balance, which is only completed by the actions of its viewers—actions, it is implied, that are a moral imperative. Interpreted in this way, Tiwanaku iconography is not a threat, like a display of trophies or a representation of violence. It is an argument, a proposition about proper behavior and moral conduct that demands not acquiescence but action. It is a call to sacrifice. And that sacrifice, particularly of labor—to construct and operate raised fields and to erect monuments—and allegiance, formed the basis of the Tiwanaku political economy and at the same time guaranteed the continued well-being of the social and natural world.

Conclusions

Tiwanaku state formation, as I have reconstructed it, resulted from a growth spiral involving work feasts related to raised-field construction and cultivation. This process began sometime during the Late Formative 1 period and was probably a general social dynamic in small-scale polities throughout the Titicaca Basin at this time. The growth spiral of Tiwanaku progressed far beyond that of other contemporaneous polities, however, because of an accident of history and geography. The adjacent Taraco Peninsula, one of the most densely populated areas in the Titicaca Basin at the time and the seat of a rival polity to Tiwanaku, was unsuited to raised-field agriculture. The leaders of the Taraco Peninsula polity were therefore unable to participate in this new form of political economy and gradually began to lose followers to the leaders of Tiwanaku.

The resulting centuries-long migration from the Taraco Peninsula to Tiwanaku in large part accounts for Tiwanaku's initial urbanism. It also had the important effect of establishing a fundamental distinction within the emerging city between the longtime residents of Tiwanaku and the newer arrivals. The former possessed rights to land and raised-field infrastructure that the latter did not. This initial distinction gradually gave rise to a class distinction, as the apex families and lineages of Tiwanaku came to accumulate disproportionate wealth and power and, eventually, to constitute an aristocracy.

The elite of Tiwanaku owed their wealth and their elevated status to their increasingly institutionalized role as hosts in work feasts related to agricultural production and, increasingly as time wore on, to monument construction. The institution of the work feast was the central feature of the emerging Tiwanaku political economy. The institution itself, and the relation of various social segments to it, became increasingly formalized and ritualized through time. By the Middle Horizon a body of thought had developed that situated that institution and its participants within the context of a developed cosmological model. The outlines of this moral economy can be discerned in the elite iconography that had emerged by the beginning of the Middle Horizon and especially in the stone sculptures from the city's monumental core: the Gateway of the Sun and the presentation stelae.

Tiwanaku was therefore what we might call a hospitality state. Its political and moral economies revolved around the institution of the work feast—an institution that no doubt became increasingly elaborate and grandiose through time. Work feasts, in the Middle Horizon, were carried out in the platform/courtyard complexes I discussed before, which were dedicated hospitality facilities attached to the residences of aristocratic families. It is possible that the presentation stelae literally stood in for the leaders or ancestral figures of those families on these occasions. The Tiwanaku polity, conceived of in this way, had no single strong leadership position or central bureaucratic institutions and only weakly developed mechanisms of social coercion. In this way it was probably very different from the contemporaneous Wari and Moche states of Peru. Its expansion beyond the southern Titicaca Basin was quite limited. It had little territorial ambition or martial drive. It was more of a city-state, albeit one with a few distant colonies and possessions, than an empire.

The Middle Horizon communities of the Tiwanaku Valley, and perhaps the Katari Valley also, represent agricultural estates founded and managed by the aristocratic lineages of Tiwanaku to augment their production of an agricultural surplus. Their inhabitants were retainers, followers, or junior members of these elite groups. The Tiwanaku Valley was in no sense an ancient social substrate that was implicated in Tiwanaku urbanism and state formation. It was entirely a creation of the city and its leadership.

The "Tiwanaku state," properly speaking, may never have existed. What did exist was a heterarchically organized group of aristocratic lineages that acted independently of one another but on occasion undertook common projects. These shared projects included the construction of unitary civic monuments, such as the Akapana and the Pumapunku, and perhaps concerted military action in the face of a common threat. However, virtually all other activity was organized independently. The colonization of the Moquegua Valley is perhaps the best-understood example of this process (see Goldstein this volume and Williams this volume). The multiethnic and heterarchical colonial pattern that has recently been recognized in Moquegua by Goldstein and Owen (Goldstein 2004; Owen 2005; Owen and Goldstein 2001) can now be seen as a result of independent colonial projects undertaken by two or more of Tiwanaku's aristocratic lineages. Other external relations involving regions beyond the southern Titicaca Basin should be expected to display an equally diverse structure.

The model of Tiwanaku as a hospitality state that I have presented is clearly provisional and tentative. I have taken full advantage of the license granted by the editors of this volume to venture rather further into speculation than I might otherwise have done. However, the model does account for many curious features of Tiwanaku as a city and as a regional phenomenon, and for particularities of its diachronic development, that have not been addressed by competing models. The model of Tiwanaku as a hospitality state meets the challenge formulated by Bermann in the quotation that begins this chapter: to account for the dramatic differences that are apparent between Tiwanaku and other major Andean polities. Hospitality state or no, this is a challenge that must be met.

References Cited

Abercrombie, Thomas
   1986   The Politics of Sacrifice: An Aymara Cosmology in Action. Unpublished Ph.D. dissertation, Department of Anthropology, University of Chicago, Chicago.

Albarracin-Jordan, Juan
   1996   Tiwanaku Settlement System: The Integration of Nested Hierarchies in the Lower Tiwanaku Valley. *Latin American Antiquity* 7(3):183–210.

Albarracin-Jordan, Juan, Carlos Lémuz Aguirre, and Jose Luis Paz Soria
   1993   Investigaciones en Kallamarca: Primer informe de prospección. *Textos antropológicos* 6:11–123.

Allen, Catherine
   1988   *The Hold Life Has*. Smithsonian Institution Press, Washington, D.C.

Bandy, Matthew S.
   2001   Population and History in the Ancient Titicaca Basin. Unpublished Ph.D. dissertation, Department of Anthropology, University of California, Berkeley.
   2004   Trade and Social Power in the Southern Titicaca Basin Formative. In *Foundations of Power in the Prehispanic Andes*, edited by Christina A. Conlee, Dennis Ogburn, and Kevin Vaughn, pp. 91–111. Archaeological Papers of the American Anthropological Association 14. American Anthropological Association, Washington, D.C.
   2005   Energetic Efficiency and Political Expediency in Titicaca Basin Raised Field Agriculture. *Journal of Anthropological Archaeology* 24(3):271–296.
   2006   Early Village Society in the Formative Period in the Southern Lake Titicaca Basin. In *Andean Archaeology*. Vol. 3, *North and South*, edited by William H. Isbell and Helaine Silverman, pp. 210–236. Springer, New York.

Bandy, Matthew S., and Christine A. Hastorf
   2007a   An Introduction to Kala Uyuni and the Taraco Peninsula Polity. In *Kala Uyuni: An Early Political Center in the Southern Lake Titicaca Basin*, edited by Matthew Bandy and Christine A. Hastorf, pp. 1–12. Contributions of the Archaeological Research Facility 64. Archaeological Research Facility, Berkeley.
   2007b   Kala Uyuni and the Titicaca Basin Formative. In *Kala Uyuni: An Early Political Center in the Southern Lake Titicaca Basin*, edited by Matthew Bandy and Christine A. Hastorf, pp. 135–144. Contributions of the Archaeological Research Facility 64. Archaeological Research Facility, Berkeley.

Bastien, Joseph W.
   1978   *Mountain of the Condor: Metaphor and Ritual in an Andean Ayllu*. West Publishing, Saint Paul.

Berenguer Rodriguez, Jose
   1985   Evidencias de inhalación de alucinógenos en esculturas Tiwanaku. *Chungara* 14:61–66.

Bermann, Marc
   1994   *Lukurmata: Household Archaeology in Prehispanic Bolivia*. Princeton University Press, Princeton, New Jersey.

Billman, Brian
   1999 Reconstructing Prehistoric Political Economies and Cycles of Political Power in the Moche Valley, Peru. In *Settlement Pattern Studies in the Americas: Fifty Years since Virú*, edited by Brian Billman and Gary Feinman, pp. 131–159. Smithsonian Institution Press, Washington, D.C.
   2002 Irrigation and the Origins of the Southern Moche State on the North Coast of Peru. *Latin American Antiquity* 13(4):371–400.

Classen, Constance
   1993 *Inca Cosmology and the Human Body*. University of Utah Press, Salt Lake City.

Couture, Nicole C.
   2002 The Construction of Power: Monumental Space and Elite Residence at Tiwanaku, Bolivia. Unpublished Ph.D. dissertation, Department of Anthropology, University of Chicago, Chicago.

Couture, Nicole C., and Kathryn Sampeck
   2003 Putuni: A History of Palace Architecture in Tiwanaku. In *Tiwanaku and Its Hinterland: Archaeology and Paleoecology of an Andean Civilization*. Vol. 2, *Urban and Rural Archaeology*, edited by Alan L. Kolata, pp. 226–263. Smithsonian Institution Press, Washington, D.C.

Dietler, Michael D., and Ingrid Herbich
   2001 Feasts and Labor Mobilization: Dissecting a Fundamental Economic Practice. In *Feasts: Archaeological and Ethnographic Perspectives on Food, Politics, and Power*, edited by Michael Dietler and Brian Hayden, pp. 240–264. Smithsonian Institution Press, Washington, D.C.

Goldstein, Paul
   2004 *Andean Diaspora: The Tiwanaku Colonies and the Origins of South American Empire*. University Press of Florida, Gainesville.

Isbell, William H.
   2004 Palaces and Politics of Huari, Tiwanaku and the Middle Horizon. In *Palaces of the Ancient New World*, edited by Susan Toby Evans and Joanne Pillsbury, pp. 191–246. Dumbarton Oaks, Washington, D.C.

Isbell, William H., and Katharina J. Schreiber
   1978 Was Huari a State? *American Antiquity* 43(3):372–389.

Janusek, John Wayne
   2003 Vessels, Time, and Society: Toward Ceramic Chronology in the Tiwanaku Heartland. In *Tiwanaku and Its Hinterland: Archaeology and Paleoecology of an Andean Civilization*. Vol. 2, *Urban and Rural Archaeology*, edited by Alan L. Kolata, pp. 30–94. Smithsonian Institution Press, Washington, D.C.
   2004 *Identity and Power in the Ancient Andes: Tiwanaku Cities through Time*. Routledge, New York.
   2006 The Changing "Nature" of Tiwanaku Religion and the Rise of an Andean State. *World Archaeology* 38(3):469–492.

Janusek, John W., Arik T. Ohnstad, and Andrew P. Roddick
   2003 Khonkho Wankane and the Rise of Tiwanaku. *Antiquity* 77(296). Electronic document, http://antiquity.ac.uk/ProjGall/janusek/janusek.html, accessed December 31, 2003.

Kolata, Alan
   1986 The Agricultural Foundations of the Tiwanaku State: A View from the Heartland. *American Antiquity* 51(4):13–28.
   1993 *The Tiwanaku: Portrait of an Andean Civilization*. Blackwell, Cambridge.
   2003 The Social Production of Tiwanaku: Political Economy and Authority in a Native Andean State. In *Tiwanaku and Its Hinterland: Archaeology and Paleoecology of an Andean Civilization*. Vol. 2, *Urban and Rural Archaeology*, edited by Alan L. Kolata, pp. 449–472. Smithsonian Institution Press, Washington, D.C.

Lémuz Aguirre, Carlos, and Jose Luis Paz Soria
   2001 Nuevas consideraciones acerca del Período Formativo en Kallamarka. *Textos antropológicos* 13:93–110.

Maruyama, Magoroh
   1963 The Second Cybernetics: Deviation-Amplifying Mutual Causal Processes. *American Scientist* 51(2):164–179.

McEwan, Gordon F.
   1989 The Wari Empire in the Southern Peruvian Highlands: A View from the Provinces. In *The Nature of Wari: A Reappraisal of the Middle Horizon Period in Peru*, edited by R. M. Czwarno, F. M. Meddens, and A. Morgan, pp. 53–71. BAR International Series 525. British Archaeological Reports, Oxford.
   2005 *Pikillacta: The Wari Empire in Cuzco*. University of Iowa Press, Iowa City.

Owen, Bruce
   2005 Distant Colonies and Explosive Collapse: The Two Stages of the Tiwanaku Diaspora in the Osmore Drainage. *Latin American Antiquity* 16(1):45–80.

Owen, Bruce, and Paul Goldstein
   2001 Tiwanaku en Moquegua: Interacciones regionales y colapso. In *Huari y Tiwanaku: Modelos vs. evidencias*, Pt. 2, edited by Peter Kaulicke and William H. Isbell, pp. 169–188. Boletín de Arqueología PUCP No. 5. Pontificia Universidad Católica del Perú, Lima.

Protzen, Jean-Pierre, and Stella Nair
   2000 On Reconstructing Tiwanaku Architecture. *Journal of the Society of Architectural Historians* 59:358–371.

2002 The Gateways of Tiwanaku: Symbols or Passages? In *Andean Archaeology*. Vol. 2, *Art, Landscape, and Society*, edited by William H. Isbell and Helaine Silverman, pp. 189–223. Springer, New York.

Schreiber, Katharina J.
1987 Conquest and Consolidation: A Comparison of the Wari and Inka Occupations of a Highland Peruvian Valley. *American Antiquity* 52:266–284.
1991 Jincamocco: A Huari Administrative Center in the South Central Highlands of Peru. In *Huari Administrative Structure: Prehistoric Monumental Architecture and State Government*, edited by W. Isbell and G. McEwan, pp. 199–213. Dumbarton Oaks, Washington, D.C.
1992 *Wari Imperialism in Middle Horizon Peru*. University of Michigan Museum of Anthropology, Ann Arbor.
2001 The Wari Empire of Middle Horizon Peru: The Epistemological Challenge of Documenting an Empire without Documentary Evidence. In *Empires: Perspectives from Archaeology and History*, edited by Susan Alcock, Terence D'Altroy, Kathleen Morrison, and Carla Sinopoli, pp. 70–92. Cambridge University Press, Cambridge.

Stanish, Charles
1994 The Hydraulic Hypothesis Revisited: Lake Titicaca Basin Raised Fields in Theoretical Perspective. *Latin American Antiquity* 5(4):312–332.
2002 Tiwanaku Political Economy. In *Andean Archaeology*. Vol. 1, *Variations in Sociopolitical Organization*, edited by William Isbell and Helaine Silverman, pp. 161–198. Kluwer Academic/Plenum Publishers, New York.
2003 *Ancient Titicaca: The Evolution of Complex Society in Southern Peru and Northern Bolivia*. University of California Press, Berkeley.

Stanish, C., E. de la Vega, Lee H. Steadman, C. Chávez Justo, K. Frye, L. Onofre Mamani, M. Seddon, and P. Calisaya Chuquimia
1997 *Archaeological Survey in the Juli-Desaguadero Region of Lake Titicaca Basin, Southern Peru*. Fieldiana Anthropology. Field Museum of Natural History, Chicago.

Steadman, Lee H.
2007 Ceramic Analysis. In *Kala Uyuni: An Early Political Center in the Southern Lake Titicaca Basin*, edited by Matthew Bandy and Christine Hastorf, pp. 67–112. Archaeological Research Facility, Berkeley.

Torres, Constantino
1987 The Iconography of the Prehispanic Snuff Trays from San Pedro de Atacama, Northern Chile. *Andean Past* 1:191–245.

Van Gijseghem, Hendrik
2005 Migration, Agency, and Social Change on a Prehistoric Frontier: The Paracas-Nasca Transition in the Southern Nasca Drainage, Peru. Unpublished Ph.D. dissertation, Department of Anthropology, University of California, Santa Barbara.
2006 A Frontier Perspective on Paracas Society and Nasca Ethnogenesis. *Latin American Antiquity* 17(4):419–444.

Vranich, Alexei
1999 Interpreting the Meaning of Ritual Spaces: The Temple Complex of Pumapunku, Tiwanaku, Bolivia. Unpublished Ph.D. dissertation, Department of Anthropology, University of Pennsylvania, Philadelphia.
2001 The Akapana Pyramid: Reconsidering Tiwanaku's Monumental Center. *Boletín de Arqueología PUCP* 5:295–308.
2005 The Development of the Ritual Core of Tiwanaku. In *Tiwanaku: Papers from the 2005 Mayer Center Symposium at the Denver Art Museum*, edited by Margaret Young-Sánchez, pp. 11–34. Denver Art Museum, Denver.
2006 The Construction and Reconstruction of Ritual Space at Tiwanaku, Bolivia (A.D. 500–1000). *Journal of Field Archaeology* 31(2):121–136.

Williams, Patrick R.
2001 Cerro Baúl: A Wari Center on the Tiwanaku Frontier. *Latin American Antiquity* 12(1):67–83.

Yoffee, Norman
2005 *Myths of the Archaic State: Evolution of the Earliest Cities, States, and Civilizations*. Cambridge University Press, Cambridge.

9
WHAT WAS TIWANAKU?

CHARLES STANISH

The culture of Tiwanaku represents one of the great civilizations of the ancient world. It is easily on par in size, complexity, and sophistication with the more well-known civilizations of the Near East, Mediterranean, and Asia. In fact, Tiwanaku eclipses many other famous civilizations of the classical world in many aspects of interest here—physical size and architectural complexity of the capital, population size, regional dominance, economic production, long-distance exchange, and the complexity of its sociopolitical organization.

In spite of this, some scholars still do not recognize what is obvious to archaeologists working elsewhere in the world who review the data—that Tiwanaku was a state society with all of the attributes common to the great ancient civilizations of the rest of the world. The reasons for these views are many and all are certainly legitimate, but several stand out. First, the traditions of scholarship in the Andes that were set up in the 1960s, as so nicely described by Moseley in his paper in this volume, have inadvertently come together to diminish the achievements of Andean civilizations such as Tiwanaku. This is reinforced by a lack of texts for cultures such as Tiwanaku. Furthermore, anthropological archaeologists working in the Andes have adopted what I call a straw-man model for premodern states. The expectations of this model can never be met because they are unrealistic and do not match any known state in world history. As a result, an analysis of Tiwanaku using the criteria found in this model will always conclude that it was not a complex, archaic state. Finally, until recently we have had few modern archaeologists of indigenous descent who have worked on Tiwanaku. In this paper I will outline the latest data for Tiwanaku and try to place it in a broader comparative and intellectual context.

RESEARCH TRADITIONS

Andeanists can understandably be a somewhat insular group, working in an area that in sheer distance alone would touch three areas of Old World first-generation state development (from the Nile to the Indus). As a result, it is not often that Andeanists refer in any depth to other cultures around the world that are structurally similar to those found in western South America. Most Andeanists are surprised to find that the iconic "city" center of Mycenae in the ancient Greek Peloponnese—the "city of kings"; the place founded by Perseus, husband of Andromeda and father of Agamemnon and Menelaus; home to palaces, guardhouses, and storehouses; and a principal city in the Trojan War—was, at its height, less than 3 ha in size. That is correct—3 ha. The architectural core of Mycenae fits inside the area bounded by the Sunken Court, Akapana, and Kalasasaya in Tiwanaku. The total, maximum size of the "city" of Mycenae was no more than 75 ha, including all surrounding domestic settlement and cemeteries. Aegean archaeologist Todd Whitelaw (2001:29) actually estimates it at a mere 40 ha. The entire settlement complex of Mycenae was about half the size of just the architectural core of Tiwanaku. In short, Tiwanaku is at least six times larger than the settlement of Mycenae and is comparable in size to the great Minoan Crete cities of the Bronze Age. Whitelaw (2001:29) estimates the maximum size of Knossos at 80 ha, about 7.5 times smaller than that currently proposed for Tiwanaku. Tiwanaku, by any comparison to many other ancient cities, is as architecturally complex and is in the general site range of non-imperial archaic states in most areas of the world.[1]

There are no historical documents available for the Middle Horizon and only vague references to the Late Intermediate periods. The lack of documents represents a huge difference between the Andes and many parts of the Old World, particularly the Near East and Mesopotamia. At Mycenae, for instance, we have the great Homeric epics to tell us that King Agamemnon led armies of thousands to Troy. We have Linear B fragments that describe the administration of state societies in Bronze Age times. If we had comparable documents for the culture of Tiwanaku, perhaps one that told of the exploits of the legendary King Taypihuanca, who with his gold-studded scepter led his army and navy to the north, defeated the combined forces of the swift-footed Taraceños and Arapans, and returned with the great trophy of the Thunderbolt Stela on a huge triumphal march around the lake, we would perhaps be more sympathetic to viewing Tiwanaku in the same way we view comparable Old World civilizations.

As mentioned, we unfortunately have few scholars of indigenous descent who work on Andean archaeology. One can imagine the frustration of someone who has a genealogical or emotional connection with Tiwanaku culture and who has to live with the dizzying array of social and political tensions that swirl around this magnificent civilization. Here is an ancient society with a capital as large as or larger than any Mycenaean or Minoan Aegean Bronze Age center and comparable in size to the city of London in the sixteenth century. It has demonstrated influence around a vast area from desert to forest, created beautiful works of art on a massive scale, carved huge stelae with stones dragged from 20 km away, and built roads, temples, and palaces, and in spite of all this evidence, foreign scholars simply will not give their ancestors credit for creating a civilization on par with those of the Mediterranean, Mesoamerica, and Mesopotamia. I am firmly convinced that if more indigenous peoples were involved in the writing of Tiwanaku history, the archaeological fairy tales of a vast empty ceremonial center would disappear as fast as they were created.

These factors have combined to create a very curious research tradition in the region that has disengaged the study of Tiwanaku and other Andean cultures from comparative anthropological and historical analysis. Some scholars think that this is appropriate and that "lo Andino" should be the basis for our studies. In my opinion, such disengagement does us a disservice and opens the doors to archaeological flights of fancy similar to those of the generation of Mayanists who argued for the "peaceful" Mayans who built "empty ceremonial" cities like Quirigua and Tikal. Archaeological interpretation must be grounded in something real. If it is not grounded in the data of history and ethnography utilizing rigid criteria of verification, then it will be no more than just-so stories that reinforce some particular social or academic fad at any moment.

Within this tradition of research in the Andes, perhaps the greatest theoretical and methodological flaw is to set up a straw-man argument in the form of the traditional state model of complex, coercive, stratified societies and to then conclude that Tiwanaku did not fit this model. I will argue below that this conception of hierarchical states is fatally flawed. It is a straw-man argument that does not represent reality anywhere on the planet, anytime in history. Once the straw-man model is rejected, the way is then open to the most creative models imaginable. Some Andean scholars, for instance, pick and choose elements from Tiwanaku's great religious traditions and architectural feats to argue that there were no political hierarchies. From a comparative anthropological and historical point of view, that is, in all due respect, an untenable theoretical position. No society of any size and complexity—certainly one that was capable of building a few square kilometers of planned urban space out of hewn volcanic rocks—has ever existed without some kind of hierarchical political structure that mobilized and organized human labor. Some scholars reduce this great capital city of a great ancient state to a place where peaceful peasants came together to eat, drink, dance, and reinforce social bonds. The reification of contemporary Western spiritual fads in scholarly work is indeed intriguing from the perspective of intellectual history but is at odds with the empirical data from Tiwanaku as well as from systematic comparative analysis of other states of similar size and complexity from the rest of the ancient world.

In this paper, I will first try to briefly summarize what we know, empirically, about Tiwanaku. Second, I will compare some of these empirical facts with other historically documented civilizations from other areas of the world. Ultimately, I conclude that while Tiwanaku, like all ancient states, had unique characteristics, it is structurally similar to the classical nonimperial civilizations in the Old World as well as to those in the Americas such as Teotihuacán, Tula, and the classic Maya states. To be sure, it is not an empire like that of the Inca. But it was certainly a centralized and complex political entity that we recognize as a first-generation state with a dominant elite and many other powerful groups that interacted in a myriad of ways.

Tiwanaku, like all ancient states, was an urbanized polity that created a huge city center for economic, political, social, religious, and cultural activities and expanded its influence, albeit selectively, over a vast area. Tiwanaku was not just a ritual gathering spot, a big place to throw ideologically charged parties, an empty religious center, an astronomical observatory, or a pilgrimage destination. Like every great capital among the world's civilizations, it had elements of most or all of these, sustained by a political and economic organization that produced, exchanged, and created valuable resources, backed by a military and religious elite that created Tiwanaku's political ideology and cultural values and offered them to, promoted them to, or forced them on peoples who lived in an area about the size of the modern U.S. state of California. And it successfully did this for almost a half millennium.

What We Know Now

Archaeologists working diligently over the past few generations have unearthed the cultures of Tiwanaku. Unlike its counterparts in the ancient classical world, there are no surviving documents from Tiwanaku times. As a result, we do not have the rich narratives that bring to life the sophistication and complexity of these cultures with ease. We have to work much harder to unlock the secrets of ancient Tiwanaku using all the tools, both theoretical and methodological, at our disposal. By combining state-of-the-art fieldwork with sophisticated theoretical work, we are able to deduce the broad structure of Tiwanaku society. The results of some of this work can be summarized into a series of empirical observations:

1. Tiwanaku was an urbanized, class-based society, centered in a huge city located on the altiplano in the eponymous site in Bolivia.

2. Tiwanaku had a large, permanent resident population that numbered at least 20,000 and probably much more. There was an additional rural population in the Tiwanaku Valley as well as people living in quasi-urban sites such as Lukurmata on the Taraco Peninsula. The total population for the Tiwanaku polity most likely reached up to six figures.

3. Tiwanaku maintained colonies on a large scale, the only one seriously studied to date being the Omo complex in Moquegua. Others include the Azapa Valley in northern Chile and Cochabamba in Bolivia.

4. Tiwanaku maintained long-term and long-distance trade relationships with autonomous and semiautonomous groups throughout a vast area in a dizzying array of ecological zones. The most famous of these is San Pedro de Atacama, where local elites adopted Tiwanaku accoutrements and maintained some kind of economic trade relationship.

5. The city of Tiwanaku hosted a class of expert craft specialists, mainly in architecture and artisan goods such as pottery, metal, and cloth. Tiwanaku artisans engaged in commodity production in pottery and cloth and possibly in other objects as well.

6. Tiwanaku artists drew off of a millennium of tradition, borrowing and reinterpreting Chavín, Pucará, and other highland cultures in the Andes. These Tiwanaku artists created works of unprecedented sophistication and beauty, most

individual perception of what Tiwanaku was in the past. Not surprisingly, those of us who see Tiwanaku as a classic archaic state tend to estimate high, while those on the other side tend to estimate low.

In this light, it is possible to briefly review the different modes of assessing Tiwanaku population:

Carrying Capacity

The work of Kolata and his associates mentioned above suggests that a very high population density was possible in the greater Titicaca region. While this in and of itself does not prove high populations, it indicates that such levels are theoretically possible. While one could alter these figures and assumptions, the fact is that the altiplano in that region, with raised fields and more rainfall, has a capacity to support a fairly dense population, at least in the greater Tiwanaku region.

Historical Data

Demographic data from the Toledo Tasa are very precise for *encomiendas* in the Titicaca region, but we do not know how dispersed these populations were. Places in the northern lake area like Saman, Taraco, and Paucarcolla have around 4,000 to 5,000 total inhabitants in the *encomienda* lists. The towns themselves were around 1 km² in size. Including the entire *encomienda* tribute list from these towns would still give a population figure below the 10,000 per square kilometer used in earlier estimates for Tiwanaku. However, these were entirely rural towns made up almost completely of farmers and herders, with no economies of scale, production areas, intensive trade, and so forth. We also know that male taxpayers would leave the area before the census takers came. Many of the males also were meeting tribute obligations, working in the gold-bearing areas of Carabaya or possibly even in the silver mines of Bolivia.

Comparative Analysis

As mentioned above, Tiwanaku is almost an order of magnitude larger than the icon of Aegean Bronze Age archaeology, Mycenae. It is also larger or about the same scale as the four great Minoan cites of Phaestos, Knossos, Malia, and Zakros. Whitelaw (2001:29) estimates Neopalatial Knossos at its height to have around 14,000 to 18,000 people in an urban area of around 80 ha. Averaged over the entire site area, he calculates a population density of 200 to 250 per hectare. That would give a density substantially larger than the 10,000 used in earlier estimates for Tiwanaku.

Skipping forward to the medieval period in England, the town of London in A.D. 1086 had approximately 17,850 people (Barron 2004) in an area substantially smaller than that estimated for Tiwanaku. In a short two centuries, that figure rose to between 50,000 and 80,000, falling again in the fourteenth century after plagues decimated Britain. Around 1300, the largest cities in Europe, Florence and Paris, had about 100,000 inhabitants each.

A famous map of the city of London in 1562 depicts an urban space of approximately 300 ha, from the Tower in the east to Somerset House in the west. The city is bounded on the south by the Thames and on the north by pasture lands. Combined with the city of Westminster about 2 km to the southwest, the urban space of greater sixteenth-century London is roughly equal to the 500 to 600 ha estimated for Tiwanaku. The population density would have been around 10,000 to 15,000 people per square kilometer, a number consistent with earlier assumptions for Tiwanaku. If London had been abandoned in the late sixteenth century, the architectural signature would look similar to that of Tiwanaku—a few stone buildings in ruins with the bulk of the former city covered in sod mounds. The analogy is not unwarranted.

Coincidentally, the population density of sixteenth-century London is about the same as that of modern Puno, Peru. Puno has about 125,000 people living in about 6 km² of area; the vast majority are single families living in single- or two-story adobe or brick houses. There are many open spaces in Puno as well. The same densities hold for Juliaca and other modern towns in the region. The problem here, of course, is the commensurability of modern towns and pre-Hispanic Tiwanaku.

From a worldwide perspective, estimates for greater Tiwanaku below 40,000 appear to be quite low compared to cities of similar geographical size and complexity. The 15,000 population range is similar to that of settlements like Cahokia, a complex settlement to be sure but hardly a fitting analogy to Tiwanaku.

Empirical Data from Survey and Excavation

What we can say is that there was an indisputable presence of about 1 km² of a relatively dense urban construction (ritual constructions, buildings, plazas, alleyways, palaces, temples, and so forth), built in carved and shaped basalt, sandstone, and andesite blocks.

We can also say that surrounding the core of Tiwanaku comprised several additional square kilometers of residential and domestic-use space. There was likewise a substantial population of nonurban villagers who lived from the edges of Tiwanaku itself up to the lakeshore, a distance of some 17 km. This is based upon the survey work of Albarracin-Jordan (1992, 1996a, 1996b) and Mathews (1992). During their Tiwanaku IV and V periods, they documented hundreds of settlements in the region between suburban Tiwanaku and the lake edge.

To the north was the Katari Valley and the Taraco Peninsula. Sites such as Lukurmata reached at least 1.5 km² in size (Stanish 1989). Dozens of other Tiwanaku sites populated the Katari Basin and the Taraco Peninsula. Bandy (2001) surveyed the Taraco Peninsula. His data indicate a population drop during the Late Formative 2 period, suggesting an out-migration to Tiwanaku, an observation that confirms the settlement pattern dynamics in the Tiwanaku Valley. During the Middle Horizon, the population rebounded to near normal levels while Tiwanaku continued to grow at a very high rate. These data strongly suggest that the initial growth of Tiwanaku was a result of a depopulation of the surrounding area, but once established as an urban center, this part of greater Tiwanaku was fully repopulated. These data support a population estimate for Tiwanaku on the high end.

Archaeologists have also excavated outside the core area of the Tiwanaku urban zone and have found fairly dense domestic settlement. The modern town of Tiwanaku is full of archaeological debris from the late Tiwanaku IV and V periods. We do not know the extent of the entire settlement complex at Tiwanaku. Certainly, there are areas near the architectural core that do not have evidence of settlement. However, there are also areas near the core with very intense domestic occupations. In particular, the work of Alconini (1995), Couture (2002), Janusek (2008), Escalante (1997), Portugal (1993), Rivera Casanovas (1994), and many others has uncovered craft production and residential areas. Tiwanaku artisans manufactured a great variety of commodities, from musical instruments to textiles. These commodities have been found in distant areas, such as San Pedro de Atacama in northern Chile some several hundred kilometers away.

So how large was Tiwanaku? My inclination is always to defer first to the empirical data and second to comparative analysis. We do not have historical census data for Tiwanaku as an urban phenomenon. From this perspective, greater Tiwanaku would have had a population of about 70,000, with perhaps half of this concentrated in the urban center at any one time. There would have been many instances of multiple residences for families, and the total population of the center would have varied according to the ritual and agricultural calendar.

The question that immediately arises is: Does demographic size matter? The answer is yes. Nonhierarchical societies simply have structural limits for growth. Such a society could not build a city like Tiwanaku. The relationship between population size and internal complexity is not linear. But at certain "tipping points" of demographic densities, structural shifts toward greater complexity are unavoidable. There does not exist a single example in the history of the world where a site as large and complex as Tiwanaku was not constructed by a fairly complex state society. In every single instance where we find sites like Tiwanaku with historical documents, we also find that there were unequivocal social and political hierarchies, backed by intensive economic production and exchange.

Looked at from another angle, there does not exist a single historically documented empty pilgrimage center or ceremonial site of even a quarter the size of Tiwanaku found outside of a state organization. Sites such as Mecca, Delphi, and others all have large permanent settlements attached to them and functioned within a regional political organization. From yet another perspective, every historically documented ancient city in the world was home to pageant and ceremony. Medieval London was the center of royal celebrations on a grand scale. One could easily pinpoint empty spaces in this city, and a creative archaeologist could discuss the more than 100 documented churches within 4 km² to argue that London in the sixteenth century was a huge ceremonial center built for overly religious peasants. Of course, we know otherwise because we have texts, and also perhaps because we value the image of our ancestral civilizations as something more than passive, praying peasants and disheveled agrarian serfs.

Based upon the data available and analogies to comparable centers the world over, the city of Tiwanaku was an architectural monument that was simultaneously a pilgrimage destination, a political center, an economic powerhouse, and a residential place for elite, specialized labor classes and a large proletariat. Like Jerusalem since the ninth century B.C., perhaps the quintessential icon of a religious center in the West, Tiwanaku was first a political and economic center that also hosted an array of highly charged religious institutions and events. Anyone who argues that Tiwanaku was an empty ceremonial center or just a pilgrimage destination holds an extraordinarily high burden of proof given the lack of any historically verified analogue from any culture on five continents throughout the course of human history.

THE STRAW-MAN MODEL OF THE COERCIVE HIERARCHICAL STATE

The term *hierarchy* is one of the most widely used and most poorly developed concepts in the archaeological literature. Scholars in archaeology in general seem to adopt an idealized concept of hierarchy best represented by those pyramid charts from the late 1970s published in the older evolutionary anthropological literature. In this model, there is a paramount or king/queen, with discrete levels of decision making layered one on top of another. These classes are, to use another term, stratified. The implication is that the highest decision maker receives and gives information through a formal network of subordinates. This model also implies that each subordinate level is subject to the control of the level above. In theory at least, each superordinate level has virtually life and death power over subordinates. Most significantly, each level has different access to resources and wealth (e.g., see Schortman 1989).

In the 1970s, archaeological theorists took this concept to a new level, looking at hierarchy not only internally within a society but regionally, over a landscape. In this model, multitiered settlement patterns represented congruent control over people's lives and resources. A typical statement is: "Simple chiefdoms have one decision-making level, or control hierarchy, above the local community; complex chiefdoms have at least two such levels" (Beck 2003:643). States were different in the degree to which force was monopolized. Some states became empires, with Rome being a kind of default model. In this theoretical construction, the state was composed of elite who exerted their will by military force and other kinds of coercion. Most importantly, there was strong structural continuity between these levels. By that, these different stages were seen as smooth and evolutionary, with states intensifying the structure of chiefdoms and with empires effectively being hyperstates that were simply larger.

This was a good model. It is parsimonious, bold, useful, and testable. Unfortunately, from a historical perspective, it is wrong; no matter where one looks in the historical literature, we never find a stratified society in which power is so elegantly and rigidly distributed. Even the most hierarchical preindustrial society in the world that we know of—say, the France of Louis XIV or Rome under Augustus—imposed limits on the power of the elite and dispersed control to various groups and institutions. There are always multiple sources of power in any society, no matter how rigid and stratified it may be or, more importantly, how powerful the elite claims to be. Kings need senates and parliaments, the non-elite resists encroachment constantly, middle classes famously usurp the power of the aristocracy, religious societies form counter-hegemonic entities that threaten the state, and so forth.

As anthropological archaeologists searched for these ideal hierarchies in the dirt, they of course came up empty-handed since they did not exist. Instead they encountered reality—multiple contemporary palaces, "corporate" elite strategies, non-elite households with lots of "elite" goods, humble tombs with priceless objects, ephemeral elite from Teotihuacán to Harappa, "network" states, nodal communities, and the like. Instead of questioning the empirical utility of the traditional hierarchy model, we Andeanists instead came to believe that "real" hierarchical states were indeed found "over there" (usually in the Mediterranean, Aegean, and Mesoamerica, where the documents told us there were indeed kings) and that the cultures that we studied "here" did not in fact have hierarchies. We therefore invented or borrowed new terms like *heterarchy, segmentary states,* and so forth to try to explain the apparent absence of centralized, hierarchical states in the pre-Inca Andes.

The reality is, to repeat, that there is no such thing in the real world as the rigid hierarchy model as used in archaeology. The case of London in the later Middle Ages is a telling example of the complexities of power and authority in a premodern state. England at this time was the quintessential centralized, premodern bureaucratic state with a king, a parliament, armies, navies, police forces, exchequers, sheriffs, taxing bodies, bishops, earls, dukes, royal courts, a strong state-supported church in which the king was head, embassies, palaces, a feudal aristocracy of landlords and knights, vassals, serfs, indentured servants, and the like. Yet authority was distributed in anything but a pyramid of power.

The work of Barron (2004) provides an excellent summary of power and authority in England and London from 1200 to 1500. As she puts it, the relationship between the king and London could be reduced to the fact that "the king needed money and the Londoners wanted self-government" (Barron 2004:9). This fundamental economic and political fact underlay much of the tension over centuries. The power of the Crown waxed and waned over time. In theory, the Crown always retained de jure rights to govern the city. If one were to read official documents from that era, it would appear that there was a clear-cut political hierarchy with the king on top. This, indeed, echoes the political ideals set out in other more fragmentary documents, such as Linear B tablets and cuneiform texts. In fact, to the contrary, there was a great deal of negotiation and formal and informal political restrictions on elite action in England at this time.

A look at how power actually was distributed in medieval England is far from the stratified pyramids that we assume. As Barron says (2004:10), because the king spoke with one voice, the Crown "had a distinct advantage in formulating and carrying out policy but, if push came to shove, the Londoners could muster a sizeable military force." A mayor and a court of aldermen, institutions that changed throughout the centuries, governed the city. There were 24 wards in the city in the early thirteenth century (Barron 2004). Under the aldermen were a number of offices such as ward beadles, rakers, scavengers, and constables. These were all answerable to the aldermen, being sworn in before them and the mayor. Mayors were elected early on by the barons of London under royal charter. Over time they were elected by groups of aldermen from each ward, with waxing and waning influence by the commoners. The history of the institution shows periods of interference by the Crown, without question, but the choice of mayor rested in the hands of the lesser elite and at times the commoner classes (Barron 2004). Sheriffs were likewise selected this way. There were times when the king tried to interfere, but the city protected its right to select the sheriffs (Barron 2004). Other members of the bureaucracy were almost all appointed by the city and not the king.

Over time a variety of democratic institutions took hold in London. In anthropological terms, we would view these as centers of non-elite resistance to authority. These institutions included those such as the Folkmoot and the Hustings Court. By the later fourteenth century, the court of common council took over from these earlier institutions (Barron 2004). Along with the aldermanic councils, these institutions sought ways to raise money for communal projects. By the fifteenth century, taxes for these projects could be raised only by consent of both the commoner and aldermanic groups (Barron 2004). These projects included piping in water to the city, the repair of granaries, and the improvement of the city walls and ditches (Barron 2004). From an archaeological perspective, significant construction of the urban area was done virtually outside of royal or "state" control.

Another check on both city and royal power was the institution of sanctuaries controlled by the church. Effectively the 100 or so churches provided havens from state authorities for criminals and even people accused of treason. In 1566, though, the sanctuary was abolished, as the combined political power of the city and Crown diminished the church's role (Barron 2004). The king did have power of life and death over some people, particularly political troublemakers. However, this power was exercised in the city only sparingly. On the ground, other elite had palaces, controlled long-distance exchange, created their own bureaucracies, and the like. Middle-class merchant groups had considerable power over everyday life, a sphere where the Crown could not interfere, no matter how much it tried. Even commoners could exact demands from the authorities, including the king, mayor, barons, and other minor aristocracy.

A historical anecdote is quite telling. In 1369 Edward sent a royal writ to the city, telling it to clean up the disgusting filth in the streets left by butchers. The aldermen effectively ignored the order for more than 20 years (Barron 2004). The king of England, the apex of a stratified hierarchical state, while capable of occasionally executing a heretic and able to raise armies and navies at will, could not even force the people in his capital city 2 km away to clean up their garbage. If this is not heterarchy or "segmentary," I don't know what is.

The oft-cited article by Fritz (1986) about the Hindu imperial capital of Vijayanagara falls into this kind of archaeological theory-building trap. He describes Vijayanagara, following the historian Stein (1980), as a "segmentary state, consisting of relatively autonomous polities." Quoting Appadurai (1978:51), he describes this urban capital of more than 10 km² of core architecture as housing a state with "no single, centralized, permanent bureaucratic organization, but a temporary affiliation of local groups, authoritatively constituted by, or in the name of the king, and empowered to make public decisions on specific matters." These three scholars from three disciplines—archaeology, anthropology, and history—contrast this segmentary model with apparently that of a nonsegmentary or stratified hierarchy model. But, as we can see, their description of the "segmentary" state fits very well, almost to a tee, sixteenth-century England. If sixteenth-century England is not a centralized state, then what is? If it is not, then the concept of a coercive, hierarchical state has no analytical meaning.

This straw-man hierarchy model is part of our discourse on Tiwanaku. Goldstein (2005) brings in Vijayanagara as a kind of analogy for Tiwanaku. He argues, following Sinopoli and Morrison (1995), that the rulers of the southern Indian state did not control domestic relations of production and had to negotiate with local elite. In his view, therefore, this state is not an example of "globalist model[s] of coercive core-centered hierarchy" but something less hierarchical. To Goldstein's credit, he clearly articulates what this globalist model is, unlike far too many of us who just assume it to be understood. In this view, a state is hierarchical, bureaucratic, and predatory—the end point of an evolutionary process. It controls production and interferes in the domestic economy. There must be provinces or colonies as part of the expansion process. These colonies must have administrators and governors.

Goldstein goes on to list several things missing from the Tiwanaku state that one would expect from this coercive state model. In his view, there are no palaces at Tiwanaku that would qualify as royalty. Goldstein also states that there is little evidence that the Tiwanaku elite interfered with domestic production. He says that there were no formal roads. Goldstein, commendably echoing most of our colleagues in this symposium, draws a very profound conclusion of what we should find at a place like Tiwanaku, given the globalist, evolutionary model:

> Neoevolutionists thus implicitly assume that horizontally distinct corporate social groups like clans or Andean ayllus wither away as their increasingly redundant functions are usurped by the state's hierarchy. Patterns of authority and group identity based on kinship and ethnicity are seen to become socially vestigial, politically impotent, and administratively irrelevant in class-based societies. (Goldstein 2005:307)

These are fascinating inferences but are not necessarily born out by the data from comparative history or anthropology. A quick read of the *Iliad* shows how important kinship and ethnicity are in structuring the state civilizations of the Aegean. The Aztec *calpulli* are famous horizontal institutions that were defined by both ethnicity and kinship. The Ottoman Empire had too many ethnic, national, and religious institutions within its midst to even count. In our other example of medieval London, the town was full of horizontal institutions that existed outside of direct royal authority, including guilds, baronial houses defined by kinship, merchant barrios, religious institutions, foreign quarters, and the like. There is literally an unlimited number of examples from history and ethnography to draw from in state societies.

In short, the empirical record shows that *ayllu*-like institutions were found throughout the great states and empires of the ancient world. Far from disappearing as an inevitable result of state development, such institutions flourished as a primary means to structure society in hierarchical, state models. They are historically varied but structurally very similar across space and time. The fact that they existed in Tiwanaku does not diminish its status as a centralized state; to the contrary, it brings in Tiwanaku as one of the great states of the ancient world.

There is likewise little evidence that the elite of most state societies interfered with domestic production of the non-elite for their own subsistence. Almost all states in premodern times tax primary producers either through corvée labor or direct tribute. It is not in any elite group's interest to tell farmers how to farm, to tell butchers how to butcher, and so forth. The elite simply take a portion of that production for their own use. Even the Inca, perhaps one of the most economically intrusive states in the ancient world, did not intervene in local production, preferring instead to use corvée labor to work state lands and installations. Local production was largely untouched. While Goldstein may be absolutely correct in deducing this feature as a component of state societies out of the *theoretical* literature, it is not an *empirically* verified component of state societies from around the world.

The Tiwanaku peoples had roads, albeit not like the ones the Inca had. The surveys from the Juli-Pomata area show that the Tiwanaku sites align along roads that were then co-opted by the Inca. The surveys to the north in the Huancané-Putina area also indicate a concentration of settlement on the road system (though these data have not been published). Our (Stanish et al. 2010) recent survey in the area between Desaguadero and Moquegua indicates that there were indeed Tiwanaku artifact scatters on sites along the road between the lake and the largest colony. However, it is quite true that this was a more informal and noncentralized kind of system than we see for the Inca. Nevertheless, while we did not find *tambos* or other kinds of way stations that dated to the Tiwanaku period, we did find a line of sites that led to Moquegua, indicating that some kind of exchange took place along this road.

I disagree about the lack of palaces as well. Call them what you want, but from a comparative perspective, if Tiwanaku structures such as the Pumapunku were not elite residences, then surely the palaces of most of the Bronze Age and early Iron Age Aegean and Mediterranean would not qualify either. Indeed, there are no royal tombs like Moche at Tiwanaku. But the Inca did not have royal tombs either. In fact, building elaborate tombs for the elite is not, and appears to never have been, a feature of highland Andean culture except for some post-Tiwanaku *chullpas* found only in the south-central Andean region. They are not found in the Tiwanaku, Pucará, Chavín, or Wari cultures, indicating a highland tradition that does not include elaborate tombs for individual dead elite like anything remotely as elaborate as among the Moche.[3]

Goldstein notes that there are no iconographic representations of secular hierarchy in Tiwanaku, unlike among the Moche. There are none in the Inca culture either until the colonial period; nor, for that matter, are any represented in Chan Chan, Teotihuacán, and many other ancient states.[4] There are no Moche-like representations of elite in Wari or Pucará art either. This also appears to be a highland tradition (although the images of people wearing puma headdresses decapitating sacrificial humans in Pucará art might come close).

If the criteria adopted by those testing Tiwanaku against the straw-man argument were applied around the world, then there would be very few ancient states and no first-generation states at all. To put it another way, by the criteria proposed above, most ancient empires and all first-generation states would be segmentary states. I adamantly believe that we have to rethink what a coercive hierarchy really is in practice. In light of the fact that the king of late medieval England could not even get his subjects to clean up their garbage, it is clear that our models of states and even empires need to be substantially revised. As I have implied, I believe that the model used by some and attacked by others is one that never has existed and that, in fact, all societies the world over had multiple axes of power and wealth.

By sticking strictly to consistent archaeological criteria of verification, it is virtually impossible to deny that Tiwanaku was an urban, stratified center of an ancient state more complex than Mycenaean Greece and certainly as complex as twelfth-to-sixteenth-century London, Minoan Crete, and other great civilizations of the ancient world.

Tiwanaku Colonies

Virtually all of the great classical civilizations of antiquity in the Old World had colonies. In reviewing the literature on the Andes, I sense that a similar straw-man logic is at work here as well. In this flawed concept, a colony is a product of a reasoned, rational policy on the part of state administrators to control an area, politically, economically, and/or militarily. A state bureaucracy of some sort decides where to put the colony, and then it amasses military and administrative resources to build an outpost that is incorporated into the political orbit of the home country. Following world-systems theory, the peripheries were completely subordinate to the core, which extracted resources and dominated the political, economic, and at times even cultural life of the periphery.

This is indeed a model that was proposed by some system theorists and incorporated into many processualist models in the 1970s, particularly those that drew off of world-systems theory. But once again, a look at historically documented colonies in the ancient world of states and empires presents a different picture.

Colonies are highly varied. They physically contain all sorts of things, including stores, forts, armies, government agents, religious buildings, residences, and specialized production areas. Sometimes the relationship between colony and home country is strong, sometimes weak; and almost always the relationship breaks down after a few generations. The earliest documented Greek colonization was far from this straw-man model of intentional, rational colonization by home capital city:

> These migration settlements were not colonies in the usually understood sense of the term. They were not organized movements, directed from and set forth by a particular city, but small bands of homeless folk dispossessed by the so-called Dorian Invasions. . . . The real colonial movements began somewhat later . . . when the Greek cities of the mainland recovered from the . . . destruction of the Mycenaean centers in the thirteenth and twelfth centuries. (White 1961:444)

Later Greek colonies, such as "Al-Mina and later Naukratis were trading posts, occupied with the consent of Assyria and her successors in Syria and Egypt. Neither the Syrian coast nor Egypt was open for the foundation of true colonies, that is, sizeable settlements of colonists on agricultural land, where an independent new community with full civic life could develop" (White 1961:446).

The most mature Greek colonies were sent out by the home city and do indeed fit aspects of the straw-man model of colonies: "The mother-city or metropolis selected the site, appointed the leader of the colony, called for volunteers, and organized the colony. The major portion of the colonists usually came from the mother-city, but contingents from other places sometimes participate" (White 1961:449). However, even the most complex of colonies quickly rid themselves of their political and economic links to the home city, and this deviates substantially from the core of the straw-man model structure: "Once the new city was founded the ties which bound it to the mother-city were those of religion and sentiment only. Colonies were in no sense a colonial empire of the mother-city; they pursued their independent ways, and many soon became more prosperous and more famous than the mother-cities" (White 1961:449).

The short of it is this: bureaucratically administered, formal colonies with politically appointed agents of the state occur virtually only in the most complex of premodern states. And even in these, the ties that bind colony and home country are quite ephemeral, weakening or disappearing in two or three generations. The vast bulk of colonies in the premodern world are far less formal. Virtually all colonies eventually develop their own identities and cease functioning as an extension of the home polity.

From this perspective, Tiwanaku likewise had colonies. The Tiwanaku colony in Moquegua has been ably described by several scholars, most notably Goldstein in a series of publications since the early 1990s. What we know, empirically, is this. There is a huge amount of Tiwanaku pottery found in a series of settlements throughout the Moquegua Valley, stretching from the coast in Ilo to up to 3,000 m in the high drainages. No other pottery styles of any iconographic complexity (with the exception of the very rare Wari sherd found on occasion) are found to coexist with the Tiwanaku pottery in these sites. There is a large site complex called Omo that contains an unusually large amount of Tiwanaku pottery, even for Moquegua. There is a site called Chen Chen that had literally thousands of cist tombs filled with Tiwanaku-style pottery and other artifacts. There is a structure on the main site of Omo that is built in a miniature style similar to that found at the Tiwanaku capital. Below Omo are very extensive fields that up to the present day provide some of the richest agricultural land in the south-central Andes.

The Wari site of Cerro Baúl is also located in the Moquegua drainage and had been ably studied and published by Luis Lumbreras, Bertha Vargas, Robert Feldman, Michael Moseley, Donna Nash, Ryan Williams, and others. It is in the same size category and is as complex as Mycenae, Tiryns, Gla, and other well-known Bronze Age Aegean sites. Moquegua is the only known place in the Andes where there are both Tiwanaku and Wari settlements (though some smaller sites in Moquegua have some pottery from both cultures). The Wari site is located on a famously defensive massif, once aptly described by Michael Moseley as the Masada of the Andes, which provides the highest level of protection available in any premodern settlement. Adjacent to Cerro Baúl is the site of Cerro Mejía, also a Wari-affiliated site. Surrounding Baúl is a series of Tiwanaku sites that were, for all intents and purposes, contemporary for a substantial period of time with the site of Wari on the summit above.

There is a very clear ritual/religious component to Cerro Baúl, as there is at Omo, Tiwanaku, Cuzco, Teotihuacán, Tenochtitlán, and virtually every other political center in the ancient world. There are also some Tiwanaku objects found at the summit as well, indicating that the site was a place where Tiwanaku and Wari peoples probably met, drank, possibly slept, and almost certainly negotiated with one another. In Moseley et al.'s excellent characterization, it was an "embassy-like delegation of nobles and attendant personnel that endured for centuries" (Moseley et al. 2005:443).

Cerro Baúl was also a defensive site that served to keep its occupants safe from the surrounding Tiwanaku settlements. The Tiwanaku-affiliated peoples did not need defensive locations, since they vastly outnumbered the Wari contingent. People who argue against conflict in the Middle Horizon or against a defensive function for Cerro Baúl fail to understand that historically, competing polities rarely have actual battles more than a mere fraction of the time. It is very common in the historical literature to note that a cooperative "live and let live" philosophy is the norm in human affairs, a norm that is occasionally punctured by outbursts of organized violence. These outbursts can indeed have enormous political and other consequences, but they are in fact quite rare. The Hundred Years' War (a total of around 115 years, with 80 of those actually violent) is called what it is precisely because it is so rare. If we use history as our guide, it is most likely that 99 percent of the time, the Tiwanaku and Wari peoples in Moquegua were interacting in peace for their mutual self-interests. That is not to say that they were not adversaries, and as such they had to maintain defensive postures vis-à-vis each other. But the historical record is replete with examples of adversaries engaged in simultaneous conflict and trade. Usually it is the political elite that promotes the first, and it is the non-elite that engages in the latter. Nevertheless, conflict and cooperation are not mutually exclusive. Once this is realized, the settlement complex around Cerro Baúl makes eminently good sense and fits in well with our historical understanding of complex societies.

I would also argue that the Wari leadership maintained Cerro Mejía to prevent sieges. This walled site is located in a manner that would precisely ensure that the only access to Cerro Baúl could not be blocked. Any attempt to do so would put the besiegers in a tactically impossible position, outflanked on low ground between the two hills of Baúl and Mejía. In premodern military terms, such a position is almost certainly fatal and one to be avoided at all costs, a point constantly reiterated by military strategists from ancient China to modern army manuals.

I would also argue that the construction of Tiwanaku sites around the base of Cerro Baúl is strategic in nature as well. It effectively cuts off Wari "expansion" outside of Baúl and ensures that an uneasy peace existed between the two peoples. Of course the Tiwanaku peoples could have built more settlements, but they did not. I would suggest that, again based upon historical analogies, the settlement system in the Cerro Baúl area preserves the outcome of protracted negotiations and understandings between the two rivals in the only place in their world where they chose to interact on a formal basis. Wari was welcome in Tiwanaku territory in this one instance because it was in each side's interests; but the Wari were apparently given their limits, and they accepted these to achieve other goals. If not, we would see many more Wari settlements up and down the valley—we do not.

According to Williams and Nash (2002), there is a Tiwanaku construction on the summit of Baúl. This is reminiscent of the Teotihuacán barrio in Kalminaljuyu, the Oaxacan barrio in Teotihuacán, the central Mexican temple in Tikal, and countless examples in the history of the Old World. In the eighteenth-century Ottoman Empire, foreign representatives and ethnic minorities were required to live in their own neighborhoods (Göçek 1987:6). The Hanseatic League had a special area in sixteenth-century London called the Steelyard. Throughout the historical world in state societies, it was common for larger settlements to host a small section of foreigners, who maintained their cultural attributes. It is found at Baúl, and the work of Janusek at Tiwanaku may have found some similar barrios.

The Tiwanaku peoples expanded into other areas in the south-central Andes as well. In their heartland, they established colonies or enclaves in the Puno Bay, in the north near Arapa and Huancané, and throughout the lowlands in areas that we barely understand. Many of the Tiwanaku sites in Cochabamba are colonies that utilized a distinctive architectural style that we see in the northern Titicaca Basin.

Some scholars have suggested that the nature of pottery production in the peripheral Tiwanaku settlements indicates a nonhierarchical relationship between colony and core. They argue that the pottery is all locally manufactured as opposed to being imported from the capital. In their view, this argues for a less centralized state, or no state control at all. I would note that this Tiwanaku pattern is precisely the pattern of pottery manufacture that we see in the Inca Empire. The leaders of Tawantinsuyu militarily captured provinces and installed artisan workshops for pottery, cloth, and metals. Their norm for ceramic manufacture was to create workshops in provincial territories, where Inca canons were executed more or less according to some standard set in Cuzco, although there was considerable borrowing from local pottery traditions. If anything, data from Tiwanaku colonies that indicate that they pursued a policy similar to the Inca simply reinforce the notion that Tiwanaku followed the same norms of state building in the Andes as the Inca. Polities such as Chavín, Wari, and others that did not follow this norm most likely were less complex than the Tiwanaku or Inca, relying instead on earlier practices of the direct movement of ceremonial and feasting objects to distant places.

Summary

The model of the coercive, hierarchical state used to assess Tiwanaku is a flawed one—one without empirical foundation. The fact is that Tiwanaku is a city comparable in size and complexity to medieval London and Bronze Age Knossos, to name but just two iconic sites of the ancient world. The people of Tiwanaku built massive agricultural fields, established colonies over hundreds of kilometers, and built huge temples and palaces adorned with monoliths and great art. They established roads and causeways. They created the Kalasasaya and the Akapana, plus numerous buildings surrounded by a great moat. The city was planned, with components that ranged from a prosaic but sophisticated sewer system to architectural feats that combined centuries of religious principles and an amazing understanding of how to move people through magnificent space. Tiwanaku peoples massed-produced ceramic art on a scale not seen before in the region. They created sophisticated metalworking, textile, and musical instrument industries and much more.

The city of Jerusalem is perhaps a better analogy for Tiwanaku. It was also the political, economic, and demographic center of kingdoms and empires from at least the ninth century B.C., and while only half the size of Tiwanaku in area, it held a population of up to 200,000 in the first century A.D. I see no structural difference in kind between Jerusalem, Tiwanaku, and any other capital of a great civilization.

Notes

[1] I have argued elsewhere (Stanish 2010) that there is a structural limit of around 100,000 people in Andean cities due to the nature of their political and economic organization. The early first-generation states of Moche, Wari (possibly Huaro), and Tiwanaku reached about half this size quickly but did not grow much beyond that. Even Inca Cuzco did not grow beyond 100,000 inhabitants, even though it was the capital of one of the most powerful empires in world history.

[2] An easy walk is about 5 km per hour with an occasional rest. At a fast walking pace, one can cover a kilometer in about 10 minutes.

[3] The only exception would be the Late Horizon *chullpas* at sites like Sillustani and Tanka Tanka.

[4] A possible exception being wooden *keros*, but most of those are colonial in date.

References Cited

Albarracin-Jordan, Juan
   1992 Prehispanic and Early Colonial Settlement Patterns in the Lower Tiwanaku Valley, Bolivia. Unpublished Ph.D. dissertation, Department of

Anthropology, Southern Methodist University, Dallas.

1996a *Tiwanaku. Arqueología regional y dinámica segmentaria.* Editores Plural, La Paz.

1996b Tiwanaku Settlement System: The Integration of Nested Hierarchies in the Lower Tiwanaku Valley. *Latin American Antiquity* 7(3):183–210.

Alconini Mujica, Sonia

1995 *Rito, símbolo e historia en la pirámide de Akapana, Tiwanaku: Un análisis de cerámica ceremonial prehispánica.* Editorial Acción, La Paz.

Appadurai, Arjun

1978 Kings, Sects and Temples in South India, 1350–1700 A.D. In *South Indian Temples: An Analytical Reconsideration*, edited by Burton Stein, pp. 47–73. Vikas, New Delhi.

Bandy, Matthew

2001 Population and History in the Ancient Titicaca Basin. Unpublished Ph.D. dissertation, Department of Anthropology, University of California, Berkeley.

Barron, Caroline

2004 *London in the Later Middle Ages: Government and People 1200–1500.* Oxford University Press, Oxford.

Beck, Robin A., Jr.

2003 Consolidation and Hierarchy: Chiefdom Variability in the Mississippian Southeast. *American Antiquity* 68(4):641–662.

Couture, Nicole C.

2002 The Construction of Power: Monumental Space and Elite Residence at Tiwanaku, Bolivia. Unpublished Ph.D. Dissertation, Department of Anthropology, University of Chicago, Chicago.

Escalante Moscoso, Javier

1997 *Arquitectura prehispánica en los Andes bolivianos.* Producciones CIMA, La Paz.

2003 Residential Architecture in La K'arana, Tiwanaku. In *Tiwanaku and Its Hinterland: Archaeological and Paleoecological Investigations of an Andean Civilization.* Vol. 2, *Urban and Rural Archaeology*, edited by Alan L. Kolata, pp. 316–326. Smithsonian Institution Press, Washington, D.C.

Fritz, John M.

1986 Authority and Meaning of a South Indian Imperial Capital. *American Anthropologist* 88(1):44–55.

Göçek, Fatma Müge

1987 *East Encounters West. France and the Ottoman Empire in the Eighteenth Century.* Oxford University Press, Oxford.

Goldstein, Paul

2005 *Andean Diaspora: The Tiwanaku Colonies and the Origins of South American Empire.* University Press of Florida, Gainesville.

Janusek, John

2008 *Ancient Tiwanaku.* Cambridge University Press, Cambridge.

Kolata, Alan

1993 *The Tiwanaku: Portrait of an Andean Civilization.* Blackwell, Cambridge, Massachusetts.

2003 The Proyecto Wila Jawira Research Program. In *Tiwanaku and Its Hinterland: Archaeology and Paleoecology of an Andean Civilization.* Vol. 2, *Urban and Rural Archaeology,* edited by Alan L. Kolata, pp. 3–17. Smithsonian Institution Press, Washington, D.C.

Kolata, Alan, and Carlos Ponce Sanginés

1992 Tiwanaku: The City at the Center. In *The Ancient Americas, Art from Sacred Landscapes*, edited by Richard F. Townsend, pp. 317–333. Art Institute of Chicago, Chicago.

Mathews, James Edward

1992 Prehispanic Settlement and Agriculture in the Middle Tiwanaku Valley, Bolivia. Unpublished Ph.D. dissertation, Department of Anthropology, University of Chicago, Chicago.

Moseley, Michael, Donna J. Nash, Patrick Ryan Williams, Susan deFrance, Ana Miranda, and Mario Ruales

2005 Burning down the Brewery: Establishing and Evacuating an Ancient Imperial Colony at Cerro Baúl, Perú. *Proceedings of the National Academy of Sciences* 102(48):17264–17271. Washington, D.C.

Parsons, Jeffrey

1968 An Estimate of Size and Population for Middle Horizon Tiahuanaco, Bolivia. *American Antiquity* 33:243–245.

Ponce Sanginés, Carlos

1981 *Tiwanaku: Espacio, tiempo y cultura: Ensayo de síntesis arqueológica.* Los Amigos del Libro, La Paz.

1995 *Tiwanaku: 200 Años de investigaciones arqueológicas.* Producciones CIMA, La Paz.

Portugal Ortiz, Max

1993 Trabajos arqueológicos de Tiwanaku, Pt. 1. *Textos antropológicos* 4:9–50.

Rivera Casanovas, Claudia

1994 Ch'iji Jawira: Evidencias sobre la producción de cerámica en Tiwanaku. Unpublished licenciatura thesis, Universidad Mayor de San Andrés, La Paz.

Shortman, Edward

1989 Interregional Interaction in Prehistory: The Need for a New Perspective. *American Antiquity* 54(1):52–65.

Sinopoli, Carla, and Kathleen Morrison

1995 Dimensions of Imperial Control: The Vijayanagara Capital. *American Anthropologist* 97(1):83–96.

Stanish, Charles

1989 Tamaño y complejidad de los asentamientos nucleares de Tiwanaku. In *Arqueología de*

Lukurmata, Vol. 2, edited by Alan Kolata, pp. 41–57. Instituto Nacional de Arqueología, La Paz.

2003 *Ancient Titicaca: The Evolution of Complex Society in Southern Peru and Northern Bolivia*. University of California Press, Berkeley.

2010 Labor Taxes, Market Systems and Urbanization in the Prehispanic Andes: A Comparative Perspective. In *Archaeological Approaches to Market Exchange in Ancient Societies*, edited by C. Garraty and B. Stark, pp. 185–205. University of Colorado Press, Boulder.

Stanish, C., E. de la Vega, M. Moseley, R. Williams, B. Vining, and K. LaFavre

2010 Tiwanaku Trade Patterns in Southern Peru. *Journal of Anthropological Archaeology* 29(4): 524–532.

Stein, Burton

1980 *Peasant State and Society in Medieval South India*. Oxford University Press, New Delhi.

White, Mary E.

1961 Greek Colonization. *Journal of Economic History* 21(4):443–454.

Whitelaw, Todd

2001 From Sites to Communities: Defining the Human Dimensions of Minoan Urbanism. In *Urbanism in the Aegean Bronze Age*, edited by K. Branigan, pp. 15–37. Sheffield Studies in Aegean Archaeology, Sheffield.

Williams, Patrick Ryan, and Donna J. Nash

2002 Imperial Interaction in the Andes: Huari and Tiwanaku at Cerro Baúl. In *Andean Archaeology*. Vol. 1, *Variations in Sociopolitical Organization*, edited by William H. Isbell and Helaine Silverman, pp. 243–265. Kluwer Academic/Plenum Publishers, New York.

10
Nature of an Andean City:
Tiwanaku and the Production of Spectacle

William H. Isbell

Constructing Knowledge About Tiwanaku

Scientific knowledge proceeds by presenting hypotheses whose inadequacy can be revealed by further research. Understandings gained in the new research help develop better hypotheses and interpretations. In this way the spiral of knowledge advances. Social sciences, including archaeology, are not particularly compliant with formal hypothesis testing and falsification, but the process of knowledge-construction still proceeds in much the same fashion. Archaeologists propose interpretations of the past, and some become the current and popular thinking about a prehistoric culture, phase, or evolutionary stage. Gradually, new research accumulates additional information. Furthermore, theoretical perspectives change, which is to say that scholars develop new perspectives regarding the meaning of archaeological remains. Campsites of the Pleistocene revealed "Man the Hunter," until feminist theory taught archaeologists to see bands of gendered individuals with complementary identities. As the currently accepted representations of the past become less and less convincing in light of new information and thinking, new alternatives are proposed. When the alternatives are more convincing than the old dogma, the old is discarded in favor of the new—which will also fall, eventually, under criticism.

Clearly, new archaeological knowledge is built on, and out of, former understandings. In the spiral of knowledge, less adequate interpretations of the past are discarded as they are replaced by newly accumulated, more convincing understandings. But some ideas and interpretations become very deeply engrained in the body of accepted knowledge, so much so that they tend to go unquestioned. Indeed, some ideas are repeated so frequently and over so many years that they seem more convincing than any data contradicting them. Yoffee (2005) refers to such untested affirmations about the archaeological past as factoids. Unfortunately, in some cases factoids become so powerful that they shape the contexts in which new research is interpreted, selecting which interpretations are acceptable and which are not until they overshadow the spiral of scientific progress, at least for a time. This describes key aspects of currently popular understandings about Tiwanaku. More objective reevaluation is urgently needed, and this paper seeks to make a critical contribution, setting the stage for the other new articles in this book.

To understand Tiwanaku's past from a less biased perspective, we must determine how erroneous factoids have become such important parts of standard knowledge. Some errors, including the implications of theories popular in earlier eras of the academy, resulted from historical accidents. Others have resulted from political agendas, professional ambitions, and the appeal of well-told stories.

Factoids of Tiwanaku: Antiquity, Precocity, Imperialism, and a European-like City

Tiwanaku profoundly impressed sixteenth-century Spanish invaders with its monumental architecture and grand stone sculptures; their weathered conditions promoted a sense of remoteness and mystery (Betanzos 1996 [1557]; Calancha 1939 [1638]; Cieza 1962 [1553]; Cobo 1979 [1653], 1990 [1653]; Polo de Ondegardo 1916 [1571]). Europeans appreciate the labor required to cut, move, and place immense blocks of stone, and they admire the organizational skills, as well as the authority, required to plan and realize imposing constructions. Similar monuments symbolized and legitimized authority in the ancient and classical Old World. Because its remains were so impressive to Europeans, Tiwanaku was described and redescribed by generations of travelers during colonial and early republican times (Castelnau 1852; D'Orbigny 2002 [1844]; Humboldt 1815; Squier 1877; Wiener 1880). Consequently, as Americanist archaeology was emerging as an academic discipline in the mid- to late nineteenth century, Tiwanaku was one of the first centers to receive professional examination (Stübel and Uhle 1892). Indeed, Tiwanaku was the first Andean "style" of art to be defined.

In the process of describing Tiwanaku, the German archaeologists showed that its style of art preceded that of the Incas. This was a groundbreaking demonstration, for many thinkers of the time believed that American civilizations were little or no older than their discovery by Europeans. But significant preconquest antiquity was firmly established for the "Tiwanaku style" in 1892. By the turn of the twentieth century it had become the fulcrum on which all other pre-Hispanic Andean cultural chronology was developed—until the advent of radiocarbon dating 50 years later.

To make a long and complex story short and simple, a couple of decades after describing Tiwanaku-style art, Max Uhle (1903b) excavated artifacts with some of the same figures that graced Tiwanaku's sculptures at the distant coastal site of Pachacamac in central Peru. Surely the world's leading expert on Tiwanaku style at that time, Uhle designated the Pachacamac images "in the style of Tiwanaku," even though they were on ceramics and textiles, not stone sculptures. To his great credit, Uhle realized that such striking similarity must mean that the two cultures cross-dated temporally. Uhle was cautious about designating Tiwanaku as the singular source of diffusion for the diagnostic art, but the art was now the "Tiwanaku style," making it easy to assume the priority of Tiwanaku's monumental sculpture over Pachacamac's pottery and textile designs. Within a few decades, Tiwanaku was universally accepted as the source of the art, wherever it was found.

At the start of the twentieth century, principles of archaeological stratigraphy were just being recognized. Uhle observed that by using the newfangled technique at Pachacamac, he could separate ceramic styles—or cultures—by excavation contexts. Some were under strata containing Tiwanaku-style objects, some were above, and some were in the same strata. Soon Uhle pieced together a sequence consisting of early or pre-Tiwanaku cultures, middle or Tiwanaku cultures, and late or post-Tiwanaku cultures, as well as a fourth phase, Inca culture, dated to the time of the Spanish invasion (Uhle 1903a). Using the broadly spread Tiwanaku style, Uhle turned his Pachacamac sequence into the first regional chronology in the Americas.

The Tiwanaku style became diagnostic of Peru's chronological Middle period, which more recently has been renamed the Middle Horizon (Kroeber 1944; Rowe 1962b). However, what is important for us to realize is that until the invention of radiocarbon dating, Tiwanaku was not just the most impressive prehistoric site in the central Andes; it was also the only style that provided a secure dating tool for organizing other styles and cultures—from northwestern Argentina to southern Ecuador—into chronologies. Artifacts diagnostic of ancient cultures were either stratigraphically earlier than the Middle period, stratigraphically later, or stratigraphically associated with, and therefore part of, the Middle period. When chronological questions could not be resolved by stratigraphy, which was frequent, determinations were based on stylistic comparisons.

Seeking to extend Uhle's (1903a) regional chronology, archaeologists made Herculean efforts to detect Tiwanaku influence in other Andean art styles. In his influential compendium on Andean archaeology, Philip Means (1931) employed the Tiwanaku style to date many less well-known Andean cultures. He argued, for example, that the art of Chavín de Huántar showed significant Tiwanaku influence but must already have evolved along distinctive lines for several centuries since the Tiwanaku infusion. As scholars repeated and exaggerated Means's systematic comparisons of all cultures with Tiwanaku, the site and its art style took on greater and greater importance—and antiquity—seeming to represent an ancient "Ur-culture" from which all others derived inspiration. But, of course, many comparisons were simply wrong, such as Means's conclusion that Chavín de Huántar was a later, Tiwanaku-influenced iconography. Today, radiocarbon dating has shown that Chavín de Huántar was built and occupied more than a millennium before the emergence of Tiwanaku. But we are following the history to see how Tiwanaku acquired its mystique.

Until the radiocarbon era, Tiwanaku was generally considered the seminal civilization of Andean culture. Often employing racist assumptions characteristic of nineteenth- and early twentieth-century scholarship, Tiwanaku was imagined to have been the center of precocious invention, from which civilization diffused to lesser Native Americans. The most exuberant claim was made by Arthur Posnansky (1910, 1911a, 1911b, 1911c, 1945, 1957), who argued that Tiwanaku was the "Cradle of American Man," erecting its spectacular monuments more than 10,000 years ago. Of course, modern archaeologists reject such pseudoscientific excesses,[1] but "precocious-Tiwanaku" thinking became deeply engrained into the fabric of South American prehistory. During the early era of radiocarbon dating, Carlos Ponce (1962, 1972, 1980) used a single excessively early date to argue that Tiwanaku culture had appeared by 1500 B.C., becoming the center that radiated complex civilization over the next millennium. Contemporary thinking is certainly less extreme, but the popularity of the conviction that Tiwanaku was the hub of cultural influence in the southern Andean highlands means that statements like "Tiwanaku's preeminence as a cultural and political capital had its origins in the late formative period (ca. 500 BC–AD 400)" (Kolata 2004:99) are not subject to rigorous tests.

In the 1950s, as radiocarbon dating was reorganizing the chronology of Andean cultures, Bolivian archaeologist Carlos Ponce (1947, 1962, 1969a, 1969b, 1972, 1976, 1980, 1999, 2001) rose to preeminence in Tiwanaku studies and dominated the field for more than half a century. Ponce was a politician as much as a prehistorian, and he sought to build a new Bolivian national identity with Tiwanaku as its symbol. He represented the site as a great city, in every way like, and evolutionarily equivalent to, the greatest Old World cities (see Isbell and Vranich 2004). Furthermore, he asserted that Tiwanaku had been the capital of a conquest state, incorporating virtually all of Bolivia into a great pre-Columbian empire; thus all indigenous Bolivians were direct descendants of Tiwanaku and should have as much pride in their past as Euro-Bolivians.[2]

Of course, for Ponce's political mystique to work, Tiwanaku had to be represented as exclusively Bolivian, with no debts to earlier cultures in Peru, Chile, or other neighboring nations. In his narratives, it was a precocious evolutionary heartland in which a collection of farming hamlets developed steadily and quickly, becoming a centralized state and then a great city that organized the entire territory through trade, conquest, and imperial administration. Ponce's image of Tiwanaku as an early and powerful political center was legitimized by repetition, including Edward Lanning's (1967) important synthesis of Andean archaeology. Lanning accepted Ponce's claims on the basis of tradition and the identification of what was believed to be Tiwanaku influence on the rise of Huari in central highland Peru (Menzel 1964; Rowe 1956, 1962b, 1967). However, during this era new archaeological data from Tiwanaku itself was extremely limited and very interpretive.[3] In this condition it was easier to think in factoids than to propose and evaluate alternative hypotheses.

As Ponce pursued his experiment in Bolivian national heritage construction, radiocarbon dating was demonstrating the temporal priority of Peru's Chavín culture (Rowe 1962a; Strong 1957; Tello 1960). Furthermore, pre-Chavín cultures were coming to light on the Pacific coast; finds included preceramic monuments from the late archaic (Bird 1948; Engel 1963; Lanning 1963; Patterson and Lanning 1964). The "early and precocious Tiwanaku" model should have been discarded, but Carlos Ponce and his disciples steadfastly defended the image by inventing a new representation. They promulgated a chronology for the Tiwanaku heartland that consisted of five phases— Tiwanaku I, II, III, IV, and V

(Ponce 1972). Naming all the phases Tiwanaku made culture synonymous with place. Thus the complex society that erected megalithic monuments and carved great stone statues appeared with the first sedentary occupation of the south altiplano heartland, not with the development of explicit defining characteristics of Tiwanaku culture as is traditional in archaeology. As stated above, Ponce (1962, 1972, 1976) cited a single radiocarbon date, one that was significantly older than the cluster of assays from comparable strata, to date a sparsely represented ceramic complex with no similarities to the pottery associated with megalithic construction as older than Chavín. This he called Tiwanaku I, an independent Bolivian hearth of Andean civilization.

Several archaeologists were critical of Ponce's chronology and its implications, but it was adopted anyway (see note 3), enduring through the 1970s, 1980s, and 1990s. In fact, the chronology employed today—which discards Tiwanaku I through III in favor of phases named Early, Middle, and Late Formative—was popularized only after Ponce's death. Currently, the old names Tiwanaku IV and V continue in use, but even they are more probably contemporary cultural variants than different temporal phases (Goldstein 2005; Knobloch this volume). John Janusek (2003:31) presents the new chronology with radiocarbon dates from the Tiwanaku heartland, while Isbell and Knobloch (2006, 2009; see also Knobloch 2002) show why the name Tiwanaku should no longer be applied to the widespread iconography that appears on Tiwanaku stone sculpture, an argument repeated very briefly below.

Ponce's original claim that Tiwanaku became a densely occupied urban zone—just like European cities—was founded on Jeff Parsons's (1968) observations that continuous ceramic refuse covered a great part of the site. This refuse was dense enough to imply a permanent resident population. Until the 1960s, all but Posnansky and a few of his followers who imagined Tiwanaku at a lower elevation believed that the site had been a vacant ceremonial center, inhabited by a few priests and monks except during pilgrimage season. No one of this era questioned the marginality of Tiwanaku's high-elevation environment. Based on a brief visit, and methods of evaluation perfected in the Valley of Mexico, Parsons cautiously suggested a population of about 20,000 residents. However, Ponce quickly affirmed comparable densities of pot sherds and other refuse across a significantly larger area, totaling some 6 km^2 surrounding Tiwanaku's megalithic monuments. He and other scholars declared that the city had housed 30,000 to 60,000 people (Kolata and Ponce 1992; Ponce 1981). Alan Kolata, director of the new Wila Jawira Project, claimed 115,000 for the greater urbanized heartland (Kolata 1993a:205).

The Wila Jawira Project (Kolata 1993a, 2003b) conducted systematic surface collection at Tiwanaku combined with instrument-based mapping, but neither this nor Ponce's surface data have been published. This makes it impossible to judge interpretive conclusions about demography based on surface artifact area and density. Nonetheless, it became "accepted knowledge" that Tiwanaku housed at least 50,000 inhabitants.

So overwhelmingly influential was the new dogma—that the south altiplano supported an immense city of 50,000 inhabitants—that the new question in Andean research became how the marginally productive altiplano could support such a great concentration of people. Rather than test the bases for the new knowledge, creative economic explanations were explored. David Browman (1978, 1980, 1981, 1985) excavated at Chiripa, a small lakefront site near Tiwanaku, but developed bold inferences about the capital city as well as a "Tiwanaku Empire." Browman reasoned that if Tiwanaku's residents could not be fed from local production, they must have obtained food from neighboring, more productive lands through long-distance trade.

Browman went on to argue that Tiwanaku City must have been occupied by craftspeople who manufactured labor-intensive goods. These high-cost articles were traded via llama caravan for significantly greater amounts of food and raw materials, which were transported back to the capital. So, during the late 1970s and 1980s, Tiwanaku was redefined not only as a great demographic center but also as a lively manufacturing depot engaged in long-distance trade. Indeed, it was imagined as abounding with workshops managed by specialists organized into craft guilds, much like ancient Rome and medieval Europe. Significantly, this change in thinking transpired almost without any new data from field research.

In the mid-1980s, innovative paleoecological research was begun in the altiplano by Clark Erickson (1984, 1985, 1987, 1988, 1992a, 1992b). The focus was ancient altiplano farming and a little-understood technique of intensification: raised-field cultivation. Erickson's results began showing that lakeshore wetlands could sustain impressive agricultural yields and, consequently, larger populations than formerly imagined for the cold, "marginal" altiplano. Alan Kolata (1987, 1993a, 1996c; Janusek and Kolata 2003; Kolata et al. 1996) was quick to explore the implications of raised-field agriculture for Tiwanaku. For more than a decade, Kolata (1987, 1991, 1993a, 1993b, 1996c, 2003b) and his students (Couture 2002, 2003, 2004; Janusek 1994, 2004; Seddon 1994, 1998) directed excavations at Tiwanaku and Lukurmata, a key secondary lakeshore center. They also supervised studies of fossil raised fields and their rehabilitation by modern development specialists working with Indian communities.[4] Unlike Erickson, who argued that community organization was sufficient for raised-field agriculture, Kolata and colleagues affirmed that the hand of hierarchical, bureaucratic management was everywhere apparent and that state-level bureaucracy was essential for large-scale raised-field farming. This discrepancy has never been resolved, along with debates about the actual productivity of raised fields, as well as issues regarding their implications for modern lakeshore economies.

In all of his narratives Kolata promoted Tiwanaku as the administrative center of a powerful and highly centralized, imperialist state (Kolata 1987, 1993b, 2003c, 2004). He credited Tiwanaku with imperial organization and with colonies established as far away as San Pedro de Atacama in Chile (Kolata 1993b). Drawing on structuralist models of the ancient Chinese capital described by Paul Wheatley (1971), and even more on the Southeast Asian palace-city of Angkor Wat (Coe 2003; Mannikka 1996), he went on to describe the Tiwanaku capital as a cosmogram, carefully planned by kings and priests, who mapped universal principles of celestial order and power onto the world of the living. Like Angkor Wat, Tiwanaku's ceremonial core was defined as a sacred island *surrounded* by a water-filled moat. Near the middle of the symbolic island towered the "World Mountain." At Tiwanaku this was the Akapana Pyramid, which represented the origin of water and fertility as rain fell from the sky, flowing down and outward to create rivers and valleys. Large internal drains and a summit covered in water-worn blue-green pebbles from the source of the valley's river were offered as proof of the mountain and water metaphors.

The implication of the cosmogram model is that universal order organized urban space as well as social hierarchy. The city was arranged in terms of a cline of the sacred, diminishing from center to periphery, with a uniformly oriented grid determining the layout of all buildings—and of course capturing the energy and essence of celestial rotation. The east–west power of the sun was primary, harnessed by processions along ascending and descending paths, passing great portals though which the fixed gaze of monumental statues amplified the celestial currents like great generators. Powerful monarchs constructed luxurious palaces within the "sacred island"—next to, or on top of, the central temples and religious processionals. They had themselves commemorated in great statues erected within shrines, with eyes fixed on the paths of power. These were the sculptures that so impressed Spanish invaders centuries later. In the cosmogram model, below the supreme kings and ministers was a hierarchy of bureaucrats managing state interests and integrating people of diverse ethnicities. Each had an economic specialization, and they supervised everything from farming to temple construction. Vigorous commerce was promoted by, and essential to, these bureaucrats. Long-distance caravans brought a myriad of products from distant provinces, but especially corn, from which beer was brewed. Inferences about Tiwanaku's social and political events emphasize feasts that focused on toasts and pledges with corn-beer imported from lower elevations.

DISCOVERING THE REAL TIWANAKU: WHAT IT WAS NOT

The previous summary presents a short history of Tiwanaku's mystique, how it developed, and why so many factoids must be overcome today. Now that we understand that much that is currently written does not represent secure knowledge, we must test the old assertions with archaeological information. Specifically, I will evaluate issues related to Tiwanaku's size, antiquity, precocity, and continuitous cultural development in its local heartland, as well as the supposed cosmogram it formed. First, did Tiwanaku culture appear in the southern altiplano at an early date, developing rapidly into a densely occupied and powerful city, with little or no influence from other Andean cultures?

Tiwanaku as Locally Developed, Densely Occupied City of Craft Specialists

Tiwanaku and the Tiwanaku Valley have a long history of occupation, but during the centuries of formative cultural development, these hamlets do not seem to have been the demographic or ritual center for the region. There was a greater concentration of people and construction along the shoreline of Lake Titicaca, especially on the Taraco Peninsula (Bandy 2001, 2006, this volume; Hastorf 1999; Isbell and Burkholder 2002). And to the south of Tiwanaku, a Late Formative center was constructed at Khonko Wankane (Janusek et al. 2003; Portugal 1937). Indeed, rather than being in a center where a unique culture evolved, Tiwanaku's people appear to have participated in a broad interaction sphere that shared distinctive ritual artifacts, with an emphasis on stelae with anthropomorphic, zoomorphic, and geometric designs; semisubterranean temples; and ceramic trumpets as well as burners, sometimes with distinctive incised and painted decorations (K. Chávez 1988, 2002; S. Chávez 1975, 2004; Chávez and Chávez 1975). Belonging to the Yaya-Mama religious tradition, after about 800 B.C. these cultural elements appear to have been distributed from southern Cuzco to northern Chile. A fragment of a stela at Charazani, in the high jungle of eastern Bolivia (Alconini 2007), may reveal an even greater area.

Between about 200 B.C. and A.D. 200–400, a Yaya-Mama center emerged, triumphed, and declined in the northern Titicaca Basin at Pucará (K. Chávez 1988, 2002; S. Chávez 1992, 2002, 2004). In fact, during the ascendancy of Pucará, Tiwanaku can probably be described as something of a cultural backwater. At Tiwanaku itself, Formative-period occupations preceding the sixth or seventh century A.D. are scarce. Early Formative pottery is absent, while ceramics of Middle Formative times are limited to rare examples from the Kk'araña sector (Janusek 2003:43–44). This suggests that Tiwanaku consisted of no more than a hamlet inhabited by a few hundred individuals during the final millennium B.C.

Late Formative 1A and 1B pottery, corresponding more or less to the first half-millennium of our era, is limited to a collection of burial vessels from a stratum below the later Kalasasaya building, about .5 km southeast of Kk'araña, as well as from some continued occupation in that sector. However, Kk'araña ceramics are not quite the same as the pots from the burials (Janusek 2003:49). Tiwanaku certainly was not yet a thriving "proto-city" but was one of several small polities emerging in the south altiplano. Bandy (2006:232) concludes that "During the Late Formative 1 period . . . the Tiwanaku Polity was probably similar to or smaller than the Taraco Peninsula Polity (the Taraco Peninsula is immediately west of the Tiwanaku Valley), and the two were likely competitors." Tiwanaku's Semisubterranean Temple was probably built during Late Formative times. If ceramic differences between Kk'araña and the cemetery relate to domestic versus mortuary wares, we can propose that in the centuries immediately preceding A.D. 550, Tiwanaku had developed into a village with a cemetery and small monumental shrine located about .5 km away.

The inference that Tiwanaku became a village with a cemetery and shrine for the first time in the Late Formative phase is supported by the discovery of only two, probably relatively late, Yaya-Mama-style sculptures within the archaeological zone. (They are the Bearded Statue [Posnansky 1945: Figures 87 and 88] found in the Semisubterranean Temple and a more recently excavated monolith on the north side of the Kalasasaya, between the Semisubterranean Temple and Kk'araña [Arellano 1991: Figure 27].) It is also possible that two statues moved to the entrance of Tiwanaku's Christian church are relatively early, but both are eroded and probably also partially recarved. More or less contemporary statues from Pokotia, about 3 km away, probably document another village in the developing interaction sphere. Had Tiwanaku been the center of early altiplano cultural development, its sculptural record should be long and abundant. However, various components of the archaeological record concur in revealing Tiwanaku as a late, but spectacular, synthesis within an ancient and extensive interaction sphere. It was not the precocious center of innovation and diffusion (see Benitez 2009).

Now, if Tiwanaku was not more than a hamlet or village during Formative times, how large did it become in Tiwanaku IV–V times? Demographic claims during the 1970s, 1980s, and 1990s (Kolata and Ponce 1992:32) placed the population of the city between 30,000 and 60,000. The figure of 50,000 (Stanish 2003) became very popular and was confidently asserted by almost all specialists. However, after a decade and a half of research and analysis, Kolata (2003a:15) reduced his early estimate to a third or half of the old total, suggesting only 15,000 to 20,000 residents. I find the smaller number much more convincing, but unfortunately the basis for this very significant revision was not described.

Certainly, recent excavation results have influenced thinking, consistently revealing relatively thin occupation strata at Tiwanaku and modest residential architecture with little domestic crowding. Furthermore, Ponce's death may have provided scholars greater intellectual independence, but surely another development was also influential.

Archaeological thinking about Native American cities has changed radically during the last century and a half. Tiwanaku's population estimate from the 1970s through the 1990s reflects the theoretical orientation of the mid-twentieth century, when American archaeologists reembraced cultural evolution and the conviction that a universal process underlies the development of complex civilization worldwide. The late-nineteenth-century notion that Native American "cities" had not been cities at all, but unique New World variants of some kind of vacant ceremonial center, was discarded during the 1960s and 1970s. Along with new research at important centers such as Teotihuacán in the Valley of Mexico, new theory presented America's prehistoric cities as part of the same evolutionary process that produced cities in Asia and Europe. Focus turned to occupational specialization, the organization of production, and urban economies of scale. Estimates of resident populations for indigenous American cities jumped to levels equivalent to demographic totals formerly reserved for archaic civilizations of the Middle East and classical Mediterranean. Almost overnight it became fashionable to affirm immense residential totals for prehistoric American centers. Conservatism was not viewed as scientific rigor but as anti-evolutionary—bordering on ethnocentric racism. Looking back on the era, I believe that a generation of Americanists went overboard claiming excessive demographic figures for cherished archaeological centers.

The claims for Tiwanaku were shaped more by enthusiasm than science.

I find a population of 15,000 to 20,000 quite convincing for Tiwanaku, even if declarations that residential refuse is distributed more or less continuously over some 6 km^2 are not exaggerations. Of course, caution is in order, because Tiwanaku's area of prehistoric refuse, variation in ceramic densities, and the chronology of this surface pottery have never been demonstrated in print. On the other hand, recent excavations at Tiwanaku have been consistent in revealing shallow cultural deposits. My thinking is as follows: Beyond the monumental civic center, Tiwanaku's modern landscape is slightly rolling, composed of low rises surrounded by shallow dales. All archaeological excavations in this periphery have been located on the rises that I believe represent eroded adobe constructions of the past, just as dales probably represent vacant areas. Consequently, I believe that only the rises were occupied by prehistoric residential architecture, although sherds and other refuse were probably dumped and carried into the dales by erosion. In all probability Tiwanaku's suburban periphery was not a continuous, dense occupation. Rather, Tiwanaku was a landscape of walled compounds separated from one another by fields, gardens, and probably also campsites for visitors. In this case, 6 km^2 of domestic trash could represent a modest number of permanent residents, especially if occupation lasted several centuries and the surface is stable or even deflating so that broken pottery is brought to the surface.

Now, if Tiwanaku was a significantly smaller city than formerly thought, was its economy based on specialized production, characterized by craft guilds manufacturing high-value goods for intensive long-distance trade, as David Browman (1978, 1980, 1984) argued? A decade of excavation results, recently reported in a great compendium volume (Kolata 2003b), demonstrates conclusively that this was never the case at Tiwanaku. The only occupational specialization resolutely documented in Tiwanaku's excavation record is ceramic production in the Ch'iji Jawira sector (Rivera 2003), and even that is more consistent with part-time, household-based production than guild-organized workshops.

Certainly, the production of specialized goods is still inadequately understood for Tiwanaku. Expertise apparent in some textiles, metal implements, and other kinds of artifacts implies skills beyond that of household part-timers. Some kind of specialized workshops must have existed at Tiwanaku or its subsidiary centers, but they are too infrequent to have been discovered by archaeological excavations. However, investigators have shown that Tiwanaku cannot be explained as a city that fulfilled multiregional demands for specialized goods by the efficiency and skill of its manufacturing economy of scale. Indeed, Tiwanaku's average citizen was not a craft specialist employed in the manufacture of specialized goods.

Tiwanaku as Precocious and Continuitous Cultural Center—Judged by Ceramics

The demographic estimates discussed above raise doubt whether Tiwanaku had a large enough population to be more than locally influential until the transformative changes that took place around A.D. 550–750. However, an independent picture of Tiwanaku's importance and influences in the southern altiplano and neighboring regions can be gained from an examination of ceramics.

The truly diagnostic pottery of Tiwanaku is the ceramics of its cultural apogee, the so-called Tiwanaku IV and V phases, consisting of several popular vessel shapes frequently decorated with characteristic painted designs (Figure 10.1). Pottery, of course, is primarily for eating and drinking, including the preparation of food as well as its storage. There is nothing more fundamental to a people than food and eating. Ceramic vessels correlate very specifically with food practices—from technologies of preparation to etiquettes of consumption, including issues such as size of the group for which food is normally prepared, means of carrying prepared food to work, which utensil to use at a feast, and what is a proper serving size. In our society, a saucepan is not for frying potatoes, coffee is not drunk from a champagne flute, and one does not eat corned-beef hash from a teacup. So if Tiwanaku were the dominant culture of the south altiplano, without significant external influences, its pottery and etiquette would have characterized the entire heartland area with little change and that only very gradually.

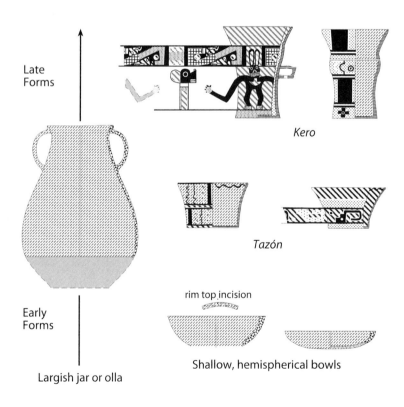

FIGURE 10.1. Tiwanaku vessel forms.

A stratigraphic study of change and continuity in Tiwanaku ceramics was conducted in the heartland settlement of Iwawi (Isbell and Burkholder 2002; Isbell et al. 2002; see also Burkholder 1997, 2001). Because Tiwanaku itself surely conducted unique rituals, and the capital is subject to more earthmoving and stratigraphic mixing than any other site in the altiplano, a site of tertiary rank in the regional settlement-size hierarchy, located only 20 km from the capital, offered better conditions for the base study of ceramic continuity.

Iwawi first gained fame as Tiwanaku's port, where great blocks of andesite stone from across Lake Titicaca were landed before being hauled inland to the city (Ponce 1972). It is also an ancient mound of residential debris about 2.5 m deep on the shore of Lake Titicaca. Excavations yielded nine strata, the lowest sterile soil that appears to have been shaped into raised fields for cultivation before the site was occupied. Stratum V divides the sequence in two. It is composed of andesite sand, probably from intensive work shaping imported stone blocks. Significantly, this grit layer probably represents a moment when construction in andesite was intensive, a major construction time at the capital.

So, do ceramic shapes demonstrate long-term continuity at Iwawi? The answer is no. Only one vessel shape continues through all of Iwawi's occupational strata: I, II, III, IV, VII, and VIII. It is a largish jar or olla (Figure 10.1; for additional illustrations of Iwawi–Tiwanaku vessel shapes, see Isbell and Burkholder 2002:217, 218, Figures 7.8 and 7.9; for Tiwanaku shapes, see Janusek 2003:57, Figure 3.27) that served as a cooking pot. Its continuity suggests that some ways of preparing food remained unchanged throughout the occupational history of the Iwawi mound. There was never such a radical change in foodways that population replacement is implied. On the other hand, there are profound changes in other shapes, especially serving wares. Apparently, food etiquette did undergo profound change at Iwawi and throughout the Tiwanaku heartland.

In the deep strata, VI through VIII, the common cooking pot is accompanied by a wide range of more or less shallow, hemispherical bowls, some with incised rims (Figure 10.1). These were probably serving bowls, for eating and drinking. But they disappear with the appearance of the sandy debitage that constitutes stratum V and are completely replaced in higher strata by the two most common Tiwanaku shapes, the *kero* and the *tazón*. *Tazones* are flat-bottomed bowls with straight or slightly belled, flaring sides, often painted, sometimes with polychrome Tiwanaku themes. They were probably food bowls. *Keros* are tall, flat-bottomed flagons, with concave sides, slightly constricted waists, and flaring rims. They were apparently drinking vessels and are more frequently decorated with polychrome Tiwanaku icons than any other pottery shape. In fact, if one were to characterize Tiwanaku culture by a single artifact, it would surely be the *kero* beer flagon.

The *kero* and *tazón* appear without antecedents at Iwawi and apparently throughout the Tiwanaku heartland. Furthermore, several other vessel shapes show up without antecedents. New ritual behavior is indicated by the appearance of the hollow-headed *incensario* with scalloped rim. But it has an earlier antecedent in solid-headed *incensarios* with scalloped rims that share features with Yaya-Mama pottery forms. So there seems to have been both continuity and change in ritual activities that may have been shamanic. Other ritual vessels—a ring-based bowl often called a *sahumador* and a small jar or *vasija* that frequently accompanies the dead to the grave—appear in stratum VI or VII but continue only into stratum IV times.

Obviously Iwawi does not reveal continuity in the ceramics of the Tiwanaku heartland. The key diagnostics of Tiwanaku, the *kero* and *tazón,* appear without antecedent in strata IV and III and overwhelm the second half of the sequence. On the other hand, Iwawi ceramics do not imply cultural replacement, for basic food preparation continued, except as indicated by the late appearance of bottles or *tinajas*. It seems that in the south altiplano, the appearance of Tiwanaku culture involved the adoption of new eating customs that consisted more of table manners and social etiquette than of basic cooking techniques or primary staples. This suggests that change in identity was taking place.

An examination of the *kero* alone may help us understand culture change in the Tiwanaku heartland. Its distinctive shape makes it easy to trace, even from a few well-preserved sherds. The *kero* is interpreted as a drinking cup and has been associated with feasting. It was probably a corn-beer flagon. Corn is characteristically a product of lower elevations than Tiwanaku, but we should not conclude that corn-beer was unknown in the altiplano before the appearance of *keros*. However, *keros* were apparently associated with specific new patterns of beer drinking. Furthermore, their more or less simultaneous popular appearance in cultures of the western Pacific coast, throughout the altiplano, and in societies residing in eastern tropical valleys suggests that corn-beer drunk from *kero* vessels involved a new etiquette that was part of a new *inter*national identity. I am reminded of the relationship between martinis, martini glasses, international business, and "happy hour." Men and women of the southern Andes, from different places and cultures, shared the knowledge and utensils for conducting socially endorsed events that were transcultural.

If *keros* were long associated with maize beer, they probably did not evolve in the cold altiplano where corn is rare and precious. Rather, we should look to warmer climates. Indeed, Cochabamba, a large valley system southeast of Tiwanaku, about 1,300 m lower in elevation, offers excellent antecedents for *kero* shapes. Apparently they date at least as early as the final millennium before our era, as indicated by collections in Cochabamba's archaeological museum (*http://www.umss.edu.bo/Sitios/ Museo/ index.html*; see also Anderson this volume). Furthermore, Cochabamba is famous for excellent corn-beer today as well as in Inca times. I believe that sometime between A.D. 550 and 750, Tiwanaku was interacting with people from the Cochabamba area and other areas as well. All were learning to consume corn-beer in terms of a specific etiquette of transcultural practices that promoted a shared new international identity.

Culture changes associated with new beer drinking must have included more than just the ceremonies of consumption. They also must have involved the distribution of corn, the technology of brewing, the meaning of inebriation, and other practices with sweeping ramifications. For example, in far-off Conchopata, in Peru's central highlands, where ritual drinking beer from *keros* also became prominent, the growing importance of brewing, in which women played a key role, had profound effects on the redefinition of gender (Isbell and Groleau 2010). Furthermore, the process linked many more cultures than those of the Tiwanaku heartland and people of the Cochabamba Valley. Since Yaya-Mama times, and perhaps earlier, altiplano peoples were involved in long-distance trade with people in complementary environments, creating a trans-Andean interaction sphere. This sphere of exchange intensified and internationalized between A.D. 550 and 750, with Tiwanaku emerging as its central place. Indeed, I believe the process involved was not at all like diffusion, with a precocious and dominant center from which influences radiated. The process was multicultural or transcultural.

Tiwanaku as Precocious and Continuitous Cultural Center—Judged by Religious Iconography

Stübel and Uhle's (1892) early archaeological description of Tiwanaku defined the religious iconography that characterizes much of Tiwanaku's monumental stone sculpture. When Uhle (1903b) found the same images on ceramics and textiles at Pachacamac, he inferred that all had spread from Tiwanaku, and he named the art Tihuanaco style (the spelling of that time). Scholars have followed his lead for a century. For example, artifacts decorated with the diagnostic figures discovered on the Peruvian coast, especially the numerous textiles preserved in its arid sands, were called Coast Tiahuanaco, implying derivation from Bolivian Tiwanaku images although recognizing significant differences (see Sawyer 1963).

Over the past century many scholars have discussed this iconography; Patricia Knobloch and I are among the most recent (Isbell and Knobloch 2006, 2009). Because the name Tiwanaku creates the impression that the iconography must have originated at, and spread from, the Tiwanaku site, we (Isbell and Knobloch 2009) prefer a more neutral name. SAIS is an acronym for Southern Andean Iconographic Series. We employ the concept *series* because it includes the principles of both tradition and horizon.

SAIS iconography consists of three principal images: (1) a Rayed Head, (2) a front-face Staff God, and (3) a Profile Attendant, who appears in several variants, including a Sacrificer with ax and severed head. All three are anthropomorphic but include animal characteristics and other special conventions such as divided eyes, internal body structures, and elaborate headdresses or crowns that suggest mythical or supernatural status. At Tiwanaku, SAIS icons appear primarily on monumental sculptures, employing fine-line incision, relief, and excision. Some closely related images appear in such high relief that they could be called sculpture-in-the-round, but these examples differ somewhat from the three typical SAIS figures. Conklin (this volume) may be correct about Tiwanaku's preference for depicting supernatural images in two-dimensional representations, or relief sculpture.

Very occasionally, SAIS images appear on Tiwanaku ceramics (Couture and Sampeck 2003; Korpisaari and Pärssinen 2005), and a fine textile from Pulacayo (Berenguer 2000), south of Tiwanaku, suggests that if preservation were better, Tiwanaku's archaeological record would include many spectacular weavings decorated with SAIS icons. Be that as it may, most archaeologists have privileged stone sculpture, imagining that it was the original and primary medium for the mythical SAIS figures.

SAIS images are widespread, occurring throughout the central and southern Andes but never in stone sculpture outside the Tiwanaku heartland. The mythical figures are found as far south as San Pedro de Atacama and as far north as Cajamarca and Lambayeque. They were produced in tapestry, embroidered and painted textiles, ceramics, wood sculptures, carved gourds, mosaic mirrors, wall murals, and other media. Everywhere, they differ slightly in the combination of media, style, and technique. But the shared group of figures implies a common, underlying ideology, probably a body of religious myths.

Now, if SAIS iconography originated at Tiwanaku, the set of icons (and myths) should be present early in the history of the site. Furthermore, if the set of figures diffused from Tiwanaku, the full repertoire of images must have been at Tiwanaku throughout the past. But this is not the case.

Prior to A.D. 550–750, only one of the SAIS icons was depicted at Tiwanaku—the Rayed Head. Furthermore, it appears only as a design on ceramic vessels and in rather idiosyncratic manners that differ significantly from later representations (Isbell and Knobloch 2006, 2009). Rather than SAIS iconography, Formative-phase Tiwanaku was characterized by art of the Yaya-Mama religious tradition, such as the two sculptures mentioned above (the Bearded Statue [Posnansky 1945: Figures 87 and 88] and the monolith on the north side of the Kalasasaya [Arellano 1991: Figure 27]).

Yaya-Mama art consists of simple sculptures, sometimes with two anthropomorphic figures or faces on them, a male and a female, apparently emphasizing sexual dualism (S. Chávez 2002; Chávez and Chávez 1975). Among the other figures that appear are a primitive version of the Rayed Head, so the presence of that image at Formative Tiwanaku is not a surprise. However, Yaya-Mama art lacks the Staff God and Profile Attendant.

The most likely antecedents and apparently earliest examples of Staff Gods and Profile Attendants are not at Tiwanaku. Unfortunately, complex issues must be simplified for this discussion. Antecedents of the Staff God and Profile Attendant icons—as well as a more typical Rayed Head—are found in Pucará art, in provincial Pucará art (of the far south coast of Peru), and on hallucinogenic paraphernalia from north Chilean Atacama Desert oases. Of course, all these are related to, and perhaps should be considered part of, the Yaya-Mama religious tradition, but they are the participants that best reveal the origins of SAIS iconography. However, none of the three is an immediate antecedent for SAIS.

Pucará art includes a male, profile Sacrificer image reminiscent of Profile Attendants, a female front-face figure reminiscent of the Staff God, and a Rayed Head much like later representations. In addition, many of the conventions of SAIS art, such as the divided eye, internal body structure, and elaborate crowns, are also typical of the Pucará figures. Temporally, all these icons belong to a four- or five-century period from about 200 B.C. to A.D. 200–400 (Isbell and Knobloch 2006, 2009). Pucará and its images are surely ancestors of the SAIS pantheon, but somewhat distant.

Provincial Pucará art is known almost exclusively from looted textiles that probably served as shrouds for mummies buried during the first centuries of our era. All probably come from the far south coast, especially the Sihuas Valley region of Arequipa (Haeberli 2001; Isbell and Knobloch 2006, 2009). The icons that appear are the Rayed Head, usually perched on a three-step pedestal, and idiosyncratic Profile Attendants. However, the woven representations usually show the icons in a grouping suggestive of a hierarchical structure that also characterizes many of the Tiwanaku sculptures.

The third and most confusing of the SAIS antecedents is the decorative art on wooden snuff tablets and other hallucinogenic paraphernalia from Chile's vast Atacama Desert. The carved images include all three of the icons and, particularly, a wide variety of Profile Attendants and Sacrificers. These shamanic instruments probably appeared in the Atacama archaeological record by about A.D. 200 to 300 and perhaps earlier, but they continued in use until the collapse of Tiwanaku, about A.D. 1100. Since few of the objects are precisely dated, it is difficult to determine whether all or only some of the images were present from the beginning of the sequence. What is apparent is that well before their appearance at Tiwanaku, best dated between A.D. 550 and 750, Atacama snuff tablets were decorated with a very typical Profile Attendant, at least.

It is not clear how, or even precisely when, the new synthetic pantheon of Staff God, Rayed Head, and Profile Attendant was formalized. Most probably it was after, or perhaps during, the transformation dated to A.D. 550 to 750 and occurred under the influence of earlier Pucará culture, provincial Pucará art, and the iconography of Atacama shamanic snuff paraphernalia. Very significantly, the same SAIS repertoire appears in the Peruvian central highlands at Huari/Conchopata at more or less the same time. So SAIS art was like the *kero* and beer drinking. It did not have a place of origin but was from the beginning multicultural. While multicultural or transcultural origins are difficult for archaeologists to understand, what is clear is that Tiwanaku was not the precocious and continuitous center for the development and diffusion of SAIS iconography and religious ideology. Like other places throughout the Andes, Tiwanaku was a recipient of the art—although it was also an innovative creator of the image repertoire, shaping old icons into a major new synthesis. Indeed, at much the same time the new pantheon of SAIS icons was formalized, Tiwanaku embarked on an unparalleled program of monumental constructions, creating a ritual landscape and pilgrimage center exceeding anything known before in the Andes.

Tiwanaku as Sacred-Island Cosmogram and Palace-City

In the following section I review claims that Tiwanaku was a city of hierarchically organized officials—from clerks to ministers to king—residing in a precisely determined pattern of concentric rings and a uniform astronomically aligned grid, where status and sanctity were mapped onto a space whose center was a symbolic "sacred island." According to this argument, supreme structural principles ordered the urban cosmogram, which included statues of the kings as well as their royal residences among the temple compounds and the World Mountain pyramid. This interpretation of Tiwanaku has been published repeatedly since 1992, and most recently in 2004, with no significant change (Kolata 1993a, 2004; Kolata and Ponce 1992). I believe its long life can be attributed in part to the convincing flow of a well-written narrative enlivened by ethnohistorical and ethnographic analogies. Indeed, the model continues to be cited even as parts of it topple in light of new information produced by some 30 years of more or less continuous field investigation. Rather than assail details, I address three main components of this model: the water-filled moat, the issue of palaces, and evidence for kings.

First, let us examine the keystone of the analogy between Tiwanaku and spectacular Southeast Asian palace-cities: the case for a moated "sacred island" at the center of the site. The notion that the core of Tiwanaku was surrounded by a water-filled moat is not new but was resurrected in light of structural analyses of Southeast Asia's sacred-island capitals, of which Angkor Wat is the most famous. However, the idea was first promulgated in the early twentieth century by Arthur Posnansky (1912, 1911a, 1911b, 1914, 1938, 1945, 1957). Trained as an engineer, Posnansky made professional-quality maps and systematic observations at Tiwanaku, recording a great deal of valuable information. Unfortunately, his scholarship was flawed by thinking that was all too popular in his time—hyper-diffusionism, racism, and outrageous ideas about the antiquity of Tiwanaku.

Posnansky (1945:30–36) believed that Tiwanaku had been such a spectacular metropolis that it could have thrived only at a lower altitude with a better climate. So the site must be so ancient that it preceded the rise of the Andes to their present elevation—3,850 m above sea level. In its heyday, Posnansky argued, Tiwanaku had been at least 200 m lower. Furthermore, Lake Titicaca was about 40 m higher than it is today, with shores washing the edge of the city, not 20 km away as it is today. Posnansky considered a steep drop to the floodplain of the Tiwanaku River as the old bank of Lake Titicaca. With lake water filling the modern river valley, Tiwanaku City had a bustling waterfront with a wharf for boats. Several deep gullies were imagined to represent the remnants of an ancient canal on which reed gondolas navigated about the ancient civic center.

Posnansky's interpretation was based on several errors regarding complex archaeological and geological data. Furthermore, by the time he arrived at Tiwanaku, railroad construction had inflicted severe damage to the ruins, exceeding centuries of Spanish-inspired mining for stone and looting for gold. Perhaps most relevant, railroad track had been laid immediately south of the Akapana Pyramid, near the course of the supposed moat. Grading and embankments for the railroad had transformed the landscape, so Posnansky (1945: Plate III) simply pro - jected the moat on his map, using dotted lines to highlight a hypothetical route at an oblique angle to, and actually crossing, the new railroad line slightly southwest of the Akapana.

When archaeologist Wendell Bennett (1934) visited Tiwanaku in the early 1930s, he repeated the moat idea by outlining it on his impressionistic site map. Subsequently, however, the moat disappeared from Tiwanaku literature, only to be resurrected decades later in support of the analogy with Angkor Wat and other Southeast Asian palace-cities (Kolata 1993a, 2003c, 2004; Kolata and Ponce 1992). Like Angkor Wat, Tiwanaku was a cosmogram surrounded by water, which defined a sacred island, which housed the World Mountain, making it the center of the universe.

First we examine the issue of water in the moat, an element without which even a symbolic island cannot be created. In several books and articles, the supposed coarse of the moat has been emphasized by darkening it on an enhanced vertical air photograph of Tiwanaku (Kolata 2003c:178, Figure 7.1, 2004:101, Figure 4.2; see also Kolata 1993a:94). These illustrations reveal a discrepancy between the route inferred by Posnansky (1945: Plate III) and the route selected by modern proponents. Recent scholars place the southern course of the moat exactly over the railroad line, while Posnansky had it crossing the line. But most importantly, the vertical air photograph obscures considerable topographic relief at Tiwanaku, hiding the fact that, especially severe in the northwest, gradient in the projected route of the moat would have drained water away from the civic center. If the moat existed as proposed, it could not have held water.

If we take the enhanced photograph (Kolata 2003c:178, Figure 7.1) on which the moat is darkened and we overlay the 1-m contour lines published on the "Topographic map of Tiwanaku showing the locations of principal structures and Proyecto Wila Jawira excavation areas" folded into the compendium volume (Kolata 2003b), we see that the northern course of the moat is 10 m lower than the southern course (Figure 10.2). Consequently, the hypothetical canal would not hold water. Any water in it would immediately run north, down the steep slope, and into the Tiwanaku River. Indeed, the contour lines show that from its northwestern corner the supposed moat drops 7 or 8 m in elevation over 200 m distance as the proposed route proceeds east. This was not a moat but several drainage gullies, probably partially natural and partially excavated (and surely providing fill for mound construction).

If the northern course of the moat is so steeply inclined that it had to function to drain the land, what of the rest of the hypothetical course? In fact, the topographic lines show that there is no justification for the moat in the western part of the civic center, in the southwestern corner, and in most of the darkened southern course. Indeed, the only more or less convincing portion of the shaded course is the eastern segment, where a deep gulley drains the land east of the civic center today, carrying water to the Tiwanaku River. Also seemingly convincing is the southeastern corner, where the darkened, hypothetical course turned west (Figure 10.2). But here the imagined course has been placed exactly over the modern railroad, constructed at the turn of the twentieth century and involving undetermined volumes of earthmoving. The pre-railroad contours, not the modern railroad landscape, are what is relevant. Fortunately, Max Uhle took photographs of the critical area in 1893 (Figure 10.3).[5] These photos show a megalithic gateway and lintel south of the Akapana, almost exactly on the hypothetical course of the moat as currently projected (Kolata 2003c:178, Figure 7.1). The upper view looks north toward the Akapana Pyramid, while the lower looks south. If a depression had marked the course of the moat before railroad construction, it would appear in one of these photographs. However, there is no trace. Furthermore, Adolf Bandelier visited Tiwanaku in 1894

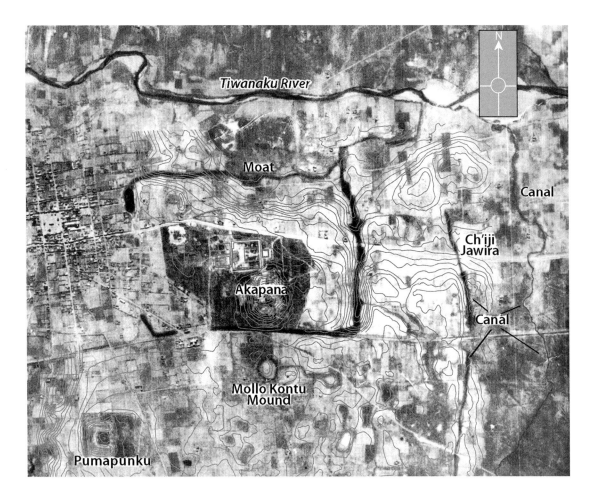

Figure 10.2. Contour map overlying an aerial picture of the monumental area of Tiwanaku.

and noted that the land south of the Akapana was flat, with no evidence for an ancient moat (Bentley 2013). In conclusion, then, there was no moat at Tiwanaku creating a sacred island around a World Mountain and palace-city. The analogy with Angkor Wat does not pass the test of field information.

Do other parts of the structuralist cosmogram argument pass rigorous scrutiny? For example, I have been informed by scholars developing new site plans that maps produced by the Wila Jawira program showing buildings on a universal orientation are proving inaccurate (Benitez and Vranich 2005). Indeed, Posnansky's turn-of-the-century plans showed modest variations in monument orientations, not strict conformance to a single grid. New studies vindicate Posnansky, while Wila Jawira maps seem to be too idealized. Of course, this is not to say that Tiwanaku's buildings were oriented haphazardly, but the notion that they expressed a cosmos based on a universal principle that organized religion, space, political power, and social status does not stand the test. Archaeologists must seek new explanations to account for actual facts.

If there was no moat, sacred island, or universal grid at Tiwanaku, is there evidence for authoritative kings who ruled in luxury, another part of the palace-city cosmogram interpretation? Of course, the best way to test this argument is to examine the facilities of rulers themselves—the palaces from which powerful lords would have ruled. Indeed, several Tiwanaku buildings have been classified as palaces by the Wila Jawira Project, especially a structure directly west of the Putuni Palace Courtyard that was fully excavated and named the Palace of the Multicolored Rooms (Kolata 1993a). Sampeck (1991: 30–35) provides excavation details, while Couture (2004; see also Couture and Sampeck 2003) discusses relationships with another less completely excavated building that was also classified as a palace, across a patio to the west.

FIGURE 10.3. Photographs from Max Uhle (1893) showing the flat area to the south of the Akapana (*courtesy of the University of Pennsylvania Museum Archives*).

The Palace of the Multicolored Rooms (Figures 10.4a, 10.5a) is poorly preserved, but a reconstruction has been created by combining Sampeck's (1991) Figures 4 and 5 with Kolata's (1993a) Figure 5.36a–b. The building was an architectural compound about 23 m long and 6 m wide,[6] divided into four elongated rooms and a fifth square space that may have been a kitchen. An open patio to the west seems to have bordered it, and there was a similar structure on the opposite side of the patio. To the east a slim corridor and an open drain narrowly separated the palace from the Putuni monument. Although some cut stones appear in floors and foundations, and fragments of a cut-stone entry lintel were found, construction was primarily of adobe, with a thatched roof probably supported by wooden beams. The walls were painted brilliant colors, including green, blue, and orange red.

Was this Palace of the Multicolored Rooms a sumptuous residence for a supreme ruler and closely related nobles? It certainly was larger than domestic residences excavated in suburban portions of Tiwanaku (Janusek 2004). By Andean palatial standards, the compound was tiny. In size, its closest comparison is the Puruchuco Palace (Figures 10.4b and 10.5b; Jimenez 1973) in the Lima Valley, occupied by a third- or fourth-order lord, subservient to the Inca, to the Inca governor, to a traditional ethnic lord, and perhaps even to his senior vassal at the moment of the Spanish invasion. The Puruchuco Palace measures about 10 by 22 m, so it actually had about twice the floor space of the Palace of the Multicolored Rooms.[7] Furthermore, the Puruchuco Palace is much more complex architecturally, with a courtyard, ramp, and elevated stage. The stage could be approached from the front by visitors, approached from the side, probably by attendants, or entered from behind, probably by the presiding lord. A narrow, almost secret hallway leads from the residential area to the rear stage entrance. In the residential area was an ample windowed room with porch and patio, as well as a curious room that was probably a wardrobe for storing fancy costumes and for dressing the lord for formal events. Finally, Puruchuco was securely walled, with an entrance designed for security and defense. None of these features are present in Tiwanaku's Palace of the Multicolored Rooms.

The Puruchuco Palace is reminiscent of Pachacamac's Palace of Tauri Chumpi (Eeckhout 1999: 123), the residence of the Inca governor of the Lima area at the moment of the Spanish invasion, except that Tauri Chumpi's palace was much larger—about 10 times the floor space of Puruchuco and 20 times that of Tiwanaku's Palace of the Multicolored Rooms (Figure 10.5c; all the palaces discussed are shown at approximately the same scale). Significantly, Tauri Chumpi's palace shares with Puruchuco many formal elements that displayed power and magnified difference—all lacking in the Tiwanaku compound. Similar elements appear in the Inca compound at La Centinela (Figure 10.5c; Wallace 1998: Figures 4 and 5), probably another governor's palace that was similar in size to Tauri Chumpi's residence.

The palaces of secondary and tertiary rulers from coastal Peru provide quantitative and qualitative attributes of late Andean palaces. A fundamental feature was an assembly space with a marked place at

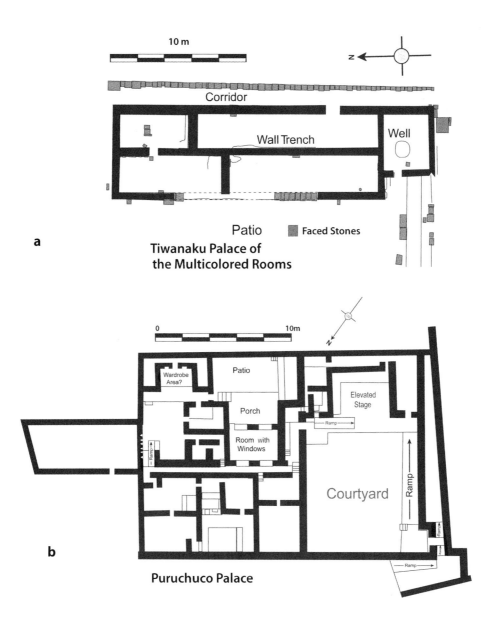

Figure 10.4. Plan view of the palace at Puruchuco.

one end. In the coastal palaces, these were raised stages, approached from below by a ramp. A private route, often hidden behind the stage, led to the elite residence, and of course there was another entrance to the housing area as well. Within the residential quarters was a second and smaller patio for household activities. Finally, the complex was protected by stout walls and a fortified entrance.

How do these second- and third-order palaces compare with first-order Andean palaces? If the *ciudadelas* of Chan Chan were the residences of the Chimu kings, as generally believed, Ciudadela Rivero (Figure 10.5e; Moore 1996: Figure 5.25;

Moseley and Mackey 1974: General Plan of Central Chan Chan) provides a well-preserved but smallish example of a royal Chimu palace. Indeed, Rivero shares significant features with the smaller palaces discussed above, including a courtyard—as well as a larger plaza—with a raised stage and ramp. But in size, Rivero is five or six times the area of Tauri Chumpi's palace, and of course the largest of Chan Chan's palaces, Gran Chimu, was three or four times the size of Rivero. So imperial Andean palaces were certainly grand.

Unfortunately, Cuzco is so damaged by modern architecture that it has not provided a clear plan for

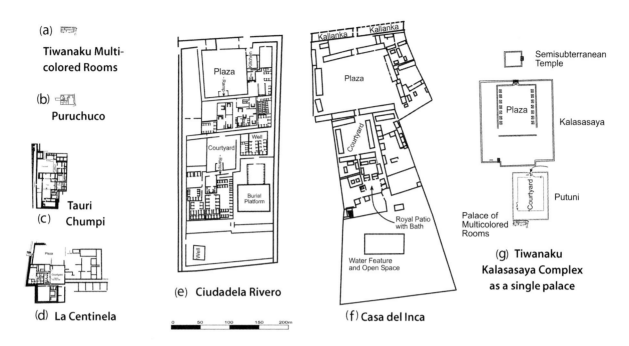

FIGURE 10.5. Comparison of monumental buildings in the Andes that have been interpreted as palaces.

an imperial palace. However, archaeologists agree that the Casa del Inca at Huanuco Pampa (Figure 10.5f; Morris and von Hagen 1993: Figure 153) was the emperor's palace during visits to the provincial administrative center, providing the best example of an Inca palace.

Huanuco Pampa's Casa del Inca is about 400 m long and 100 to 200 m wide, so it is more or less on a spatial par with Ciudadela Rivero, although the enclosure was much less crowded, especially the expansive area in the rear that may have been a garden/zoo/entertainment space (Figure 10.5f). But Ciudadela Rivero and the Casa del Inca share important features: two assembly spaces, a large plaza just inside the complex, and a smaller inner courtyard deeper within. The raised stage characteristic of coastal palaces is absent in the Inca compound, but we know that the Inca habilitated temporary spaces for festivities with movable furnishings, including awnings and benches (MacCormack 1991). Consequently, it seems likely that the plaza and the courtyard of Inca palaces functioned in much the same manner as those in Chimu palaces and that first-order palaces of late pre-Hispanic times shared a spatial order that required a large outer and a small inner assembly area.

Now returning to Tiwanaku and the Palace of the Multicolored Rooms, royal power and wealth are not simple functions of the size of the footprint of the palace—but there certainly seems to be a correlation. In view of the size of Tiwanaku's Palace of the Multicolored Rooms, even smaller than the third- or fourth-order palaces of Inca-period central coastal Peru, it seems that the residents of Tiwanaku's core were not kings or even immensely wealthy and powerful.

If Tiwanaku's supreme lords lived in palaces that were smaller than Puruchuco, their wealth and power was simply not comparable to that of the best-known Andean rulers, the Inca and Chimu emperors. If the Palace of the Multicolored Rooms and its western neighbor were Tiwanaku's ultimate residences, then the leaders of Tiwanaku were probably not kings but were more likely members of some kind of collective form of government—perhaps a council of elders or some kind of Andean version of senators. But more importantly, the sacred-island, palace-city interpretation fails again.

Before going on to the third test study, the issue of kings at Tiwanaku, an alternative understanding of Tiwanaku's architecture may be possible. Perhaps archaeologists have misread the landscape of the civic center (Isbell 2004b) in attempting to identify palaces. As determined above, a diagnostic of first-order, late pre-Hispanic palaces is a large outer, and a small inner, assembly space, separated by walls and gateways or by differences in elevation (Figure 5e–f). Residential quarters were located deeper within the complex, beyond the courtyard.

Inspecting the context of the Palace of the Multicolored Rooms shows that it lies immediately west of a small megalithic courtyard, the Putuni monument. The Putuni, in turn, lies immediately west of a large megalithic plaza complex, the Kalasasaya (Figure 10.5g; see also Isbell 2004b: Figure 21). Each of these monuments has always been considered a separate building and may well have been, at least sometime in Tiwanaku's history. But their spatial organization corresponds with a larger outer, and a smaller inner, assembly area, if access to the Putuni was through the Kalasasaya. Indeed, the back (or west) side of the Kalasasaya is the Balconera Wall, an addition to the building that is generally considered to be late and that includes megalithic "orthostat" stones marking positions on the western horizon apparently used for solar cylindrical observations (Benitez 2008, 2009). This architectural modification could easily have obscured a direct relationship between the Kalasasaya and Putuni, although a small stairway does still descend the back of the Kalasasaya toward the front of the Putuni. If the Kalasasaya and Putuni were parts of a palace complex, then the Palace of the Multicolored Rooms was a tiny part of the royal residential compound. Its small size and simple organization would represent only a fraction of Tiwanaku's royal power and wealth.[8]

How should we understand Tiwanaku's civic center and the possible space of rulership? This remains an enigma. One interpretation suggests that rule was not concentrated into the hands of a single lord but was probably dispersed among elders or senators in a council-based government. In this vision of the past, residences surrounding Tiwanaku's sacred inner-city temples were modest, certainly by comparison with the dwellings of Chimu and Inca kings. But an alternative possibility is that most of the buildings constituting Tiwanaku's civic center were, at some time, part of a single palace complex. If this were the case, kingship must have been absolute, with a ruler powerful and wealthy beyond imagination. In fact, Tiwanaku would seem to be a palace-city more like the Southeast Asian capitals, even if not a sacred island.

A point that seems to support the palace-city understanding of Tiwanaku comes from the provincial capital in Moquegua, with its monumental building Omo M10. Interestingly, this complex is formally similar to late palaces with a large outer plaza and a smaller inner courtyard (Figure 10.6). It consists of three sequential spaces. First is a large walled plaza; second is a smaller courtyard; and finally there is a compound of walled spaces surrounding a sunken patio. Paul Goldstein (1993, 2005) believes that the building was a temple, although I have emphasized its similarity to late palaces (Isbell 2004b). This evidence seems to support the idea of a grand palace with an outer plaza and an inner courtyard at Tiwanaku, although it is not definitive. Until more evidence is available, it seems prudent to suppose that Tiwanaku's elite residences were modest and associated with council members rather than supreme kings.

We now turn to the issue of kings themselves; evidence for kings will also inform inferences about royal residences, so this study may help resolve the enigma of Tiwanaku palaces. Most obviously, mortuary remains from Tiwanaku would determine the presence of monarchs if spectacular royal tombs were discovered. However, to date, no Tiwanaku burial that approaches the magnitude of a royal interment has been reported. This favors a collective form of government for Tiwanaku, but it is not definitive. Some scholars point to three-sided rooms in the Kalasasaya plaza that were found empty by archaeologists, and to megalithic chambers built into the Putuni platform, also discovered empty, arguing that valuable contents—perhaps royal mummies—were removed as the city was abandoned (Kolata 1993a). But this is speculation in need of additional proof.

Perhaps the burial of a Tiwanaku governor has been documented in a distant province. In 1916 a buried treasure was found on San Sebastian Hill in Cochabamba. It consisted of a golden costume composed of a staff and bowl, a headdress, wide bracelets and anklets, epaulettes, two circular breastplates, a sandal, and sequins from a perishable skirt and vest. According to the finder's account, a body had been buried, apparently in extended position, dressed in the attire. For decades this "treasure" has been interpreted as the mortuary outfit of a high-ranking Tiwanaku official, a provincial governor, or a comparable official of state in Cochabamba (Berenguer 2000; Money 1991). Now, if the Tiwanaku center was adorned with statues of kings, and provincial offi-

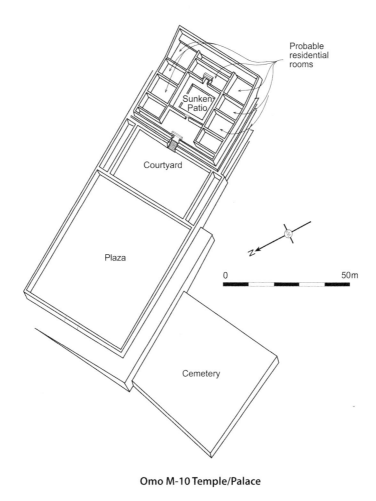

FIGURE 10.6. Omo M10 complex in Moquegua.

cials as far away as Cochabamba were buried in uniforms of gold, rulership must have been powerful and affluent, as in the Chimu and Inca empires. But are Tiwanaku's statues and Cochabamba's golden costume correctly interpreted as Tiwanaku rulers?

Critical examination of the San Sebastian gold costume reveals nothing identifying it as Tiwanaku. Except for a skirt with circular sequins, a feature reconstructed for the costume, there is nothing similar to Tiwanaku's great statues among the golden clothing. The altiplano statues wear headbands that appear to represent woven cloth, but the San Sebastian outfit has a gold forehead ornament consisting of a human head or face. Although its nose and mouth are not inconsistent with Tiwanaku, it has a cutout window above the forehead showing a step pyramid that is reminiscent of metallic plaques from northwestern Argentina (González 1992: Figures 337 and 339). The face has two little feet below its chin and broad winglike projections from both sides. There are no analogues in Tiwanaku's IV–V art, unless one exaggerates vague similarity with the headdress of the anticephalic idols (Posnansky 1945: Figure 130). More importantly, none of Tiwanaku's statues or other human figures wears wide bracelets and anklets, epaulettes, circular breastplates, or sandals like the Cochabamba costume. Their vests are not covered with gold sequins but with textile designs of the same kind well-known from archaeological examples of weavings. Finally, the staff and bowl accompanying the Cochabamba outfit, shown in the hands of the costumed wearer by the artists responsible for a popular reconstructive drawing (Berenguer 2000:72–73), are without comparison in Tiwanaku. I conclude that the outfit is not Tiwanaku and consequently very unlikely to represent a regional Tiwanaku political official from Cochabamba. The San Sebastian treasure provides no evidence for powerful kings at the pinnacle of Tiwanaku's government.

So mortuary remains do not imply great Tiwanaku kings, but negative information is only circumstantial. Now, what of Tiwanaku's impressive stone statues, carved during Tiwanaku's IV and V phases? They have been identified as Tiwanaku's great monarchs by some scholars (Kolata 1993a).

Typically, Tiwanaku IV–V monolithic statues stand rigidly, with arms resting on the sides and stomach and with each hand grasping an object. Archaeologists generally agree that the objects are probably a *kero,* or beer flagon, and a snuff tray for inhaling hallucinogens (Berenguer 1987), although Constantino Torres (2007) has shown that the *kero* might be a bag of hallucinogenic powder with a pair of snuffing tubes projecting from its opening. To the degree that these identifications are correct, the statues do not seem to emphasize insignia of kingship but rather shamanic symbols. Furthermore, the presentation is not that of rule but of a presiding host who offers a toast. Just as we use the term *speaker* to designate the leader of an assembly, Tiwanaku's stone carvers seem to have stated "host, who offers drink and drugs" to designate the social status of the images (see Bandy this volume). Rather than kings, Tiwanaku's famous statues more likely represent the hosts of shamanic ritual feasts. Perhaps they participated in a governing council and lived in modest palaces in the civic center. The case grows stronger, but proof is still wanting. The enigma of Tiwanaku rule remains to be resolved.

On a final note, a less hierarchical and centralized concept of Tiwanaku government seems to be supported by recent thinking about the Tiwanaku heartland, as well as about colonization and expansionism. Ideas that intrusive Tiwanaku colonies were placed in Chile's northern oases such as San Pedro de Atacama have been discarded in favor of inferences about trade partnerships and cultural fields (Stovel 2002). Even Cochabamba may not have been colonized by Tiwanaku settlers (Higueras-Hare 1996). The single convincing case of Tiwanaku colonists on the Peruvian coast is at Moquegua, but Goldstein (2005) now argues that it was established without backing from a centralized government (Goldstein this volume). So, formerly popular conquest and colonization models of a Tiwanaku Empire seem to be collapsing in the light of new research and thinking. Indeed, the inference that Tiwanaku was a cosmogram capital with luxurious palaces and supreme kings has scored poorly in our review of the current information.

What Tiwanaku Was—Some New Understanding of the City

Tiwanaku was a large city, probably composed of 15,000 to 20,000 permanent residents plus a significant number of visitors. Some citizens produced crafts, especially ceramics, but mostly within household contexts. The city was a political center where rulers made and enforced decisions within an urban heartland and in territories farther away, probably including the coastal Moquegua Valley. Tiwanaku was a religious center with great monuments that focused cosmic power and transferred it to humans—especially to the priests/shamans, politicians, residents, and pilgrims of the city. Formalized drinking of corn-beer and probably also hallucinogenic ceremonies intensified personal experience and promoted a new international identity. But, unfortunately, in modern times, Tiwanaku became an icon of New Age mystery, of diffusionist chronology, of nationalist origins, and of ideal-type cultural comparisons, resulting in the creation of popular but erroneous factoids. To correct understandings of Tiwanaku's past, we must take care not to bend knowledge too far in the opposite direction, but we do require new perspectives that are not based on our expectations but on Tiwanaku materiality itself.

If Tiwanaku was not a sacred-island cosmogram and a paragon of structural imperatives mapped onto the real world, how can archaeologists explain its astonishing megalithic edifices? They are the most impressive monuments of the Andean past, rivaled only by Inca constructions at Sacsayhuaman and Ollantaytambo. Indeed, an alternative approach to explaining Tiwanaku and its monumentality is emerging. Pilgrimage and oracle centers are documented as key features of ancient Andean landscapes (Bauer and Stanish 2001; Nesbit 2003; Silverman 1990, 1994, 2000b; Topic and Topic 1992; Topic et al. 2002; see also Hemming 1970 and Zárate 1968 [1556] for descriptions of Hernando Pizarro's 1533 entry into Pachacamac, a famous oracular temple-city), but late-twentieth-century cultural evolution focused archaeological attention on ideal stages that minimize this kind of organization except as legitimization for political power. However, Alexei Vranich (1999, 2001, 2002, 2006; Isbell and Vranich 2004) argues that Tiwanaku's landscape is better understood as an exhibition and emotional experience than as a cosmological structure, offering a different and more phenomenological approach to the ancient capital.

Many observers have pointed out that Tiwanaku's buildings were never finished, but Vranich argues that this was intentional. In fact, many constructions were remodeled before being completed. Of course, this makes no sense if the city was a cosmogram of structural imperatives, for structure is immutable. But if the spatial organization is explained as choreographed routes for visitors, combining history and nature with built environment to produce eternally emerging experiences, change was essential. Tiwanaku's civic center was cultural practice; participation involved spectacular vistas that included buildings, mountain peaks, and sunsets, as well as themes from politics and history, surely shaped by costumed performances, alcohol, and drugs. I will return to this point below, but enactments by permanent residents probably incorporated visiting pilgrims. Unfortunately, archaeologists know little about oracular shrines and Andean practices of pilgrimage. In fact, given that the word *pilgrimage* has such strong Old World implications, it may not even be the right concept to use in the Andes.

Following Vranich's argument, Tiwanaku was a specialized producer, but not so much of manufactured items—as emphasized by economically driven, cross-cultural models of urbanism. Tiwanaku produced spectacle. It was a city visited by vast numbers of pilgrims. Presumably, the resident population was first and foremost involved in planning and supervising the experience of the city, involving symbolic landscapes, oracular prognostications, costumed enactments, feasts, and other ritual activities—which included ingestion of hallucinogens by at least some visitors and residents.

In a restudy of Tiwanaku's monuments, Vranich and colleagues (Benitez and Vranich 2005) are finding that building plans, monoliths, gateways, paths, and vistas are not oriented to an abstract and absolute grid as the Wila Jawira Project believed. Rather, some buildings are even slightly trapezoidal so that both of their sides point to the same horizonal mountain peak. Walls, orthostats, and architraves divide the solar year, mark lunar extremes, and frame solstice sunsets over distant horizon features. The descent into the Semisubterranean Temple framed the southern pole, around which the Milky Way revolves, as though the dark constellation animals marched out of the earth, up its steps, and through the sky, only to descend again into the temple depression. The Pumapunku, probably the entrance to the city, provided pedestrians a view of sacred Illimani Mountain to the east and sacred Lake Titicaca to the west—probably creating Tiwanaku's sacred space. Some vistas were public, experienced by thousands. But others were unique, selecting a single individual or special entourage with a single beam of light.

This current interpretation of Tiwanaku is driven more by information about the site than any of the former models, all of which have fared poorly when critiqued in light of actual archaeological evidence. I suspect that these long-popular interpretations fail in large part because they all employ analogies from other world civilizations. While each analogy focused our attention on some aspect of ancient cities—economy, resident population, rulership, religion—and provided interpretations to be tested, each argument sought to impose knowledge on Tiwanaku rather than infer from the remains as they present themselves. Today, at last, archaeological investigation of Tiwanaku is accumulating enough information to support more phenomenological thinking and a new image of Tiwanaku as spectacle.

Investigation of Tiwanaku as oracular spectacle and host to pilgrims requires archaeologists to ask new kinds of questions that do not focus on traditional concerns with urban craft production, the degree of hierarchical centralization in government, or even symbolic representation of ideology. We must understand human practice and experience, asking about Andean pilgrimage and the cultural practices in which it was embedded. What was involved in an Andean pilgrimage? Who went on them? When, how, and for how long? What was the benefit? How was pilgrimage financed and by whom? Silverman (2000a:247, Figure 7) discusses a fascinating sculpture she interprets as a Nazca family on pilgrimage. (Also see the photo facing page 1 of Silverman and Proulx 2002 for another view of the same model, with additional commentary.) All the travelers—father, mother, and daughter—carry ritual items, especially panpipes and parrots. No supplies for the trip are apparent, unless the daughter's load includes them. Is this an omission of the mundane and obvious, or did Andean pilgrims depend on facilities along the route?

I suspect that a key element for understanding urban dynamics at Tiwanaku is the question of how pilgrimage was conducted and financed. Did pilgrims travel with great entourages that included food, tents, cooks, and clothing for lengthy stays? Indeed, colonial accounts imply that days and perhaps even months of fasting—probably limited to abstention from sex, salt, and capsicum peppers—were normal before pilgrims could enter an important sanctuary to receive prognostications. If so, the issue of interim room and board is overwhelming, as is the issue of whether pilgrims labored in construction or other activities during these periods of consecration.

How many pilgrims came to Tiwanaku annually? From how far away? Was the flow constant; periodic in accord with an annual calendar; based on unpredictable events such as illnesses, deaths, and the ascension of new lords among the constituents? Were stays short, lengthy, or variable? What transpired during a stay? Did pilgrims demonstrate devotion by providing wealth or labor to a shrine? Could a powerful patron buy a dispensation or favorable prognostication with a pledge to add a great stone to a wall or build a segment of a monument? If so, how was the pledge fulfilled? Even more immediately, did pilgrims supply their own subsistence and perhaps even provision the permanent residents of Tiwanaku through gifts of food? Or did pilgrims depend on facilities along the route of travel? Perhaps ethnicities participating in pilgrimage maintained a facility at Tiwanaku, where members were attended during their visits. The possibilities are many, and they have not been explored by archaeologists, in spite of the fact that Morris (Morris and Thompson 1985) recognized temporary housing, large-scale storage, and feasting as key determinants of the Inca provincial city of Huanuco Pampa. Jason Nesbit (2003) is one of very few Andean prehistorians exploring techniques for detecting temporary pilgrims and determining their activities at oracle centers. If we are to understand Tiwanaku, I am convinced that we must ask and determine who were permanent residents and who were temporaries. Where and how were pilgrims housed? For how long? Who financed what and how?

Were there different kinds of pilgrimages in the Andes? Perhaps there were visits to confirm ascension to office for high priests and lords. I am impressed that some of the carefully designed experiences Vranich and colleagues have detected at Tiwanaku were constructed for thousands, but others seem intended to single out one individual. In fact, I can imagine an aspirant to a priestly title spending nights of observation, devotion, and formal instruction at a particular spot in the Semisubterranean Temple, witnessing the march of the Milky Way while repeating the appropriate myths and routines of divination. I can also imagine confirmation of a new lordship, sanctified by the last beam of sunlight cast over a homeland mountain peak, shining through the gateway of the Kalasasaya onto the new ruler, as the solstice sun began its reverse direction, symbolically initiating a new era. Such a shamanic spectacle could single out one person but be witnessed by thousands and appear entirely miraculous. If the pretender were dressed in a reflective, golden outfit, the spectacle resonates with myths about the origins of Inca kingship.

In conclusion, our examination of Tiwanaku's archaeological record indicates that Tiwanaku was unlikely to have housed more than 15,000 to 20,000 persons, although future distinctions must be drawn between permanent residents and pilgrims, including perhaps long-stay pilgrims. Economically, Tiwanaku was not a center for manufacturing or a city with an economy of scale providing goods to a vast hinterland, as predicted by economic models. What it produced was spectacle that was eternally changing.

As a capital city, Tiwanaku was not the ancient and precocious center of innovation and diffusion imagined by investigators mired in Eurocentric models of diffusionism. Tiwanaku was a transcultural and panregional phenomenon that cannot be understood in isolation. While interregional interaction seems very old in the south-central Andes, a great transformation promoted a new spatial center at Tiwanaku as the Late Formative 2 turned into the Tiwanaku IV–V period—between A.D. 550 and 750. Changes included ceramic innovations and new foodways, including an international protocol for corn-beer drinking.

As ceramics and foodways were changing, new religious images appeared at Tiwanaku and elsewhere, formalized into a new pantheon composed of Staff God, Rayed Head, and Profile Attendants. Megalithic monuments became vastly more impressive and also more numerous in the capital. Sculptures and architraves that required astonishing stoneworking skills appeared. But the monuments did not inscribe a static cosmogram; they participated in constantly changing practices creating spectacles for visitors—almost surely vast numbers of pilgrims who inundated the city in accord with needs and schedules we do not understand. The experiences provided by Tiwanaku integrated people with architectural monuments as well as with nature, especially horizontal phenomena such as mountain peaks, the setting sun, lunar extremes, and rotation of the Milky Way. There were surely historical components—associations with past events and people—as well as future prognostications. Some spectacles involved thousands, while some singled out individuals, bathing them in special sunlight. Amid this monumentality there is little indication of extremely centralized and hierarchical rule or even truly sumptuous lifestyles. Instead, the magnitude of burials and palaces, as well as the symbols decorating statues and mortuary clothing, suggests the supremacy of shamanic practices, including altered states provoked by hallucinatory preparations. Supreme prominence was given to hosts of what may have been ecstatic festivities, in which spectators were participants. Government may have taken the form of a council of elders, heads of houses, and/or shamans.

Further understandings of Tiwanaku require new investigations that will ask new questions. Foremost among them are questions about pilgrimage, as well as its finance and organization. Were pilgrims the consumers of Tiwanaku's spectacles, and were its permanent residents the producers? Can archaeologists distinguish them? How were they distributed at Tiwanaku, and in what ways did they depend on one another? As archaeologists gain better understandings of Andean oracle centers and pilgrimage, only then will we understand Tiwanaku—and perhaps other cities of ancient South America. In the meantime, it should be clear that former interpretations of Tiwanaku have served more to show what the city was *not* than to demonstrate what it was.

Notes

[1] Although many of Posnansky's interpretations are flights of fancy, his descriptive information about Tiwanaku is excellent; it includes invaluable maps, drawings, and photographs.

[2] Ponce went on to argue that Tiwanaku had conquered far beyond the borders of Bolivia and that a northern center of Tiwanaku-related culture, Huari, in the central highlands of Peru, was a provincial administrative capital of the Tiwanaku Empire. This has been shown to be wrong. Tiwanaku and Huari were capitals of contemporary states whose development was interrelated in complex and yet-to-be-determined ways, but the two were politically independent.

[3] Ponce served in numerous national political offices. He controlled the privilege of excavating at Tiwanaku and in most of the surrounding Bolivian nation. His assistants directed excavations in his name and were allowed to publish what he approved. His voice was strong enough to shut out alternatives and competitors. To his credit, in the late 1980s he endorsed the Wila Jawira Project of Alan Kolata, which conducted investigations over a period of two decades, although there seems to have been an expectation that interpretations would not deviate excessively from his own.

[4] The success of raised-field agriculture in the altiplano, as a modern development strategy, is unclear. As Stanish (2003) pointed out, self-motivated raised-field agriculture has not survived the early flurry of propaganda and programmatic subsidies of the late 1980s and 1990s. Consequently, inferences about prehistoric production based on the first experimental fields were obviously premature. Indeed, while the technique seems destined to disappear again, as it apparently did in the distant past, we need more than a couple of decades of history to make a convincing evaluation.

[5] I want to thank Alexei Vranich for bringing these two photographs to my attention. His study of Uhle's notes and photographs at the University of Pennsylvania Museum provide him a profound knowledge of the site.

[6] A modestly large suburban American home has about 2,000 square feet. The Palace of the Multicolored Rooms totaled slightly more than 1,000 square feet.

[7] The Puruchuco Palace had about 2,000 square feet.

[8] Even if the two megalithic buildings were not part of one great palace, it seems likely that the Palace of the Multicolored Rooms and other buildings facing onto the patio to its west were part of a single elite residential complex. Indeed, there are several ways that the outlines and space of a single Tiwanaku palace can be defined.

References Cited

Alconini Mujica, Sonia
- 2007 Sacred Spaces and Public Architecture of Power in Charazani: The Inkas in the Eastern Margins of the Empire. Paper presented at the 2007 Annual Meeting of the Society for American Archaeology, Austin, Texas.

Arellano Lopez, Jorge
- 1991 The New Cultural Contexts of Tiahuanaco. In *Huari Administrative Structure: Prehistoric Monumental Architecture and State Government*, edited by William H. Isbell and Gordon F. McEwan, pp. 259–280. Dumbarton Oaks, Washington, D.C.

Bandelier, Adolph
- 1911 The Ruins of Tiahuanaco. *Proceedings of the American Antiquarian Society* 21:218–265.

Bandy, Matthew
- 2001 Population and History in the Ancient Titicaca Basin. Unpublished Ph.D. dissertation, Department of Anthropology, University of California, Berkeley.
- 2006 Early Village Society in the Formative Period in the Southern Lake Titicaca Basin. In *Andean Archaeology*. Vol. 3, *North and South,* edited by William H. Isbell and Helaine Silverman, pp. 210–236. Springer, New York.

Bauer, Brian S., and Charles Stanish
- 2001 *Ritual and Pilgrimage in the Ancient Andes: The Islands of the Sun and the Moon.* University of Texas, Austin.

Benitez, Leonardo R.
- 2005 Architectural Observations and Archaeoastronomy at Tiwanaku. Lecture delivered at the State University of New York at Binghamton, March 28, 2005.
- 2008 A Unique Lunisolar Observatory and Calendar in Precolumbian Bolivia. Unpublished paper, University of Pennsylvania Museum of Anthropology.
- 2009 Descendants of the Sun: Calendars, Myths, and the Tiwanaku State. In *Tiwanaku: Papers from the 2005 Mayer Center Symposium at the Denver Art Museum*, edited by M. Young-Sanchez, pp. 49–82. Frederick and Jan Mayer Center for Pre-Columbian and Spanish Colonial Art at the Denver Art Museum, Denver.

Benitez, Leonardo, and Alexei Vranich
- 2005 Urban Planning and Conveying the Sacred at Tiwanaku. Paper presented at the Twenty-Fourth Northeast Conference on Andean Archaeology and Ethnohistory, American University, Washington, D.C.

Bennett, Wendell C.
- 1934 Excavations at Tiahuanaco. *Anthropological Papers of the American Museum of Natural History* 35:329–507.

Bentley, Nicolas
- 2013 The Tiwanaku of A. F. Bandelier. In *Advances in Titicaca Basin Archaeology 2*, edited by Alexei Vranich and Abigail Levine. Cotsen Institute of Archaeology Press, Los Angeles.

Berenguer Rodriguez, José
- 1987 Consumo nasal de alucinógenos en Tiwanaku: Una aproximación iconográfica. *Boletín del Museo Chileno de Arte Precolombino* 2:33–53.
- 2000 Tiwanaku: Lords of the Sacred Lake. Impresion Morgan Impresiores, Santiago de Chile.

Betanzos, Juan de
- 1996 [1557] *Narrative of the Incas*. University of Texas Press, Austin.

Bird, Junius B.
- 1948 Preceramic Cultures in Chicama and Virú. In *A Reappraisal of Peruvian Archaeology*, edited by Wendell C. Bennett, pp. 21–28. Memoir 4. Society for American Archaeology, Menasha, Wisconsin.

Browman, David
- 1978 Toward the Development of the Tiwanaku State. In *Advances in Andean Archaeology*, edited by David Browman, pp. 327–349. Mouton, The Hague.
- 1980 Tiwanaku Expansion and Altiplano Economic Patterns. *Estudios arqueológicos* 5:107–120.
- 1981 New Light on Ancient Tiwanaku. *American Scientist* 69:408–419.
- 1984 Tiwanaku: Development of Interzonal Trade and Economic Expansion in the Altiplano. In *Social and Economic Organization in the Prehispanic Andes*, edited by David Browman, Richard Burger, and Mario Rivera, pp. 117–142. International Series 194. British Archaeological Reports, Oxford.
- 1985 Cultural Primacy of Tiwanaku in the Development of Later Peruvian States. *Dialogo andino* 4:59–71.

Bueno Mendoza, Alberto
- 1983 El antiguo Valle de Pachacamac: Espacio, tiempo y cultura (tercera parte). *Boletín de Lima* 5:3–12.

Burkholder, Jo Ellen
- 1997 Tiwanaku and the Anatomy of Time: A Ceramic Chronology from the Iwawi Site, Department of La Paz, Bolivia. Unpublished Ph.D. dissertation, State University of New York, Binghamton.
- 2001 La cerámica de Tiwanaku: ¿Qué indica su variabilidad? In *Huari y Tiwanaku: Modelos vs. evidencias*, Pt. 2, edited by Peter Kaulicke and William H. Isbell, pp. 217–250. Boletín de Arque-

ología PUCP No. 5. Pontificia Universidad Católica del Perú, Lima.

Calancha, Antonio de la
1939 [1638] *Crónica moralizada de la Ordén de San Agustín del Perú*. Imprenta Artistica, La Paz.

Castelnau, Francis de
1852 *Antiquités des Incas et autres peuples anciens, recueillies pendant l'expédition dans les parties centrales de l'Amerique du Sud. Part III, Expédition dans les parties centrales de l'Amérique du Sud, de Rio de Janeiro à Lima, et de Lima au Para: exécuté par ordre du gouvernement Français pendant les années 1843 à 1847. 1850–1855.* 15 vols. P. Bertrand, Libraire-editeur, Paris.

Chávez, Karen L. Mohr
1988 The Significance of Chiripa in Lake Titicaca Basin Developments. *Expedition* 30:17–26.
2002 Local Differences and Regional Similarities in Pottery of the Yaya-Mama Religious Tradition. Paper presented at the symposium "The Yaya-Mama Religious Tradition in the Lake Titicaca Basin: Interdisciplinary Perspectives, in Honor of Karen L. Mohr Chávez," at the 2002 meetings of the Society for American Archaeology, Denver.

Chávez, Sergio J.
1975 The Arapa and Thunderbolt Stelae: A Case of Stylistic Identity with Implications for Pucara Influences in the Area of Tiahuanaco. *Ñawpa Pacha* 13:3–24.
1992 The Conventionalized Rules in Pucara Pottery Technology and Iconography: Implications for Socio-Political Development in the Northern Lake Titicaca Basin. Unpublished Ph.D. dissertation, Department of Anthropology, Michigan State University, East Lansing.
1997 Preliminary Results of the Excavations of Two Sites within the Ch'isi Temple Domain and of a New Temple on the Copacabana Peninsula, Bolivia. Paper presented at Sixty-Second Annual Meeting of the Society for American Archaeology, Nashville, Tennessee.
2002 The Identification of the Camelid Woman and the Feline Man: Themes, Motifs, and Designs in Pucara Style Pottery. In *Andean Archaeology*. Vol. 2, *Art, Landscape and Society*, edited by Helaine Silverman and William H. Isbell, pp. 35–69. Kleuwer Academic/Plenum Publishers, New York.
2004 The Yaya-Mama Religious Tradition as an Antecedent of Tiwanaku. In *Tiwanaku: Ancestors of the Inca*, edited by Margaret Young-Sánchez, pp. 70–75, 81–85, 90–93. Denver Art Museum and University of Nebraska Press, Lincoln.

Chávez, Sergio Jorge, and Karen Lynne Mohr Chávez
1975 A Carved Stela from Taraco, Puno, Peru, and the Definition of an Early Style of Stone Sculpture from the Altiplano of Peru and Bolivia. *Ñawpa Pacha* 13:45–83.

Cieza de León, Pedro de
1962 [1553] *La crónica del Perú (parte primera)*. Espana-Calpe, Madrid.

Cobo, Bernabè
1979 [1653] *History of the Inca Empire*. Translated and edited by Roland Hamilton. University of Texas Press, Austin.
1990 [1653] *Inca Religion and Custom*. Translated and edited by Roland Hamilton. University of Texas Press, Austin.

Coe, Michael D.
2003 *Angkor and the Khmer Civilization*. Thames and Hudson, New York.

Courty, Georges
1904 Sur las hauts plateaus de Bolivie: Le sol et les habitants. *Bulletin de la Société de Géographie Commerciale* 26:614–619.

Couture, Nicole C.
2002 The Construction of Power: Monumental Space and Elite Residence at Tiwanaku, Bolivia. Unpublished Ph.D. dissertation, Department of Anthropology, University of Chicago, Chicago.
2003 Ritual, Monumentalism, and Residence at Mollo Kuntu, Tiwanaku. In *Tiwanaku and Its Hinterland: Archaeology and Paleoecology of an Andean Civilization*. Vol. 2, *Urban and Rural Archaeology*, edited by Alan L. Kolata, pp. 202–225. Smithsonian Institution Press, Washington, D.C.
2004 Monumental Space, Courtly Style, and Elite Life at Tiwanaku. In *Tiwanaku: Ancestors of the Inca*, edited by Margaret Young-Sánchez, pp. 127–135, 139–143, 146–149. University of Nebraska Press, Lincoln.

Couture, Nicole C., and Kathryn Sampeck
2003 Putuni: A History of Palace Architecture at Tiwanaku. In *Tiwanaku and Its Hinterland: Archaeology and Paleoecology of an Andean Civilization*. Vol. 2, *Urban and Rural Archaeology*, edited by Alan L. Kolata, pp. 226–263. Smithsonian Institution Press, Washington, D.C.

D'Orbigny, Alcide
2002 [1844] *Viaje a la América Meridional: Brasil, Republica del Uruguay, Republica Argentina, la Patagonia, Republica de Chile, Republica de Bolivia, Republica del Perú: Realizado de 1826 a 1833*. Instituto Frances de Estudios Andinos, Editores Plural, La Paz.

Eeckhout, Peter
　1999　Le Temple de Pachacamac sous l'Empire Inca. *Journal de la Société des Américanistes* 84:18–50.

Engel, Frederic
　1963　*A Preceramic Settlement on the Central Coast of Peru: Asis, Unit 1.* Transactions of the American Philosophical Society 53, Part 3. American Philosophical Society, Philadelphia.

Erickson, Clark
　1984　Waru-Waru: Una tecnología agrícola del altiplano prehispánico. *Boletín del Instituto de Estudios Aymaras* 2(18):4–37.
　1985　Applications of Prehistoric Andean Technology: Experiments in Raised Field Agriculture, Huatta, Lake Titicaca. In *Prehistoric Intensive Agriculture in the Tropics,* edited by Ian Farrington, pp. 209–232. International Series 232. British Archaeological Reports, Oxford.
　1987　The Dating of Raised Field Agriculture in the Lake Titicaca Basin of Peru. In *Pre-Hispanic Agricultural Fields in the Andean Region,* edited by William M. Denevan, Kent Mathewson, and Gregory Knapp, pp. 373–383. International Series No. 359. British Archaeological Reports, Oxford.
　1988　An Archaeological Investigation of Raised Field Agriculture in the Lake Titicaca Basin of Peru. Unpublished Ph.D. dissertation, Department of Anthropology, University of Illinois, Urbana.
　1992a　Applied Archaeology and Rural Development: Archaeology's Potential Contribution to the Future. *Journal of the Steward Anthropology Society* 20:1–16.
　1992b　Prehistoric Landscape Management in the Andean Highlands: Ridged Field Agriculture and Its Environmental Impact. *Population and Environment* 13:285–300.

Goldstein, Paul S.
　1993　Tiwanaku Temples and State Expansion: A Tiwanaku Sunken-Court Temple in Moquegua, Peru. *Latin American Antiquity* 4(3):22–47.
　2005　*Andean Diaspora: The Tiwanaku Colonies and the Origins of South American Empire.* University Press of Florida, Gainesville.

González, Alberto Rex
　1992　*Las placas metálicas de los Andes del Sur: Contribución al estudio de las religiones precolombinos.* Verlag Philipp Von Zabern, Mainz am Rhein.

Haeberli, Joerg
　2001　Tiempo y tradición en Arequipa, Perú, y El surgimiento de la cronología del tema de la deidad central. In *Huari y Tiwanaku: Modelos vs. evidencias,* Pt. 2, edited by Peter Kaulicke and William H. Isbell, pp. 89–137. Boletín Arqueología PUCP No. 5. Pontífica Universidad Católica del Perú, Lima.

Hastorf, Christine A. (editor)
　1999　*Early Settlement at Chiripa, Bolivia: Research of the Taraco Archaeological Project.* Contributions of the University of California Archaeological Research Facility No. 57. University of California Archaeological Research Facility, Berkeley.

Hemming, John
　1970　*The Conquest of the Incas.* Harcourt, Brace, Jovanovich, New York.

Higueras-Hare, Alvaro
　1996　Prehispanic Settlement and Land Use in Cochabamba, Bolivia. Unpublished Ph.D. dissertation, Department of Anthropology, University of Pittsburgh, Pittsburgh.

Humboldt, Alexander von
　1815　*Personal Narrative of Travels to the Equinoctial Regions of the New Continent, during the Years 1799–1804 by Alexander de Humboldt and Aimé Bonpland.* Translated by Helen Maria Williams. M. Carey, Philadelphia.

Isbell, William H.
　2004a　Cultural Evolution in the Lake Titicaca Basin: Empirical Facts and Theoretical Expectations. *Reviews in Anthropology* 33:209–241.
　2004b　Palaces and Politics of Huari, Tiwanaku and the Andean Middle Horizon. In *Palaces of the Ancient New World,* edited by Susan Toby Evans and Joanne Pillsbury, pp. 191–246. Dumbarton Oaks, Washington, D.C.
　2014　A Community of Potters or Multicrafting Wives of Polygynous Lords? In *Craft Production: Producer and Multi-Craft Perspectives,* edited by Izumi Shimada. University of Utah Press, Salt Lake City, in press.

Isbell, William H., and Jo Ellen Burkholder
　2002　Iwawi and Tiwanaku. In *Andean Archaeology.* Vol. 1, *Variations in Sociopolitical Organization,* edited by William H. Isbell and Helaine Silverman, pp. 199–241. Kluwer Academic/Plenum Publishers, New York.

Isbell, William H., Jo Ellen Burkholder, and Juan Albarracin-Jordan
　2002　Iwawi y Tiwanaku. *Gaceta arqueológica andina* 26:139–170.

Isbell, William H., and Amy Groleau
　2010　The Wari Brewer Woman: Feasting, Gender, Offerings, and Memory. In *Inside Ancient Kitchens: New Directions in the Study of Daily Means and Feasts,* edited by E. A. Klarich, pp. 191–220. University Press of Colorado, Boulder.

Isbell, William H., and Patricia J. Knobloch
　2006　Missing Links, Imaginary Links: Staff God Imagery in the South Andean Past. In *Andean Archaeology.* Vol. 3, *North and South,* edited by

William H. Isbell and Helaine Silverman, pp. 307–351. Springer, New York.

2009 The Origin, Development and Dating of Tiahuanaco-Huari Iconography. In *Tiwanaku: Papers from the 2005 Mayer Center Symposium at the Denver Art Museum*, edited by M. Young-Sánchez, pp. 163–210. Frederick and Jan Mayer Center for Pre-Columbian and Spanish Colonial Art at the Denver Art Museum, Denver.

Isbell, William H., and Alexei Vranich

2004 Experiencing the Cities of Wari and Tiwanaku. In *Andean Archaeology*, edited by Helaine Silverman, pp. 167–182. Blackwell Publishing, Malden, Massachusetts.

Janusek, John Wayne

1994 State and Local Power in a Prehispanic Andean Polity: Changing Patterns of Urban Residence in Tiwanaku and Lukurmata, Bolivia. Unpublished Ph.D. dissertation, Department of Anthropology, University of Chicago, Chicago.

2003 Vessels, Time, and Society: Toward a Ceramic Chronology in the Tiwanaku Heartland. In *Tiwanaku and Its Hinterland: Archaeology and Paleoecology of an Andean Civilization*. Vol. 2, *Urban and Rural Archaeology*, edited by Alan L. Kolata, pp. 30–89. Smithsonian Institution Press, Washington, D.C.

2004 *Identity and Power in the Ancient Andes: Tiwanaku Cities through Time*. Routledge, New York.

Janusek, John Wayne, and Alan Kolata

2003 Prehispanic Rural History in the Katari Valley. In *Tiwanaku and Its Hinterland: Archaeology and Paleoecology of an Andean Civilization*. Vol. 2, *Urban and Rural Archaeology*, edited by Alan L. Kolata, pp. 129–167. Smithsonian Institution Press, Washington, D.C.

Janusek, John W., Arik T. Ohnstad, and Andrew P. Roddick

2003 Khonkho Wankane and the Rise of Tiwanaku. *Antiquity* 77(296). Electronic document, *http://antiquity.ac.uk/ProjGall/janusek/janusek.html*, accessed July 30, 2013.

Jimenez Borja, Arturo

1973 *Puruchuco*. Editorial Jurídica S.A., Lima.

Knobloch, Patricia J.

2002 Who Was Who in the Middle Horizon Andean Prehistory. Electronic document, *http://www.rohan.sdsu.edu/~bharley/ WWWHome.html*, accessed July 30, 2013.

Kolata, Alan

1987 Tiwanaku and Its Hinterland. *Archaeology* 40: 36–41.

1989a The Agricultural Foundation of the Tiwanaku State: A View from the Heartland. *American Antiquity* 54:748–762.

1989b *Arqueología de Lukurmata*, Vol. 2. Instituto Nacional de Arqueología de Bolivia, La Paz.

1991 The Technology and Organization of Agricultural Production in the Tiwanaku State. *Latin American Antiquity* 2:99–125.

1993a *The Tiwanaku: Portrait of an Andean Civilization*. Blackwell, Cambridge, Massachusetts.

1993b Understanding Tiwanaku: Conquest, Colonization and Clientage in the South Central Andes. In *Latin American Horizons*, edited by Don Stephen Rice, pp. 193–224. Dumbarton Oaks, Washington, D.C.

1996a Mimesis and Monumentalism in Native Andean Cities. *RES: Anthropology and Aesthetics* 29/30: 223–236.

1996b Proyecto Wila Jawira: An Introduction to the History, Problems, and Strategies of Research. In *Tiwanaku and Its Hinterland: Archaeology and Paleoecology of an Andean Civilization*. Vol. 1, *Agroecology*, edited by Alan L. Kolata, pp. 1–22. Smithsonian Institution, Washington, D.C.

1996c (editor) *Tiwanaku and Its Hinterland: Archaeology and Paleoecology of an Andean Civilization*. Vol.1, Agroecology. Smithsonian Institution Press, Washington D.C.

2003a The Proyecto Wila Jawira Research Progran. In *Tiwanaku and Its Hinterland: Archaeology and Paleoecology of an Andean Civilization*. Vol. 2, *Urban and Rural Archaeology*, edited by Alan L. Kolata, pp. 3–17. Smithsonian Institution Press, Washington, D.C.

2003b (editor) *Tiwanaku and Its Hinterland: Archaeology and Paleoecology of an Andean Civilization*. Vol. 2, *Urban and Rural Archaeology*. Smithsonian Institution Press, Washington, D.C.

2003c Tiwanaku Ceremonial Architecture and Urban Organization. In *Tiwanaku and Its Hinterland: Archaeology and Paleoecology of an Andean Civilization*. Vol. 2, *Urban and Rural Archaeology*, edited by Alan Kolata, pp. 175–201. Smithsonian Institution Press, Washington, D.C.

2004 The Flow of Cosmic Power: Religion, Ritual and the People of Tiwanaku. In *Tiwanaku: Ancestors of the Inca*, edited by Margaret Young-Sánchez, pp. 96–113, 121–125. University of Nebraska Press, Lincoln.

Kolata, Alan, and Carlos Ponce Sanginés

1992 Tiwanaku: The City at the Center. In *The Ancient Americas: Art from Sacred Landscapes*, edited by Richard F. Townsend, pp. 317–333. Art Institute of Chicago, Chicago.

Kolata, Alan L., Oswaldo Rivera, Juan Carlos Ramírez, and Evelyn Gamio

1996 Rehabilitating Raised-Field Agriculture in the Southern Lake Titicaca Basin of Bolivia: Theory,

Practice and Results. In *Tiwanaku and Its Hinterland: Archaeology and Paleoecology of an Andean Civilization*. Vol. 1, *Agroecology*, edited by Alan L. Kolata, pp. 203–230. Smithsonian Institution Press, Washington, D.C.

Korpisaari, Antti, and Martti Pärssinen (editors)
   2005 *Pariti: Isla, misterio y poder: El tesoro cerámico de la cultura Tiwanaku*. Producciones CIMA, La Paz.

Kroeber, Alfred L.
   1944 *Peruvian Archaeology in 1942*. Viking Fund Publications in Anthropology No. 4. Viking Fund, New York.

Lanning, Edward P.
   1963 A Pre-Agricultural Occupation on the Central Coast of Peru. *American Antiquity* 28:360–371.
   1967 Peru before the Incas. Prentice-Hall, Englewood Cliffs, New Jersey.

MacCormack, Sabine
   1991 *Religion in the Andes: Vision and Imagination in Early Colonial Peru*. Princeton University Press, Princeton, New Jersey.

Mannikka, Eleanor
   1996 *Angkor Wat: Time, Space, and Kingship*. University of Hawaii Press, Honolulu.

Means, Philip Ainsworth
   1931 *Ancient Civilizations of the Andes*. Charles Scribner's Sons, New York.

Menzel, Dorothy
   1964 Style and Time in the Middle Horizon. *Ñawpa Pacha* 2:1–106.

Money, Mary
   1991 El "Tesoro de San Sebastián": Una tumba importante de la cultura Tiwanaku. *Beiträge zur Allgemeinen und Vergleichenden Archäologie, Deutschen Archäologischen Instituts*, Bonn 11: 189–198.

Moore, Jerry D.
   1996 *Architecture and Power in the Ancient Andes: The Archaeology of Public Buildings*. Cambridge University Press, Cambridge.

Morris, Craig, and Donald E. Thompson
   1985 *Huánuco Pampa: An Inca City and Its Hinterland*. Thames and Hudson, London.

Morris, Craig, and Adriana von Hagen
   1993 *The Inka Empire and Its Andean Origins*. Abbeville Press, New York.

Moseley, Michael E., and Carol J. Mackey
   1974 *Twenty-Four Architectural Plans of Chan Chan, Peru: Structure and Form at the Capitol of Chimor*. Peabody Museum Press, Peabody Museum of Archaeology and Ethnology, Harvard University, Cambridge, Massachusetts.

Nesbit, Jason
   2003 Cerro Icchal: An Andean Place of Ritual. Unpublished master's thesis, Department of Anthropology, Trent University, Peterborough, Ontario.

Oakland Rodman, Amy
   1992 Textiles and Ethnicity: Tiwanaku in San Pedro de Atacama, North Chile. *Latin American Antiquity* 3:316–340.

Parsons, Jeffrey R.
   1968 An Estimate of Size and Population for the Middle Horizon Tiahuanaco, Bolivia. *American Antiquity* 33:243–245.

Patterson, Thomas C., and Edward P. Lanning
   1964 Changing Settlement Patterns on the Central Peruvian Coast. *Ñawpa Pacha* 2:113–123.

Polo de Ondegardo, Juan
   1916 [1571] Relacíon de de los fundamentos acerca del notable daño que resulta de no guardar a los indios sus fueros. In *Colección de libros y documentos referentes a la historia del Perú*, edited by Horacio H. Urteaga, pp. 45–188. Sanmarti, Lima.

Ponce Sanginés, Carlos
   1947 Cerámica Tiwanacota. *Revista geográfica americana* 28:204–214.
   1962 Fechas radiocarbonicas. Unpublished manuscript, Centro de Investigaciones Arqueológicos en Tiwanaku, La Paz.
   1969a *Descripción sumaria del Templete Semisubterranel de Tiwanaku*. Centro de Investigaciones Arqueológicas en Tiwanaku No. 2. Centro de Investigaciones Arqueológicas en Tiwanaku, La Paz.
   1969b La ciudad de Tiwanaku (La Paz). *Arte y arqueología* 1:5–32.
   1972 *Tiwanaku: Espacio, tiempo y cultura*. Academia Nacional de Ciencias de Bolivia, La Paz.
   1976 *La cerámica de la Epoca I de Tiwanaku*. Instituto Nacional de Arqueología Publicación No. 18. Instituto Nacional de Arqueología, La Paz.
   1980 *Panorama de la arqueología boliviana*. Libreria y Editorial "Juventud," La Paz.
   1981 *Tiwanaku: Espacio, tiempo y cultura: Ensayo de síntesis arqueológica*. Los Amigos del Libro, La Paz.
   1999 *Los jefes de estado de Tiwanaku y su nomina*. Producciones CIMA Deposito legal no. 4-1-1528-99. Producciones CIMA, La Paz.
   2001 *Tiwanaku y su facinante desarollo cultural: Ensayo de síntesis arqueológica*. Producciones CIMA, La Paz.

Portugal Zamora, Maks
   1937 Estudio sintetico sobre el ultimo descubrimiento arqueologico en Huancane-Khonko. *Revista de Bolivia* 10 (2).

Posnansky, Arthur
   1910 *Guía para el visitante de los monumentos prehistóricos de Tihuanacu e Islas del Sol y la Luna (Titicaca y Koaty)* Imprenta y Litografía Boliviana-Hugo Heitmann, La Paz.

1911a *El clima del altiplano y la extensión del Lago Titicaca con relación á Tihuanacu en épocas prehistóricas.* Imprenta de Ismael Argote, La Paz.

1911b *Razas y monumentos del altiplano andino. Trabajos del Cuarto Congreso Sientifico* (1° Panamericano) 11, pp. 2–142.

1911c *Tihuanacu y la civilización prehistórica en el altiplano andino.* Imprenta de la Verdad, La Paz.

1912 *Guía general ullustrada para la investigación de los monuments prehistóricas de Tihuanacu é Illas del Sol y la Luna* (*Titicaca y Koaty*) *con breves apuntes sobre los chullpas, urus, y excritura antigua del los aborigenas del altiplano andino.* Imprenta y Litografía Boliviana, La Paz.

1914 *Una metrópoli prehistórica en America del Sur. Eine praehistorische Metropole in Südamerika.* Dietrich Reimer, Berlin.

1938 *Antropología y scoiología de las razas interandinas y de las regiones adyacentes.* 2nd ed. Instituto "Tihuanacu" de Antropología, Etnología y Prehistoria. Editorial "Renacimiento," La Paz.

1945 *Tihuanacu: The Cradle of American Man.* Vols. 1 and 2. American Museum of Natural History, New York.

1957 *Tihuanacu: The Cradle of American Man.* Vols. 3 and 4. Minesterio de Educación, La Paz.

Rivera Casanovas, Claudia
2003 Ch'iji Jawira: A Case of Ceramic Specialization in the Tiwanaku Urban Periphery. In *Tiwanaku and Its Hinterland: Archaeology and Paleoecology of an Andean Civilization.* Vol. 2, *Urban and Rural Archaeology,* edited by Alan L. Kolata, pp. 296–315. Smithsonian Institution Press, Washington, D.C.

Rowe, John H.
1956 Archaeological Explorations in Southern Peru, 1954–55. *American Antiquity* 22:135–151.
1962a *Chavin Art: An Inquiry into Its Form and Meaning.* Museum of Primitive Art, New York.
1962b Stages and Periods in Archaeological Interpretation. *Southwestern Journal of Anthropology* 18: 40–54.
1963 Urban Settlement in Ancient Peru. *Ñawpa Pacha* 1:1–28.
1967 An Interpretation of Radiocarbon Measurements on Archaeological Samples from Peru. Reprinted in *Peruvian Archaeology: Selected Readings,* edited by John H. Rowe and Dorothy Menzel, pp. 16–30. Peek Publications, Palo Alto. Originally published 1966, *Proceedings of the Sixth International Conference, Radiocarbon and Tritium Dating.* U.S. Atomic Energy Commission, Springfield, Virginia.

Sampeck, Kathryn E.
1991 Excavations at Putuni, Tiwanaku, Bolivia. Unpublished master's thesis, Department of Anthropology, University of Chicago, Chicago.

Sawyer, Alan
1963 Tiwanaku Tapestry Design. *Textile Museum Journal* 1:27–38.

Seddon, Matthew Thomas
1994 Excavation of the Raised Fields of the Rio Catari Sub-Basin, Bolivia. Unpublished master's thesis, Department of Anthropology, University of Chicago, Chicago.
1998 *Ritual, Power and the Development of a Complex Society: The Island of the Sun and the Tiwanaku State.* University of Chicago, Chicago.

Silverman, Helaine
1990 The Early Nazca Pilgrimage Center of Cahuachi and the Nazca Lines: Anthropological and Archaeological Perspectives. In *The Lines of Nazca,* edited by Anthony Aveni, pp. 207–244. American Philosophical Society, Philadelphia.
1994 The Archaeological Identification of Cahuachi as a Pilgrimage Site. *World Archaeology* 26:1–18.
2000a Nasca: Geografía sagrada, ancestros y agua. In *Los dioses del antiguo Peru,* edited by Krzystof Makowski, pp. 239–275. Coleccion Arte y Tesoros del Peru, Banco de Crédito del Perú, Lima.
2000b Pilgrimage and Sacred Landscapes in Ancient Nasca Society. Paper presented at Dumbarton Oaks Symposium "Pilgrimage and Ritual Landscape in America," October 7–8, 2000, Washington, D.C.

Silverman, Helaine, and Donald Proulx
2002 *The Nasca.* Blackwell Publishers, Malden, Massachusetts.

Squier, E. George
1877 *Peru: Incidents of Travel and Explorations in the Land of the Incas.* Harper and Brothers, New York.

Stanish, Charles
2003 *Ancient Titicaca: The Evolution of Complex Society in Southern Peru and Northern Bolivia.* University of California Press, Berkeley.

Stovel, Emily
2002 The Importance of Being Atacameño: Political Identity and Mortuary Ceramics in Northern Chile. Unpublished Ph.D. dissertation, State University of New York, Binghamton.

Strong, William Duncan
1957 *Paracas, Nazca, and Tiahuanacoid Cultural Relations in South Coastal Peru.* Memoirs of the Society for American Archaeology 13. Society for American Archaeology, Washington, D.C.

Stübel, M., and Max Uhle
- 1892 *Die Ruinenstätte von Tiahuanaco im Hochlande des Alten Peru: Eine Kulturgeschichtliche Studie.* Verlag von Karl W. Hiersemann, Leipzig.

Tello, Julio C.
- 1942 Disertación del Dr. Julio C. Tello, por Mibe. *Huamanga* 8(48):62–63.
- 1960 *Chavín: Cultura matriz de la civilización andina.* Universidad Nacional Mayor de San Marcos, Lima.

Topic, John R., and Theresa Lang Topic
- 1992 The Rise and Decline of Cerro Amaru: An Andean Shrine during the Early Intermediate Period and Middle Horizon. In *Ancient Images, Ancient Thought: The Archaeology of Ideology*, edited by A. Sean Goldsmith, Sandra Garvie, David Selin, and Jeannette Smith, pp. 167–180. University of Calgary Archaeological Association, Calgary.

Topic, John R., Theresa Lange Topic, and Alfredo Melly Cava
- 2002 Catequil: The Archaeology, Ethnohistory, and Ethnography of a Major Provincial Huaca. In *Andean Archaeology.* Vol. 1, *Variations in Sociopolitical Organization*, edited by William H. Isbell and Helaine Silverman, pp. 303–336. Kluwer Academic/Plenum Publishers, New York.

Torres, Constantino Manuel
- 2007 La relación entre plantas visionarias e iconografía en el arte de Tiwanaku. Paper presented at the Series Iconográficas de los Andes del Sur: Un Coloquio sobre Arte y\ Arqueología Precolombina, Universidad de Chile, Santiago.

Uhle, Max
- 1903a Ancient South American Civilization. *Harpers Monthly Magazine.* October:780–786.
- 1903b Pachacamac: *Report of the William Pepper, M.D., L.L.D. Peruvian Expedition of 1896.* University of Pennsylvania, Philadelphia.

Vranich, Alexei
- 1999 Interpreting the Meaning of Ritual Spaces: The Temple Complex of Pumapunku, Tiwanaku, Bolivia. Unpublished Ph.D. dissertation, Department of Anthropology, University of Pennsylvania, Philadelphia.
- 2001 La pirámide de Akapana: Reconsiderando el centro monumental de Tiwanaku. In *Huari y Tiwanaku: Modelos vs. evidencias*, Pt. 2, edited by Peter Kaulicke and William H. Isbell, pp. 295–308. Boletín de Arqueología PUCP No. 5. Pontificia Universidad Católica del Perú, Lima.
- 2002 Visualizing the Monumental: Seeing What Is Not There. In *Experimental Archaeology: Replicating Past Objects, Behaviors, and Processes,* edited by James R. Mathieu, pp. 83–94. BAR International Series 1035. British Archaeological Reports, Oxford.
- 2005 Understanding the Architecture of Tiwanaku. Lecture delivered at the State University of New York at Binghamton.
- 2006 The Construction and Reconstruction of Ritual Space at Tiwanaku, Bolivia (A.D. 500–1000). *Journal of Field Archaeology* 31(2):121–136.

Wallace, Dwight
- 1998 The Inca Compound at La Centinela, Chincha. *Andean Past* 5:9–33.

Wheatley, Paul
- 1971 *The Pivot of the Four Quarters: A Preliminary Enquiry into the Origins and Character of the Ancient Chinese City.* Aldine, Chicago.

Wiener, Charles
- 1880 *Pérou et Bolivie: Récit de voyages Suivi d'études archéologiques et ethnographiques et de notes sur l'écriture et les langues des populations indiennes.* Librairie Hachette et Cie, Paris.

Yoffee, Norman
- 2005 *Myths of the Archaic State: Evolution of the Earliest Cities, States, and Civilizations.* Cambridge University Press, Cambridge.

Zárate, Agustin de
- 1968 [1556] *The Discovery and Conquest of Peru.* Edited by J. M. Cohen. Penguin Books, Baltimore.

11

Social Diversity, Ritual Encounter, and the Contingent Production of Tiwanaku

John W. Janusek

"No point of view on the totality is conceivable."
—Jean-Paul Sartre, *Being and Nothingness-*

"What is your vision of Tiwanaku?" This was the question presented to me when I was invited to write a chapter for this volume. After readily agreeing, I began to think about the conclusions of a comprehensive book on Tiwanaku I was then completing. In writing that book I became aware of the intellectual distortion involved in "wrapping up" a civilization in a few hundred pages and was reminded of the not-so-subtle political interests of anthropologies of "cultural patterns" in vogue during the early part of the twentieth century. In that book I argue for an epistemic relativism in which, without abandoning objectivity or empirical research, we realize that all knowledge of the world—including a past world such as Tiwanaku—is socially constructed. Indeed, there are multiple valid perspectives on any place or social order. I certainly have a vision of New York, as I do of a lot of places I've never lived in or even visited, but my vision is different from that of an inhabitant of Manhattan, whose vision differs from that of a Brooklyn resident, whose vision differs from that of a Newark resident, a Texan president of the United States, or a farmer living near Dubuque, Iowa. Let us say that I am that Iowan farmer: What can I possibly say in a few pages that will be valuable?

I believe the value of a book project such as this resides not so much in the individual chapters as in the discord apparent among the different perspectives of the Andean archaeologists represented in this volume, as well as in the surprising resonances that emerge from among those perspectives. While none of us actually lived in the pre-Hispanic phenomenon we describe here, we have either worked there producing data on its past or have thought a lot about that data and the civilization. I offer a brief synopsis of my current thinking on Tiwanaku based on (1) my past research at the primary center and at many sites and places in the landscape around it, and (2) my current research in the Machaca region just south of the Tiwanaku Valley, across the Kimsachata-Chilla mountain range. I focus on the primary center of Tiwanaku.

Tiwanaku was an always-changing center with a long history of significance that endures today. Indeed, every June 21 the site is the focus of pilgrimage for tourists, New Agers, urbanites, and local community members alike to ring in Aymara New Year. On January 21, 2006, the inauguration of Bolivia's first native president, Evo Morales, took place on the reconstructed Kalasasaya complex in the "ruins" of Tiwanaku, a place that clearly remains culturally and politically potent. Thus, to interpret Tiwanaku during its political peak as the center of an emergent Andean state is to isolate a sequence of human generations and historical moments in a much longer *durée*. I simply touch on Tiwanaku's long-term history here, a theme I develop elsewhere (see Janusek 2004a, 2004b, 2004c, 2006b, 2008a). Tiwanaku enjoyed generations when certain predominant practices, values, and materialities achieved relative "continuity." It also involved particular junctures—notably its rise to power in A.D. 500–600, its transformation at around A.D. 800–900, and its disintegration after A.D. 1000–1100—when profound changes in predominant practices, values, and materialities took the day. Any view of Tiwanaku must take into account both its long-term protean character and certain recurring continuities. A core element of the latter, I argue, is its role as a place of encounter.

Gathering evidence indicates that Tiwanaku was a place of social convergence and ritual encounter with a long and historically contingent history. At its peak in the Tiwanaku period (A.D. 500–1000), it was a place of lively interaction for its diversely affiliated inhabitants and their variable activities and affiliations. It was a place of recurring cyclical rituals where perhaps thousands descended in major ceremonies that involved worship at its various temples, ceremonial feasting, monumental construction, economic exchange, political networking, the trading of news and gossip, and a direct, immediate experience of community—the vast, imagined community that constituted Tiwanaku—which, more than a hundred years ago, Emile Durkheim termed collective effervescence. Tiwanaku came to warp place and time, in a manner reminiscent of Eliade's sacred space (1959) but in a more complex, less structurally determined way. It was a ceremonial city and pilgrimage site (Janusek 2008a, 2008b); a locus of political power, economic interaction, and devout ritual activity; and a mythicized, exciting, transformative place that people essentialized from afar (as they now do New York). Upon visiting it and inculcating its lessons and experiences, they returned to a "different home" (Turner 1974).

Background

In past writings I developed a model in which Tiwanaku was the urban center of an emergent macrocommunity comprised of diverse kin-based groups, ethnic-like macro-communities, and other forms of social affiliation. While politically centralized and ultimately centered on a core of elite factions, the Tiwanaku political community emerged as a "hospitality state" (Bandy this volume) grounded in a feasting economy (Janusek 2004b, 2006c) that involved populist practices and flexible strategies of incorporation. Tiwanaku itself, I suggest, modeled the greater Tiwanaku political community. Inhabitants of the emergent center internalized Tiwanaku state culture, if to varying degrees, as their own world knowledge, daily practices, and notions of personhood. Yet those inhabitants, who hailed from diverse places and ethnicities and who continued to forge unique social networks and affiliations, differentiated themselves from others in status, craft, place, and other domains of group identity. Tiwanaku was an ongoing project of cultural production for groups of multiple scales, statuses, interests, and modes of affiliating with—indeed modes of *being*—Tiwanaku.

Here I examine the means by which Tiwanaku formed a coherent political community that lasted centuries during its pre-Hispanic apogee, the Tiwanaku period (A.D. 500–1100). Clearly, something evocative, seductive, and powerful—and something more realistic than simply a "monopoly of military force" (e.g., Carneiro 1970; Service 1975)—was at work in Tiwanaku's emergence, popularity, and influence. Based on evidence from Tiwanaku and ongoing research in the Machaca region of Bolivia (Janusek 2008a), I argue that it was the power of ritual encounters and spiritual experience that drove Tiwanaku's immense popularity and increasingly vast influence throughout the south-central Andes. In saying this, I do not suggest that ritual practice and religious ideology were the sole "prime movers" in Tiwanaku state formation. Rather, recurring rounds of ritual events and social gatherings, organized according to effective calendar systems, provided key settings for a wealth of activities, including economic transactions and object-driven "tournaments of value" (*sensu* Appadurai 1986); political jockeying and volatile tournaments of power; rituals of consumption involving heaping plates of food and full cups of alcoholic drink; and plain old socializing, hanging out with kith and friends, catching up on news and gossip, schmoozing with political leaders, currying potential trade partners, clients, and in-laws (that is, setting up marriage alliances), gaining direct and immediate experience of *collective effervescence*, and having fun. Such rituals were *total social phenomena* in Marcel Mauss's sense: overdetermined and socially prescribed moments of dense social, transformative experience. Tiwanaku's prosperity was invested in, and its long-term success was on account of, recurring cycles of such momentous events. Tiwanaku political power, economic prosperity, and cultural influence were outcomes of the popularity and attraction of its vibrant social and ritual life.

Tiwanaku was a bold project of pan-regional community formation. As the first such formation of its kind in the south-central Andes, it was a project of social integration, for which the center of Tiwanaku served as a principal (though not the only; see Korpisaari and Pärssinen 2005 and Seddon 1998) place of social and ritual encounter (Janusek 2008b). Tiwanaku did not develop sui generis. It emerged as the principal center of the Lake Titicaca Basin in Late Formative 2 (A.D. 250–500), as one of several ritual-political centers that had for centuries formed a field of interacting ritual-political communities and anchored multiple overlapping interaction circuits in the Lake Titicaca Basin (Bandy 2001; Janusek 2004c; Lémuz 2001). Tiwanaku leaders co-opted many of those networks, through which valued objects and ideas continuously traveled, and by some strategic twist came to specify those objects and ideas as their own creations (Ohnstad and Janusek 2007). Similar to any contemporary city worth its weight in symbolic and material capital in our current global network, Tiwanaku presented itself as an ideal place with which to identify and to which to make regular pilgrimage.

Like other Formative centers, Tiwanaku positioned itself as a center par excellence of social encounter and spiritual experience. Yet it managed to trump its peers and to remain the center of cultural, economic, and political life in the basin for several hundred years. This belies Tiwanaku's populism and prestige and the fundamental egalitarian ethic of reciprocal obligation that informed relations among individuals and groups of different status. Yet Tiwanaku also came to form a hegemonic political community that encouraged—indeed that ultimately demanded—specified congeries of devout persons and ruled subjects.

Social Diversity and Cosmopolitanism

Material expressions of local group identity, cultural affiliation, and social diversity emphasize Tiwanaku's cosmopolitan characteristics. Marking status and plying specific trades were practices that established a group's identity and position in Tiwanaku society, and bounded residential compounds and more encompassing neighborhoods of such compounds were salient spatial and social contexts for their performance. It is likely that individuals, households, or craft production groups formed differentiated groups *within* encompassing compounds or neighborhoods. However, determining this will require the excavation of much or all of an entire compound, something that remains to be done.

Tiwanaku residential groups maintained multiple nested and overlapping affiliations, of which a position in Tiwanaku's social hierarchy and a role in its political economy—that is, particular subject positions within the hegemonic system—were but parts. Other palpable aspects of group identity formation at Tiwanaku were enacted in recurring local traditions and histories, a place of residence in the urban landscape, daily and periodic interaction networks, and enduring ties to homelands and other areas beyond Tiwanaku. Some can be characterized as ethnicity, which I consider a specific manifestation of identity that is relatively broad in scope and most salient in an interregional interaction network or a hegemonic political community (*sensu* Comaroff and Comaroff 1991).

Archaeological evidence for the expression of group differentiation in Tiwanaku residential sectors, aside from that manifested in local spatial arrangements, occupations, and status markers, was found in local stylistic assemblages, dietary habits, mortuary practices, and styles of body modification. Deborah Blom and I argue elsewhere that the archaeological detection of social identity requires an analysis that conjoins multiple cultural practices (Janusek and Blom 2006). Since these patterns have been discussed at length elsewhere (Blom 2005; Janusek 2002, 2004b; Rivera 2003), I merely summarize them here.

First, the stylistic aspects of ceramic assemblages, including characteristics of technical production, vessel form, and iconographic depiction, differed significantly among many bounded residential sectors (Janusek 2002; Rivera 2003). Of significance, ceramic assemblages in Ch'iji Jawira, at the far eastern edge of Tiwanaku, were most unusual. Among other things, the latter included high frequencies (about 18 percent of analyzed assemblages) of non-Tiwanaku and "hybrid" vessel sherds associated with the Cochabamba region of relatively warm valleys approximately 200 km east of Tiwanaku. Vessels of nonlocal manufacture or with nonlocal influence included cooking ollas, storage/fermentation vessels, and painted ceremonial wares.

Second, Tiwanaku inhabitants maintained diverse diets. Melanie Wright and colleagues (2003) determined through archaeobotanical analysis that proportions of crop remains varied significantly among bounded residential sectors. High-altitude *Chenopodium* (quinoa) grains were most frequently represented and best distributed at Tiwanaku, followed by tubers and maize. In particular, the distribution of maize was anomalous. As a grain that grows well only in valley regions below the altiplano, maize was an exotic crop that we expected to find only in high-status residential areas such as Putuni. It was used in great quantities to produce fermented *chicha* beer for ritual events. Yet maize was most frequent in Akapana East 2 and was best distributed in Ch'iji Jawira, which also yielded relatively high proportions of nonlocal wares from the valleys in which maize grows. Thus identities that transcended social status in Tiwanaku's local universe fostered the acquisition of valued consumable goods in Tiwanaku. These identities may have thrived on recurring long-distance interactions conducted via llama caravans and enduring links to distant homelands.

It is significant that some deceased were buried under living spaces in Tiwanaku and that not all were relegated to discrete cemeteries as in many societies, including modern Western nation-states. Evidence for this was found in Akapana, Putuni, Akapana East, Ch'iji Jawira, and other Tiwanaku-affiliated sites (Couture and Sampeck 2003; Janusek 2004b; Kolata 1993; Manzanilla 1992; Rivera 2003). This recurring mortuary pattern indicates that keeping certain deceased individuals close to home was an important element of life, identity, and local memory for at least some of Tiwanaku's residential groups. Human burial beneath or near inhabited dwellings was a practice that was vibrant during the pre-Tiwanaku Late Formative in the region and most likely originated during the preceding Early and Middle Formative periods and perhaps sooner (Hastorf 2003). The desire to keep the corpses of the deceased and their mortuary contexts near living spaces indicates that memorialization and periodic commemoration of ancestors and deceased relatives was important to social groups in Tiwanaku. In Putuni and Akapana East 2, mortuary contexts were constructed so as to remain visible for the living (Couture 2002; Janusek 2004b): in Putuni several consisted of aboveground niches surrounding its ceremonial courtyard, and in Akapana East 2 a subpatio multiple interment was marked on the living surface by a stone. These patterns suggest that local groups periodically remembered and bestowed offerings on deceased members, some of whom were likely considered progenitor ancestors. Mortuary patterns indicate that local social memory, however fabricated and enacted, was critical in fostering identity in Tiwanaku.

Body modification was a potent and highly personal way of marking identity, and perhaps in particular, ethnicity in Tiwanaku society (Blom 2005; Blom et al. 1998; Janusek and Blom 2006). If woven clothing was the most potent manner of "wearing" social identity in Tiwanaku, its lack of preservation in the Andean highlands leaves us to consider other aspects of bodily adornment, of which cranial modification appears to have been most critical. Bioarchaeologists have identified three broad head shapes for Tiwanaku populations: modified "annular" skulls produced by turban-like headbands and "tabular" skulls produced by wooden contraptions, as well as unmodified skulls. Head-shape styles crosscut age, sex, and social status. All of these styles were common in Tiwanaku, in some cases within the same compound. Cranial modification appears to have expressed regional scales of identity akin to ethnicity. Humans with annular skulls were most frequently located at Tiwanaku-affiliated sites in the Katari Valley north of Tiwanaku and in nearby regions, while humans with tabular skulls represented 100 percent of human burials excavated in the Tiwanaku colony of Moquegua some 200 km to the west.

Blom and I (2006) hypothesize that Tiwanaku was a focal place of convergence for people of multiple bodily styles, as well as differing statuses, specializations, mortuary traditions, and social networks. These bodily forms indexed linkages to broader regional identities with discrete affiliations to nonlocal places and societies. The fact that people "wearing" all styles were buried in Tiwanaku, even within the same compound or neighborhood, indicates that people of diverse ethnicities lived and worked together (if in different capacities or statuses) and most likely intermarried in the center.

The best local evidence for the expression of ethnicity in Tiwanaku comes from Ch'iji Jawira (Rivera 2003). Among its distinctive serving-ceremonial assemblages were high frequencies of so-called Cochabamba Tiwanaku wares associated with the Cochabamba Valley region some 200 km southwest. Also notable was the absence here of ceramic incense burners, ritual vessels ubiquitous in other Tiwanaku residential compounds. In addition to such differences, the area's peripheral location and specialized activities may indicate that resident specialists maintained close affiliations elsewhere, especially the temperate Cochabamba region. Pending chemical analysis of human remains at Tiwanaku, it is hypothesized that, like those with shared styles of body modification in Tiwanaku, inhabitants of Ch'iji Jawira may have originally emigrated from Cochabamba or its environs (Janusek 2002, 2004b: 164). In that case, the roughly concentric gradient of urban space and status in Tiwanaku was simultaneously a gradient of cultural affiliation that separated relatively "pure" Tiwanaku groups, such as those in Akapana, Putuni, and Akapana East 1M, from groups in the settlement periphery and outside of the moat with strong "foreign" ties. This same gradient also defined the history of the settlement by distinguishing the new neighborhoods of the periphery from the long-established compounds and monuments of the core, thereby focusing social legitimacy and power centripetally on the latter and defining an urban historical consciousness not unlike other past cities, such as Tenochtitlán and Rome.

Ceremony and Ritual Commensalism

Monumental Spaces

Ongoing research on the Late Formative (100 B.C.–A.D. 500) foundations of altiplano cultural development indicates that Tiwanaku emerged amid a regional peer-polity network of multicommunity polities (Bandy 2001; Janusek 2004b; Stanish 1999). While these polities remain to be precisely defined, it appears that they were diverse in character, shifting in regional influence, and grounded in periodic communal rituals. Khonkho Wankane, a Late Formative center 25 km directly south of Tiwanaku, is a key case in point (see Smith this volume). Excavations here reveal a moderately occupied ceremonial center that was built in Late Formative 1, restructured in Late Formative 2, and decreased in size just before Tiwanaku's rise to prominence (Janusek 2006b). With a small permanent occupation, Khonkho became populous during periodic ritual events, when people from distant regions came to participate in ritual celebrations and construction activities (see evidence for temporarily occupied structures in Janusek 2003, 2004b). These were auspicious and socially dense moments when inclusive regional identities were invigorated, when regional power structures were temporarily crystallized, and when pan-community histories were created, reproduced, or refabricated. Over cycles of such events, persons and communities acquired new forms and modes of being.

Ritual activity was pivotal at Tiwanaku in the Late Formative and Tiwanaku periods. Tiwanaku's Late Formative components, if less intensively investigated than Khonkho's, demonstrate a parallel trajectory of expansion, construction, and transformation (Couture 2002; Janusek 2006b). In Late Formative 1 (100 B.C.–A.D. 250), both sites incorporated sunken courtyards for periodic ceremonies, many of which involved ritual consumption (Zovar 2007). New monumental complexes at Khonkho and Tiwanaku in Late Formative 2 followed a predominantly east–west orientation. In part, this represents the increasing importance of a solar cult and of effective calendar keeping (Benitez 2005), which implies renewed attention to coordinating ritual activities and productive systems (namely farming, herding, and fishing) (Janusek 2006b). New temples transformed the character of monumentality in that sunken courtyards were now incorporated within massive stone-lined platforms. Further, platform-courtyard complexes, such as the Dual-Court Complex at Khonkho and the Kalasasaya at Tiwanaku, abutted massive plazas for major ceremonial and (likely) political events. These transformations afforded an increasing theatricality to movement through ritual spaces, as well as a greater sense of mystery in personal encounters with the ritual specialists and massive carved stone stelae enclosed within (Ohnstad and Janusek 2007). They encouraged pilgrims and others to inculcate new ritual attitudes and indeed to become new types of persons—ideal subjects—appropriate to this emergent cosmology.

By the beginning of the Tiwanaku period (A.D. 500–600), Khonkho had waned in importance while the scale and diversity of monumentality had exploded at Tiwanaku. The massive terreplein complexes of Akapana and Pumapunku took to even greater heights the monumentality of Late Formative temples, yet in their total physicality they materialized the religious significance and cosmological meanings developed in the Late Formative. Some traditional practices, notably the production and carving of massive stone effigy monoliths, were now largely restricted, perhaps by sumptuary laws, to Tiwanaku itself. Emphasizing the potency of Tiwanaku's sun cult, stone monoliths and monolithic portals now depicted celestial imagery. Calendar keeping, likely of great significance in affording Tiwanaku's strategic "edge" in Late Formative 2, remained critical for coordinating religious, productive, and political cycles and in conferring legitimacy on the ritualists who produced such esoteric knowledge. As much is clear in the construction of a celestial observatory on the western edge of the Kalasasaya (Ponce 1990; Posnansky 1945), in which the famous Sun Portal likely stood (Benitez 2005).

As Tiwanaku became an urban settlement, temples and shrines for local worship were built among the city's residential compounds (Janusek 2004b: 110–112). Extensive plazas attached to the Akapana and Pumapunku (Vranich 1999), later elite-affiliated platform-courtyard complexes for ceremonial feasting in Putuni (Couture 2002; Couture and Sampeck 2003) and Akapana East (Janusek 2004b: 218–219), and sunken courtyards southwest of the Akapana all attest to Tiwanaku's vibrant ceremonial life and the diverse religious affiliations, ritual practices, and social statuses of its affiliated populations. These data point to the enduring importance of periodic rituals and, increasingly through time, of rituals of consumption (Janusek 2006c) as recurring events that shaped sociopolitical dynamics in the south-central Andes. From its formative foundations through its disintegration, and in a refabricated form today, Tiwanaku was and remains a profound spiritual-ritual phenomenon.

Nondomestic Residential Spaces

Complementary research on Tiwanaku's residential components emphasizes that Tiwanaku was not simply either an empty ceremonial center or densely inhabited city. Two ongoing projects at the site address the character of Tiwanaku residential occupations in the urban periphery. The Mollo Kontu Project, directed by Couture and Blom, investigates residential organization in the southeastern quadrant of the city, which harbored several interconnected *qochas* (Couture and Blom 2004). Like *qochas* today, these may have supplemented farming by sustaining gardens or may have supported camelid herds. Excavations in Mollo Kontu South indicate that residential occupation organized into supra-household compounds characterized parts of this sector during the Middle Horizon (Couture and Sampeck 2003). Nevertheless, new excavations in Mollo Kontu Mound reveal very complex strata of lenses and middens, in some cases associated with human burials and other features. Project investigators have located no clear dwellings or other types of structures. Artifactual data point to the likelihood that the area was used from the end of the Late Formative through the Tiwanaku periods, with strata comprising long-term palimpsests of ephemeral or temporary occupation. Quite possibly, this area was densely inhabited during some of Tiwanaku's recurring calendrical ceremonies, when pilgrims, entrepreneurs, and llama caravan traders descended on the center (Janusek 2008a, 2008b). In this scenario, the *qochas* provided feed for the llamas and alpacas that temporarily inhabited Tiwanaku.

The Proyecto Arqueológico Pumapunku y Akapana (PAPA), directed by Alexei Vranich, conducted a second archaeological investigation at the site of Muru Ut Pata on the northeastern edge of Tiwanaku. PAPA member Katherine Davis set out to investigate domestic life in a local community at the edge of the Tiwanaku urban district. Supporting previous findings by Wendell Bennett (1934), Stig Rydén (1947), and me (2004b, below), Davis found abundant evidence for refuse disposal in sheet middens and refuse/ash pits. Local activities included domestic, craft-related, and ritual practices. Further, her excavations yielded rectilinear structures similar to those found at Tiwanaku. Yet, as she argues, it is not clear that these were residential dwellings. Nor is it clear that they were organized into a compound or bounded neighborhood group, as were other residential areas of the site (Katherine Davis, personal communication 2006). This evidence does not negate what we know about residential life in Tiwanaku, but like recent evidence from Mollo Kontu, it offers an important caveat regarding the ubiquitous applicability of a compound-based residential model across Tiwanaku.

Tiwanaku residential organization was complex, and the site was not simply a grid-organized urban center focused on a monumental core (Benitez and Vranich 2005). As mentioned above, many structures at Tiwanaku cannot be securely categorized as dwellings. Furthermore, many structures, in particular those occupied late in the Middle Horizon, appear to have been temporarily or periodically occupied. A prime example was the Tiwanaku V occupation of Akapana East (Janusek 2003, 2004b). In this area, compounds once dedicated to primary or secondary residential activity were entirely transformed in a major project of urban renewal. Renewal here produced relatively extensive open spaces associated with a variety of structures, few of which can be unequivocally considered dwellings. Several small rectangular structures encountered in Akapana East 1 revealed only the slightest of compacted surfaces and few of the domestic features associated with typical dwellings. I have argued that these structures were only periodically occupied and used in some manner for important ritual occasions. Drawing an analogy with similar contemporary structures in Bolivian towns, I argue that they served as storage (for costumes, jars of native *chicha* beer, and so on), workspace (for example, to prepare feasts), or housing for visitors during important Tiwanaku ritual events. The fact that most such structures were located in late (Tiwanaku V) contexts, postdating A.D. 800, in relation to a growing frequency of liquid fermentation and serving wares (Janusek 2003; Mathews 2003), suggests that they were closely tied to the increasing importance of rituals of consumption in Tiwanaku.

Rydén Redux and the Ubiquitous Tiwanaku Ash Pit

If compound-bounded dwelling areas are not ubiquitous throughout Tiwanaku, the refuse middens and ash pits that Bennett and Rydén first noted are. On separate occasions in the 1930s, Wendell Bennett and Stig Rydén excavated isolated units at Tiwanaku in part to locate its "invisible" habitations. Bennett was struck to find that among isolated features and a couple of possible foundations, Tiwanaku cultural strata comprised enormous quantities of refuse and superimposed layers of middens. He (1934:480) arrived at the influential conclusion that Tiwanaku was a "vacant ceremonial center" composed of an "aggregation of temples." Rydén (1947) reached the more prescient conclusion that these middens were the product of recurring "ritual meals" at the site. Setting out to do "household archaeology" in the early 1990s, I discovered at least as many refuse pits and middens as the nicely preserved primary domestic contexts I sought.

As Tiwanaku transformed into an urban settlement in A.D. 500–800 (Tiwanaku IV), material refuse became an ever-present element of its expanding settlement landscape. It is not surprising that as Tiwanaku changed from one among many ritual-political centers in a multicommunity political field to the primary urban center in the south-central Andes, dealing with refuse became an increasingly important part of life there. This pattern characterizes emergent urbanism worldwide, in that population nucleation and intensified production tend to produce great quantities of material "stuff" per hectare. Excavations that seek to investigate Tiwanaku household life, from Bennett and Rydén through Janusek to Couture and Davis, inevitably yield far more than primary residential deposition. They also yield extensive refuse lenses, sheet middens, and ash pits (Couture and Blom 2004; Davis 2006; Janusek 2004b; Rivera 2003). Combining the total residential area excavated to date at Tiwanaku, I estimate that approximately 40 to 50 percent consisted of secondary deposition.

So-called ash pits stand out in Tiwanaku. Excavation in residential sectors of the site is inevitably hampered to some degree by encountering Tiwanaku refuse pits that had destroyed huge sections of prior occupations. Refuse deposits in general are rare in Late Formative contexts and are less common at other Tiwanaku sites. Ash pits were particularly common in Akapana East (including Akapana East 1M, 1, and 2), Kk'araña, Ch'iji Jawira, and Mollo Kontu. Many ash pits are amorphous, consisting of huge excavated depressions with abundant exhausted artifacts, broken or eroded adobe bricks, and camelid dung. I interpret these as borrow pits that yielded adobe construction material and then served as handy deposits for refuse. Other ash pits consisted of old subterranean wells, storage bins, and other pits that had been converted into ash pits upon their obsolescence. In all cases in which such features were recovered in Tiwanaku, they had been ultimately filled with ash and refuse—in wells up to 6 m in depth.

In nature and quantity, the refuse found in Tiwanaku sheet middens (common in Ch'iji Jawira) and ash pits is diagnostic of some of the activity that took place in Tiwanaku's settlement peripheries. Pellets of camelid dung were frequent components of most secondary contexts. For centuries camelid dung has been a critical source of fuel in this part of the Andes, and its high temperature combustion makes it ideal as much for domestic hearths as for ceramic and other material production (Winterhalder 1978). The ash itself tends to be colored a blue to green hue of gray. This color was uncommon in Late Formative contexts in the southern basin, and at Khonkho it was located only in one area of the site that other material patterns suggest was for communal production of food and drink for rituals of consumption focused in nearby temple complexes (Zovar 2007). Pending chemical analysis, I suggest that it derives from the high-temperature combustion of llama dung (also Katherine Davis, personal communication 2005). This parallels other evidence from Tiwanaku ash pits. They also yielded immense quantities of cooking, storage/fermentation, and serving-ceremonial-ware sherds; splintered and butchered camelid, guinea pig, and bird bones; exhausted bone and stone implements; and preserved food remains (including maize kernels and cobs and quinoa seeds; Wright et al. 2003). Some contained "perfectly good" items such as adobe bricks, reconstructable vessels, and cut-stone blocks. Most such pits revealed less than four depositional strata, indicating that they were filled relatively quickly in few dumping events. In a few pits, pieces of the same vessel were located in multiple strata.

The amount and variety of refuse located in Tiwanaku's sheet middens and ash pits were enormous. I believe they are the product, in part, of recurring feasts and other rituals that occurred at multiple social scales and in multiple spatial contexts at Tiwanaku. In relation to the relatively sparse density of primary dwelling areas in the settlement, it is clear that the refuse represents more than domestic garbage. It is difficult to prove this point definitively because many of these contexts are located in or near residential spaces, in some cases contemporaneous with primary residential occupations and in other cases preceding or postdating them. They are not limited to spatially segmented or artifactually differentiated feasting spaces or contexts; rather they are everywhere. Evidence suggests that Tiwanaku middens and ash pits, which involved significant labor input, were the product of periodic ritual events, including local residential and more inclusive center-wide feasts for which people of diverse compounds, neighborhoods, and perhaps Andean regions would have gathered. Thus Rydén was precocious: "ritual meals" apparently were a central element of Tiwanaku culture from its Late Formative beginnings through its Middle Horizon hegemony.

The Regional Perspective: Historical and Archaeological Evidence

Recent Social Organization in the South-Central Andes

Tiwanaku's significance and character are best contextualized by examining later, historically documented sociopolitical organization in the region. Tiwanaku's sociopolitical disintegration in A.D. 1000–1200 was a process of cultural regeneration that ultimately produced a regional landscape of relatively dispersed, locally hierarchical, and pastorally focused communities (Albarracin-Jordan 1996; Janusek 2004a, 2004b). Important changes, including successive phases of Inca and Spanish hegemony, changed local social-spatial organization and economic-ethnic relations over the next few centuries.

Nevertheless, Tiwanaku cultural and political disintegration initiated a trajectory of regional social-spatial change that remains vital today. The ultimate phase of this trajectory, which occurred under Spanish colonial rule, was the creation of nucleated settlements, or *reducciones*, to facilitate state control and economic appropriation. Prior to this, centers of social convergence that had emerged after Tiwanaku's collapse ranged from major settlements to nonsettled ceremonial spaces such as mountaintops, cemeteries, and local chapels (see Stanish 2003). The fundamental basis of social status, economy, and identification was the *ayllu*, an Andean permutation of "community" that referred (variably across space and societies) to a corporate group, referred to as kin, that identified with shared economic resources, political interests, ritual places (and rites), and deceased ancestors. *Ayllu* members tended to live in local hamlets and villages distributed across the landscape. They were organized according to scalar "hierarchies of encompassment" (Abercrombie 1998) and sociopolitical hierarchies of distinction. An *ayllu* and its leadership claimed a particular social place, status, and in some cases productive activity through membership in extensive regional interaction networks and encompassing sociopolitical systems.

This post-Tiwanaku social world gave rise to a novel expression of "urbanism" that remains vibrant today and that may well partake of Tiwanaku's more ancient form of ceremonial urbanism. Major towns in the south-central Andes, each termed a pueblo or *marka*, were centers of social-ritual convergence and symbolic places of social unity for the dispersed communities that identified with them. Each maintained a relatively small permanent occupation but formed symbolic and ceremonial "anchors" for *ayllu* identities. Yet each *ayllu* maintained representative residential spaces in the local town—in some cases spatially mirroring their location in the regional landscape—and houses pertaining to a particular *ayllu* or hamlet tended to cluster in specific neighborhoods. These towns were densely populated only during key ceremonial occasions. Nonlocal people, usually now either members of the various rural communities surrounding the town or stake-claiming community members now living in nearby cities, came to reside temporarily in the town while helping prepare meals, orchestrate dances, ferment or provide drinks, or simply have a good, raucous time.

Structures providing residence, workspace, and storage (such as for costumes and alcohol) for such events were extremely important in these centers and may be analogous to those archaeologically encountered in Tiwanaku's Akapana East, Muru Ut Pata, and other sectors. Permanent populations in these recent towns were relatively small overall, but they pulsated periodically and exploded momentarily during important calendrical and other ceremonies. At these times, plazas, streets, and the residential compounds of feast hosts were jammed with people from outlying places and communities, and routine life was abandoned to music, dancing, and drinking. But many such rituals are also important contexts for exchanging or selling goods, social "networking," and, most explicitly, forming and transforming power relations. During such events, social status and other forms of identity, ethnic or otherwise, were affirmed, contested, and transformed. Feast hosting itself remains critical to becoming a respected adult member who "is heard" in a community and is the key way to build a political career for more ambitious persons. The Machac Mara ritual at Khonkho Wankane (unlike Tiwanaku's mestizo and urban-focused carnival) is a "total" social event (Janusek 2006a; *sensu* Mauss 1967) that involves feasting, economic interaction, social networking, and the annual election of regional native leaders.

Settlement Organization in the Tiwanaku Region

Tiwanaku's regional setting facilitated a similar pulsating ceremonial urbanism, if in a different cultural field that was more regionally integrated and centrally coordinated. Tiwanaku was fundamentally unlike centers such as Teotihuacán in that its expansion in the Middle Horizon was characterized not by demographic implosion (Sanders et al. 1979) but by regional population growth and settlement increase in the Tiwanaku and adjacent valleys. Survey to date in the Tiwanaku Valley (the upper valley is currently being investigated) has revealed nearly 300 sites dating to the Tiwanaku period, a dramatic increase in number from the Late Formative (Albarracin-Jordan 1996; Albarracin-Jordan and Mathews 1990; Mathews 2003). Human settlement was well distributed across valley resource zones and comprised multiple size-based tiers. Pedestrian survey and multiple statistical analyses (McAndrews et al. 1997) indicate that Tiwanaku Valley settlements formed clusters centered on small towns, all of which clustered around Tiwanaku, which served as both primary local center and state capital (Janusek and Blom 2006). These patterns indicate that the pre-Hispanic Tiwanaku Valley comprised several multisettlement, semi-autonomous sociopolitical and ritual communities. This is reminiscent of later *ayllus*, which in turn centered on one or more central places for periodic religious ceremonies and rituals of consumption.

Urban and rural domains of Tiwanaku social organization were inextricably intertwined, as they have been in recent Andean communities. There is convincing evidence that some groups immigrated to Tiwanaku and that local activities, affiliations, and memories helped forge the increasingly hierarchical and hegemonic state system. There is further evidence that local urban ties to distant places played a major role in Tiwanaku's rise to power, vitality, and political-religious longevity. Much like contemporary pueblos, Tiwanaku was indebted to the local, nonurban, and "foreign" populations that identified with it. It anchored the social coherence of its vast political community in great part through periodic feasts and ceremonies. Tiwanaku was a ceremonial center, an urban phenomenon, and a concrete symbol. Like later pueblos, Tiwanaku was an "incomplete center" with which local communities identified, to which they periodically paid homage, and to which they occasionally came for key religious ceremonies and feasts. This was Tiwanaku's strength and ultimately its liability.

Thus ritual was not ephemeral in relation to political and economic activities. In fact, as they do in the recent and contemporary Andes, past feasts and rituals formed the situational matrix for social networking, economic interchange, and political events. One can imagine that periodic ceremonies in Tiwanaku were times when llama caravans laden with goods from disparate regions descended on the center. Extensive herds may have been put up in the Mollo Kontu sector or outside of the center near one of several marshy springs in the surrounding valley. One can also imagine that some periodic ceremonies were times when representatives of multiple communities comprising a vast regional community united and when political decisions were made. Further archaeological research promises to shed more light on these potential aspects of pre-Hispanic Tiwanaku.

Conclusions

At its peak in the later centuries of the first millennium, Tiwanaku was a ceremonial city. On the surface, this is a deceptively bland remark on its variegated manifestations over time and its manifold significance for innumerable individuals, groups, ethnicities, and polities over generations, up through today. Tiwanaku was a city to the extent that, from its Late Formative foundations, it grew exponentially in extent and population, as well as in social, economic, and spatial complexity, throughout the Tiwanaku period. From A.D. 400 to 800, Tiwanaku was transformed from one of multiple interacting ritual-political centers in the southern Lake Titicaca Basin into an extensive and socioeconomically diverse and politically focused urban center—indeed, the principal center of social life, cultural life, and political activity in the south-central Andes.

Yet Tiwanaku also condensed multivalent social realities to produce novel subjectivities, create congeries of devout persons (differentiated by age, gender, kin group, and so on), synthesize new material values (religious or otherwise), subsidize artistic production (in textiles, ceramics, or stonework), and provide the technical means (for example, ceremonial events, fermented beverages, or psychotropic substances) to facilitate social transcendence and spiritual redemption at the places most important for a particular region or subjectivity (for example, the temples at Tiwanaku; local shrines in Moquegua, Cochabamba, Puno Bay, and the Island of the Sun). In these and other senses, Tiwanaku put the "ceremonial" in "ceremonial city" and the "productive" in "productive economy," which was as much about creating particular types of "citizens" and human values as it was about constructing raised fields for farming or patron–client networks to secure desiderata.

I argue elsewhere that a critical force driving Tiwanaku's far-reaching prestige and influence, beginning in the Late Formative, was its role as a pilgrimage center for dispersed communities and populations (Janusek 2008b). Comparison with Khonkho Wankane supports this conclusion. In a sense, Tiwanaku's eventual distinction as the principal center for the south-central Andes during the Middle Horizon can be interpreted as part of a long-term historical transformation from local (Late Formative 1) to regional (Late Formative 2) to pan-regional ceremonial center (Tiwanaku IV). In forging a vast community sui generis, Tiwanaku leaders and adherents alike may have promoted its cult as utopian, as an idealized place positively different from others of its kind and from the places its adherents and potential affiliates inhabited. It was a pilgrimage site writ large yet was resolutely different from many other pilgrimage sites in simultaneously forming the center of urban political, economic, and religious life for this vast political community.

Most important, Tiwanaku was perpetually changing, and this historical process was not the product of a teleological progression. Its ultimate transformation from a *primus inter pares* to a distinctive primate center involved fortuitous conjunctions of regional sociopolitical circumstances, historical events, environmental conditions, and strategic transformations of traditional materialities, practices, and ideals. We can include among the latter: (1) a profoundly seductive spiritual cult that meshed past with novel representations (for example, an early chthonic with a solar complex); (2) an effective celestial-based calendar kept by ritual specialists to schedule recurring rituals and to facilitate the coordination of diverse productive economies; (3) a novel and synthetic monumentality that incorporated ancient sunken courts within massive platform complexes associated with large plazas for communal gathering; (4) a feasting economy that promoted an ethic of elite generosity and "social egalitarianism" as much in its recurrence at multiple scales as in the ubiquitous distribution and use of Tiwanaku serving-ceremonial vessels; and (5) an incipient hegemony that delegated (or left) direct control over production in the hands of local leaders and communities (Janusek 2002), thereby promoting social expression in regional affiliations, material styles, and religious observation. Yet Tiwanaku produced a specific range of ritual persons and political subjects, if differentiated by gender, ethnicity, and so on, and more rigorously so throughout the Tiwanaku period.

Tiwanaku was a place of social convergence and ritual encounter with a long and contingent history. A central point in interpreting Tiwanaku is that it did not begin its illustrious career as a state political "capital." Rather, its statehood was an unforeseen consequence of a long history of historical conjunctions, religious transformations, political machinations, and multiple forms of local participation and affiliation, which together ultimately produced, to a great extent unwittingly, what we now call the Tiwanaku state. To this extent, I agree with Norman Yoffee (2005:16), who writes that in many early states, "centrality is mainly concerned with the creation of new symbols of social identity, ideologies of power, and representations of history." While this is by no means a definitive vision of Tiwanaku, nor could it ever be as Sartre alluded, it may add something to the bourgeoning perspectives and visions of this fascinating Andean civilization that are collated in this volume.

Acknowledgments

I am grateful to Alexei Vranich and Chip Stanish for inviting me to participate in the symposium "Contending Visions of Tiwanaku," which the Cotsen Institute of Archaeology at UCLA sponsored in May 2006. Intense debates and discussions gave rise to many interesting ideas in that two-day session. Gratitude is also owed to my many sources of research funding, including the National Science Foundation (BCS-0514624), the National Geographic Society, the Howard Heinz Foundation, the Mary G. and Curtiss T. Brennan Foundation, and the Vanderbilt University Discovery Grant program.

References Cited

Abercrombie, T. A.
 1998 *Pathways of Memory and Power: Ethnography and History among an Andean People*. University of Wisconsin Press, Madison.

Albarracin-Jordan, Juan
 1996 *Tiwanaku. Arqueología regional y dinámica segmentaria*. Editores Plural, La Paz.

Albarracin-Jordan, J. V., and J. E. Mathews
 1990 *Asentamientos prehispánicos del Valle de Tiwanaku*, Vol. 1. Producciones CIMA, La Paz.

Appadurai, A.
 1986 Commodities and the Politics of Value. In *The Social Life of Things: Commodities in Cultural Perspective*, edited by A. Appadurai, pp. 3–63. Cambridge University Press, Cambridge.

Bandy, M. S.
 2001 Population and History in the Ancient Titicaca Basin. Unpublished Ph.D. dissertation, Department of Anthropology, University of California, Berkeley.

Benitez, Leonardo
 2005 Time and Calendrics at Tiwanaku: An Archaeoastronomical Study. Paper presented at the 70th Annual Meeting of the Society for American Archaeology, Salt Lake City.

Benitez, Leonardo, and Alexei Vranich
 2005 Urban Planning and Conveying the Sacred at Tiwanaku. Paper presented at the 24th Northeast Conference for Andean Archaeology and

Ethnohistory, American University, Washington D.C.

Bennett, W. C.
1934 Excavations at Tiahuanaco. *Anthropological Papers of the American Museum of Natural History* 34(3):359–494.

Blom, D. E.
2005 Embodying Borders: Human Body Modification and Diversity in Tiwanaku Society. *Journal of Anthropological Archaeology* 24:1–34.

Blom, D. E., B. Hallgrímsson, L. Keng, M. C. Lozada C., and J. E. Buikstra
1998 Tiwanaku "Colonization": Bioarchaeological Implications for Migration in the Moquegua Valley, Peru. *World Archaeology* 30(2):238–261.

Carneiro, R.
1970 A Theory of the Origin of the State. *Science* 169: 733–738.

Comaroff, J., and J. Comaroff
1991 *Of Revelation and Revolution: Christianity, Colonialism, and Consciousness in South Africa*. University of Chicago Press, Chicago.

Couture, Nicole
2002 The Construction of Power: Monumental Space and Elite Residence at Tiwanaku, Bolivia. Unpublished Ph.D. dissertation, Department of Anthropology, University of Chicago, Chicago.

Couture, N. C., and D. E. Blom
2004 Informe sobre los trabajos realizados por el Proyecto Jacha Marka en los años de 2001 y 2002. Unpublished research report presented to the Vice Ministry of Culture, Bolivia.

Couture, Nicole and Kathryn Sampeck
2003 Putuni: A History of Palace Architecture in Tiwanaku. In *Tiwanaku and Its Hinterland: Archaeology and Paleoecology of an Andean Civilization*. Vol. 2, *Urban and Rural Archaeology*, edited by Alan L. Kolata, pp. 226–263. Smithsonian Institution Press, Washington, D.C.

Eliade, M.
1959 *The Sacred and the Profane: The Nature of Religion*. Harcourt, Brace and World, New York.

Hastorf, C. A.
2003 Community with the Ancestors: Ceremonies and Social Memory in the Middle Formative at Chiripa, Bolivia. *Journal of Anthropological Archaeology* 22:305–332.

Janusek, John Wayne
2002 Out of Many, One: Style and Social Boundaries in Tiwanaku. *Latin American Antiquity* 13(1): 35–61.

2003 The Changing Face of Tiwanaku Residential Life: State and Social Identity in an Andean City. In *Tiwanaku and Its Hinterland: Archaeology and Paleoecology of an Andean Civilization*. Vol. 2, *Urban and Rural Archaeology*, edited by Alan L. Kolata, pp. 264–295. Smithsonian Institution Press, Washington, D.C.

2004a Collapse as Cultural Revolution: Power and Identity in the Tiwanaku to Pacajes Transition. In *Foundations of Power in the Prehispanic Andes*, edited by C. A. Conlee, D. Ogburn, and K. Vaughn. American Anthropological Association, Arlington, Virginia.

2004b *Identity and Power in the Ancient Andes: Tiwanaku Cities through Time*. Routledge, New York.

2004c Tiwanaku and Its Precursors: Recent Research and Emerging Perspectives. *Journal of Archaeological Research* 12:121–183.

2006a Blood for Sun and Earth, Festival for Community: Archaeological Implications of a Bolivian Solstice Ritual as a "Total Social Phenomenon." Paper presented at the Annual Conference of the American Anthropological Association, San Jose, California.

2006b The Changing "Nature" of Tiwanaku Religion and the Rise of an Andean State. *World Archaeology* 38(3):469–492.

2006c Consumiendo el estado: Politica comensalista en una antigua entidad politica andina. *Textos antropológicos* 15(2):23–38.

2008a *Ancient Tiwanaku*. Cambridge University Press, Cambridge.

2008b Patios hundidios, encuentros rituales, y el auge de Tiwanaku como un centro pan-regional andino. *Boletín de Arqueología PUCP* 9:161–184.

Janusek, J. W., and D. E. Blom
2006 Identifying Tiwanaku Urban Populations: Style, Identity, and Ceremony in Andean Cities. In *Urbanization in the Preindustrial World: Cross-Cultural Approaches*, edited by G. Storey, pp. 233–251. University of Alabama Press, Tuscaloosa.

Kolata, A. L.
1993 *The Tiwanaku: Portrait of an Andean Civilization*. Blackwell, Cambridge, Massachusetts.

Korpisaari, Antti, and Marti Pärssinen (editors)
2005 *Pariti: Isla, misterio y poder: El tesoro cerámico de la cultura Tiwanaku*. Producciones CIMA, La Paz.

Lémuz Aguirre, C.
2001 Patrones de asentamiento arqueológico en la peninsula de Santiago de Huata, Boliva. Unpublished licenciatura thesis, Universidad Mayor de San Andres, La Paz.

Manzanilla, L.
1992 *Akapana: Una pirámide en el centro del mundo*. Instituto de Investigaciones Antropológicas, Universidad Nacional Autónoma de México, Mexico City.

Mathews, J. E.
  2003 Prehistoric Settlement Patterns in the Middle Tiwanaku Valley. In *Tiwanaku and Its Hinterland: Archaeology and Paleoecology of an Andean Civilization*. Vol. 2, *Urban and Rural Archaeology*, edited by Alan L. Kolata, pp. 112–128. Smithsonian Institution Press, Washington, D.C.

Mauss, M.
  1967 *The Gift: Forms and Functions of Exchange in Archaic Societies*. W. W. Norton, New York.

McAndrews, T., J. Albarracin-Jordan, and M. Bermann
  1997 Regional Settlement Patterns in the Tiwanaku Valley of Bolivia. *Journal of Field Archaeology* 24:67–84.

Ohnstad, A., and J. W. Janusek
  2007 The Development of Tiwanaku Style out of the Ideological and Political-Economic Landscapes of the Lake Titicaca Basin. Paper presented at the colloquium, Southern Andean Iconographic Series, Santiago.

Ponce Sanginés, Carlos
  1990 *Descripción sumaria del Templete Semisuterraneo de Tiwanaku*. 6th ed. Juventud, La Paz.

Posnansky, Arthur
  1945 *Tihuanacu: The Cradle of American Man*, Vols. 1 and 2. J. J. Augustin, New York.

Rivera Casanovas, Claudia
  2003 Ch'iji Jawira: A Case of Ceramic Specialization in the Tiwankau Urban Periphery. In *Tiwanaku and Its Hinterland: Archaeology and Paleoecology of an Andean Civilization*. Vol. 2, *Urban and Rural Archaeology*, edited by Alan L. Kolata, pp. 296–315. Smithsonian Institution Press, Washington, D.C.

Rydén, S.
  1947 *Archaeological Researches in the Highlands of Bolivia*. Elanders Boktryckeri Aktiebolag, Göteborg.

Sanders, W. T., J. R. Parsons, and R. S. Santley
  1979 *The Basin of Mexico: Ecological Processes in the Evolution of a Civilization*. Academic Press, New York.

Sartre, Jean-Paul
  1992 [1956] *Being and Nothingness: A Phenomenological Essay on Ontology*. Translated by H. E. Barnes. Washington Square Press, New York.

Seddon, Michael Thomas
  1998 Ritual, Power, and the Development of a Complex Society. Unpublished Ph.D. dissertation, Department of Anthropology, University of Chicago, Chicago.

Service, E.
  1975 *Origins of the State and Civilization: The Process of Cultural Evolution*. Norton, New York.

Stanish, C.
  1999 Settlement Pattern Shifts and Political Ranking in the Lake Titicaca Basin, Peru. In *Settlement Pattern Studies in the Americas*, edited by B. R. Billman and G. M. Feinman, pp. 116–128. Smithsonian Institution Press, Washington, D.C.
  2003 *Ancient Titicaca: The Evolution of Social Complexity in Southern Peru and Northern Bolivia*. University of California Press, Berkeley.

Turner, Victor
  1974 *Dramas, Fields, and Metaphors: Symbolic Action in Human Society*. Cornell University Press, Ithaca.

Vranich, A.
  1999 Interpreting the Meaning of Ritual Spaces: The Temple Complex of Pumapunku, Tiwanaku, Bolivia. Unpublished Ph.D. dissertation, Department of Anthropology, University of Pennsylvania, Philadelphia.

Winterhalder, B. P., and R. B. Thomas
  1978 *Geoecology of South Highland Peru: A Human Adaptation Perspective*. University of Colorado, Institute of Arctic and Alpine Research, Boulder.

Wright, M. F., C. A. Hastorf, and H. Lennstrom
  2003 Pre-Hispanic Agriculture and Plant Use at Tiwanaku: Social and Political Implications. In *Tiwanaku and Its Hinterland: Archaeology and Paleoecology of an Andean Civilization*. Vol. 2, *Urban and Rural Archaeology*, edited by Alan L. Kolata, pp. 384–403. Smithsonian Institution Press, Washington, D.C.

Yoffee, Norman
  2005 *Myths of the Archaic State: Evolution of the Earliest Cities, States, and Civilizations*. Cambridge University Press, Cambridge.

Zovar, Jennifer
  2007 La transformación de la vivienda: Arquitectura doméstica en Khonkho Wankane, Bolivia. In *Arqueología del área ventro sur andina: Actas del Simposio Internacional 30 de Junio–2 de Julio de 2005, Arequipa, Peru ANDES*, edited by Mariusz S. Ziółkowski, Justin Jennings, Luis Agusto Belan Franco, and Andrea Drusini, pp. 359–386. Boletín del Centro de Estudios Precolombinos de la Universidad de Varsovia No. 7. Warsaw University Press, Warsaw.

12

Tiwanaku's Coming of Age: Refining Time and Style in the Altiplano

Patricia J. Knobloch

Since Arthur Posnansky's (1945) assertion that Tiwanaku was more ancient than the Andes, the dating of Tiwanaku has been characterized by excessive antiquity. Early radiocarbon dating brought the city of Tiwanaku into the first millennium, though nationalistic goals in Bolivian archaeology (Ponce 1979) continued to promote excessive antiquity through liberal interpretation of the dates. In recent years, the early Tiwanaku ceramic phases have been redefined, renamed, and redated (Janusek 2003b), but the legacy of liberal interpretation of radiocarbon dates and excessive antiquity has been difficult to correct.

This paper questions the currently popular dating of the Tiwanaku city by refining the temporal range of the Tiwanaku period represented by the Late Formative 2 and Tiwanaku IV and V phases. The focus of the paper is on recalibrating the dates from recent heartland Tiwanaku excavations (Janusek 2003b: Tables 3.1, 3.2) with the most current calibration curve and on evaluating their contexts and associations. Detailed evaluation of the contexts distinguishes between primary and secondary associations and is followed by a review of the associated remains—especially ceramic styles—to determine how each ^{14}C sample and its respective date is best interpreted. By "primary association" of a charcoal sample, I mean carbon that virtually could not be earlier material somehow incorporated into a deposit, or a later intrusion. "Primary association" refers to charcoal surely formed and incorporated into a deposit when it was created. Excellent examples include straw in an adobe brick, fibers in a textile, and soot on a pot. These criteria may seem demanding, but they are necessary for a thoroughly rigorous evaluation of what radiocarbon dates mean in terms of real time. The goal of my paper is to correlate stylistic seriations, recalibrated ^{14}C dates,[1] and observations about archaeological contexts into a "best fit" explanation for the dating of critical phases from proto-urbanism to collapse—Late Formative 2 (LF2), Tiwanaku IV (TIV), and Tiwanaku V (TV). The results offer a new temporal framework for Tiwanaku occupation and provide the most probable chronology for dating key events in the city itself (Figure 12.1), as well as its relations with surrounding cultures.

Late Formative 2

The LF2 period is identified by the Qeya pottery style that documents the transition from incised outlining to painted outlining of motifs (Figures 12.2–12.4). Tiwanaku occupation during LF2 is still limited to a few locations such as the Putuni and Akapana East. These LF2 occupations correlate with the Rayed Head icon that may have syncretized with the Atacameño iconography of northern Chile into the Tiwanaku style.

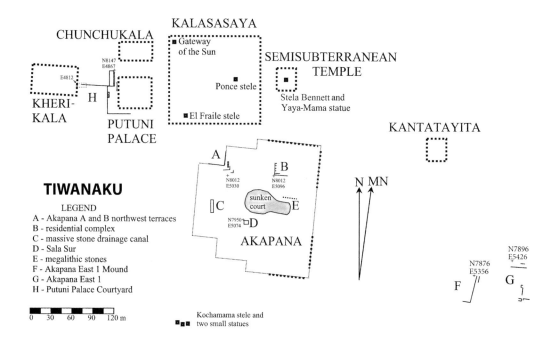

FIGURE 12.1. Map of Tiwanaku (drawn using Posnansky 1945).

FIGURE 12.2. A museum-curated example of a Qeya-style vessel with incised decoration of a Rayed Head deity. The rays are stylized geometric appendages in a crown band surrounding the face (VA10463, Museen Dahlem, Staatliche Museen zu Berlin; collected in 1890; photo by P. J. Knobloch, 1985).

FIGURE 12.3. A museum-curated example of a Qeya-style *escudilla* with avian mythical figures on the interior rim. Height 14.1 cm; diameter 22.8 cm (VA16708, Museen Dahlem, Staatliche Museen zu Berlin; collected in 1904; photo by P. J. Knobloch, 1985).

Putuni

Putuni excavations provide at least one reliable example of LF2 presence in the area. Three excavations by Kathryn Sampeck and Nicole Couture (Couture 2002; Couture and Sampeck 2003) were located in the Putuni Palace Courtyard, an area between the Putuni and Kherikala rectangular enclosures (Figure 12.5).[2] In one excavation, Feature 134 was a cache of 19 LF2 vessels (fully illustrated in Couture and Sampeck 2003: Figures 9.3–9.6). The prepared pit was 2 m below the surface, not associated with architecture and too disturbed by Late Tiwanaku IV (LTIV) phase burials to determine associated occupation evidence. There are no associated carbon dates. Slip, possibly paste, and Lukurmata vessel sherds are similar but can date anywhere from LF2 to TV (Couture and Sampeck 2003:230). A second excavation exposed a 50-cm-thick clay platform that was dated to LF2 by a piece of charcoal from its surface, OS11306 (cal A.D. 542–598).[3] However, as a secondary association sample, the charcoal may have been deposited after

FIGURE 12.4. A museum-curated example of a Qeya-style *escudilla* with avian mythical figures on the interior rim. Height 14.1 cm; diameter 22.8 cm (VA16708, Museen Dahlem, Staatliche Museen zu Berlin; collected in 1904; photo by P. J. Knobloch, 1985).

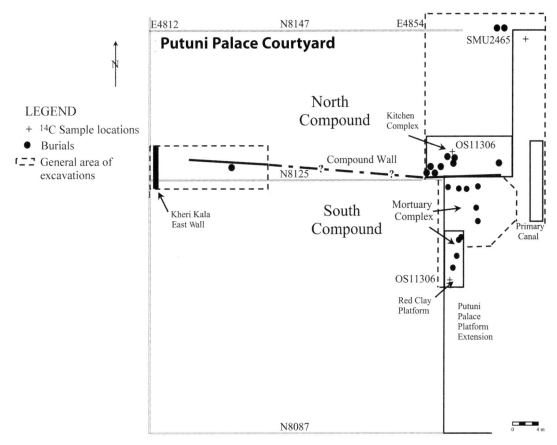

FIGURE 12.5. Map of the Putuni Palace Courtyard area excavated by Nicole Couture and Kathryn Sampeck, between the Kherikala enclosure to the west and the Putuni Palace to the east, indicating Late Formative 2– and Tiwanaku IV–period occupations.

formation of the platform and originated from earlier or later activity. Of the 307 sherds found on this surface, 54 were serving ware and 8 were from decorated *sahumadors* (Couture 2002: Tables 4.1– 4.3), but only 1, a non-Qeya-style everted bowl fragment, was illustrated (Couture and Sampeck 2003: Figure 9.8). A third excavation was near the Kherikala structure, where the lowest excavated levels produced thin outdoor surfaces with a few ceramics. The only decorated sherd was illustrated (Couture and Sampeck 2003: Figure 9.9) but again was not diagnostic of the Qeya style. Finally, 1990 excavations of deep wells and shaft tombs uncovered some decorated Qeya sherds, but they have not been published (Couture 2002:129, Footnote 23).

Akapana East 1

In the middle area of this excavation (Figure 12.6; see inset), two early floor surfaces and three structures, oriented 6 to 8 degrees east of north, were uncovered. At 85–95 cm and 75–85 cm below surface, the two floors were almost sterile except for one LF2 Qeya-style *incensario* sherd 2 cm above the earlier floor and consequently buried by the second floor (Janusek 2003b: Figure 3.23a)[4] (Figures 12.7, 12.8). Adobe collapse covered the floors up to 40–50 cm thick (Janusek 1994:106–108). Tiwanaku IV- style ceramics were found in the fill but not illustrated. Five incomplete bodies were found buried by the adobe fill. Janusek interprets the deposition as dedicatory, but the lack of artifacts and its haphazard context, including a mandible broken in two with parts about 1 m apart, might suggest greater violence. Analysis of repetitious cut marks indicated a process of defleshing the bones (Blom et al. 2003: 442), perhaps by scavengers. Later generations attempted some leveling of the area for reoccupation. Atop this leveled, low mound surface was a secondary deposit of charcoal that produced a ^{14}C sample, SMU2471 (cal A.D. 573–772). The sample should at least cap the damaged occupation with the LF2 Qeya sherd that was below the fill and the mound, dating it as pre-A.D. 750, and might cap the TIV ceramics in the fill, also as pre-A.D. 750. However, the charcoal is not in primary association and comes from a disturbed leveling activity, so it is also possible that the date is of little relevance to the TIV ceramic materials.

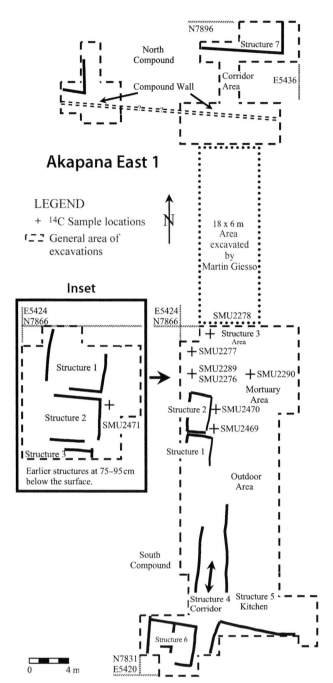

FIGURE 12.6. Map of the Akapana East 1 area excavated by John Janusek. The inset indicates earlier, underlying structures.

Lukurmata

LF2-style pottery was found at Lukurmata (Bermann 2003: Figure 13.6a, b; Janusek 2003b: Figures 3.24, 3.25). The end of the LF period is marked by one carbon sample, ETH3177 (cal A.D. 656–826), from structure 29, about 4 m east of the main exca-

FIGURE 12.7. A museum-curated example of a Qeya-style *incensario* with stylized mythical icons painted on the exterior and a modeled feline head at the scalloped rim. Height 12.1 cm (VA34847, Museen Dahlem, Staatliche Museen zu Berlin; collected in 1913; photo by P. J. Knobloch, 1985).

vation unit, which revealed a structure described as LF2 (Janusek 2003b: Table 3.3). The only description of structure 29 is in a table that indicates association with structures 30–32 (also undescribed) located 15 cm above structures 25–28 (Bermann 2003: Table 13.6). Inconsistent with stratigraphic logic, structures 25–28 were assigned to Early Tiwanaku IV (ETIV). A tanware bowl with the volute motif was illustrated (Berman 1994: Figure 11.20), but tanware is not currently useful for stylistic dating. Until structure 29 data are published, this radiocarbon date appears to be in stratigraphic conflict with the stylistic date based on ceramics and is consequently of limited use.

Other Sites

Late Formative 2 at Marcapata (1 km east of Akapana) (M. Giesso personal communication to Couture, 2002) was a shaft tomb used intensively in TIV–V but that also contained a Qeya *vasija* (Figure 12.9) (Couture 2002:127; Janusek 2003b: Figure

FIGURE 12.8. A museum-curated example of a Qeya-style *incensario* with stylized mythical icons painted on the exterior and a modeled feline head at the scalloped rim. The interior was blackened or fire clouded. Height 16.5 cm (VA12283, Museen Dahlem, Staatliche Museen zu Berlin; collected in 1894; photo by P. J. Knobloch, 1985).

FIGURE 12.9. A museum-curated example of a Qeya-style *vasija*. Height 18 cm (VA30824, Museen Dahlem, Staatliche Museen zu Berlin; collected in 1908; photo by P. J. Knobloch, 1985).

3.18). Other LF2 pottery, including Qeya-style vessels (Rivera Casanova 2003: Figures 11.2, 11.17), was located at Ch'iji Jawira, Kk'araña (Janusek 2003b: Figure 3.23b, c, e), and Tilata (Janusek 2003b: Figure 3.23d; see Mathews 2003: Figure 5.3, site TMV-101). Thus several of the excavations by Alan Kolata's Wila Jawira Project located limited amounts of LF2 Qeya evidence but without significant habitation remains. As Couture (2002:128) points out, "More excavations of early levels need to be conducted not only in the central district, but across the site as a whole, to verify these results."

To summarize LF2 dating, the OS11306 (cal A.D. 542–598) sample suggests but does not confirm a time-depth into the sixth century, whereas SMU2471 (cal A.D. 573–772) was located well above depositions that buried a LF2 Qeya sherd to confirm that it predated the ninth century.

The Tiwanaku Period

The Tiwanaku period (TIV and TV) is characterized by red-slipped wares with new shapes such as *keros, tinajas* (Figure 12.10), and *tazones*.

The Akapana Pyramid

As the visual edifice that dominates the Tiwanaku site, the Akapana was shaped into an impressive pyramid of stepped terraces interpreted as a man-made, sacred mountain (Kolata 2003:183–188).[5] In recent decades, several excavations were conducted in the Akapana, including in the central northwest corner along the first and second terrace walls, a multiroom summit complex, one small room enclosure, and an unpublished burial near a massive drainage canal. Linda Manzanilla (1992; Manzanilla et al. 1990) and Sonia Alconini (1995) have published maps, ceramic analyses, and detailed descriptions.

Akapana's Northwest Terrace Excavations (Akapana A and B). This excavation explored the pyramid's lower terraced construction and also revealed numerous features—skeletal remains, burials, and offerings—that have been interpreted in diverse ways. Consequently, the chronological evaluation is important though complicated.

Three ^{14}C dates, ETH5640 (cal A.D. 865–994), SMU2330 (cal A.D. 894–1149), and SMU2329 (cal

Figure 12.10. A museum-curated example of a Tiwanaku-style red-slipped *tinaja*. Height 17.6 cm; diameter 13.6 cm (VA16709, Museen Dahlem, Staatliche Museen zu Berlin; collected in 1904; photo by P. J. Knobloch, 1985).

A.D. 532–898), come from the base of wall 1; one ^{14}C date, SMU2367 (cal A.D. 867–1023), was atop wall 1; and four more ^{14}C dates, SMU2293 (cal A.D. 602–822), SMU2285 (cal A.D. 526–890), ETH6306 (cal A.D. 584–670), and ETH5639 (cal A.D. 868–994), were associated with the "ceramic smash" on terrace 1. Few detailed maps of the area were published, but Manzanilla's photos, plus Alconini's maps and the north and east coordinates for ^{14}C dates (Janusek 2003b: Table 3.1), provide enough information to reconstruct an accurate layout to evaluate the contexts of these dates (Figure 12.10).[6] There are two Feature 8s (see Blom et al. 2003: Figures 18.1, 18.2), which I have labeled Feature 8a and Feature 8b, respectively. For now, I have placed Feature 8b and Feature 9 on the first terrace, south of the east–west wall. Figure 12.11 was based on Alconini's (1995: Figures 3, 4) maps, with the same alignment of the walls but using photographs whenever possible to ensure greater accuracy.

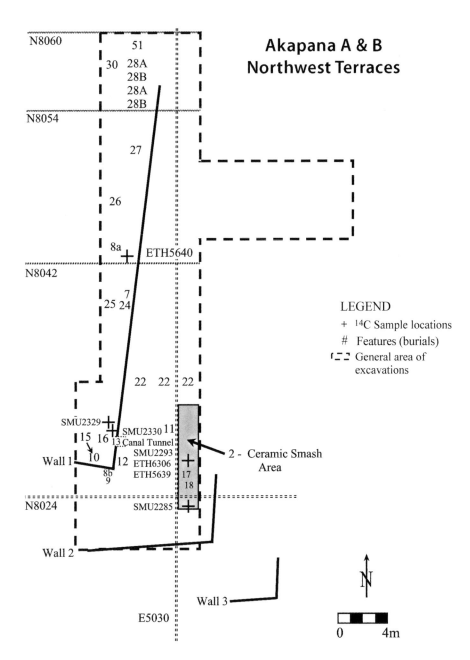

FIGURE 12.11. Map of the Akapana A and B sectors in the northwestern terrace area, excavated by Linda Manzanilla and María Renée Baudoin.

Wall 1 consists of a north–south section that turns west at its southern end and continues in that direction. The first terrace is above and to the east and south of the wall sections, respectively. Manzanilla (1992: Figure 6) provides the most informative image of the entire location with a photo taken from the northwest that clearly shows the northern limit of wall 1. The photo gives the impression of a partially dismantled wall with eroded adobe covering its ashlars to a depth of as much as 2 m (Figure 12.12).

Several deposits of human and camelid bones were discovered along the base of wall 1. On the first terrace between wall 1 and wall 2 was a 70-cm-thick deposit of broken ceramics covering an area 9.2 by 2 m and labeled Feature 2, or "ceramic smash" (Manzanilla 1992:94). I will discuss the features along the base of wall 1 first and then those associated with the "ceramic smash" on the first terrace.

Along the base of wall 1 are several numbered features, some of which are burials that were also

FIGURE 12.12. The Akapana A and B sectors' northwestern terrace area with: (a) a view of the top surface of wall 1, the first terrace, and wall 2, looking southeast; (b) north–south section of wall 1, looking northeast (photos by P. J. Knobloch, 2000).

numbered. Feature 8a is burial 1 and burial 2 (Blom et al. 2003:437–438, Figures 18.1, 18.4–18.6; Manzanilla 1992:71, 74, Figures 42, 43), consisting of partial and disarticulated skeletons of two males and two camelids, two illustrated Tiwanaku IV-style polychrome *keros* (Manzanilla 1992: Figure 56; Manzanilla reports two and Blom et al. report three *keros*), unillustrated polychrome jar and bowl sherds, and a ^{14}C sample in secondary association, ETH 5640 (cal A.D. 865–994).[7] Osteological analysis produced evidence of bone crushing and cut marks. Since the carbon sample is a secondary association within this context and dates the level prior to further soil deposition, the ceramics within this same context most likely predate A.D. 1000 but could also predate A.D. 850.

Feature 12, burial 8 (Manzanilla 1992:74, Figure 48), is a partial human skeleton with a skull. Alconini's (1995:101, Figure 4) map provides the location for this burial as N8028 E5025, with a secondary association ^{14}C sample SMU2367 (cal A.D. 867–1023).[8] No discussion of ceramics was published.

Feature 13 (N8028 E5024) is a complete, articulated canine skeleton found at the mouth of the wall's canal with a secondary ^{14}C sample, SMU2330 (cal A.D. 894–1149). The coordinates for this sample are from a square 2 m farther north at N8030 E5025 (Janusek 2003b: Table 3.1), but perhaps the carbon sample came from the southern edge of the square close to the canine skeleton. If this carbon sample dates the latest possible activities on the surface prior to the soil deposition that buried it, then the canine skeleton predates A.D. 1150.

Feature 16 is burial 10 (Manzanilla 1992:74, Figure 51), a group of mixed bones that included four adults, one juvenile, one child, and some camelids. A few TIV ceramics were associated and none were illustrated (Alconini 1995:101). A ^{14}C sample, SMU2329 (cal A.D. 532–898), was in a secondary association with these bones but was possibly part of an original bundle that included the ceramics. If so, then the bundle predates A.D. 900. Unfortunately, the deposit was too mixed and disturbed to provide certainty.

Other skeletal deposits without ^{14}C samples provide evidence for understanding the mechanics of the secondary deposition. Briefly, they can be listed as:

1. Feature 7 is burial 3 (Manzanilla 1992:74, Figures 44, 45), a deposit of three humans (undescribed) with decorated *keros* and *incensarios* that have not been illustrated. Of interest were two disarticulated camelid skeletons under the human bodies and two articulated camelid skeletons placed on top.

2. Features 8b and 9 are burials 4 and 5, respectively (Blom et al. 2003:438, Figures 18.2, 18.7–18.9; Manzanilla 1992:74, Figure 46), consisting of partial and disarticulated skeletons of two humans. Burial 4 was male and burial 5 had one human skull, other human bones, one camelid, and some sherds. These remains had been scattered on the surface and showed cut marks and carnivore bites.

3. Feature 10 is burial 6 (Manzanilla 1992:74, Figure 47), a partial skeleton, including a mostly articulated torso with some utilitarian sherds, one decorated sherd, and camelid bones. Feature 15 lay below Feature 10. Feature 16 (Manzanilla 1992: Figure 51) is west of Feature 13 (Manzanilla 1992: Figure 52). Therefore, the east coordinate shown for Feature 13 is probably E5024.

4. Feature 15 is burial 9 (Manzanilla 1992:74, Figure 49) and represents the only complete skeleton and undisturbed burial of a small child, who died of a bone disease. In the photo, the body appears to have been placed in a pit.

5. Feature 28B was excavated at the northern end of wall 1 and contained three adult skulls, arm and leg bones, camelid bones, and decorated ceramics atop a completely articulated camelid skeleton (Kolata 2003: Figure 7.19B; Manzanilla 1992:83). No burial number was published. Alconini (1995: Figure 5) illustrates a Tiwanaku IV *sahumador* and *kero* (Janusek 2003b: Figures 3.60 and 3.41, respectively), one decorated sherd, and several Tiwanaku V–style ceramics (Alconini 1995: Figure 6).[9] In the square north of this feature, an exquisite Tiwanaku IV–style portrait cup was uncovered (Janusek 2003b: Figure 3.63A; Manzanilla 1992: Figure 53) (Figure 12.13). Consequently, Feature 28B contains a mixture of Tiwanaku IV– and Tiwanaku V–style pottery.

6. Feature 27 consists of TIV ceramics and camelid bones (Alconini 1995:101–102).

FIGURE 12.13. A museum-curated example of a portrait cup. Height 11.9 cm (VA2787, Museen Dahlem, Staatliche Museen zu Berlin; collected in 1880; photo by P. J. Knobloch, 1985).

Other, sparse features contain some human and camelid skeletal remains: Feature 22 (burial 12), Feature 24, Feature 25 with TIV keros (Alconini 1995: Figure 9), and Features 26, 28a, and 30 (Alconini 1995:82, 101–102, Table 3).

To summarize the activities along the base of wall 1, only one undisturbed burial, Feature 15, was discovered along wall 1, protected by Feature 10. Features 10, 13, 16, and 28B were deposited on a "floor" surface, level 4, associated with the bottom of wall 1 and the canal opening. This "floor" is assumed to have been the activity surface during occupation. In spite of this "floor" context, Feature 13 with SMU 2330 (cal A.D. 894–1149), and Feature 16 with SMU 2329 (cal A.D. 532–898), do not provide any consistency in dating the overall context of level 4. Features 7 and 8a were assigned to level 2A, which was deposited directly on top of the level 4 surface (Manzanilla 1992: Figure 10). Perhaps Features 24 and 27 were also at this level. Since there are no profile drawings that indicate that grave pits were dug into the adobe fill and level 4, the skeletal remains probably represent deposits placed against the wall. Left exposed, the bodies could be looted, scavenged, and buried by natural erosion. The canine from the same level was more likely a scavenger and not an offering.[10] Considering all the evidence of disturbance on these skeletons, it is not surprising that the carbon sample associations are all secondary, as it is equally possible that the carbon samples were originally bundled with the bones or mixed into the features later. Sample SMU2329 (cal A.D. 532–898) has a very broad sigma range and could represent a mixing of older remains predating A.D. 900. Together with ETH5640 (cal A.D. 865–994) and SMU2330 (cal A.D. 894–1149), deposition of the skeletal remains may predate A.D. 1000, or with little doubt A.D. 1150. Only ETH5640 (cal A.D. 865–994) may be associated with discarded Tiwanaku IV–style ceramics dating between A.D. 850 and A.D. 1000, but there is no convincing excavation evidence that details the association. The canine in proximity to SMU2330 (cal A.D. 894–1149) may represent continued exposure of level 4 after A.D. 1000. Feature 12 is atop the wall with SMU2367 (cal A.D. 867–1023) but provides no associated context or artifacts for dating.

The "ceramic smash" on terrace 1 was Feature 2 and has also been referred to as the *kero* smash; it consists of TIV-style ceramics (Alconini 1995: Figures 12–22), predominately *keros* (Figure 12.14). It produced two ^{14}C samples, SMU2293 (cal A.D. 602–822) and SMU2285 (cal A.D. 526–890). Above Feature 2 were adjacent skeletal remains labeled Features 17 and 18 (Alconini 1995:101). Feature 17 is a cranial fragment with some ETIV ceramics—not illustrated—and associated with a ^{14}C sample, ETH 6306 (cal A.D. 584–670).[11] Feature 18 is burial 11 (Manzanilla 1992:88, Figure 55), consisting of a partial, almost articulated adult. Blom et al. (2003:438–439, Figure 18.10) reported evidence for the weathering of these bones, important in light of the fact that the body appeared splayed out over the ceramic pile. Feature 11 is a secondary group burial, burial 7, deposited later (Alconini 1995:102; Manzanilla 1992: 74, 83, Figure 50) and associated with TIV ceramics—not illustrated—and a ^{14}C sample, ETH5639 (cal A.D. 868–994). The composition and contexts of these four ^{14}C samples are not described, so they may be secondary associations. The collection of dates range from A.D. 550 to 1000, but there is a dis-

FIGURE 12.14. A museum-curated example of a Tiwanaku-style *kero* with a rounded double torus. Height: 14.1 cm; diameter 14.5 cm (*VA34897*, Museen Dahlem, Staatliche Museen zu Berlin; collected in 1913; photo by P. J. Knobloch, 1985).

continuity between the earlier date of Feature 17, collected with ETIV ceramics but located stratigraphically above the two later dates collected with TIV pottery of the "ceramic smash." This probably indicates disturbance.[12] The apparent lack of TV ceramics is important for stylistic chronology, although the ^{14}C samples suggest that TIV-style materials were deposited as late as the tenth century.

Akapana's Summit. There were three areas of excavations that produced ^{14}C samples: a residential area, a possible burial, and a U-shaped enclosure, or Sala Sur.

On the northeastern corner of the Akapana summit, excavations exposed the foundations and floors of an L-shaped group of conjoined rooms bordering the south and west sides of a paved patio. Both Manzanilla (1992: Figure 23) and Alconini (1995: Figure 32) provide excellent maps. Alconini (1995:76, 82, 102) dated the occupation of this residential area based on a ceramic stylistic seriation of five style phases: A, B, B/D, C, and D. These correlate with Janusek's seriation as ETIV for A, TIV for B, transitional TIV/V for C, and LTV for D. Phase B/D represents a group of pottery offerings that are stylistically between phase B and D ceramics and similar to phase C ceramics. Examples of phase B/D ceramics came from Features 20 and 24 (Alconini 1995:123, 141, Figures 49 and 51, respectively). Feature 24 is located northwest of Feature 25, or room 8. Akapana phases B and C ceramics were deposited along the exterior west side of Features 18, 19, and 21 of rooms 4, 5, and 6, respectively, as well as near Features 17 and 23, from rooms 3 and 7, respectively. A few phase B ceramics are illustrated (Alconini 1995: Figure 38, bottom).[13] Many phase C or transitional TIV–TV ceramics are illustrated (Alconini 1995: Figures 35–38 top, Figures 39–42). Unfortunately, no excavation profile drawings were provided to define the thickness or proximity of the occupation layers, and no carbon dates were associated with the ceramics.

Feature 11 was layered with camelid bones a few centimeters thick (Manzanilla 1992: Figure 25). Two carbon samples were obtained within this room. Manzanilla cited one date from Ríos (1991) as INAH972 (cal A.D. 852–1142), from the northeastern corner, and Janusek reported the other as SMU2473 (cal A.D. 1014–1398), from the southeastern corner.[14] There is a large burned area in the room that might represent the original source or primary context for the charcoal samples. The extremely recent SMU2473 (cal A.D. 1014–1398) indicates that the room may have been used to deposit llama carcasses long after Tiwanaku occupation. This room contained a tiny copper fox figurine, copper pins, hammered silver sheets, a bone labret, plant remains (Kolata 2003:189; Manzanilla 1992: 59), and examples of Akapana phase D or TV ceramics (Alconini 1995: Figures 43–48). One rare vessel form is a TV or Akapana phase D pedestal bowl (Janusek 2003b: Figure 3.64, type 13; Alconini 1995: Figure 53, type 6.6) with an interlocking fret design. There is also a modeled puma head from a TIV *incensario* (Manzanilla 1992: Figure 31). This slight mix of TIV and TV ceramics could be associated with the lengthy INAH972 (cal A.D. 852–1142).

Feature 30, excavated under the paved patio, revealed six flexed adult burials facing north. Five were located in an east–west line to the south of the sixth (Alconini 1995:143). This sixth held a Tiwanaku IV puma *incensario* similar to one found in Feature 11. However, Manzanilla (1992:61–62, Figures 38, 39) cites Marc Bermann's (1989) contradictory comment that these burials date to LF2 (his Tiwanaku III). Manzanilla also noted carbonized material on the interior of the *incensario* that should have been AMS dated. Manzanilla and Woodard (1990) interpreted the L-shaped complex of conjoined rooms as a priestly residence.

Also from Akapana's summit, SMU2468 (cal A.D. 648–766) was obtained near human remains found 2 m northwest of a stone drainage canal (Kolata 2003: Figure 7.10; Manzanilla 1992:42–45, Figure 13). No ceramic associations are discussed. Another date, SMU2336 (cal A.D. 766–971),[15] is associated with a U-shaped enclosure, or Sala Sur, but is not given a primary designation. Two features, 15 and 16, produced ceramics, including an LF2–ETIV *escudilla*, several incised blackware sherds (Alconini 1995: Figure 54), and a condor head sherd from a *sahumador* (Manzanilla 1992:46, Figures 14–16). If the Sala Sur activities belong to LTIV–ETV (Janusek 2003b: Table 3.1), then the ^{14}C sample does not date the LF2–ETIV *escudilla*, or LF2 pottery manufacture continued into the eighth century A.D.

Summary of Akapana Pyramid. Alan Kolata (2003: 186) suggested that the canine skeleton, Feature 13, in proximity to SMU2330 (cal A.D. 894–1149), indicated that drainage from the canal ended and that pyramid functions stopped sometime prior to TV. Excavations in 2006 indicate that the canal was never completed and never used to drain water (Alexei Vranich, personal communication 2007), so the canine death does not indicate an end to the Akapana's functions. Accurate interpretation of the other ^{14}C samples is thwarted by their secondary associations as well as a general lack of ceramic descriptions from dated contexts such as SMU2329 (cal A.D. 532–898) and ETH6306 (cal A.D. 584-670), whereas SMU2367 (cal A.D. 867–1023) and SMU2468 (cal A.D. 648–766) had no ceramics. At best, it seems that activities associated with ceramics of both TIV and TV overlapped from A.D. 850 to A.D. 1000, with TV extending into the eleventh century.

Akapana East

The Wila Jawira Project conducted excavations in two areas east of the Akapana that produced ^{14}C samples: Akapana East 1 (AkE1) (Figure 12.6) and Akapana East 1 Mound (AkE1-M) (Janusek 2003a: Figure 10.1) (Figure 12.15), where excavations yielded information about residential and domestic occupation (Janusek 1994, 2003b, 2004).

Akapana East 1 Mound. The AkE1-M excavations, located in what was interpreted as the southeast corner of a walled compound, included three structures, a thoroughfare, and a drainage ditch (Janusek 2004: Figure 7.4A) (Figure 12.15). The base of the wall of the compound correlates with the lowest occupation levels (John Janusek, personal communication 2007).

Structure 1's patio area produced approximately 100 diagnostic TIV ceramics from the first-floor level above sterile soil (Janusek 1994: Table 7.8); a ^{14}C sample, B55491 (cal A.D. 532–674), from the second-floor level, and eight more floor levels that were so compact they literally "peeled up" (John Janusek, personal communication 2006). The ceramics included ETIV examples (Janusek 1994: Table 7.8, Figures 7.11, 7.12).[16] The charcoal is a secondary association and may not date the ceramics from the second floor or below, but it comes from undisturbed stratigraphy and does indicate that ceramics above level 2 should not date earlier than the sixth century. Examples of TIV pottery came from floor levels 4 (Janusek 1994: Figure 7.12A–D) and 5 (Janusek 1994: Figure 7.12E–G), while examples from floor level 6 (Janusek 1994: Figures 7.12H–J) and above show "gradual transformation toward" LTV (Janusek 1994:134). Janusek (1994:134) states that structure 1's occupation dates from ETIV (A.D. 500–600) through LTV (A.D. 600–800). However, photos indicate that the occupation is rather shallow (Janusek 2003a: Figure 10.6). Since the platform, or *patilla*, in the Sala Sur is 30 cm thick (Janusek 1994:130), there may be only 40 to 50 cm of total deposition, which seems inadequate for three to four centuries of occupation.

Three ^{14}C samples were found in secondary refuse deposits in and near structure 2: SMU2333 (cal A.D. 72–651), SMU2331 (cal A.D. 1021–1316), and SMU2332 (cal A.D. 985–1190). SMU2332 was found associated with a feature in an occupation level above structure 2, but there is no discussion of ceramics from the context (Janusek 1994:377). AkE1-M's structure 4 was built over structure 3 and included examples of Tiwanaku V– style *keros* (Janusek 1994:376–377, Figures 11.1, 11.2) but no ^{14}C samples. Though Janusek (1994:376–377) suggested that the TV *keros* could be associated with the SMU2332 (cal A.D. 985–1190) sample, the 18-m separation raises reasonable doubt.

Akapana East 1. After LF2, Akapana East 1 was used for adobe brick manufacture and as a dump space with "ephemeral hearths, a deep well, and over twenty deep, amorphous pits" (Janusek 2004:143) The pits held immense quantities of storage, serving, and ceremonial ceramics, as well as food remains and ash, deposited as one event to fill a pit (Janusek 2004:143–144). This evidence implies Akapana-related feasting activities. After a period of disuse, residential structures and occupation resumed as the population increased during Tiwanaku V (Figure 12.6). A thick wall divided AkE1 into two multi-roomed households with outdoor kitchen and mortuary space in the southern compound and an elite edifice with a sunken court in the northern compound. Photos of the excavations indicate about 20 cm of deposition covering the features (Janusek 2003a: Figures 10.20, 10.21, 10.28). The southern structures were occupied and abandoned at different times, indicating an unstable occupation period, perhaps over two or three generations.

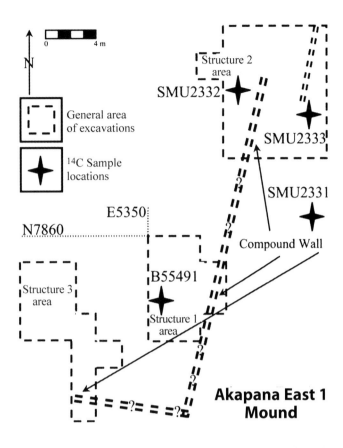

FIGURE 12.15. Map of Akapana East 1 Mound area excavated by John Janusek.

Six carbon samples came from the southern compound. SMU2469 (cal A.D. 778–990) was found outside of structure 1's northeastern corner. SMU 2278 (cal A.D. 708–968), SMU2289 (cal A.D. 865–987), SMU2277 (cal A.D. 895–1017), SMU2290 (cal A.D. 886–1033), and SMU2276 (cal A.D. 974–1133) were from secondary deposition in outdoor refuse pits. In rounding these ranges to the closest 50 years, the dates cover activities from A.D. 700 to A.D. 1150, with the most overlap from A.D. 900 to A.D. 1000. Of these samples, only SMU2469 (cal A.D. 778–990) was associated with TV "elaborate vessels" (Janusek 1994:425–426) that were excavated within the same square (N7855 E5426) though not yet published. The other samples are clustered in an area with little ceramics of temporal significance, and even SMU 2290 (cal A.D. 886– 1033) from the mortuary area is in a grid square lacking burials (Blom et al. 2003: 441–442). The published illustrations (Janusek 1994: Figures 10.22–10.26; 2003a: Figure 10.24) show Tiwanaku V and foreign-style ceramics but without exact provenience. Given the lack of evidence for multiple levels of occupation—other than the previous LF2 structures—these ^{14}C samples were probably produced during the Tiwanaku occupation. At best the majority of the carbon samples probably represent activities coinciding with site abandonment about A.D. 1000, while SMU 2469 (cal A.D. 778–990) may date an occupation using Tiwanaku V-style ceramics from A.D. 800 to 1000. Sometime later, occupation resumed, as implied by SMU2470 (cal A.D. 1217–1499) (see Janusek 1994:377).

Summary of Akapana East. Radiocarbon dates B55491 (cal A.D. 532–674) and SMU2471 (cal A.D. 573–772) might date Tiwanaku's stylistic beginnings, but these samples were secondary associations that could have been old when they entered the contexts in which they were excavated. Only B55491 (cal A.D. 532–674) occurred above and below compacted floor levels and may—without reasonable doubt—provide a beginning date in the sixth or seventh century A.D. for TIV artifacts found in upper levels. However, given all the ^{14}C samples outside of structure 1's northeast corner in AkE1, a more effectual approach to interpreting the Tiwanaku IV and V data is to discern a pattern among many samples rather than one. Without the extreme dates, those reported so far indicate a general pattern of ninth- and tenth-century activity: SMU2469 (cal A.D. 778–990), SMU2278 (cal A.D. 708–968), SMU2289 (cal A.D. 865–987), SMU2277 (cal A.D. 895–1017), SMU2290 (cal A.D. 886–1033), and SMU2276 (cal A.D. 974–1133). Of course, additional illustrations of ceramics from the same contexts as these radiocarbon dates would help clarify chronology, including the relationship between TIV and TV styles.

The Putuni Palace Courtyard

In the Putuni Palace Courtyard (PPC), Tiwanaku IV and V occupations were stratigraphically distinct. TIV activities occurred in two areas, the "north compound" and the "south compound," which are separated by a west-to-east wall (Figure 12.5). Two end sections—a west section under the West Palace and an east section along the southern edge of the kitchen complex—define this wall. In the south compound are two areas: a mortuary zone created after the deposition of the clay platform and a habitation area. Photos (Couture and Sampeck 2003: Figures 9.11, 9.15) show that it must have been very difficult to discern the sequence of events in this area of so much activity. After leveling the TIV areas, the TV occupation built palaces in the northern compound area above the kitchen and a platform extension on the west side of the Putuni above the mortuary zone and clay platform (Figure 12.16).

PPC Tiwanaku IV: Kitchen Complex and Red Clay Platform. The most difficult issue for evaluating the chronological implications of these excavations is determining how the kitchen complex was temporally differentiated from the red clay platform in the southern compound.[17] For example, an LF2–ETIV burnished, tan *escudilla* with vertical bands on its rim was found above the surface of the clay platform (Couture and Sampeck 2003:231), while another came from the kitchen (Couture 2002: Figure 5.13c; Couture and Sampeck 2003: Figure 9.13c).[18] However, a fine red-slipped, polished, and everted *tazón* (Couture and Sampeck 2003: Figure 9.8) typical of TIV–TV was found on the surface of the platform, implying contemporaneity with the kitchen, which has been dated to TIV.

Charred wood from the floor in the east room of the kitchen complex (Features 107 and 108) provided ^{14}C sample OS10643 (cal A.D. 779–895), a primary depositional association with the kitchen hearths and ash pits. The date supports post–A.D. 800 kitchen activity as well as the beginning of the Tiwanaku period. This date caps the LF2 occupation interpreted previously to have ended by the ninth century.

North of the kitchen complex, two giant urn burials were uncovered. The northern compound was dated to the LTIV period and produced over 1,000 sherds from serving and ceremonial vessels, but only two *escudilla* sherds were illustrated (Couture 2002: Table 5.3; Couture and Sampeck 2003: Figure 9.13).

PPC Tiwanaku IV: Mortuary Complex. In the southern compound, an elite mortuary area with 10 tombs (see Figure 12.5) produced many ceramics assigned to LTIV (Couture and Sampeck 2003: 238–243, Figures 9.21–9.30). These are well illustrated, but they have no associated ^{14}C dates. Among the illustrations are two *escudilla* sherds with wider rims and wavy line decorations (Couture and Sampeck 2003: Figure 9.21a) that are stylistically distinct from those mentioned previously from the kitchen complex and above the clay platform. Skeletal remains were not found in these looted tombs, and Couture (2002: 198–200) suggests that original burials were bundled corpses that were removed prior to the ritual closing of the north and south compounds to prepare for building the Putuni platform extension.[19]

PPC Tiwanaku IV: Putuni's Northwestern Sector. Under the north wall of the Putuni platform in the northwestern area was a layer of occupation with two refuse pits that produced ^{14}C sample SMU2369 (cal A.D. 599–894).[20] The lack of associated cultural material and the sample's apparent secondary deposition means that the date is useful only to place construction of the Putuni platform after A.D. 600, although possibly as late as post–A.D. 900.

PPC Tiwanaku V: Putuni Palaces. The construction of the palaces and platform extension on the west side of the Putuni began with a well-prepared foundation (Figure 12.16) that involved leveling or filling in the

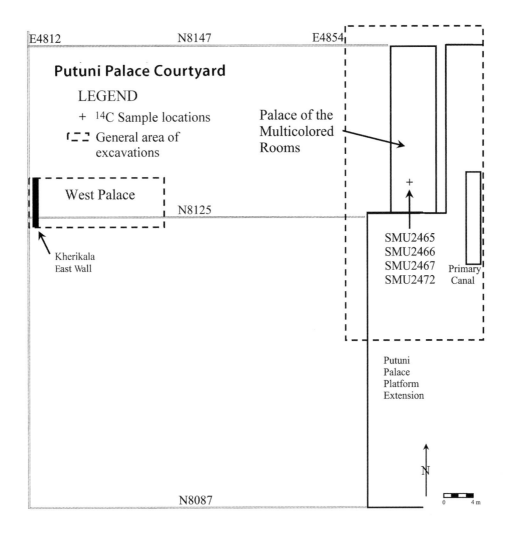

FIGURE 12.16. Map of Putuni Palace Courtyard area excavated by Couture and Sampeck, between the Kherikala enclosure to the west and the Putuni Palace to the east, indicating Tiwanaku V–period occupations.

area. The "entire Late Tiwanaku IV occupation, including walls, canals, and the elite mortuary complex" was covered by "a thick and nearly continuous stratum of greenish gravel composed of small and medium sized pebbles" (Couture and Sampeck 2003:248, referencing Janusek and Earnest 1990:238; Sampeck 1991: 24). So clearly distinguished stratigraphically, Putuni Palace Courtyard finds provide valuable information about stylistic changes in ceramics as well as absolute dating in the Tiwanaku period.

Above the gravel layer were built two structures: the Palace of the Multicolored Rooms (also called the Putuni East Palace; Janusek 2004: Figure 7.2E) and the West Palace. The Multicolored Rooms Palace was truly elaborate, with frequent refurbishing of walls in brilliant colors, a fragment of an elegantly carved lintel, appearance of precious metals, and an immense canal system for water access and sewage disposal. Six burials were associated with this structure. The Feature 38 burial contained a sheet gold square with a low-relief face in typical Tiwanaku style: a Y-shaped eyebrow/nose and a full-lipped, slightly open, rectangular mouth.[21] The Feature 18 burial was a bell-shaped subfloor tomb with its opening in the palace floor, confirming it as contemporary with palace activities. It produced three radiocarbon samples—SMU2465 (cal A.D. 899–1028), SMU2466 (cal A.D. 867–992), and SMU2467 (cal A.D. 895–1019), approximately A.D. 900–1000—as well as TV ceramics. This pottery includes a large decorated *tinaja*, a burnished black pitcher in the shape of a llama, and a set of 10 extremely fine recurved *tazones* (Couture and Sampeck 2003:255, Figure 9.44, which reproduces only two of the *tazones*). Couture's Table 6.2 (2002:276) indicates that the large painted *tinaja* was probably decorated with a volute (as seen with Couture 2002: Figure 6.4). Other illustrations of ceramics from this palace (Couture 2002: Figures 6.22, 6.23) show decorated *tinajas* (similar to ones from the West Palace; Couture 2002: Figures 6.29, 6.30; Couture and Sampeck 2003: Figures 9.47, 9.48), *keros*, and three more recurved *tazones*. The recurved *tazón* with an interlocking fret motif or profile heads is the hallmark of TV at Putuni and the Akapana, "similar in importance to the *escudilla* in the LTIV elite mortuary complex" (Couture and Sampeck 2003:255).

Since the Palace of the Multicolored Rooms produced three very comparable carbon dates, iconography from other associated ceramics is especially valuable for providing a thorough TV-style description. Several illustrations of TV pottery from the adjacent West Palace were published (Couture 2002: Figures 6.27, 6.31–6.34; Couture and Sampeck 2003: Figures 9.49–9.51). Couture (2002:298) points out that during TV, *keros* predominated in the palace areas, *escudillas* decreased, and *mechachuas*[22] increased. Occupation ended abruptly in the palaces when the roofs were burned and quantities of *tinajas* storing llama meat were smashed (Couture 2002: 303).[23] A final ^{14}C sample, SMU2472 (cal A.D. 772–996), represents wood from a roof collapse that was probably cut in the late ninth or tenth century and burned toward the end of this time range.

Summary of the Putuni Palace Courtyard. The ^{14}C sample on the clay platform, OS11306 (cal A.D. 542–598), suggests an LF2 date for construction, but the sample is a secondary association potentially different in origin. I suggest that this platform was more contemporary with the kitchen activities. Carbon sample OS10643 (cal A.D. 779–895) is one of the few primary association dates for Tiwanaku. It represents a moment near the beginning of the Tiwanaku style and early in the history of Putuni-area occupation. The cluster of ^{14}C samples—SMU2465 (cal A.D. 899–1028), SMU2466 (cal A.D. 867–992), and SMU2467 (cal A.D. 895–1019)—provides one of the best temporal associations for *keros* designated TV.

And, as mentioned above, the SMU2472 (cal A.D. 772–996) suggests that occupation terminated around the end of the tenth century. Stratigraphy and dates do provide some support for the temporal distinction of stylistic changes in ceramics from an earlier TIV style preceding construction of the Putuni platform extension and palaces to a later TV style from the palaces and extension. However, the scarcity of ceramic illustrations means that this stylistic change has not been convincingly documented.

Lukurmata

In 1986 the Wila Jawira Project conducted several excavations in the area of this hilltop shrine in the Katari Valley north of Tiwanaku. Bermann's (1990, 1994, 2003) research centered in the ridge southwest of the Semisubterranean Temple, and Janusek's (1994, 2003a) research centered on the terraced area to the south designated Misiton I and II, although project members worked in both locations.

Lukurmata Tiwanaku IV: Ridge. The TIV ridge excavation produced two carbon samples: SMU2113 (cal A.D. 618–1024), which Bermann did not publish; and ETH3179 (cal A.D. 812–991), which Bermann (1994:266, Appendix III) published as ETH3174. This latter sample was a primary deposit in a hearth west of structure 38 in patio B (Bermann 1994: 184–187, Figure 12.9, hearth). The hearth produced only plainware sherds but is associated with structures 33–39 (Bermann 1990:57, 1994:178), which contained decorated, red-slipped *keros* (Bermann 1990: Figures 99, 100) and vessels with the black-on-orange volute motif (Bermann 1990: Figures 99d, 101–104, 1994: Figures 12.26–12.29). Another TIV sherd (Bermann 1994: Figure 11.5) displays a human arm and hand holding a *topo*, as illustrated by Posnansky (1957:3–4: Plates XXIIb–XXIId) and Janusek (2003b: Figure 3.76).[24] Since the area was sealed by 50 cm of natural deposit and the ^{14}C sample was a primary deposit, structures 36–39 and patio B probably date TIV occupation between A.D. 800 and 1000.

Lukurmata Tiwanaku IV: Misiton I. Misiton 1 was located on a terrace. The excavation of N2342 E2970 was illustrated with a profile drawing (Janusek 1994:414, Figure A.2). An important secondary association ^{14}C date, B55490 (cal A.D. 684–885), was embedded in the first surface of a workshop complex (Janusek 1994:194–195) and provides a beginning date of no earlier than approximately A.D. 700 for events in the levels above. The associated ceramics and the first two occupation levels are described but not illustrated. After two more occupations and a walled patio area, numerous ceramic illustrations are published from a stratum (Janusek 1994: Figures 8.5, 8.18–8.23A, B, E) to support a TIV-style occupation that includes an *escudilla* similar to examples found at Putuni (Janusek 1994: Figure 8.18F). The 50 cm of occupation between the B55490 sample and the walled patio could mean that the TIV style appeared significantly later than A.D. 700.

Lukurmata Tiwanaku IV: Misiton 2. The primary excavation area is located 50 m northwest of Misiton 1 along the same terrace.[25] In 1991 Janusek (1994: 215–237, Figures A.3, A.4 for profile drawings) uncovered two construction events. The TV occupation of conjoined, rectangular storage rooms will be discussed later. The TIV occupation was located at the edge of the northern terrace and consisted of a residential area including structure 42, a 3-m-diameter circular house with an interior hearth that produced a primary association ^{14}C sample, SMU1920 (cal A.D. 778–986).[26] TIV-style vessels such as *keros* were associated with this structure but have not been illustrated.[27] This occupation is correlated with the occupation of structures 33–39 from Bermann's ridge excavations. Associated with the residential occupation was another ^{14}C sample, SMU2117 (cal A.D. 899–1045), a primary association recovered from a large outdoor hearth about 1 m east of structure 42.

Northwest of structure 42, a small excavation (N2371-73 E2882; Bermann 1990:308–310; Bermann and Graffam 1989:157) uncovered a 20-cm-thick midden layer containing utilitarian ceramics similar to those from structures 33–39 and "vessels decorated in what is clearly a Tiwanaku IV style" (Bermann 1990:309). Above this early occupation was a 2- to 15-cm silty clay layer, and then structure 42 and other residential structures were built. This stratigraphy indicates that structure 42 and its associated residential occupation occurred after the beginning of TIV. So the SMU2117 (cal A.D. 899–1045) date indicates TIV occupation from A.D. 900 to 1050. The stratigraphic evidence below structure 42 and the SMU1920 (cal A.D. 778–986) date may extend TIV back to A.D. 800.

Lukurmata Tiwanaku V: Ridge. Evidence for this phase came from a refuse pit 100 m south of the Semisubterranean Temple, or Bennett's section K (Bennett 1936; Bermann 1990: Figure 7; 1994: Figure 11.9). The pit was 1.9 m in diameter and 85 cm deep. At level 18, a burning event took place within the pit, and a ^{14}C sample that represents a primary association, ETH3180 (cal A.D. 1018–1188), was collected. Some pottery was illustrated (Bermann 1994: Figures 13.1–13.3), including a *kero* base described as a non-Tiwanaku-style *incensario* (Bermann 1990:327; 1994: Figure 13.3). This vessel can now be identified as an LTIV-style *kero* with a basal band of white camelid skull motifs (Janusek 2003b:62, Figures 3.43, 3.44). Another sherd displayed a TV-style flamingo motif (Bermann 1994: Figure 13.2b). Other TV evidence on the ridge came from bell-shaped tombs within the main excavation that were dated by diagnostic ceramics (Bermann 1994:220–223). Though Bermann describes several *keros*, including a polychrome one decorated with pumas, none is illustrated, unless his Figure 11.2 (Bermann 1994:151) is one, although it is referenced simply to have come from a TV Lukurmata tomb (Janusek 2003a:62) (Figure 12.17). The exact association of ETH3180 (cal A.D. 1018–1188) in level 18 with the TIV and TV sherds was not published, so the temporal sequence remains undetermined.

Lukurmata Tiwanaku V: Misiton 2. The later storage structures built to the south of the residential area discussed above were occupied either at the end of activities in structure 42 or after its abandonment. The storage complex was expertly constructed of cut-stone and cobblestone walls (Janusek 2004: 228–233, Figure 8.1A).[28] Two ^{14}C samples were collected from areas outside the structures: B55489 (cal A.D. 1151–1296) came from a midden, and B55488 (cal A.D. 1046–1225) came from a hearth—a primary deposit—associated with occupation that followed a period of abandonment at the site. Janusek (1994:224, Footnote 1) dismissed the very late B55489 midden date as odd and probably intrusive, but the B55488 date caps the end of occupation in the area as no later than A.D. 1250.

Summary of Lukurmata. Unlike the shallow and disturbed deposits at the AkE1 excavations, Lukurmata ridge structures were found beneath 50 cm of natural deposition in stable, horizontal stratified layers, disturbed only by several easily discernible burial pits from later occupation. The Lukurmata ridge excavations provided a primary associated ^{14}C date from a hearth in a building that belonged to a group of single-roomed structures and within a stratigraphic level producing TIV ceramics. Consequently, ETH3179 (cal A.D. 812–991) provides a reliable date for TIV ceramics. Misiton 2 also furnished two primary associated ^{14}C samples: SMU1920 (cal A.D. 778–986) from a house hearth, although its related TIV ceramics must be published to confirm stylistic designation; and SMU2117 (cal A.D. 899–1045), which is less clearly defined, again due to a lack of illustrated ceramics, although TIV style is implied. Consequently, Lukurmata data provide evidence for placement of TIV in the ninth and tenth centuries. Tiwanaku V ceramic evidence was found but not well associated with any ^{14}C samples, most of which imply post-Tiwanaku events.

Concluding Remarks

This review has evaluated excavation contexts and the nature of ^{14}C samples' association with contexts containing LF2-, TIV-, and TV-style pottery—although excavation details and many collected ceramics critical for this study of absolute chronology remain unpublished. All ^{14}C samples were recalibrated, and the standard deviations were narrowed to 1σ range (or at least 85 percent of 1σ range) to produce a "best fit" explanation of the radiocarbon chronology. That chronology is as follows:

LF2: A.D. 500–800
TIV: A.D. 800–1000
TV: A.D. 800–1100

These results are significantly different from currently popular dates for the first two phases: LF2, usually designated A.D. 300–500, and TIV, usually designated A.D. 500–800. Only TV remains almost the same as formerly dated, A.D. 800–1150. The almost total overlap of TIV and TV is supported by the ^{14}C dates from coastal Moquegua and the co-occurrence of the both styles in many excavation contexts.[29]

Although beyond the scope of this paper, ^{14}C samples from the sites of Omo and Chen Chen can be subjected to the same rigorous treatment employed here (Goldstein and Owen 2001; Owen and Goldstein 2001) (see Table 12.1). Omo and Chen Chen styles are assigned to Tiwanaku IV and V. Their radiocarbon dates imply lengthy use for the Omo-style pottery, within an approximate range of A.D. 800 to 1100 (eliminating the B36639 date) but a briefer temporal span for Chen Chen–style pottery, within an approximate range of A.D. 900 to 1000. Consequently, it is increasingly convincing that Tiwanaku IV and V do not represent temporally distinct units. The pottery styles assigned to these supposedly temporal phases were simultaneous, or largely overlapping, and probably represent different workshops, ethnicities, or other social distinctions. A more detailed unit of analysis, such as design elements or temper attributes, may produce evidence for what kinds of social relations characterized these

FIGURE 12.17. A museum-curated example of a Tiwanaku-style *kero* with a Rayed Head deity icon. Height 19.5 cm; diameter 15 cm (VA64431, Museen Dahlem, Staatliche Museen zu Berlin; collected in 1938; photo by P. J. Knobloch, 1985).

Table 12.1 Comparison of Correlated ^{14}C Samples for Omo and Chen Chen Styles

OMO STYLE		CHEN CHEN STYLE	
LAB CODE	CAL A.D. (85–100% OF 1)	LAB CODE	CAL A.D. (85–100% OF 1)
B36639	565–670	AA37175	911–973
B129938	692–873	B39679	892–988
B134693	812–991	B26650	896–1023
B129939	882–995	B129619	899–1020
AA38032	898–995	AA38031	899–1019
B127211	962–1136	AA40628	974–1025
B120264	977–1147	AA37173	951–1038
B60762	989–1148	B134694	897–1045

social groups (Knobloch 2000). Research and analyses by Linda Manzanilla (1992), Jo Ellen Burkholder (2001), and Sonia Alconini (1995) represent steps toward this kind of greater understanding.

This review indicates that Tiwanaku's magnificent society developed its urban core and regional state control within a shorter time than formerly believed, perhaps from just A.D. 800 to 1000. During this time, Tiwanaku society experienced an increase in associated settlement sizes (Albarracin-Jordan and Mathews 1990) and population growth that placed greater demands on the controlling authorities at the capital. The city of Tiwanaku participated in and managed diverse allegiances with communities in the Moquegua Valley on the south coast (Goldstein and Owen 2001; Owen and Goldstein 2001), in neighboring Katari Valley (Bandy 2001), in locations along Lake Titicaca (Korpisaari and Pärssinen 2005; Seddon 2004), and elsewhere. So brief a temporal range for such marvelous accomplishments may be criticized, yet it is longer and represents no more impressive accomplishments in politics and architecture than that of the Inca. From Pachacuti's reign (A.D. 1438–1463) to colonial conquest in 1532—a span of 100 years—the Inca dominated the entire central Andes and constructed monumental Cuzco, as well as Machu Picchu, Sacsahuaman, Ollantaytambo, and many other wonders (Rowe 1963 [1947]:202–205, 225). Indeed, two centuries for the city of Tiwanaku, and its Tiwanaku IV and V styles, is not unreasonable.

ACKNOWLEDGMENTS

I am indebted to the late Deter Eisleb for his kind generosity in allowing me to study and photograph the Berlin collections and for permission to publish these photos. For helping me compile a list of ^{14}C dates and accurately denoting them for the "Who Was Who in the Middle Horizon Andean Prehistory" website (*http://www-rohan.sdsu.edu/~bharley/WWWHome.html*), I would like to thank Paula Reimer, Christopher Ramsey, and Joerg Haeberli. This list was then translated into the present article owing to the gracious invitation from Charles Stanish and Alexei Vranich to participate in their Tiwanaku conference at UCLA's Cotsen Institute in 2006. John Janusek was my expert reference; he reviewed the data presented here and gave freely of his time and past data analysis. He and Antti Korpisaari also provided welcome critical comments on a 2007 draft of this paper. For the incentive to write this article, clarify it with analytical comments, and complete its final version, I am greatly indebted to William Isbell for his unwavering encouragement and generous editorial expertise.

Notes

[1] In the text, ^{14}C dates are written with lab code numbers and a cal A.D. representing 85 to 100 percent of a 1σ range. This approach avoids the temporal overlaps of 2σ spans that can mask patterns of sequential order within the few centuries discussed here. The dates presented are also rounded to the nearest 50 years, so 25 becomes 50 and so on. The CALIB5.0.2 program was used and was set to Southern Hemisphere standards (McCormac et al. 2004; Stuiver and Reimer 1993; Stuiver et al. 2005). Graphs are found at http://www-rohan.sdsu.edu/~bharley/WWWWHEN.html..

[2] The name Putuni refers to the Putuni platform and courtyard (approximately 60 m by 75 m).

[3] Janusek (personal communication 2007) notes this ^{14}C sample with ETIV evidence.

[4] Though described here as an *incensario*, I believe this sherd is the same sherd Janusek (2003b: Figure 3.23a) illustrates as a *sahumador* (Janusek 2003b: Figures 3.16b, 3.19a) and that Bennett (1934: Figure 13b) calls a "flat bottom cup." Since Tiwanaku *incensarios* have a modeled head, frequently a scalloped rim, and one handle (Janusek 2003b: Figure 3.62a, b), the Qeya vessel form is probably antecedent to the Tiwanaku form of *incensarios* and not *sahumadors*. See Bermann's (1994: Figure 9.5a) description of a Qeya-style incised *incensario*. The Qeya *incensario* in my Figure 12.8 has a blackened interior from burning inside the vessel.

[5] Excavations on the Akapana confirm the construction of its terraced walls, stairs, and canals. However, with only magnetic survey and with no excavations to original sterile construction levels, it seems premature to conclude that the Akapana did not begin as a natural hill.

[6] Only two unresolved issues remain. Issue 1: Alconini (1995: Figure 4) placed Feature 10 in N8028 E5026. However, a photo of this burial (Manzanilla 1992: Figure 47) shows it located against the base of the east–west section of wall 1, or N8026 E5022. Compare Figure 47, showing a protruding stone block in the upper left corner of the photo, with photo D (Manzanilla 1992) to locate the same protruding stone block and wall section. This comparison also indicates that Feature 10 was located a few centimeters above Features 13 and 15, which were on surface 4D, which was aligned with the base of wall 1's canal opening. Issue 2: Alconini (1995: Figure 4) placed Feature 8b and Feature 9, which represent burials 4 and 5, to either side of a line on her map representing the southern end of wall 1's north–south section. However, Manzanilla's (1992: Figure 46) drawing of these burials shows them as south of the east–west section of this wall, on top of the first terrace. More discrepancies occur in the reprinted information on this same drawing (Blom et al. 2003:436, Figure 18.2). The phrase "First Terrace" replaces the original "Muro 1," and north and east coordinates are given as N8027 E5025, which would place this excavation unit along the north–south wall.

[7] Janusek (2003b: Table 3.1) notes the location of this sample as at the "summit" of Akapana rather than at the base of terrace 1 but provides the correct NE coordinates. Therefore, I assume the "summit" note is a typographical error. Also, Janusek's (2003b) Tables 3.1 and 3.3 list "Established Phase" ceramic associations for carbon samples that are not from the original excavation notes provided to me by Janusek (personal communication 2007). I employ these original notes for ceramic styles and dates, and readers can compare the original with subsequently published designations.

[8] Janusek (2003b: Table 3.1) assigned this feature to N7962 E4971, a location atop the Akapana, though he described it as a llama offering at the base of terrace 1. I am assuming the coordinates are a typographical error.

[9] Alconini (1995: Figures 7, 8) illustrates a vessel associated with Feature 28 that she describes as reminiscent of Yaya-Mama-style iconography, although only very generally.

[10] A great deal of interpretation regarding skeletal remains deals with "offerings" and "ancestor worship." I recommend James Whitley's (2002) circumspect view that there are "too many ancestors in contemporary archaeological interpretation, and they are being asked to do too much." The same might be said of broken pottery as offerings; it could simply be the result of garbage removal.

[11] Janusek (2003b: Table 3.1) notes that ETH6306 is from Feature 17 at the "base of terrace 1" with "Tiw IV" ceramics, but his original notes indicate "terrace 1, base," or preferably the surface of terrace 1 and the base of wall 2, and "E Tiw IV" (personal communication, 2007).

[12] Vranich (2001) concurs with the interpretation that all these materials were disturbed, based on his "revetment and fill" construction model for the Akapana. In contrast with Kolata and Manzanilla, who date the "ceramic smash" as abandonment of the Akapana, Vranich suggests that the material was part of the fill used to construct the pyramid's terrace revetments. However, only one revetment on the first terrace has been excavated at the eastern side. The facade is built of large cut stones with larger blocks for capstones. The interior cross walls that remain are quite small and do not provide support for the facade. Therefore, the cross walls were built to create small chambers, perhaps to contain fill. The rectangular footprint of the "ceramic smash" indicates that a facade with interior cross walls may once have delineated that area on top of the first terrace. Consequently, the broader width of the first terrace may have been a purposeful architectural skirt of chambers that on receiving fill became part of the revetment-like surfacing. Further excavation in the narrower terraces is needed to determine if Vranich's "revetment and fill" model is valid for the entire pyramid. Otherwise, the chambers could represent tombs arranged on a single terrace level, and the weathered skeleton an open tomb that was never filled.

[13] Confusingly, three rows of sherd drawings are attributed to the "top" or "bottom" location in the figure. Consequently,

readers do not know whether to interpret the middle row of sherds as part of the top or the bottom.

[14] SMU2473 and Feature 11 are published as associated with LTV/Pacajes material (Janusek 2003b: Table 3.1), but Janusek's original notes indicate "TV" only (personal communication, 2007).

[15] SMU2336 has been published with conflicting lab report dates: B.P. 1243 ± 113 (cal A.D. 766–971) (Janusek 2003b: Table 3.1) and B.P. 710 ± 110 (cal A.D. 1265–1403) (Alconini 1995: Figure 56). The former is the correct date (Janusek, personal communication 2007).

[16] Figure 7.11B is best viewed in Janusek 2001 Figure 5, a photograph that shows a white curling line emanating from the feline's mouth like a tongue.

[17] Janusek's notes (personal communication 2007) for ^{14}C sample OS11306 (cal A.D. 542–598), also found on the clay platform's surface, indicate ETIV ceramic evidence.

[18] Similar examples are in Alconini's Akapana A phase, or transitional LF2–TIV by Janusek's (2003b: Figure 3.49, from Alconini 1995:78–79, Figure 60) definition.

[19] Extensive human and animal remains were found on the surface areas of the north compound after the kitchen complex and canals were destroyed (Couture and Sampeck 2003:245–248). Though Couture and Sampeck describe the remains as offerings, the lack of grave goods, incomplete skeletons, and exposed surface may indicate a more violent event that destroyed the occupation.

[20] Not located on maps in Figure 12.5 or Figure 12.16.

[21] This mask or pectoral contrasts with Wari-style versions with dashed eyebrows, tubular noses, and thin-lipped mouths found at Asángaro, Peru (Ponce 1948:37, Figure 40).

[22] A *sahumador* with a hollow tube fired onto the interior base (Janusek 2003b: Figure 3.61a, b).

[23] The elite grave goods indicate lack of a long-distance, northern trade for *Spondylus* shell, in contrast to southern trade for lapis lazuli. The northern boundary may also be defined by the presence of most obsidian from the northern Cotalli resource but not farther north from Quispisisa (Giesso 2003: 368–371, Figure 15.5, Tables 15.4–15.6). Perhaps "middlemen" partners controlled altiplano access to exotic, north coast materials. Then again, centuries of looting make the presence of any rich artifacts remarkable.

[24] Bermann identifies the image as the arm of the Sacrificer holding a trophy head, but I believe he has inverted the sherd.

[25] This location was designated with NE coordinates of ^{14}C samples and profile drawing captions (Janusek 1994:414–415).

[26] There is an error in the coordinates: SMU1920 was given N2371 E2884, whereas its origin, Feature 1, was given N2369 E2884 (see Janusek 1994:220).

[27] Illustrations of Lukurmata residential pottery by Janusek (1994: Figures 8.33, 8.34) may include examples from Bermann's earlier excavations.

[28] To follow the NE coordinate positions that are lacking on Janusek's map, the upper left corner is N2377 E2882 and the bottom right corner is N2357 E2892.

[29] For an earlier discussion of the contemporaneity of classic and decadent Tiwanaku, see Knobloch 1989 [1988]:121.

References Cited

Albarracin-Jordan, J. V., and J. E. Mathews
1990 *Asentamientos prehispánicos del Valle de Tiwanaku*, Vol. 1. Producciones CIMA, La Paz.

Alconini Mújica, S.
1995 *Rito, símbolo e historia en la pirámide de Akapana, Tiwanaku. Un análisis de la cerámica ceremonial prehispánica*. Editorial Acción, La Paz.

Bandy, Matthew
2001 Population and History in the Ancient Titicaca Basin. Unpublished Ph.D. dissertation, Department of Anthropology, University of California, Berkeley.

Bennett, Wendell C.
1934 Excavations at Tiahuanaco. *Anthropological Papers of the American Museum of Natural History* 34(3):359–494.
1936 Excavations in Bolivia. *Anthropological Papers of the American Museum of Natural History* 35(4) 329–507.

Bermann, Marc
1989 Visión de las casas del período Tiwanaku en Lukurmata. In *La tecnología y organización de la producción agrícola en el estado de Tiwanaku*, Vol. 2, edited by A. Kokata, pp.113–151. Instituto Nacional de Arqueología, La Paz.
1990 Prehispanic Household and Empire at Lukurmata, Bolivia. Unpublished Ph.D. dissertation, University of Michigan, Ann Arbor.
1994 *Lukurmata: Household Archaeology in Prehispanic Bolivia*. Princeton University Press, Princeton, New Jersey.
2003 The Archaeology of Households in Lukurmata. In *Tiwanaku and Its Hinterland: Archaeology and Paleoecology of an Andean Civilization*. Vol. 2, *Urban and Rural Archaeology*, edited by Alan L. Kolata, pp. 327–340. Smithsonian Institution Press, Washington, D.C.

Bermann, Marc, and G. Graffam
1989 Arquitectura residencial en las terrazas de Lukurmata. In *Arqueología de Lukurmata*, Vol. 2, edited by A. Kokata, pp. 153–173. Instituto Nacional de Arqueología, La Paz.

Blom, D., J. Janusek, and J. Buikstra
2003 A Reevaluation of Human Remains from Tiwanaku. In *Tiwanaku and Its Hinterland: Archaeology and Paleoecology of an Andean Civilization*. Vol. 2, *Urban and Rural Archaeology*, edited by

Alan L. Kolata, pp. 435–446. Smithsonian Institution Press, Washington, D.C.

Burkholder, Jo Ellen
2001 La cerámica de Tiwanaku: ¿Qué indica su variabilidad? In *Huari y Tiwanaku: Modelos vs. Evidencias*, Pt. 2, edited by P. Kaulicke and W. H. Isbell, pp. 217–250. Boletín de Arqueología PUCP No. 5. Pontificia Universidad Católica del Perú, Lima.

Couture, Nicole
2002 The Construction of Power: Monumental Space and Elite Residence at Tiwanaku, Bolivia. Unpublished Ph.D. dissertation, Department of Anthropology, University of Chicago, Chicago.

Couture, Nicole C., and Kathryn Sampeck
2003 Putuni: A History of Palace Architecture at Tiwanaku. In *Tiwanaku and Its Hinterland: Archaeology and Paleoecology of an Andean Civilization*. Vol. 2, *Urban and Rural Archaeology*, edited by Alan L. Kolata, pp. 226–263. Smithsonian Institution Press, Washington, D.C.

Eisleb, Dieter, and Renate Strelow
1980 *Altperuanische Kulturen Tiahuanaco*, Vol. 3. Museum für Völkerkunde, Berlin.

Giesso, Martin
2003 Stone Tool Production in the Tiwanaku Heartland. In *Tiwanaku and Its Hinterland: Archaeology and Paleoecology of an Andean Civilization*. Vol. 2, *Urban and Rural Archaeology*, edited by Alan L. Kolata, pp. 363–383. Smithsonian Institution Press, Washington, D.C.

Goldstein, P.aul, and Bruce Owen
2001 Tiwanaku in Moquegua: Las colonias altiplánicas. In *Huari y Tiwanaku: Modelos vs. Evidencias*, Pt. 2, edited by P. Kaulicke and W. H. Isbell, pp. 139–168. Boletín de Arqueología PUCP No. 5. Pontificia Universidad Católica del Perú, Lima.

Janusek, John Wayne
1994 State and Local Power in a Prehispanic Andean Polity: Changing Patterns of Urban Residence in Tiwanaku and Lukurmata, Bolivia. Unpublished Ph.D. dissertation, Department of Anthropology, University of Chicago, Chicago.
2001 Diversidad residencial y el surgimiento de la complejidad en Tiwanaku. In *Huari y Tiwanaku: Modelos vs. evidencias*, Pt. 2, edited by P. Kaulicke and W. H. Isbell, pp. 251–294. Boletín de Arqueología PUCP 5. Pontificia Universidad Católica del Perú, Lima.
2003a The Changing Face of Tiwanaku Residential Life: State and Local identity in an Andean City. In *Tiwanaku and Its Hinterland: Archaeology and Paleoecology of an Andean Civilization*. Vol. 2, *Urban and Rural Archaeology*, edited by Alan L. Kolata, pp. 264–295. Smithsonian Institution Press, Washington, D.C.
2003b Vessels, Time, and Society: Toward a Ceramic Chronology in the Tiwanaku Heartland. In *Tiwanaku and Its Hinterland: Archaeology and Paleoecology of an Andean Civilization*. Vol. 2, *Urban and Rural Archaeology*, edited by Alan L. Kolata, pp. 30–91. Smithsonian Institution Press, Washington, D.C.
2004 *Identity and Power in the Ancient Andes: Tiwanaku Cities Through Time*. Routledge, New York.

Janusek, J., and H. Earnest
1990 Excavations in the Putuni: The 1988 Season. In Tiwanaku and Its Hinterland, edited by Alan Kolata, pp. 236–246. Second preliminary report of the Proyecto Wila Jawira submitted to the Instituto Nacional de Arqueología de Bolivia, the National Science Foundation, and the National Endowment for the Humanities. Unpublished report, the Institute of Archaeology, La Paz, Bolivia, and the funding agencies in Washington, D.C.

Knobloch, Patricia J.
1989 [1988] Artisans of the Realm. In *Ancient Art of the Andean World*, edited by S. Masuda and I. Shimada, pp. 107–123. Iwanami Shoten Publishers, Tokyo. Electronic document, *http://www-rohan.sdsu.edu/~bharley/ArtisansoftheRealm.html*.
2000 La cronología del contacto y encuentros cercanos de Wari. In *Huari y Tiwanaku: Modelos vs. evidencias*, Pt. 1, edited by P. Kaulicke and W. H. Isbell, pp. 69–87. Boletín de Arqueología PUCP No. 4. Pontificia Universidad Católica del Perú, Lima.
2002 Who Was Who in the Middle Horizon Andean Prehistory. Electronic document, *http://www.rohan.sdsu.edu/~bharley/WWWHome.html*, accessed July 30, 2013.

Kolata, Alan L.
2003 Tiwanaku Ceremonial Architecture and Urban Organization. In *Tiwanaku and Its Hinterland: Archaeology and Paleoecology of an Andean Civilization*. Vol. 2, *Urban and Rural Archaeology*, edited by Alan L. Kolata, pp. 175–201. Smithsonian Institution Press, Washington, D.C.

Korpisaari, Antti, and Martti Pärssinen
2005 *Pariti: Isla, misterio y poder: El tesoro cerámica de la cultura Tiwanaku*. Producciones CIMA, La Paz.

Manzanilla, Linda
1992 *Akapana: Una pirámide en el centro del mundo*. Instituto de Investigaciones Antropológicas, Universidad Nacional Autónoma de México, Mexico City.

Manzanilla, L., L. Barba, and M. R. Baudoin
1990 Investigaciones en la pirámide de Akapana, Tiwanaku, Bolivia. *Gaceta arqueológicas andina* 20:83–107.

Manzanilla, L., and E. Woodard
  1990   Restos humanos asociados a la Pirámide de Akapana (Tiwanaku, Bolivia). *Latin American Antiquity* 1(2):133–149.

Mathews, James E.
  2003   Prehistoric Settlement Patterns in the Middle Tiwanaku Valley. In *Tiwanaku and Its Hinterland: Archaeology and Paleoecology of an Andean Civilization*. Vol. 2, *Urban and Rural Archaeology*, edited by Alan L. Kolata, pp. 112–128. Smithsonian Institution Press, Washington, D.C.

McCormac, F. G., A. G. Hogg, P. G. Blackwell, C. E. Buck, T. F. G. Higham, and P. J. Reimer
  2004   SHCal04 Southern Hemisphere Calibration 0–11.0 cal kyr BP. *Radiocarbon* 46:1087–1092.

Owen, Bruce, and Paul Goldstein
  2001   Tiwanaku en Moquegua: Interacciones regionales y colapso. In *Huari y Tiwanaku: Modelos vs. evidencias*, Pt. 2, edited by P. Kaulicke and W. H. Isbell, pp.169–188. Boletín de Arqueología PUCP No. 5. Pontificia Universidad Católica del Perú, Lima.

Ponce Sanginés, Carlos
  1948   *Cerámica Tiwanacota: Vasos con decoración prosopomorfa*. Emecé Edictores, Buenos Aires.
  1979   *Nueva perspectiva para el estudio de la expansión de la cultura Tiwanaku*. Instituto Nacional de Arqueología 29. Instituto Nacional de Arqueología, La Paz.

Posnansky, Arthur
  1945   *Tihuanacu: The Cradle of Man*, Vols. 1 and 2. American Museum of Natural History, New York.
  1957   *Tihuanacu: La cuna del hombre americano*, Vols. 3 and 4. Ministerio de Educación, La Paz.

Ríos Paredes, M.
  1991   *Informe de la muestra de radiocarbono procedente de la pirámide de Akapana, Tiwanaku, Bolivia*. INAH, Subdirección de Servicios Académicos, Laboratorios de Fechamiento, Mexico City.

Rivera Casanovas, Claudia
  2003   Ch'iji Jawira: A Case of Ceramic Specialization in the Tiwanaku Urban Periphery. In *Tiwanaku and Its Hinterland: Archaeology and Paleoecology of an Andean Civilization*, Vol. 2, *Urban and Rural Archaeology*, edited by Alan L. Kolata, pp. 296–315. Smithsonian Institution Press, Washington, D.C.

Rowe, John H.
  1963 [1947]   Inca Culture at the Time of the Spanish Conquest. In *Handbook of South American Indians*. Vol. 2, *The Andean Civilizations*, edited by J. Steward, pp. 183–330. Bureau of American Ethnology Bulletin 143. Cooper Square Publishers, New York.

Sampeck, K.
  1991   Excavations at Putuni, Tiwanaku, Bolivia. Unpublished master's thesis, Department of Anthropology, University of Chicago, Chicago.

Seddon, Matthew
  2004   Excavations at the Site of Chucaripupata: A Tiwanaku IV and V Temple and Domestic Occupation. In *Archaeological Research on the Islands of the Sun and Moon, Lake Titicaca, Bolivia: Final Results of the Proyecto Tiksi Kjarka*, edited by C. Stanish and B. Bauer, pp. 93–137. Monograph 52. Cotsen Institute of Archaeology, UCLA, Los Angeles.

Stuiver, M., and Reimer, P. J.
  1993   Extended ^{14}C Database and Revised CALIB Radiocarbon Calibration Program. *Radiocarbon* 35: 215–230.

Stuiver, M., P. J. Reimer, and R. W. Reimer. CALIB 5.0.2.
  2005   Electronic document, *http://calib.qub.ac.uk/calib/calib.html*, accessed September 10, 2005.

Vranich, Alexei
  2001   La pirámide de Akapana: Reconsiderando el centro monumental de Tiwanaku. In *Huari y Tiwanaku: Modelos vs. evidencias*, Pt. 2, edited by Peter Kaulicke and William H. Isbell, pp. 295–308. Boletín de Arqueología PUCP No. 5. Pontificia Universidad Católica del Perú, Lima.

Whitley, James
  2002   Too Many Ancestors. *Antiquity* 76(291):119–126.

13
Concluding Thoughts

Alexei Vranich

The unheralded rise and fall of Tiwanaku is a story related a thousand times over to enthralled visitors to the site as well as to groups of schoolchildren and the occasional politician. Unfortunately, supporting data are so scarce that a motivated guide can easily fashion an engaging tale—all too often with a panache that overrides archaeological data—that has a far broader appeal to the public than the hedged and cautious interpretations of a scholarly publication. Concomitantly, Tiwanaku's appeal as a mysterious, thought-provoking ancient primary state has multiplied exponentially in academic circles, resulting in pressure on investigators to provide a compelling narrative sustained by the solid fabric of a linear description and a satisfying outcome relevant to the values and climate of the time.

This is not to say that the data are too scarce to develop empirically based claims and theories; on the contrary, scholars probably know more about Tiwanaku than any other pre-Columbian site in the continent. As the field becomes more specialized, a researcher can easily spend a lifetime delving into one single facet of this complex site. Nevertheless, no single perspective, regardless of how well thought out and formulated, can describe the entire phenomenon. The intent of this volume, then, is to see if multiple perspectives on the same event can resist succumbing to the allure of the single narrative that, when read as whole, presents a composite and well-informed vision of an archaeological society.

The burden of the past and the intrusion of the modern are topics repeated throughout the volume, to the point of trying the patience of even the most empathic audience. To ground these concerns in a meaningful context, the contributions by Vranich (chapter 1) and Moseley (chapter 2) provide background, from the contact period to the present, exploring how politics and personalities continue to be factors influencing research design and interpretation. Fortunately, the concerns do not wallow at the level of a helpless lament or turn into a literary critique of biases and circular reasoning but deserve and detain the attention of the reader. Accepting the heavy burden of history, each author uses the hand he or she has been dealt, entertaining the hope of answering the question: "What was Tiwanaku?" Geographically, the contributions can be assembled into two groups: research at the site (Janusek, Stanish, Isbell, Conklin, Bandy, Knobloch) and research in the "enclaves" beyond the southern Titicaca Basin (Anderson, Goldstein, Williams, Seddon). The general trend among contributors has been to eschew the traditional variables used to measure social complexity, such as population density, social stratification control, and intensification of resources, and to favor exploring other lines of evidence, in particular the potential of ritual and performance as a means of developing consensus among a large and diverse group of people. Andean scholars expatiate with minuteness on the variety and importance of ritual, festivals, and feasting in modern communities and in pre-Columbian empires; however, the challenge remains to find an objective manner in which to reframe such activities as a social prime mover.

Research in the Hinterlands

The only local example we have of complex and expansive Andean society is that of the Inca, which, as Moseley points out, became the first indigenous analogue for Tiwanaku. This analogue served well for a time, but the paucity of comments on the Inca in this volume indicates that the field has taken a change in direction. The case for the misuse of analogy has been well made—with some of the worst abuse committed at Tiwanaku—and in many ways new data from the hinterlands demonstrate that the Inca Empire is not necessarily a good fit. The meteoritic rise of the Inca was for the most part the result of quick negotiations (both peaceful and violent) between numerically superior conquerors and smaller indigenous groups. Nevertheless, in the case of Tiwanaku, we appear to have a subtler situation. Several authors in this volume describe a process that could be summarized as a relationship between people and ritual objects that evolved over generations. An island in the middle of a lake at 13,000 feet above sea level and a temperate valley in the eastern Andean slopes are about as different as two locations can be, yet Seddon (chapter 7) and Anderson (chapter 6) describe the same process of a gradual incorporation of the Tiwanaku *kero* into ritual life.

The hyper-arid climate of Moquegua provides the ideal setting in which to study the effects of Tiwanaku on both a local indigenous population and the contemporary Wari state. The identification of highland people in the extensive cemeteries in Moquegua allows for a series of more detailed questions: What was the relationship of these highland peoples to the site of Tiwanaku? Who were they within Tiwanaku society? What was their connection to the existing indigenous population of the valley? What was their link to the other foreign groups that clustered around the modest but irrefutably Tiwanaku ritual building at Omo? Undoubtedly, scholars will examine and categorize other social combinations, but the implication is that Tiwanaku can be defined and, owing to the difficulties of working in the southern basin, will need to be defined with data from outside the heartland.

The Site

We have not discovered, nor do we fully understand, the mechanism that directed the energies of diverse communities toward creating a singular awe-inspiring setting. Clearly, something obligated or convinced people to expend a substantial amount of time and labor on the intangible metaphysical claims of cosmology. Even though evidence from the hinterlands appears to be rather ephemeral, we need to return our focus to the ruins and imagine the necessary level of organization and the amount of labor behind the largest lithic constructions on the continent.

At the time of this publication, the site remains a politically problematic place for both national and international scholars. There were several exemplary research projects in the period between the end of Ponce's tenure and the present difficulties; the results can be found in most libraries and in dense reports from recent Bolivian excavations that can be located with a bit of time and patience. Notwithstanding, new data will be scarce and will continue to lag behind the flow of information from the hinterland. Many basic issues will remain unstudied and unresolved—for example, the actual dimensions of the site, details of the ceramic chronology, and absolute dates for monumental construction.

If this volume is an accurate index of the state of affairs in the field, the study of the site of Tiwanaku does not require new data—though it would be warmly welcomed. Rather, the contributions in this volume reflect the need to reframe existing data. In addition to enduring misconceptions (or factoids, as Isbell terms them in chapter 10) that refuse to die, there is a more influential narrative with origins both in politics and academia. Buttressed by the discovery of an uneven but extensive distribution of surface artifacts, nearly every publication frames the history of research during the second half of the twentieth century as a gradual, scientifically based rebuttal of the empty ceremonial center claim. In this climate, reconsidering previous models breaks with the idea that knowledge and cultural sensitivity are cumulative; to some, even reconsidering previous models signals a dangerous turn toward a biased past. Personally, I find it strange that the filthy and plague-prone cities of medieval Europe should be held as the apogee of human accomplishment. If we compare this to the initial description of Cuzco—clean streets, fresh running water, and no poverty—the Andean form of "urbanism" is clearly at odds with that of the Old World. Several chapters propose alternative routes to understanding this complexity and explore the applicability of analogues from various parts of the world, even going so far as to invent new terms as a means of summarizing a complex situation in a single sound-bite. The authors ground these new perspectives in existing data in desperate need of fresh eyes: Knobloch (chapter 12) reviews nearly every available publication for descriptions of excavated context, and Conklin (chapter 5) and Bandy (chapter 8) use material available to any scholar freely—in fact, to any visitor to the site freely —to explore basic concepts of spatial and social organization. Their data, derived from the study of textiles, architecture, and iconography, are generally marginalized within the field of archaeology, but as these contributions have shown, they can significantly contribute to our understanding as much as conventional excavation data when written without jargon and when framed within anthropological questions.

Conclusion

Ever since the ruins of Tiwanaku were identified as the primary site of a widely distributed artifact style, the dimensions of the polity have been changing form. More accurately, the Tiwanaku phenomenon —be it a state, an empire, or a sphere of influence— has been diminishing in size. The existence of a "coastal Tiwanaku" disappeared with the realization of the importance of the site of Huari. Over the years, the ubiquitous graphic of the Tiwanaku "empire" had changed accordingly, from the crisp boundaries of a polygonal shape covering the entire southern Andes, to a fuzzy form with graded edges centered on the Titicaca Basin, to an amorphous shape around the shoreline of the lake with thin tendrils leading to single destinations. Furthermore, in chronological time, the Tiwanaku phenomenon has been reduced on both ends of the historical calendar. The extreme carbon date of 1500 B.C. has been discarded as an accidental outlier, and the period during which Tiwanaku was one of many small centers may be extended to the fourth century A.D. Knobloch's detailed analysis in this volume defines the "expansive period" of Tiwanaku to a two-century period between A.D. 800 and 1000. Based on ^{14}C dates from Moquegua, the final days of Tiwanaku have also retreated from a high-water mark of A.D. 1200 to a period ranging from the tenth to the twelfth century. Rather than reduce the importance and relevance of Tiwanaku, this conceptual territorial and temporal loss has made this highland phenomenon far more interesting than the usual route of growth, expansion, and then quick collapse that seems to characterize short-lived (by Old World standards) Andean polities. Which leads us to ask: Was Tiwanaku an extension of Formative-period institutions, or was there a fundamental structural change into a previously unknown form? Even in this new form, Tiwanaku continues to generate questions with global implications for generations of scholars to come.

INDEX

Note: Page numbers in ***bold italics*** indicate illustrations or tables.

adobe bricks, 30, 96, 204, 222
Agrarian Reform Act (Bolivia), 8
agriculture. *See also* food
   cycles in, population shifts and, 142–143
   Huaracane, 48
   Inca, 32
   raised-field, 141–143, 171, 189n4
   segmentary organization and, 44
   Tiwanaku, ***29,*** 31–32
   urbanity and, 141–143
   Wari, ***29,*** 31, 32
Akapana, 113, 119, 136, 148, 164, ***180,*** 200, 202
Akapana A+B, 216–221, ***217, 218***
Akapana East, 200, 203, 205, 214, ***214,*** 222–224, ***223***
Akapana Pyramid, 5, 7, ***71,*** 171, 179, 221–222
Akapana Summit, 221
Alto Ramirez, 67
Alur, 42
Angkor Wat, 171, 178, 179, 180
animals. *See also* camelids
   as food sources, 99–100
   in iconography, ***145,*** 145–146, 176, ***212, 213***
   remains of, 100, 217, 218, 219, 221, 231n19
apex families, 143
Arani, ***89***
archaic state, 42, ***43***
architecture. *See also* monumental construction; residential architecture
   at Cochabamba, 96–98, ***97***
   ideological symbolism in, 97–98
   orientation in, 97
   tapia construction in, 96, ***97,*** 105

   Tiwanaku, 70–71, ***71***
   as unfinished, 187
   Wari, 71
architrave, 68, ***68,*** 187, 189
ash pits, 34, 202, 203–204, 222, 224
astronomy, 70–71, 84, 120
attendant figures, ***77,*** 77–78, ***145,*** 146, 176–177, 178
Ayacucho, 32, 34
ayllus, 43–44, 51, 160, 205
Aymara
   Europeans and, 3
   Evo Morales and, 1
   libation ritual, 116, 118, 144
   mesas, 116
   towns, 140
Azapa, 59, 153

bags, coca, 83
Bearded Statue, 172, 177
beer, 117, 122, 137–138, 144, 145, 146, 175–176, 200, 203
Bennett Stela, 71–72, ***72,*** 137–139
Berkeley School, 13, 14, 15–16, 18, 20, 22
birds
   in diet, 99
   representations of, in ceramics and structures, ***145,*** 145–146, ***212, 213,*** 227
body modification, 200, 201. *See also* cranial deformation
bones. *See* mortuary
bowls, ***139,*** 139–140, ***174,*** 175. *See also* ceramics; *tazones* (bowls)
breechcloth, 66–67, ***67***

239

240

bricks, 30, 96, 204, 222
bronze tools, 36
burial. *See* mortuary

Cahokia, 156
Calle Linares Lintel, 68
Cambodia, 171, 178, 179, 180
camelids
   in ceramics, 227
   dung of, 204
   flutes made from bones of, 98
   as food, 99–100
   mandibles of, 45, 98, *98*
   in mortuary, 37, 102, 119
   remains of, 100, 119, 217, 218, 219, 221
   as textile fiber, *75,* 77
canals, *28, 29,* 31, 32, 44, 121, *122,* 124, 179, 216, 221–222
canine remains, 218–219, 220, 221–222
Caraparial, *89,* 90, 92, 103, 104
carbon dating
   at Akapana A+B, 216–221
   at Akapana East, 214, 222–224
   at Akapana Pyramid, 221–222
   at Akapana Summit, 221
   Berkeley School and, 20
   at Chen Chen, 228, *229*
   at Cochabamba, *91,* 108n2
   horizon concept and, 16
   of *khipu,* 81
   at Lukurmata, 214–215, 226–228
   in Moquegua Archaeological Survey, *48, 49–50*
   at Omo, 228, *229*
   primary associations in, 211, 214, 226, 227, 228
   at Putuni, 213–214, 224–226
   at Quillacollo, *91*
   Rowe and, 15, 22
   secondary associations and, 211, 213–214, 218, 219, 222, 223, 226
   at Sierra Mokho, *91*
   and social axis of style variation, 20
   written format used for, 230n1
carrying capacity, 154, 156
Casa del Inca, 183, *183*
cemetery. *See* mortuary
centrality, of Tiwanaku, 11, 16–18
ceramics
   activity sets in, 45–46
   at Akapana A+B, 216–221, *219*
   at Akapana East, 214, *215,* 222–224
   at Akapana Summit, 221
   Berkeley School and, 22
   as burial offerings, 102–103, *103,* 230n10
   Caraparial, 90
   at Cerro Baúl, 55

Chen Chen, 53, 94
at Ch'iji Jawira, 199–200
Cochabamba, 87, *92,* 92–96, *93, 94, 95*
commensality and, *139,* 139–140
fineware, 92–96, *93, 95*
frequency of, *57*
household, 56–57, *57*
Huaracane, *57*
inferences about cultural importance of Tiwanaku from, *174,* 174–176
at Iwawi, 175
at Lukurmata, 214–215, 226–228, *228*
at Marcapata, *215,* 215–216
in mortuary, 37–38, 175
Omo, 36, 94
Pachacamac, 13
Piñami, 92–96, *93, 94, 95, 105*
at Putuni, 213–214, 224–226
Qeya, 211, *212, 213,* 214, 230n4
Quillacollo, 92–96, *93, 95*
religious iconography in, 177
in ritual, 121–124, *124*
social hierarchy and, 36–37, 199–200
Tiwanaku, 36, 37
utilitarian, 95–96
vessel shapes in, *174,* 174–175
in Virú Valley Project, 13–14
Wari, 36–37
ceremony, 78, 117, 144, 201–204
Cerro Baúl
   ceramics at, 36, 55
   colonization at, 55
   as defensive site, 163
   Huari at, *28*
   metal tools at, 35
   mortuary at, 37–38
   obsidian tools at, 35
   population of, 32
   residential architecture at, *33,* 34
   stylistic variation at, 21
   Tiwanaku monumental structure at, 30
   Wari monumental construction at, 30, *31,* 58
Cerro Mejía, *28, 33*
   as defensive site, 163
   metal tools at, 35
   monumental architecture at, 30–31
   mortuary at, 37
   obsidian tools at, 35
   residential architecture at, 34
Cerro Petroglifo, *28,* 55
   monumental architecture at, 31
   residential architecture at, 34
Cerro Trapiche, 32, 48, *49,* 55, 56, *56, 57, 57*
Chaco War, 4, 5
challadores, 94, 102, 104, 105

ch'allas, 116, 117, 118, *118,* 119
Chan Chan, 21, 136, 161, 182
Charazani, 172
Chavín de Huántar, 14, 16, 17, 21, 66, *66,* 73, 85n2, 161, 169
Chen Chen, *29*
   agriculture at, *29,* 31–32
   carbon dating at, 228, *229*
   ceramics, 53, 94
   colonization, *51,* 162
   as colony, 162
   dating of, 228, *229*
   geoglyphs at, *52*
   metal tools at, 36
   in Moquegua Archaeological Survey, *50*
   mortuary at, 37, 48, 55, 58
   residential architecture at, 32
   social distinctions at, 21
chicha, 117, 122, 137–138, 144, 145, 146, 175–176, 200, 203
Ch'iji Jawira, 199–200, 201, 203, 216
Chimu, 182, 183, 184, 185
Chiribaya, *50,* 59n1
Chola state, 43, 45
chronology, 15, 169–170. *See also* carbon dating
Chucaripupata, 121–128, *122, 123, 124, 125, 126,* 129
chullpas, 108n9, 161
Ciudadela Rivero, 182, 183, *183*
class. *See* social hierarchy
clothing. *See also* textiles
   design concepts in, 77–82, *78, 79, 80, 81, 82*
   fibers used in, 77
   geometry in, 78, 79, *80,* 81, 82, *82*
   hats, 82–83, *83*
   Inca, 81, *85*
   loomsmanship of, 75–77, *76*
   models for, 69, *69,* 85n1
   pre-Tiwanaku, *67,* 67–68
   prototypical figures on, *74,* 75
   on statues, 185
   at temple events, 70–71
   textile structure of, 75, *75,* 83, *83*
   Tiwanaku, 73–82, *74, 75, 77, 78, 79, 80, 82*
   on Tiwanaku stelae, 68–69, 71–72, *72*
   tunics, 65–66
   Wari, 73–82, *74, 75, 77, 79, 80, 82*
coca, 116, 117, 144
coca bags, 83
Cochabamba, *88,* 176, 184, 186, 201, 206
   architecture in, 96–98, *97*
   carbon dating at, *91,* 108n2
   ceramics in, 87, *92,* 92–96, *93, 94, 95*
   mortuary at, 100–104, *101, 102, 103*
   Piñami site at, 52
   sites in, *89*
   variability in, 89–90

colonization
   European, 3–4
   in Greece, 162
   household assemblages and, 55–57
   in Moquegua, *51,* 148
   mortuary and, 57–58
   standard conceptual model of, 161–162
   Tiwanaku versus Wari, 54–58, *56, 57*
   vectors of, *42*
   Wari, 38
commensality
   agriculture and, 141–143
   ceramics and, *139,* 139–140
   iconography and, 137–139
   monolith hand details and, 137–139
   Putuni and, 136
   ritual, ceremony and, 201–204
Conchopata, 176, 178
cooking, 57, 96. *See also* food; hearth
corn beer, 117, 122, 137–138, 144, 145, 146, 175–176, 200, 203
corporate states, 87–89, 106–107
cosmopolitanism, 199–201
cotton, *75,* 77, 81
craft specialists, Tiwanaku as city of, 172–174
cranial deformation, 19, 46, 104, 200
creation myth, of Inca, 2–3
Cuzco, 3, 12, 16–17, 117, 136, 182–183, 229

dating. *See* carbon dating
Decapitator, 2
demographics, 32, 47, 59, 172–173, 205. *See also* colonization; migration; population
diaspora, 38, 45–54, 51, 58
diet, 99–100. *See also* food
directional indicators, 144–145, *145,* 145–147, *146*
drinking vessels. *See* ceramics; *keros* (drinking vessels)
Dual-Court Complex, 201. *See also* Khonkho Wankane
dumping space, 203, 204, 222
dung, 204

eating. *See* food
El Fraile monolith, 137–139
elites, 20, 21, 35, 136, 143–144, 147, 158–159, 161, 198, 207
El Paso, *28, 30*
England, 156, 157–158, 159–160
escudilla, 212, 213, 224, 226, 227
Estuquiña, *50*
ethnicity, 54, 104, 201
European invasion/colonization, 3–4
exclusionary states, 87–89

factionalism, 38, 59
feasting, 121–122, 130, 205. *See also* food; "work feasts"

flutes, 45, 98, 174
food. *See also* agriculture; diet
    agricultural cycles and, 142–143
    camelids as, 99–100
    ceremony and, 201
    commensality and, 139–140
    maize as, 99
    preparation, 96
    social hierarchy and, 200
    storage, 203

Gateway of the Sun
    in age of traveler-scholars, 4
    animals in, *145,* 145–146
    attendant figures in, *77,* 77–78, *145,* 146
    in clothing designs, *77,* 77–82, *78, 80, 81, 82*
    directional indicators on, *145,* 145–147, *146*
    undulating band in, *81,* 81–82, *82*
gender. *See also* women
    mortuary and, 46, 104
    religious iconography and, 177
geoglyphs, 50, *52*
geometry, in clothing design, 78, 79, *80,* 81, 82, *82*
Gran Chimu, 182
guest–host relations, 139–140

hallucinogens, 98, 177, 178, 186, 189
hands, in monoliths, 137–139, *138*
hats, 82–83, *83. See also* clothing; textiles
hearth, 32, *34,* 204, 222, 224, 226, 227, 228
heat, 204
hierarchical state, 158–161, 178
hierarchy. *See* social hierarchy
horizon concept
    Chavín de Huántar and, 17
    Huari and, 16
    Kroeber and, 14
    phasing and, 17–18
    Rowe and, 15
    seriation and, 22
    Uhle and, 13
hospitality state, 147. *See also* commensality
host–guest relations, 139–140
huacas, 117, *118*
Huacas del Sol y de la Luna, 17
Huanuco Pampa, 183, 188
Huaracane, 32, *47,* 47–48, *49, 50,* 56, 57, *57*
Huari (site), *28. See also* Wari (culture and people)
    chronology and, 15
    stylistic influences in, 16, 18
hyper-diffusion, 4

Ica Valley, 15, 16
Illataco, 90, 92, *93,* 94, *94, 95,* 95–96, 106
Inca Empire
    agriculture of, Wari and, 32
    clothing of, 81, *85*
    Europeans and, 3–4
    ritual and power in, 117–118, *118*
    at Tiwanaku, 2–3, 11
incensarios, 94, 102, 175, 221, 227, 230n4. *See also* ceramics
India, 160
infrastructure, as political statement, 27–34, *28, 29, 30, 31, 33, 34*
Inti Raymi, 117
invasion, European, 3–4
irrigation, *29,* 31, 44. *See also* agriculture; canals
Iruhito, 142
Isla Esteves, 128
Island of the Sun, *54,* 114, 121, 206
Iwawi, 175

jarras, 95, 102. *See also* ceramics
jaw scrapers, 45, 98, *98*

Kalasasaya, 5, 7–9, 113, 119, 125, *126, 127,* 128, 164, 172, 177, *183,* 184, 201
Kalasasaya bowls, *139,* 139–140
Kala Uyuni, 139, 142
Kallamarka, 142
Kantatayita Architrave, 68, *68,* 75, 136
keros, 36, 37, 52, *53,* 94, *94,* 102, *103,* 113, 119, 122, *123,* 137, 174, 175–176, 218, 219, *219,* 226, 227. *See also* ceramics
Kherikala, 119, 136, 213, *213,* 214, *225. See also* Putuni
khipu, 81, *81*
Khonkho Wankane, *67,* 67–68, 142, 172, 201, 205
kin collectives, 44
Kk'araña, 172, 203, 216

La Cantera, *30,* 55, 59n2
La Centinela, 181, *183*
livestock storage, 202
llamas. *See* camelids
llama vessels, *54*
London, 156, 157–158, 159–160
loom, *76*
Los Cerrillos, 48
Los Joyeros, 48, *49*
Lukurmata, 119, 157, 214–215, *215,* 226–228

Machaca, 198
Machac Mara, 205
maize, *50,* 99, 106, 107, 200, 204. *See also* agriculture; food

maize beer, 117, 122, 137–138, 144, 145, 146, 175–176, 200, 203
Manco Capac, 3

mandible scrapers, 45, 98, *98*
Maravillas, 128
Marcapata, *215,* 215–216
markas, 140
marriage, 46, 55, 115, 198
mathematics, 81, *81. See also* geometry
mechachuas, 226
mesas, 116
mestizaje, 56, 57
metal trade, 35–36
middens, 203, 204, 222, 227
migration
   agriculture and, 142–143
   back-and-forth, 46
   corporate state and, 44, 106
   diaspora and, 51
   hegemony and, 206
   return, 46, 47
moat, 178–180, *180*
Moche Valley, 12, 17–18, 20, 143, 161
models, for dress, 69, *69,* 85n1
Mojocoya, 90, 92, *93*
Mollo Kontu Mound, *180,* 202–203, 206
Monochrome style, 92, *93, 95*
monoliths. *See also* monumental construction; stelae; *specific structures*
   ceremony and, 202
   commensality and, 137–139
   Inca Empire and, 2–3
   social status of figures depicted in, 186
   in traveler-scholar age, 4
Montalvo, *49*
monumental construction. *See also* Akapana Pyramid; Gateway of the Sun
   commensality in, 136
   modularity in, 136
   as political statement, *30,* 30–31, *31*
   Tiwanaku, 30, 31
   Wari, 30–31, *31*
Moquegua Archaeological Survey (MAS), 47–48
Morales, Evo, 1–2, 8, 9, 197
Moroccan marriage, 115
mortuary
   at Akapana A+B, 216–219
   burial styles, *101,* 101–102, 103
   camelids in, 37, 102, 119
   ceramics at, 37–38, 175
   at Chen Chen, 37, 48, 55, 58
   at Chucaripupata, 124
   at Cochabamba, 100–104, *101, 102, 103*
   colonization and, 55, 57–58
   elite, 224, 225, 226
   gender and, 46, 104
   kings in, 184–185
   offerings, 102–103, *103,* 104, 230n10
   orientation in, 102
   Piñami, 101–102, *102*
   at Putuni, 224, 225
   in residential architecture, 200
   social hierarchy and, 37–38, 104, 200
   urn burials, 102
Muru Ut Pata, 202, 205
Mycenae, 151–152

numerology, 78

obsidian, 35, 55, 231n23
offerings
   mortuary, 102–103, *103,* 104, 230n10
   ritual and, 116–117
olla, 96, 102, *174. See also* ceramics
Ollantaytambo, 186
ollitas, 102, 104. *See also* ceramics
Omereque, *89, 91,* 92, 103, 106
Omo, *29*
   carbon dating at, *49–50,* 228, *229*
   ceramics at, 36, 94
   as colony, 162
   cranial deformation patterns at, 19
   geoglyphs at, *52*
   lack of diaspora in, 48
   M10, 19, *49–50, 52,* 58, 184, *185*
   monumental architecture at, 30, *30*
   residential architecture at, 32, *34*
   ritual structure at, 128
orientation. *See also* directional indicators
   in architecture, 97
   in mortuary, 102
origin center concept
   Huari as, 16
   phasing and, 17–18
   Uhle and, 13
orthogonal cellular form, 34

pacarina, 3
Pachacamac, 12, 13, 14, 168, 176, 181
Pachacuti, 12, 229
pago, 6, 116
Palace of the Multicolored Rooms, 180–181, *182, 183, 184,* 189n8, 225, 226
PAPA. *See* Proyecto Arqueológico Pumapunku y Akapana (PAPA)
phasing, 17–18
Pikillacta, 35, 71
pilgrimage, 84, 136, 153, 158, 186–188
Piñami, 52, *89,* 90–100, *91, 92, 93, 94, 95, 97, 98, 99,* 101–102, *102, 105,* 106–107
pluralism, 38, 43, 44–45, 45–54
political statement
   infrastructure as, 27–34, *28, 29, 30, 31, 33, 34*

monumental construction as, *30,* 30–31, *31*
   mortuary as, 37–38
   residential architecture as, 32, 34
Ponce monolith, 137, *137,* 137–139, *138,* 144–145, *145*
population
   carrying capacity and, 154, 156
   of Cerro Baúl, 32
   shifts, agriculture and, 142–143
   of Tiwanaku, 153, 154–156, 173
portrait cup, 219, *219*
primary associations, in carbon dating, 211, 214, 226, 227, 228
Profiled Attendant. *See* attendant figures
"proto-states," 42
Proyecto Arqueológico Pumapunku y Akapana (PAPA), 202–203
Pucará, 66–67, *67,* 85n2, 161, 172, 177
Pulacayo, 177
Pumapunku, 3, 7, 113, 119, 136, 148, 161, *180,* 202
Punanave, 128
Puno Bay, 128, 206
Puruchuco Palace, 181, *182,* 183, 189n7
Putuni, 113, 119, 136, 180, 184, 200, 202, *213,* 213–214. *See also* Kherikala
Putuni Palace Courtyard, 224–226, *225*
pyramid, Akapana, 5, 7, *71,* 171, 179, 221–222

Qeya pottery, 211, *212, 213,* 214, 230n4
qochas, 202
Quebrada Vitoria, 68, *69*
Quillacollo, *89,* 90, 91, *91,* 92, 96, 103, 108n2
quinoa, 200, 204

radiocarbon dating. *See* carbon dating
Rayed Head, 137, 144–145, *145,* 177, 178, 189, 211, *212, 228*
reciprocity, 144
refuse middens, 203, 204, 222, 227
religious iconography, 73, *73,* 176–178, 177. *See also* Gateway of the Sun; monoliths
research traditions, 151–153
residential architecture. *See also* architecture
   at Cerro Baúl, *33,* 34
   at Cochabamba, 96–98, *97*
   elite, 184, 189n8
   at Lukurmata, 227
   mortuary in, 200
   nondomestic, 202
   orthogonal cellular form of, 34
   rank and status in, 32, 34
   social hierarchy and, 34
   state interaction and, 58
   Tiwanaku, 32, 34, *34*
   Wari, 32, 34, 71
Río Muerto, *49,* 50, *50, 53,* 55

ritual
   appropriation of, 119–128
   ceramics in, 121–124, *124*
   at Chucaripupata, 121
   defined, 114
   feasts, 121–122
   ideological spread and, 128–129
   Inca, 117–118, *118*
   offerings and, 116–117
   order and, 117
   political transformation of, 128–129
   polity and, 129–131
   power and, 115, 116–119, 128–129
   royal, 114–115
   state formation and, 114–116
   structures, 113
roads, 161

sacred-island cosmogram, 178–186
Sacsayhuaman, 186
sahumador, 122, 175, 214, 219, 230n4
SAIS. *See* Southern Andean Iconographic Series (SAIS)
Sala Sur, 221, 222
sami, 82, 144, *145,* 145–147, *146*
San Jose de Moro, 21
San Pedro de Atacama, *74,* 171, 186
San Sebastian Hill, 184–185
Sauces style, 92, *93, 95,* 96
scrapers, 98
secondary associations, in carbon dating, 211, 213–214, 218, 219, 222, 223, 226
segmentary state, 42, *43,* 43–44, 45
Semisubterranean Temple. *See* Sunken Temple
seriation
   assumptions of, 22–23
   carbon dating and, 20
   horizon concept and, 22
   phasing and, 17–18
   Rowe and, 15–16
   style and, 19
settlement organization, 205–206
sherds. *See* ceramics
Sierra Mokho, *89, 91,* 92, 108n2
Similake, 142
snuff spoons, 98, *99,* 178
social axis, of stylistic variation, *19,* 20–21, 23
social diversity, 199–201
social hierarchy
   body modification and, 200
   ceramics and, 36–37, 199–200
   food and, 200
   metal trade and, 35–36
   mortuary and, 37–38, 104, 200
   obsidian tools and, 35
   residential architecture and, 34

of Tiwanaku diaspora, 38
   tunics and, 66–67, 78
solstice festival, 7–9
Southern Andean Iconographic Series (SAIS), 176–178
spoons, 37, 45, 98, *99*
spout forms, 17, 20
Staff God, 2, 176, 177, 178
status. *See* social hierarchy
Stela Bennett. *See* Bennett Stela
stelae, *67,* 67–68, 68–69, 71–72, *72,* 172. *See also* monoliths
storage facilities, 34, 100, 227
style variation, 18–21, *19, 22*
Sun Gate. *See* Gateway of the Sun
Sunken Temple, 113, 119, 120, 121, 128, 172, 187

Tahuantinsuyu, 12
tapia construction, 96, *97,* 105
Taraco Peninsula, 140, 141, 142
Tauri Chumpi, 181, 182, *183*
Taypihuanca, 152
tazones (bowls), 36, 37, 93, 94, 102, *103, 174,* 175, 224, 226. *See also* ceramics
textiles. *See also* clothing
   Chavín, 66, *66,* 73
   early, *66,* 66–68
   Khonkho, *67,* 67–68
   Pucará, 66–67, *67*
   religious, 73, *73,* 177
   SAIS images on, 177
   on statues, 185
   structures of, 75, *75,* 83, *83*
   Wari, *73,* 73–83, *74, 75, 76, 77, 79, 80, 81, 82, 83*
Thunderbolt Stela, 152
Tilata, 216
tinaja, 102, 122, 124, 226
tinku, 51–52
tombs. *See* mortuary
topo, 226
tourism, 7
traveler-scholars, 4
Tres Quebradas, *49*
trompos, 98, *99*
Tumilaca, 32, *34,* 37, 48, *50, 51,* 59n1, 59n3
tunic, 65–66, 73–82, *74, 75, 77, 78, 79, 80, 82, 85. See also* clothing; textiles
tupu pins, 35, 68
Tupuraya style, 92, *93, 95,* 103
typology, 22

Umasuyu, 54
UNESCO, 7
Urco, 54
urn burials, 102. *See also* mortuary
Uru, 44

vasijas, 102, **215,** 215–216. *See also* ceramics
Vijayanagara, 160
Viracocha, 3, 11
Virú Valley Project, 13–15

Wari (culture and people). *See also* Huari (site)
   agrarian investments of, at Moquegua, *29,* 31, 32
   architecture, 71
   ceramics, 36–37
   Cerro Mejía site of, 30–31
   Cerro Petroglifo site of, 31, 34
   chichería patio group, 56, *56*
   coca bags, 83
   as colonists, 38, *42*
   colonization by, 21, 38, *51*
      versus Tiwanaku, 54–58, *56, 57*
   dualism of, with Tiwanaku, 83–85, *84*
   fibers used in clothing of, 77
   hats, 82–83, *83*
   khipu, 81, *81*
   loom, *76*
   metal trade of, 35
   monumental construction by, at Moquegua, 30–31, *31*
   in Moquegua Archaeological Survey, *50*
   obsidian tools of, at Moquegua, 35
   residential architecture of, 32, 34, 71
   stone art, 69, *70*
   textiles, *73,* 73–83, *74, 75, 76, 77, 79, 80, 81, 82, 83*
   tunic, 73–82, *74, 75, 77, 79, 80, 82*
War of the Chaco, 4, 5
War of the Pacific, 4–5
waste, 203, 204, 222, 227
water resources. *See* canals; irrigation
weaving, 67, 75–77, *76. See also* clothing; textiles
Wila Jawira Project, 155, 170, 179, 180, 187, 189n3, 216, 222, 226
women, 45–46, 56, 68, 104, 115, 176. *See also* gender
"work feasts," 142–143, 143–144
World Mountain, 171, 178, 179, 180

yatiri, 116, 117
Yaway, 32, 48
Yaya-Mama style, 172, 176, 177

UCLA COTSEN INSTITUTE OF ARCHAEOLOGY PRESS
MONOGRAPHS
Contributions in Field Research and Current Issues in Archaeological Method and Theory

Monograph 78 *Visions of Tiwanaku,* Alexei Vranich and Charles Stanish (eds.)
Monograph 77 *Advances in Titicaca Basin Archaeology–2,* Alexei Vranich and Abigail R. Levine (eds.)
Monograph 76 *The Dead Tell Tales,* María Cecilia Lozada and Barra O'Donnabhain (eds.)
Monograph 75 *The Stones of Tiahuanaco,* Jean-Pierre Protzen and Stella Nair
Monograph 74 *Rock Art at Little Lake: An Ancient Crossroads in the California Desert,* Jo Anne Van Tilburg, Gordon E. Hull, and John C. Bretney
Monograph 73 *The History of the Peoples of the Eastern Desert,* Hans Barnard and Kim Duistermaat (eds.)
Monograph 71 *Crucible of Pueblos: The Early Pueblo Period in the Northern Southwest,* Richard H. Wilshusen, Gregson Schachner, and James R. Allison (eds.)
Monograph 70 *Chotuna and Chornancap: Excavating an Ancient Peruvian Legend,* Christopher B. Donnan
Monograph 69 *An Investigation into Early Desert Pastoralism: Excavations at the Camel Site, Negev,* Steven A. Rosen
Monograph 68 *The Chanka: Archaeological Research in Andahuaylas (Apurimac), Peru,* Brian S. Bauer, Lucas C. Kellett, and Miriam Aráoz Silva
Monograph 67 *Inca Rituals and Sacred Mountains: A Study of the World's Highest Archaeological Sites,* Johan Reinhard and Maria Costanza Ceruti
Monograph 66 *Gallinazo: An Early Cultural Tradition on the Peruvian North Coast,* Jean-François Millaire with Magali Morlion
Monograph 65 *Settlement and Subsistence in Early Formative Soconusco,* Richard G. Lesure (ed.)
Monograph 64 *The South American Camelids,* Duccio Bonavia
Monograph 63 *Andean Civilization: A Tribute to Michael E. Moseley,* Joyce Marcus and Patrick Ryan Williams (eds.)
Monograph 62 *Excavations at Cerro Azul, Peru: The Architecture and Pottery,* Joyce Marcus
Monograph 61 *Chavín: Art, Architecture, and Culture,* William J Conklin and Jeffrey Quilter (eds.)
Monograph 60 *Rethinking Mycenaean Palaces II: Revised and Expanded Second Edition,* Michael L. Galaty and William A. Parkinson (eds.)
Monograph 59 *Moche Tombs at Dos Cabezas,* Christopher B. Donnan
Monograph 58 *Moche Fineline Painting from San José de Moro,* Donna McClelland, Donald McClelland, and Christopher B. Donnan
Monograph 57 *Kasapata and the Archaic Period of the Cuzco Valley,* Brian S. Bauer (ed.)
Monograph 56 *Berenike 1999/2000,* Steven E. Sidebotham and Willeke Wendrich (eds.)
Monograph 55 *Roman Footprints at Berenike: Archaeobotanical Evidence of Subsistence and Trade in the Eastern Desert of Egypt,* René T. J. Cappers
Monograph 54 *Advances in Titicaca Basin Archaeology 1,* Charles Stanish, Amanda B. Cohen, and Mark S. Aldenderfer
Monograph 53 *Us and Them: Archaeology and Ethnicity in the Andes,* Richard Martin Reycraft
Monograph 52 *Archaeological Research on the Islands of the Sun and Moon, Lake Titicaca, Bolivia: Final Results from the Proyecto Tiksi Kjarka,* Charles Stanish and Brian S. Bauer (eds.)
Monograph 51 *Maya Zooarchaeology: New Directions in Theory and Method,* Kitty F. Emery (ed.)
Monograph 50 *Settlement Archaeology and Political Economy at Tres Zapotes, Veracruz, Mexico,* Christopher A. Pool (ed.)
Monograph 49 *Perspectives on Ancient Maya Rural Complexity,* Gyles Iannone and Samuel V. Connell (eds.)
Monograph 48 *Yeki bud, yeki nabud: Essays on the Archaeology of Iran in Honor of William M. Sumner,* Naomi F. Miller and Kamyar Abdi (eds.)
Monograph 47 *Archaeology in the Borderlands: Investigation in Caucasia and Beyond,* Adam T. Smith and Karen S. Rubinson (eds.)
Monograph 46 *Domestic Ritual in Ancient Mesoamerica,* Patricia Plunket (ed.)
Monograph 45 *Pathways to Prismatic Blades,* Kenneth Hirth and Bradford Andrews (eds.)
Monograph 44 *Ceramic Production and Circulation in the Greater Southwest,* Donna M. Glowacki and Hector Neff (eds.)
Monograph 43 *Pottery of Postclassic Cholula, Mexico,* Geoffrey McCafferty
Monograph 42 *Pompeian Households: An Analysis of the Material Culture,* Penelope M. Allison
Monograph 41 *Rethinking Mycenaean Palaces: New Interpretations of an Old Idea,* Michael L. Galaty and William A. Parkinson (eds.)
Monograph 40 *Prehistory of Agriculture: New Experimental and Ethnographic Approaches,* Patricia C. Anderson (ed.)
Monograph 39 *Recent Advances in the Archaeology of the Northern Andes: In Memory of Gerardo Reichel-Dolmatoff,* Augusto Oyuela-Caycedo and J. Scott Raymond (eds.)
Monograph 38 *Approaches to the Historical Archaeology of Mexico, Central and South America,* Janine Gasco, Greg Charles Smith, and Patricia Fournier-Garcia
Monograph 37 *Hawaiian Adze Production and Distribution: Implications for the Development of Chiefdoms,* Barbara Lass

Monograph 36 *New Light on Old Art: Recent Advances in Hunter-Gatherer Rock Art Research*, D. W. Whitley and L. L. Loendorf (eds.)
Monograph 35 *Pottery of Prehistoric Honduras: Regional Classification and Analysis*, J. S. Henderson and M. Beaudry-Corbett
Monograph 34 *Settlement Archaeology of Cerro de las Mesas, Veracruz, Mexico*, Barbara Stark (ed.)
Monograph 33 *Girikihaciyan: A Halafian Site in Southeastern Turkey*, P. J. Watson and S. LeBlanc
Monograph 32 *Western Pomo Prehistory: Excavations at Albion Head, Nightbirds' Retreat and Three Chop Village, Mendocino County, California*, Thomas N. Layton
Monograph 31 *Investigaciones Arqueológicos de la Costa Sur de Guatemala*, David S. Whitley and Marilyn P. Beaudry (eds.)
Monograph 30 *Archaeology of the Three Springs Valley, California: A Study in Functional Cultural History*, Brian D. Dillon and Matthew A. Boxt
Monograph 29 *Obsidian Dates IV: A Compendium of Obsidian Hydration Readings from the UCLA Obsidian Hydration Laboratory*, Clement W. Meighan and Janet L. Scalise (eds.)
Monograph 28 *Archaeological Field Research in the Upper Mantaro, Peru, 1982–1983: Investigations of Inka Expansion and Exchange*, Timothy Earle et al. (eds.)
Monograph 27 *Andean Archaeology: Papers in Memory of Clifford Evans*, Ramiro Matos M., Solveig Turpin, and Herbert Eling, Jr. (eds.)
Monograph 26 *Excavations at Mission San Antonio 1976–1978*, Robert L. Hoover and Julio J. Costello (eds.)
Monograph 25 *Prehistoric Production and Exchange in the Aegean and Eastern Mediterranean*, A. Bernard Knapp and Tamara Stech (eds.)
Monograph 24 *Pots and Potters: Current Approaches in Ceramic Archaeology*, Prudence Rice
Monograph 23 *Pictographs and Petroglyphs of the Oregon Country, Part 2*, J. Malcolm Loring and Louise Loring
Monograph 22 *The Archaeology of Two Northern California Sites*, Delmer E. Sanburg, F. K. Mulligan, Joseph Chartkoff, and Kerry Chartkoff
Monograph 21 *Pictographs and Petroglyphs of the Oregon Country, Part 1*, J. Malcolm Loring and Louise Loring
Monograph 20 *Messages from the Past: Studies in California Rock Art*, Clement W. Meighan (ed.)
Monograph 19 *Prehistoric Indian Rock Art: Issues and Concerns*, Jo Anne Van Tilburg and Clement W. Meighan (eds.)
Monograph 18 *Studies in Cypriote Archaeology*, Jane C. Biers and David Soren
Monograph 17 *Excavations in Northern Belize, Central America*, Raymond Sidrys
Monograph 16 *Obsidian Dates III: A Compendium of Obsidian Hydration Determinations Made at the UCLA Obsidian Hydration Laboratory*, Clement Meighan and Glenn Russell
Monograph 15 *Inland Chumash Archaeological Investigations*, David S. Whitley, E. L. McCann, and C. W. Clewlow, Jr. (eds.)
Monograph 14 *Papers in Cycladic Prehistory*, Jack L. Davis and John F. Cherry (eds.)
Monograph 13 *Archaeological Investigations at the Ring Brothers Site Complex, Thousand Oaks, California*, C. W. Clewlow, Jr., David S. Whitley, and Ellen L. McCann (eds.)
Monograph 12 *The Running Springs Ranch Site: Archaeological Investigations at VEN-65 and VEN-261*, Jack Prichett and Allen McIntyre
Monograph 11 *The Archaeology of Oak Park, Ventura County, California*, C. William Clewlow, Jr., and David S. Whitley (eds.)
Monograph 10 *Rock Art of East Mexico and Central America: An Annotated Bibliography*, Matthias Strecker
Monograph 9 *The Late Minoan I Destruction of Crete: Metal Groups and Stratigraphic Considerations*, Hara Georgiou
Monograph 8 *Papers on the Economy and Architecture of the Ancient Maya*, Raymond Sidrys (ed.)
Monograph 7 *History and Prehistory at Grass Valley, Nevada*, C. W. Clewlow, Jr., Helen F. Wells, and Richard Ambro (eds.)
Monograph 6 *Obsidian Dates II: A Compendium of Obsidian Hydration Determinations Made at the UCLA Obsidian Hydration Laboratory*, C. W. Meighan and P. I. Vanderhoeven (eds.)
Monograph 5 *The Archaeology of Oak Park, Ventura County, California*, C. W. Clewlow, Jr., Allen Pastron, and Helen F. Wells (eds.)